She Rises

A Daily Devotional
Overcoming Every Dark Night

Renee Bollas

January

January 1

There's this happiness all wrapped up in a big bundle of fur that I want to tell you about.

His name is Smiley. Smiley was born without eyes, a condition often associated with dwarfism. His legs are a little bowed, his head is a little large and he stands "a little crooked," his owner said. He was one of 85 dogs rescued from a puppy mill in a small town in Ontario. They found homes for all of the dogs.

Well, all except for one.

Smiley was rejected. No one wanted him.

The lady who found him decided to keep him. She knew instantly he was special. She believed in him.

Smiley became a therapy dog!

He goes to nursing homes. He sits with people who need a listening ear. He visits children with special needs. He encourages them to do new things. Helps them achieve new levels. He makes them smile.

Special needs create opportunity for special deeds.

Smiley's disability gave him the ability to serve a very special group of people.

Without his disability, he would NEVER have served them or even met them. They have opened up so many doors for him.

He was rejected my man, but chosen by God.

God has a very special plan for his life.

God has a plan for your life as well. A path chosen just for you.

Be YOU! Blind, gimping, not a good speaker? Make noises? Have tics?

Different? Yes! Different is good!

Embrace it! Make it yours. Make it your message to the world.

These things make you relatable.

On a side note, we as women strive to look like everyone else. We want to have that perfect body.

There is no such thing.

Strive to be YOU!

YOU are perfect. Just. The. Way. You. Are.

If Smiley could see, I guarantee he would've been adopted into a loving family. He would've had a good life. Comfortable. And easy.

His special needs gave him so much more! His life is so much fuller than the average pup. He is much stronger in every way.

The same is true for you.

Disabilities create need. And weakness. They make life more difficult. No doubt about it.

2 Corinthians 12:9-10...My power works best in weakness...That's why I take pleasure in my weaknesses, and in the insults, hardships, persecutions, and troubles that I suffer for Christ. For when I am weak, then I am strong.

We become stronger on the inside. Our faith grows exponentially.

God is giving us unique opportunities. He is enabling us to reach people others can't. People who are just like us. Opening doors to touch so many more people in need.

Smiley rose above his circumstances. And God is using him in a big way.

He will do the same in your life as well.

Proverbs 31:15 She rises...

God wants us to rise above our circumstances as well. He will help us to overcome every obstacle we face. He will use it for our good and His glory.

Dear Jesus, how can I use this disability in my own life? Who can I reach out to? How can I serve you best? Lead me to cross paths with someone I can help along the way. I know that you have a purpose for it. All Your ways are good. Please help me to see this as You do.

January 2

Luke 13:11-12 There was a woman who had a spirit of infirmity eighteen years, and was bent over and could in no way raise herself up. But when Jesus saw her, He called her to Him and said to her, "Woman, you are loosed from your infirmity"... "So ought not this woman,...whom Satan has bound-think of it-for eighteen years, be loosed from this bond...?"

This woman had a desperate need of strength. Her need for strength could've been a physical one. However, it is more likely her need arose from the influence that was upon her thought life. Although she was being taught by Jesus Himself; the enemy could still influence her thoughts, feelings and decisions. She "could in no way raise herself up." She was not able to get herself out of this situation. She had no power to fix this on her own. She had no favorable circumstances; nor did she have resources, financial or otherwise. She may not have been in a rational state of mind to make sound decisions. She may have been bound by thoughts of defeat and hopelessness that she couldn't overcome. Instead of growing strong and climbing higher, she was spiraling downward. The enemy was rendering her useless.

The enemy can do the same thing to us. His tactics have not changed.

Perhaps there was a tragic event that happened in the past, or perhaps many little worries and insecurities have added up and seem insurmountable. Satan whispers in our ear that we will never get beyond this. Things will never get better. He tells us we can't do this anymore. He clouds our judgment. The voice of the enemy quickly forces out the voice of Truth.

Jesus saw her.

The Bible doesn't tell us exactly what her infirmity was. I think that's important. There are times in our lives when only Jesus knows exactly what's going on. He knows the whole truth of our situation. He knows the challenges and obstacles we face on a daily basis. Outward appearances can be misleading. We may look like we have it all together; but inwardly we are falling apart. We put on our happy face and smile, but all the while our heart is breaking. Jesus knows, and He cares. He knows you personally. You have never slipped His mind.

Jesus called her.

It is vital that we know the nature of the One who is calling. The Name of Jesus is power. He is strength. He is certain when everything else is uncertain. Although everything is against us, He is so for us. He gives us all that we need to endure. He quickens our mind to make sound decisions. He gives us supernatural physical strength to accomplish all He has called us to do today. He will never leave us. He is our ability to climb up and out.

Jesus healed her.

"Woman you are loosed from your infirmity!" Although Satan had her shackled, Jesus set her free. Jesus called and she responded. She made a deliberate choice to heed the voice of her Master. In doing so she was filled with supernatural strength.

Luke 13:13 And He laid His hands on her, and immediately she was made straight, and glorified God.

The same is true for us. We have strength to understand, to refrain from corrupt desires, to bear trials and ultimately to do great things for God.

Ephesians 1:18 the eyes of your understanding being enlightened...

All of our thoughts, feelings and desires are under control of the Spirit. He enables us to see things through His eyes. We are able to make wise decisions. We are lifted up and encouraged.

We are able to refrain from corrupt desires.

1 Corinthians 10:13 And God is faithful; He will not let you be tempted beyond what you can bear. But when you are tempted, He will also provide a way out so that you can stand up under it.

We are able to bear trials.

Philippians 4:13 I can do all things through Christ who strengthens me.

Romans 8:28 We know all things work together for good for those who love God and are called according to His purpose.

God uses all things for good, even the bad things. He wants to use the weak times to show us how strong He is.

We are able to do great things for God.

What has He called you to do? Heed the voice of the Lord. He wants to set you free from those discouraging thoughts.

Ephesians 3:20 Now to Him who is able to do exceedingly abundantly above all that we ask or think, according to the power that works in us...

We want to make this year count for Christ!

I like what Oswald Chambers said: "My determined purpose is to be my utmost for His highest-My best for His glory!"

January 3

My son Camden was diagnosed with Autism at the age of 2. Of the many challenges this disability presents, irrational fears are at the top of his list.

He was afraid of everything.

Especially that I would leave him somewhere. By himself.

Everywhere we went, he would ask me one question.

"Are you staying?"

The apple doesn't fall far from the tree.

I discovered he is much more like me than I care to admit.

I began to realize that was the question that continually emanated from my own heart.

"Lord, are you staying?"

As I traveled through this vast wilderness called Autism, I wondered if He was going to leave me there. In that scary place.

Irrational?

Maybe.

Even so, I needed continual reassurance. At times, I still do.

He is so faithful.

Always had one answer for me.

I am with you. I am here. The whole way. I will never leave you.

Every day He spoke softly to my heart. Gently whispering assuring words of comfort.

Revelation 22:2 In the middle of its street, and on either side of the river, was the tree of life, which bore twelve fruits, each tree yielding its fruit every month. The leaves of the tree were for the healing of the nations.

His word is life. Cling to it. Soak it in. Only He can bring vitality to the lost. Fill the hungry with good things. Heal the broken.

Dear God I pray the pages of this book will be as leaves from the tree of life. May they flutter into the lives of the reader; bringing healing to the deepest recesses of the soul. Open the eyes of the blind. Take Your daughters, who are unable to carry on, by the hand and lift them up. Help them to get back in the race. Give the deaf ears to hear. Raise the dead. Lift these poor spirits. Mend the torn places. Fill the empty. Lift high the arms of the weak. Encourage the downtrodden. Strengthen the feeble knees. Overflow the hopeless. Heal the brokenhearted. Put a new song in their mouth; praise to their God.

January 4

Joshua 1:2 "Moses My servant is dead. Now therefore, arise, go over this Jordan, you and all this people, to the land which I am giving to them, the children of Israel."

This could be a good picture for us...last year is gone!

Let's move on from it. Yes, we had some setbacks. Yes, we had some deviations. Yes, maybe we even had some BIG mistakes...all those are things are gone. Did we miss some opportunities? Yes we did. But, looking back at them in despair and regret and sulking will not change one thing. It will only keep us wallowing in self-pity. It will render us inactive to the things the Lord has for us right here and right now.

The Lord is saying to Joshua, "Let's go! Look ahead! I have some new opportunities for you!"

He is pointing forward!

And God is saying the same thing to us!

Philippians 3:13 Brethren, I do not count myself to have apprehended; but one thing I do, forgetting those things which are behind and reaching forward to those things which are ahead...

Forget those things that are behind! Reach forward! The Lord has new things for us this year.

Have you been feeling down?

Maybe you're depressed?

Listen, condemnation is from the enemy.

Conviction is from the Spirit.

What does that mean? The enemy wants us to be depressed. He doesn't want us to do anything to lift up our heads. He wants us to stay in bed with the covers over our head. If thoughts like, "I can't believe I did that...I can't believe I didn't do that" keep playing in your head over and over...That's condemnation.

Conviction says, "I can't believe I did that...AND I'm going to make sure I do something about it!" I'm going to bring a change to ensure it doesn't happen again. OR "I can't believe I didn't do that...I will make the most of the next opportunity."

Do something about it!

Get up! Take the first step!

Joshua 1:3 I promise you what I promised Moses: 'Wherever you set foot, you will be on land I have given you—

Every step you take to accomplish a goal or a small task is a step ordained by God. He gave you this "land," this task or goal.

He will complete it.

God will be with you every step of this conquest. Take the next step. He is in it.

January 5

Acts 20:24 None of these things move me. My life is worth nothing to me unless I use it for finishing the work assigned me by the Lord Jesus—the work of telling others the Good News about the wonderful grace of God.

When my son was first diagnosed with Autism, I began a journal.

The very first page reads:

"I don't know how anyone could make it through this without You, Lord. I will use this for Your glory. I want to reach any who are suffering and have a child who has Autism. I want to give them hope and peace."

I continued with: Someone at Kennedy Krieger doesn't know God (Kennedy Krieger is where I took Camden to be evaluated for Autism).

As I waded through this desolation there was one thing I was keenly aware of: God has a purpose for it.

I knew in my heart of hearts God would use it for His good.

Romans 8:28 And we know that all things work together for good to those who love God, to those who are the called according to His purpose.

The sole goal of our lives is to know God and make Him known.

I determined that I could not allow Autism to get in the way of this goal.

No obstacle or tragedy can keep me from doing what God called me to do.

In fact, the thing I saw as an obstacle actually turned out to be the very place that God wanted to spread His message. There was a whole group of suffering mothers He desired to reach.

But He had to reach my heart first.

I had to come to the place of fully knowing God had a purpose for this.

Indeed He has a purpose for everything.

The hard part is accepting His way of doing things.

Isaiah 55:8-9 I don't think the way you think. The way you work isn't the way I work." God's Decree. "For as the sky soars high above earth, so the way I work surpasses the way you work, and the way I think is beyond the way you think.

Wherever God has you, He wants to use you. Allow Him to take you behind the scenes.

2 Corinthians 4:17-18 For our light affliction, which is but for a moment, is working for us a far more exceeding and eternal weight of glory, while we do not look at the things which are seen, but at the things which are not seen. For the things which are seen are temporary, but the things which are not seen are eternal.

I had to take my eyes off of the things I could see. I needed to accept His way of doing things.

He will ask the same of you. These hard things have eternal value. Sit tight. Don't fret.

God is in full control.

Dear God, my God, my Daddy, please open my eyes to see you have a purpose for this situation in my life. Increase my trust in You. Help me to be patient as you work this out for good and for Your glory. Draw me closer to you Father.

January 6

Mark 13:26,33 "Then they will see the Son of Man coming in the clouds with great power and glory. "Take heed, watch and pray; for you do not know when the time is..."

Jesus is coming back. He has given each of us a mission to complete.

There are 3 things that keep us from completing our "mission."

Comfort:

In America, we live in such an environment of comfort we cannot see our need for Jesus. We tend to be so distracted. This word "watch" could be translated "sleepless". We're being lulled into a false sense of security. We're falling asleep on the job! In our American culture we have everything we need physically. For the most part that ease actually robs us. We have no pressing needs to be met. Therefore we have no need to seek Jesus. If you have everything you need, praise God. But keep your relationship with Him vibrant. Be vigilant to keep it fresh. Our marriages don't just happen to be raining rose pedals. We have to keep them warm and exciting. It's the same way in our relationship with Jesus. We have to consciously make the effort. The closer we are to Jesus the more we'll hear Him speak.

Disaster:

Autism was the single greatest disaster to ever strike my family. It threatened every aspect of my life. No area was untouched. I did not think I would ever recover.

Romans 5:3 We can rejoice, too, when we run into problems and trials, for we know that they help us develop endurance. And endurance develops strength of character, and character strengthens our confident hope of salvation.

Endurance has many descriptions. This is the definition I love best: a woman who is not swerved from her deliberate purpose and her loyalty to faith, not even by the greatest trials and sufferings.

We can't allow even the greatest disasters to divert us from God's purpose for our lives.

Half-heartedness:

2 Chronicles 31:21 And in every work that he began in the service of the house of God, in the law and in the commandment, to seek his God, he did it with all his heart. So he prospered.

We have to direct our thoughts. They are so prone to wandering. We need to direct all of our attention to this mission that He called us to. Give it our all.

Dear Lord wake us up! We want to be ready for Your return. Help us to get others ready as well. We want to be watchful. Put us on guard. Stir our hearts. Implant a Holy desire for You. Show us the areas we need to concentrate on. Help us to overcome every disaster and trial that comes our way. When we are tempted to swerve, help us to remain loyal to you at all cost.

January 7

Acts 3:4 and fixing his eyes on him [the lame man], Peter said, "Look at us!"

Peter demanded the lame man's attention.

This verse broke my heart. This man didn't consider himself worthy of even being looked at. He had become accustomed to people recoiling at him. They turned away so they didn't have to look at him.

Have you ever done that? I am guilty. We've got to change this.

Peer into this man's heart for a moment and you will see his soul is lifeless. His heart has been broken. He has gone into protect mode. He is empty; longing for someone to notice him but unwilling to risk being rejected again. It's easier for him to look down rather than to look up and confirm that he is not even worth looking at.

Slow down and look into the depths of his soul.

We don't look at each other anymore. We're too busy. God slow us down. Let us not be too preoccupied to look into someone's eyes. We aren't that important.

When we don't look people in the eye, we send a message to them that they aren't important. We tell them:

My phone is more important than you are.

You are not significant.

I don't care about you.

Your problems don't concern me.

You are a waste of time.

You are not valuable.

I don't want to get close to you. You're not like me. You're different.

This man had been ignored his entire life. He was just used to being treated like dirt. Being ignored was part of his every day routine. His life didn't count for anything. He felt little. Worthlessness defined his very being. He never aspired to be anything because the message had been sent long ago that he wouldn't amount to much. He believed it.

If you feel like that, God wants you to know through this man's life that you matter. You are very important. You have great value. He cares about you deeply. Your problems are His problems. He wants to help you. You are worthy of His time. He is never too busy for you.

We have to slow down and look people in the eye.

I had to remind myself to look my husband in the eye.

How about the clerk at the store?

The homeless man on the street begging for attention.

Or the disabled woman in a wheelchair. Take notice.

Matthew 25:38-40 'When did we see You a stranger and take You in, or naked and clothe You? 'Or when did we see You sick, or in prison, and come to You?' "And the King will answer and say to them, 'Assuredly, I say to you, inasmuch as you did it to one of the least of these My brethren, you did it to Me.'

The word least can be defined as being the smallest in importance, the most insignificant, and looked over, looked through, looked down upon person you can think of. When picking sides for a team they will be the last one chosen; relegated to a side only by default. They will be the last one invited over for dinner, invited into a conversation, and the one thought to have the least to offer.

I was a stranger and you invited me into your thought process. You actually considered what it would be like to be me. As unpleasant as that thought was, you went beyond and smiled. You offered your right hand of fellowship to me.

I was hungry, but more often the need is not physical. It is a pining in the soul for acceptance and love. Being shunned by the world forces a child to hide. It forces an adult to isolate themselves. There was a need and you met it. You gave yourself.

Give a letter. Make a phone call. Extend an invite for coffee. Reach out of your comfort zone.

I was not like you but you did it anyway.

Oh God, give me Your eyes to see people as You see them. They are sensitive souls that I need to be gentle with. They are precious in Your sight. You love them. Teach me how to respond compassionately. I want to extend Your hands to help. You took the time for me. Let me not disregard anyone. They are precious in Your sight.

January 8

Camden age 5: "Isaac was blind."

This was the statement Camden made after reading him the story in Genesis 22.

You may know the story well. God called Abraham to sacrifice his only son. He didn't hesitate. He went right away. We know the story so well because it highlights Abraham's faithful obedience.

When I recounted this story to Camden I got a new perspective. When I got to the part where Isaac said, "Father, I see the knife and the wood, but where is the Lamb?" Camden covered his eyes and exclaimed, "Isaac was blind!"

Indeed, Isaac could not see how God would provide. Nevertheless, he continued on with his father.

Isaac continued on at the word of his father.

He trusted his father. Implicitly. He knew his father loved him. Abraham surely raised Isaac to know God. I don't think we can say enough about Isaac's faith. There is no mention of him protesting. Not even a hint of fear. After all, it was his life that was being required.

Isaac was asked to sacrifice his life.

When this same request came to me, I could not "see" either. In a sense, God asked me to give up my son. When my son was diagnosed with Autism I felt God asking me to give up all of my hopes and dreams for him. I couldn't believe he was asking this of me.

I begged Him, "Ask me anything, but not this."

Like Isaac, I couldn't see what the Lord was doing.

Is God asking you to face something you never thought you would have to face? You can trust the word of Your Heavenly Father.

Jeremiah 29:11 For I know the plans I have for you," says the LORD. "They are plans for good and not for disaster, to give you a future and a hope."

We hear it all the time, "God has a plan for your life." It's important to understand that God knows the whole plan. He sees what you will need in advance. He will provide for every detail. There is nothing that will be left out. He is not caught off guard. We only see right here and now. He sees the beginning. He sees the end. And He sees everything in between.

He not only sees, but He foresees. He knows everything that you will need in the future. You can trust that it will be provided for. You don't have to see how. You only have to trust that He will.

God's eyes see further than mine.

Oh Lord, you see my future. Help me to trust that Your plan for me is good. Everything You do is good. Even when it looks really bad. You are for me. I want to trust You. Even when I cannot see. God please increase my faith. I don't see all the details right now. Everything is foggy. Bring clarity to my soul. Fill me with understanding. I love You Lord. I will trust You. My Dad.

January 9

John 16:21 A woman when she is in travail hath sorrow, because her hour is come: but as soon as she is delivered of the child, she remembereth no more the anguish, for joy that a man is born into the world.

I don't know about you but there have been times, such as childbirth, when I think to myself, "what was I thinking???" Ok maybe I'm the only one? My decisions produced pain. Sometimes, if given the choice to make over again, we may not choose the same thing. But that is precisely the point. If we had all the information at the beginning, we wouldn't choose pain. No sane person would.

Travail means to bring forth, bear, and produce fruit from seed; to birth.

When Jesus births something new in your life it is often painful. It is not easy. Sometimes we must endure the most difficult trials.

He uses demanding situations, hard places, and painful circumstances to change us. We want circumstances to change, but God wants us to change.

Affliction molds us into the image of our Savior.

When Jesus births something new in your life, it will produce a joy that no one can steal from you. Your heart shall have a true rejoicing. The world gives us a fleeting happiness that cannot compare to the permanent gladness the Lord has to offer. It is a joy that's full; a joy that's deep and a joy that is lasting.

Should you find yourself in a painful situation, remember Jesus is birthing something new in your Spirit. Something lasting. And valuable.

God give me perseverance during this trial. Put a word of praise in my heart. It will be worth the pain in the end. Fill me with joy unspeakable. Right here and right now. In the midst of my suffering I will praise You.

January 10

Little things can add up...

Romans 16:1-2 I commend to you Phoebe our sister, who is a servant of the church in Cenchrea, that you may receive her in the Lord in a manner worthy of the saints, and assist her in whatever business she has need of you; for indeed she has been a helper of many and of myself also.

God wants to point some people out. He wants to give them special recognition. He recorded their names in the Bible for all of time and eternity. We should take notice. Phoebe is one of them.

Phoebe was a servant. She was in a humble position, but she used this low position to affect a beautiful change in the lives of many. She was a doer of little things. Sometimes the littlest things can have the biggest impact. A simple note can lift a person out of the pit of despair. It merely says I care enough about you to sit down and write to you. Maybe Phoebe encouraged people with kind words. An encourager can change the course of someone's life; especially when sharing a word from God. That simple word can restore hope. It can give strength for another day. Maybe your many words are used with a child who cannot speak. God wants you to know He is recording them all. Perhaps all of your errands are spent on one who can't do anything for himself; God sees all that you do. Even when no one else does.

Phoebe was a helper of many. This word helper was a title given to a citizen in Athens who was responsible for seeing to the welfare of resident aliens who had no civic rights. She was a guardian of the people who were thought very little of. She wasn't serving the King or some important dignitary; but rather, the despised and rejected.

What was it that motivated her? It was her love for Jesus. The fire in her heart was for the Lord. No one was overlooked. Not one person was deemed unworthy of her time. No one was ever reckoned an inconvenience, but rather an opportunity to share the love of Jesus. If our motivation for service is anything but our love for Jesus, we are doing it for the wrong reason.

These citizens used their own resources to take care of the aliens. I sometimes want to complain about giving my time or my energy or my money, but I have to remember it ALL belongs to the Lord. It was given to me by Him and could easily be taken away. Phoebe gave of herself willingly.

God loves a cheerful giver.

Phoebe means radiant. Her name is an indicator of her legacy. She was a shining star for Jesus.

Philippians 2:14 Do all things without complaining and disputing, so that you may become blameless and pure, "children of God without fault in a warped and crooked generation." Then you will shine among them like stars in the sky...

Let's shine for Jesus today!

Dear Lord Jesus, help me to be like my sister Phoebe. Radiant. Humble me to know that there is no task that is beneath me. Everything is for Your glory. I want to be an encourager. Give me your special words that touch hearts. Use me to bring relief to those who are worn. Weary. I desire to have a servant's heart. Your heart. Overflow my heart with Your unconditional love. I want to give my all for you. As You gave Your all for me.

January 11

1 Timothy 6:6 Now godliness with contentment is great gain.

We decided to have lunch at Bob Evans. We are so happy to be able to go into a restaurant again that we pretty much allow Camden to choose the things he likes. On this particular day Ray ordered Strawberry "bread" aka a piece of cake. I'm not sure if Ray even got a single bite when Camden did a hostile takeover. After that he had a pancake, French fries and followed that up with Reese's cup sundae. I really didn't want him to have the ice cream but just to keep the peace I conceded. So we managed to make it through breakfast without causing a scene. On the way out is a wall filled with bags of candy that shouts out to children of all ages. Camden playfully stated, "I want Gummy Bears." The mother in me had to draw the line. Very matter of factly I said, "No. You've already had enough sugar today." He pushed a little more. "But I want Gummy Bears." Again, I restated that he had enough. Now he was shouting, "I want gummy bears!" He began to stomp and cause a commotion. His tantrum continued in the car; he began to kick the seat and fussed the whole way home. He had quickly forgotten the blessing of all that he had. I gave him a lecture on the ride home. He still refused to be thankful. I sent him to his room until he could have a thankful heart. I ran some errands and when I returned there was a handwritten sign on his door.

It read, "NO MOM."

I had to chuckle. How often do we do this to God?

When we don't get our way we refuse Him access.

Instead of praising Him for what we do have, we shut Him out until He gives us our way. We give Him the cold shoulder. We refuse to talk with Him. We don't want to meet with Him. Anger starts building up. Instead of thanking Him for all of His wonderful blessings, we look at the one thing He hasn't given us. Then we begin to dwell on that. Pretty soon we can't see anything else. It consumes us. That one thing separates us from God.

Thankfulness is a choice.

Have you been demanding Gummy Bears?

Make a list of all that God has blessed you with and you'll be thanking Him.

Lord I stop here and now to thank you for all the magnificent gifts that you have blessed me with. I am so undeserving of them, but you give them anyways. You overflow me with blessings and I want to bless you back. Forgive me for my ungratefulness. You are so good to me.

January 12

God needs strong women. It's a fact.

Daniel 11:32...the people who know their God shall be strong, and carry out great exploits and those of the people who understand shall instruct many...

Exploits: bold and daring feats.

Bold and daring? Me?

I didn't think so.

When we are cut down by an illness, cut open by painful news we need hope.

We may be facing the trial of a lifetime. An unplanned illness. Disability. Monumental struggle.

Everything taken.

All our dreams washed away.

God still wants to use us.

Right here. Right in this place.

How?

We possess Christ.

He is our strength to get up and carry on. Not just exist. But to persevere.

God wants us to do great things with the hand we've been dealt.

Philippians 3:8 MSG...Yes, all the things I once thought were so important are gone from my life. Compared to the high privilege of knowing Christ Jesus as my Master, firsthand, everything I once thought I had going for me is insignificant—dog dung. I've dumped it all in the trash so that I could embrace Christ and be embraced by him.

God has a call on your life.

We can cling to the way things used to be or let them go.

Remember Lots wife.

Don't look back at your old life. Let it go.

You will never be the same again.

That's the point. God doesn't want you to stay static. He wants you to change.

Maybe you're shackled to your house. Invite someone in.

If you're on a sickbed, become an intercessor. Be His prayer warrior. If you were busy running here and there you wouldn't have time to pray.

God places you where He needs you.

He takes us through the desert so our souls will thirst for Him. The true and living God.

Live a life of love. Reach out to someone else.

Help her take a breath. Be her stability. Take her by the hand.

1 Corinthians 15:3-4 For I delivered to you first of all that which I also received: that Christ died for our sins according to the Scriptures, and that He was buried, and that He rose again the third day according to the Scriptures...

She needs this hope you have.

So many have fallen into despair. They've been taken captive by thoughts of hopelessness. Unable to continue on. Defeated. Cast down. Weak.

When we are helping others, we take our eyes off of ourselves. God reveals His greater purpose. He wants us to help someone else.

All those things we thought were important are utterly meaningless.

This is the true meaning of life: We desperately need God.

When we're desperate for Him the world fades away.

God allows us to go through various trials to purify us. These trials give us a good picture of what's inside our heart. Pictures don't lie.

Out of the abundance of the heart, the mouth speaks.

What comes out of our heart during a trial?

For me, many ugly things came to the surface.

Self-pity. Why me?

I became angry at my circumstances. My faith was weak.

But God didn't want me to stay that way.

No way.

He wanted to purge these things.

God needs strong women.

We have a choice to make.

Cling to the past or reach forward to the future.

Let go of our will. Bury it. Or hold onto it and remain unchanged.

Be determined to make something good out of this!

God please change me! I don't want to stay the same. Help me go through this change with grace. Make me a strong woman after Your heart. Use me to make a difference in the life of another sister. I choose you and Your way. I lay the past at Your feet. Take it. I look forward to what You are going to do next.

January 13

Colossians 4:12 Epaphras, who is one of you and a slave of Christ, greets you. He is always struggling in prayer on your behalf, so that you may stand mature and fully assured in all the will of God.

Epaphras is struggling in prayer. In the old language the word used was agonize. In other words, Epaphras is always agonizing in prayer. Do you find prayer to be agonizing at times? Most of the time? The root of this word means conflict, fight, contention, and race.

These are not words I would equate with prayer.

I want to be a prayer warrior. I want to give it my all. I believe there is no greater tool to help in time of need than prayer. It wreaks havoc on the enemies' plans. It disrupts his schemes. It shields his victims. Prayer brings us to the throne of God. It makes us strong. It prepares us for battle. No wonder the enemy strives to stop us. He does anything to divert us from prayer. He creates situations in our lives that make it agonizing to get to prayer. But we just need to press on. Fight for your time with the Lord! Don't allow his schemes to stop you. Be urgent.

Ephesians 6:12 For we are not fighting against flesh-and-blood enemies, but against evil rulers and authorities of the unseen world, against mighty powers in this dark world, and against evil spirits in the heavenly places.

Recognize his diversions. Be persistent.

Your prayers matter.

God help me to recognize how vital my prayers are. People are depending on them. Help me to be aware of the enemy's schemes. Guard me from them. Make me vigilant. Increase my desire to pray. Make it fervent. My little prayers can change big things. You are bigger than the enemy. Put your strong hand up to divert him from my path today.

January 14

It wasn't until my phone died that I realized how much time I spent with it; which creates a real conflict in my spiritual life.

Without it for nearly two weeks, I was lost.

I had become so dependent on it. I didn't realize just how much.

A little too much.

Everywhere I go, I reach for it.

Feel my pocket. Yep. Still there. Get in the car. Yep. Still there. Get out of car. Yep. Got it.

Get out of bed. Yep. There you are. Go to bed. Yep. Good night. Still there.

It's my connection to the world.

I didn't realize how important it was until it was gone.

My life has become exponentially more difficult without it.

Everything takes double the effort. Way more work than necessary.

I actually feel lost.

Confused.

Unsettled.

In much the same way, this is what happens when we lose our connection to God.

One morning I went to my computer and this message showed up:

You're not connected...

I realized God was trying to get my attention.

I discovered my phone was causing me to lose my connection.

Technology is awesome. Don't get me wrong.

But when we connect to it instead of God, it hurts us.

It hurts Him. Nothing seems right.

It is fighting for my time with God.

When we reach for it first thing in the morning instead of reaching out to Him, there's a problem.

If we spend more time with our phone than we do with God, something needs to change.

We need to take care of that connection problem today.

Until we do, our lives will be so much more difficult. Twice as hard as they need to be.

Do you know why?

We try to do God's work without His power.

We can't do anything without Him!

Here is what the Lord spoke to me:

Connect to Me first.

I want to be the Apple of your eye. The One that turns your head.

Reach for Me.

First.

Make sure I'm with you. Be certain you're connected to Me throughout the day.

When you need direction, I Am the Way. I'll be your MapQuest.

If you're looking for advice, seek My face before you seek Facebook.

When you feel like you've lost contact, come to Me. I am your connection to everyone and everything.

When you can't find Me, search for Me with all your heart.

There is no replacement. I Am the only source of power.

When you've had the Real, everything else is just cheap imitation.

John 6:68...Lord, to whom shall we go?

Real answers are only found in one place, the throne of God.

We need to call to Him before we call to anyone else.

John 6:63 "It is the Spirit who gives life; the flesh profits nothing. The words that I speak to you are spirit, and they are life.

He really is all we need.

Before any more time goes by, restore that connection with Him.

Jeremiah 33:3 'Call to Me, and I will answer you, and show you great and mighty things, which you do not know.'

January 15

Constant: something that remains steady, a situation that does not change.

I heard the pelting. It definitely wasn't rain. Rain sloshes. I opened the front door.

Little ice balls scattering everywhere.

My anxieties heighten.

With my mission trip to Cambodia under a week away, I decided to check the weather. It was not looking good. It's that season. January on the East Coast is unpredictable at best.

Anything could happen. And sure enough the weather forecast was calling for freezing rain. Ice. And snow. Temperatures hovering in the low 30's.

I begin to panic. I can deal with the rain. The plane can still take off. But ice? It's a no go. And my worst nightmare ensues. (And that is being stuck for hours on an airplane with Camden, with another 15 hour flight ahead to Korea and then 6 more hours to Cambodia.)

Ok. Breathe Renee.

Exhale.

Suddenly I am reminded of something. I am in control of none of this.

My God is in control of all of it.

Delays are often part of His plan.

Not mine.

I like predictable. My ticket says I leave at 11:50 a.m. on 1/15. That's the plan. I've already got it set on my calendar. It's in my mind. It settles it you see.

God sees a little different.

Isaiah 55:8 For My thoughts are not your thoughts, neither are your ways my ways...

My "ticket" may take me to my destination a bit slower than I anticipated.

We have ideas. All well intentioned.

I think back to all of my well planned aspirations. Like graduation. Does anyone really know when you graduated? If it was "on time"? Oh, that's right I didn't graduate.

God had another plan for me.

I am so thankful He knows better than me.

We often give God time frames. Sarah did. Elizabeth did too.

We plan to marry by a certain time. Have kids by another.

And something comes along to unexpectedly disrupt it all.

We can worry. Fuss. Get anxious. Get angry. Worry some more.

Or we can rest. Leave it in His hands.

Trust Him with it all.

He will give us what we need to make it through. All the way to the end.

Either He is in control of all of it, or none.

I began to think back. ALL of God's delays, disruptions and even cancellations turned out to be for the best.

His best. My best.

If you have experienced a delay or cancellation to your "plan" take this time to thank Him.

Thank Him. Thank Him.

Yes, a "wintry mix" may wreck your plan. But not His.

Changes come.

There is only one "constant" in our lives.

Only One who never changes.

Rest in this: His plan is perfect.

Our God is constant. Reliable. Steady.

And for the record, I checked the weather...0 % chance of ice, snow or even rain on the day of departure.

My how things change in just a few days.

January 16

John 9:34...they cast him out.

Jesus always goes searching for the one who is cast out. He pursues the one who may feel excluded. Sometimes we can feel like we're on the sidelines. Some of our children are cast out of playgroups and even church groups. But it may not be something that drastic. Our situation just makes us feel left out. Maybe it's just that you can't go to the same places anymore. Maybe people just don't understand you. They have no idea what you're going through every day. They truly don't. You make it look easy. Or they only see a glimpse because you leave before the meltdown actually takes place. How many times have you heard, "If he was my kid I would_____." Or how about, "He just needs a good spanking"? My all-time favorite, "Just give him to me for a week and he wouldn't act like that." These words hurt more than they could ever know. They actually deflated me of my hope. I felt like I was failing my son; like I wasn't doing enough. After hearing them enough, I began to slowly withdraw myself from these possible scenarios; making me feel like the cast out.

John 9:36 Jesus heard that they had cast him out; and when He had found him, He said to him, "Do you believe in the Son of God?"

Jesus found him.

This man was blind but he received a greater healing than just his sight. This disability opened the eyes of his understanding to see his need for a Savior. He needed Jesus. No one else could help him. That's what I found to be in my life. I knew God. I had a wonderful relationship with Him. But if it weren't for this disability I would never have grasped how much I truly needed Him.

While I did withdraw myself for a time, Jesus found me where I was at.

He asked me a simple question, "Do you trust Me?"

I answered, "Yes! Yes I do!"

He asks you this same question. Do you trust Him?

God will never fail you.

He will find you where you are. You can worship and exalt Him even if He never heals; never changes the situation. He will change you. He will give you what you need. He sees and He cares enough to go searching for you. Just like me, He'll bring you into His arms. Your safe place.

January 17

Exodus 2:9 Then Pharaoh's daughter said to her, "Take this child away and nurse him for me, and I will give you your wages." So the woman took the child and nursed him.

As Christian parents, God calls us to essentially take our children away. Separate them from the world. Teach them God's way.

It is not always easy. It is very challenging. We never know what a day may hold. Being a mom is exhausting. It taxes every ounce of your patience and you know what? I wouldn't trade it for the world. You see, the world may look down upon us. Even more so if you homeschool your child. I cannot tell you the countless comments I received throughout the past year. I think my favorite was from the nurse at Patient First. She stated with her most concerned voice, "How does he get socialization? You need to make sure he is around other children." I did my best to defend myself. I tried my best to convince her I am a caring loving mom who makes sure he gets socialization. By the time I left the conversation I felt thoroughly put down and worthless. But you know what? God spoke very clearly to me. Are you doing what I called you to do? I sheepishly answered, "Yes, I am." Sternly He said, "Don't you worry about what other people think. You seek My approval and My approval is the only one that counts. Since when do you seek the accolades of the world?"

They will NEVER approve of what I'm doing. Children are seen as an inconvenience, especially special needs children. God loves them so immensely. God loves you so deeply and He cherishes what you are doing. God puts great value on being a mom. God puts a significant value on a homeschooling mom. It is not treasured by society, but it is cherished by God. And if today finds you exhausted please hear these words:

Isaiah 40:27-31 27 Why do you say, O Jacob, And speak, O Israel: "My way is hidden from the LORD, And my just claim is passed over by my God"? Have you not known? Have you not heard? The everlasting God, the LORD, The Creator of the ends of the earth, Neither faints nor is weary. His understanding is unsearchable. He gives power to the weak, And to those who have no might He increases strength. Even the youths shall faint and be weary, And the young men shall utterly fall, But those who wait on the LORD Shall renew their strength; They shall mount up with wings like eagles, They shall run and not be weary, They shall walk and not faint.

God knows you're tired. It is ok to rest. Sometimes we feel guilty for needing a break. God said, "I want to renew your strength. I want to breathe new life into you; strength for another day. I see you. I know what it takes every day to be you. No one else sees it. I see. You keep persevering. I will reward you.

Take this child and nurse him for me. Nurse him. Feed him the pure milk of the word.

ABC'S AND 123'S ARE IMPORTANT BUT NOTHING TRUMPS THE WORD OF GOD.

I found out 4 years ago the power of God's word:

John 1:1 In the beginning was the word. The word was with God and the word was God.

Every time we share God's word, even if it's one little scripture we are giving them Jesus. The name of Jesus was one of the first words my son ever spoke. And when I didn't know if he would ever speak another word I found peace in knowing that at least he could speak that precious Name. There's power in that Name. God told me, "Don't look at your abilities, look at MY abilities. Just teach him My word."

Luke 1:37 Nothing is impossible with God

Whatever goal you're trying to reach, God is going to help you get there. His Word never fails to produce fruit. I've truly seen miracles. God will work in your child as well.

If you're lacking in your teaching skills, God is able to make up the difference. He just is and we just need to trust Him in that.

If today finds you doubting your calling, perhaps you are searching for an answer, or maybe you need validation...

Proverbs 22:6 Train up a child in the way he should go, And when he is old he will not depart from it.

The final piece of our verse from Exodus 2:9 Take this child and nurse him and I will give you your reward.

What is our reward?

1 Thessalonians 2:19 After all, what gives us hope and joy, and what will be our proud reward and crown as we stand before our Lord Jesus when he returns? It is you [my child]!

The salvation of our children is ALL that matters. Let us stay focused on what is important.

The way is difficult. God knows. He chose you because He knew you had what it would take to meet this child's every need.

He will reward your efforts. Nothing goes unseen by Him.

Let's keep giving them Jesus!

January 18

Jesus is in control of your destiny.

You were formed for a divine purpose. You are not some accident. If you or your child has a disability or an ailment it is not by chance. If your husband lost his job, it's no surprise to God. Maybe you're new to the area? God has you here for a reason.

He knew this would happen before your birth. It's not a random act. God is not caught off guard. God in His sovereignty allows things in our lives so that it can bring Him glory. When I stopped trying to figure out how my son would live up to the "American Dream" and be the next whiz kid, I felt so free. Each of us is unique in every way. Not every child will excel in Math and that's ok. Not everyone has perfect health. In fact, some have extremely poor health.

Isaiah 44:1...GOD who made you has something to say to you; the God who formed you in the womb wants to help you.

Don't be afraid...

Wherever you find yourself, God is going to help you get through this.

Revelation 19:6 And I heard, as it were, the voice of a great multitude, as the sound of many waters and as the sound of mighty thundering, saying, "Alleluia! For the Lord God Omnipotent reigns!

I love the meaning of this word "Omnipotent!" It means God still holds sway over everything. No matter what things may look like, He still has influence over everyone and everything. Sometimes things have to fall apart first so you can clearly see only He can put them back together.

Colossians 1:17... in him all things hold together.

Without Him things quickly fall apart; that includes relationships, marriages and children.

Don't take Him out of the equation. You're in this together. You are not alone.

Isaiah 44:3 For I will pour water on him who is thirsty, And floods on the dry ground; I will pour out My Spirit..., and My blessing on your children.

Wherever the Lord has you today I pray He saturates your soul with the knowledge that He is still in control. If you're struggling, remember He is still sitting on the throne of your life, and you can praise Him.

Lord Jesus, you still have the authority over every situation in my life. Crush Satan under Your feet in every area he is trying to usurp Your rule. Take every thought captive. You are on the throne of my life. Silence the voice of the enemy that would tell me otherwise. Be a shield round about me. A wall of fire around my family. You alone oh Lord make me dwell in safety.

January 19

Mark 5:2,3,5 And as soon as He got out of the boat, there met Him out of the tombs a man [under the power] of an unclean spirit. This man continually lived among the tombs, and no one could subdue him anymore, even with a chain... Night and day among the tombs and on the mountains he was always shrieking and screaming and beating and bruising and cutting himself with stones.

This was a very troubled man. He was hurting himself, and doing irrational things. Things that don't make sense.

While this man was being controlled by an unclean spirit, our thought life can cause us to act in much the same way. The enemy of our soul can taint our thoughts. Lies of the enemy can cause us to beat ourselves up. Put ourselves down. Even endanger ourselves.

He can cause us to question our own self-worth. Or lack thereof.

Why do we put ourselves down; constantly beat ourselves up?

How do we come to think so little of ourselves?

Where does all the self-loathing come from?

I pondered my own life.

I was abandoned as a baby. My mom was left to raise my brother and I on her own. Later on in life, I was cheated on. Deserted. These things left scars on my heart.

The enemy used these things to speak lies into my life.

Telling me I was not good enough. I must not be smart enough. Or pretty enough. Or worth enough.

He planted tares among the wheat so to speak. I could no longer tell truth from lies.

The enemy was holding sway over my thought life. He caused me to think poorly of myself.

I constantly sought affirmation from others. I needed their approval.

I didn't get it. I never did. I never will.

It wasn't until I lifted my eyes and saw my self-worth in the eyes of Jesus that I stopped seeking the approval of man. I don't need man's acknowledgement anymore. Nor do you.

Jeremiah 1:5 Before I [God] formed you in the womb I knew [and] approved of you [as My chosen instrument]...

We have a greater approval.

Jeremiah 31:3... I [God] have loved you with an everlasting love...

Forever love. Not a conditional love.

When we fail Him (notice I didn't say if), He doesn't love us less. We are His precious daughters. Forever.

God, open my eyes to see how much you love me. I don't want to be held captive by these lies anymore. Set me free! My value is not found in the way others treat me. My worth is found in being Your daughter. I only want to seek Your approval. Your unconditional love sustains me. Help me to see myself the way You see me. Redeem every last thing the enemy has stolen from me. I am a chosen instrument to speak in Your name. Use my testimony for Your glory.

January 20

Camden and I were learning a wonderful story about a young man who wanted to know how to obtain life. This guy had a lot of possessions. In other words he had a bunch of "stuff." Basically Jesus tells him to keep His word, give up all of his "stuff" and follow Him. In a sense, Jesus was asking him to trade. When we trade with Him, He always gives us something better. He wants us to bring Him what is most precious to us. For this guy it happened to be his "stuff". But for us it can be our hopes, job, dreams or plans. He wants us to be willing to give it all up for Him. We think what we have is great, but we need to grasp that what He has is so much better. It is something beyond what our minds can fathom. He wants our plans. His are better. He wants our heart; all of it. He wants everything. This man went away sad. This guy's "stuff" happened to mean a great deal to him. He was unwilling to give up everything he had.

Jesus is all or He is nothing.

He wants us to be willing to surrender all for Him. He gave all for us.

Is Jesus asking you to part with something?

Make the trade. It's a good deal. It will be worth it. Give Him all. The return is worth more than you can imagine.

January 21

Camden: "Mama look. I found a dime. That means I have $50 dollars and 10 cents."

The boy saved all of his money to take on his mission trip to Cambodia.

And he believes with all his heart that little dime matters.

And you know what?

I couldn't wait to see what God would do with that little dime!

I am reminded of a little boy who came to Jesus with 2 little fish. His "little dimes."

He offered them with the same open hands. Essentially saying, "It's all I have, and I want You to have it."

The Lord took those little fish from that willing heart. And He fed 5000 people with them.

Or how about a scared woman offering her words? It was all she had.

Esther.

She just gave what she had. Her words. Those words saved a generation.

What "little dime" do you have to offer?

It may not be much in the eyes of the world, but it means the world to the Lord. He sees the heart behind it. Your heart to please Him. To help in some small way.

Perhaps you homeschool. That's your "little dime." Maybe you're not seeing any progress. That may be so by the world's standards. But God doesn't see as man sees. He looks at the heart. You are raising a child for Him. He is doing something so beyond what you could imagine.

Maybe you're secluded at home. Unable to get out because your child has a disability. All you have are your little prayers. "Little dimes" that don't look like much. God is using them in unbelievable ways.

Some day you will see.

Lord, all of us come with our "little dimes." Blogs we write, pictures we paint, hair we cut, songs we sing, Bible studies, and other insignificant things. Here they are Lord. We ask you to multiply their impact for Your Kingdom. Use them in ways we could only dream. Help us to open our hands and give them to You willingly. Use our "little dimes" as you choose. In big ways or small. All we have is Yours. We would have nothing without You.

January 22

Nehemiah hears of a great need. He saw people in great distress and he wants to help. He was facing a monumental task of his own and he knew it. It would surely be a battle. But, he didn't back away.

Nehemiah 1:4...I was fasting and praying...

I love how Nehemiah can always be found praying. I know that was the success behind all of his accomplishments. We can learn a lot from him.

Prayer prepares us.

Whatever you need to accomplish today, pray first. It sounds so simple but we tend to forget. Doing any work for the Lord is a battle. No matter how big or small. For Nehemiah, the battle was won before he ever went onto the battlefield. What a good example for us. Before we begin to teach our child we should pray for them to understand. Before we head out to do ministry we should pray first. Before we make a decision we should pray first. It is God who gives supernatural discernment. He is able to warn you of things that lie ahead.

Prayer prepares others.

This is just as important. Prayer gave the king a willing heart. Nehemiah broke through to him in prayer. He didn't depend on his own wisdom. In the heat of the moment, he prayed. He asked God to tell him what to say. We have to do the same. Our anxiety can take over and we might say the wrong thing. Prayer will bring clarity. In the moment, God will give you wisdom on what to say and also what not to say.

Prayer prepares the way.

If you've been running into some roadblocks, prayer may show you a way around. If your supplies have been short, He may provide in a way you don't expect. If you're lacking in ability, prayer will surely show you that your abilities are irrelevant when He is in control.

Nehemiah used every opportunity to pray and call upon God. We should do the same. When we can't reach someone, God can. Whether it's a physical distance or personal strain in a relationship, God can close the gap. He can bridge it. He can touch a heart in a way that nothing else can. Whenever we are doing anything at all for the Lord, prayer is a necessity that we can't overlook nor push to the back-burner. Prayer is our source of strength and preparation for the attacks that will come.

God help me. Strengthen me. Breakthrough. Tell me what to say. Lead in every aspect of this situation. I will follow. Spirit of truth come down. Reveal Yourself in a supernatural way. Open the eyes of the blind. Blind seeing eyes if necessary. I need you. I will depend on you solely Lord.

January 23

1 Kings 17:12 But she said, "I swear by the LORD your God that I don't have a single piece of bread in the house. And I have only a handful of flour left in the jar and a little cooking oil in the bottom of the jug. I was just gathering a few sticks to cook this last meal, and then my son and I will die."

This woman must've felt overwhelmed. She wanted to help Elijah, but she didn't even have enough for her own family. She did not have water to give. She didn't have food. Her needs were too much to handle and then Elijah was asking for her to give him something to eat. She was in a dark pit.

Do you ever feel like that?

You want to help, but you have nothing to give?

You don't even know how *you're* going to make it.

Look what happened when she trusted the word of the Lord.

She gave what she had.

She poured it out.

He multiplied it.

It didn't look like anything to her, but in the hand of God it ended up being a lot!

Elijah said, "Don't bring me just a few jars...bring me a lot!"

DON'T UNDERESTIMATE GOD!

Ask big things from God... it honors Him!

BRING MORE THAN WHAT YOU THINK HE CAN DO!

Bring higher expectations.

Ephesians 3:20 Now to Him who is able to do exceedingly abundantly above all that we think or ask...to Him be the glory.

1 Kings 17:13 And Elijah said to her, "Do not fear; go [and] do as you have said, but make me a small cake from it first, and bring [it] to me; and afterward make [some] for yourself and your son.

Don't be afraid to put others first. Jesus did. It cost Him his life. Giving will cost you. Make no mistake about it. But it will profoundly change you. It will change your perspective. You will see how good you truly have it. You will see God work in the most unexpected ways.

1 Kings 17:14 "For thus says the LORD God of Israel: 'The bin of flour shall not be used up, nor shall the jar of oil run dry, until the day the LORD sends rain on the earth.' "

When you give out of your poverty, you will see how God provides supernaturally. It is not a law that we can reason out with human understanding. It never is.

Whether you are giving your time, your energy, your help, your money...

You cannot out give God.

January 24

Romans 12:2...be transformed by the renewing of your mind.

Renew your mind! Another word for renew is renovate. The first thought that came to mind was "This Old House", on the home improvement channel. I love watching that channel. Often they renovate old dilapidated houses and turn them into gorgeous new homes. The changes are astounding. That is what the Lord wants to do with us. He wants to take this run down, tired, and worn out house and give it new look! Are there still some old things lingering in your life? Are you being defeated by the same old thoughts? Is discouragement stealing your joy? Has depression robbed you of a happy heart? Is pride threatening to ruin your marriage? Has an overwhelming feeling of hopelessness taken over your thought life? God wants to transform us! He wants to make us into His image! He wants to use this time and season in your life to forever change you! He never wants you to be the same again! Well, immediately we wonder...HOW? It is a matter of the will. Are you ready? You decide...Change makes us uncomfortable. If you don't decide, the condition of the house continues to deteriorate; sometimes rapidly.

Every good renovation starts with a vision or a grand plan of what the finished product will look like. Often we limit God's plan in our life simply because of our small view of what He can do. Sister, He wants to work in a big way in your life! He wants to use you in a big way! Let's not limit Him with our unbelief.

Ephesians 3:20...He is able to do exceedingly abundantly above all that we ask or think!

Let's not limit Him based on our current circumstances. Instead, sit down with the Master planner and ask Him to show you His blueprint; as you put away yours.

Hebrews 10:19 we have boldness to enter the Holiest by the blood of Jesus...

Be bold and ask great things from God! It honors God when we ask Him to do the impossible!

James 4:2...you do not have because you do not ask...

Ask!

Most renovations begin with the kitchen. Typically kitchens are where the most money is spent. Consider the cost, you can't begin the renovation and quit half the way through. That will spell disaster. More time will be required on the kitchen than any other area. The kitchen is usually the heart of the home. Isn't that true with us? Mom is the heart of the home. The kitchen is where all of our food and drink comes from. If this area is run down, nothing in the whole house will function properly. If Mom is falling apart, so is the rest of the family. We hesitate to fix the kitchen because we know it will cost the most. Let's jump in and go for it. Make the sacrifice. Do you find yourself trying to "eat on the way to work"? Listen to a few songs and ask the Lord to "bless the day and bless the kids...Amen." Nothing wrong with that, but is it God's best? We don't want just a little bit of Jesus, but rather, let's see exactly how much of Him we can take in every day. Watch how His Word comes alive during the day in unexpected ways. He wants to give you living water to refresh someone else today. Go to bed early so you can get up early and spend some extra time with Him. It is worth the sacrifice!

Or sometimes small changes can make a big impact. Like, when we put a beautiful plant in an empty corner. It brings that corner to life. A fresh coat of paint can bring a room to life. Why not consider a little spruce up in your marriage? A word of kindness goes so far. A compliment always brings a smile. How about a special candlelit dinner just for two? Write a love letter from your heart. Be creative. That man is a precious gift to you from the Lord...and so worth the effort. That child needs to hear you love her. She wants to know you're not too busy for her. Although these things may seem trivial, they build a firm foundation. Satan seeks to put cracks in this foundation. He wants to divide the house.

Luke 11:17...a house divided...falls.

But, the Lord is able to mend that which is broken. He takes what we have and works with it. Maybe you feel like there is nothing there for Him to even work with. He says perfect. He is the only one who can create something out of nothing! He sees the beginning and He sees the end. We don't.

Psalm 138:8 The Lord will perfect (complete) that which concerns me...

The Master builder never abandons the original blueprint. His plan in your life is unstoppable. He began the good work and He will be faithful to complete it!

Let the work begin! Let's make our lives count for Kingdom, and when the year is through, hear the voice of our Master say, "Well done good and faithful servant."

January 25

Have you ever waited so long for God to act that you begin to question whether He will?

I have. I wonder if I have misinterpreted what He said. I've seized hold of a promise. I cling to it with everything I have in me. It just hasn't happened yet.

Did I hear You wrong?

Did You really say it?

Is it ever going to happen?

As all these questions emanated from my longing heart I glanced out the window. Is that a rainbow? I did a double take. It was a rainbow, but I could only see a piece of it. A thick line of clouds blocked most of it. I decided to try to get a better look. I went outside. I took my camera along. I didn't get a good shot. It was incomplete. Clouds were blocking it.

Rainbows are a picture of God's promises. Sometimes God's promises look like they will never be completed. I'm certain that's the way Sarah felt.

Romans 9:9 For this is the word of promise: "At this time I will come and Sarah shall have a son..."

When she was given that promise, it looked impossible. Every outward circumstance contradicted the fulfillment. But we know she did get what was promised. You will too.

This word "shall" is a verb that speaks of something that will happen in the future.

When God gives you a promise it will definitely happen.

The word 'maybe' isn't found in God's vocabulary.

When God chooses, He is able to create something out of nothing if need be.

Essentially He is saying, 'I am going to do this. It is in the works. It will come into existence. There may be a few clouds blocking your view right now, but it will surely come to pass.'

Sometimes it seems so far off.

The question begs to be asked, "When?"

It will be at a fixed and definite time. It will be at an opportune time. It will be at the right time.

Our God is never late; always right on time, every time.

Luke 1:45 "Blessed is she who believed, for there will be a fulfillment of those things which were told her from the Lord."

January 26

Romans 8:28 And we know that all things work together for good to those who love God, to those who are the called according to His purpose.

Do ALL things really work together for good?

Even Autism? Cancer? Divorce? Abortion? Abandonment?

Let's take a look at these words "work together". In the old language 'synergeo' means to unite or mix together.

In other words, God takes each and every detail of our lives, the good, the bad and the ugly and "mixes" them together and brings something good out of it.

I think of Joseph. He was thrown in a pit and left for dead by his own brothers. He spent much of his life in a dark prison cell. He was falsely accused. Went back to prison.

Is all of this part of the mix? How can anything good come from those things?

Let me give you an example.

I baked some brownies, they didn't start out beautiful. They started with individual ingredients: vanilla, oil, salt, sugar, eggs, flour and baking powder. Have you ever tasted vanilla by itself? It tastes terrible. How about baking powder? It's the worst. On their own, these things taste awful. But when they are "united" or "mixed together" our loving Heavenly Father makes them good. There are 2 prerequisites to this though.

First, this promise is only for "those who love God." It is not for those who know some things about Him or merely acknowledge His existence, but for those who love Him.

Second, it is for the "the called according to His purpose." The "called" have a job to do. It is a divinely appointed, selected, and handpicked job. Sometimes that job is difficult. Or scary. We decide to run from it. And that takes us out of the will of God. Sometimes our fears take hold of us. They own us. We decide to cower in the corner. We don't take that step of faith to do what God called us to do.

1 John 4:18 There is no fear in love; but perfect love casts out fear, because fear involves torment.

Love and trust go hand in hand.

Psalm 34:8 Oh, taste and see that the LORD is good; blessed is the [wo]man who trusts in Him!

You won't know until you try.

Choose to trust God. He is greater than all of Your fears.

Surrender. Give Him your fear. Your plan. Your time frame. Your health. Your child. Your desire.

God is taking all the "bad" things and uniting them together in His great big mixing bowl.

If you remove even one of these "ingredients" the result of the brownie would not be the same. Especially the baking powder. No rise. Likewise in our lives. We need those difficult things. Trials and adversity are part of the mix. They sweeten our knowledge of God. Each one makes us crave for more of God in our lives.

Paul found it to be so.

Philippians 1:12 And I want you to know, my dear brothers and sisters, that everything that has happened to me here has helped to spread the Good News.

You won't believe the finished product.

January 27

Recently I took Camden to the Wilmer Eye Clinic for a few tests; nothing serious. While sitting in the waiting room I noticed an iPad or similar tablet that was left in an empty chair. I was very concerned since there was an older gentleman sitting there just a few moments prior. Certain he had forgotten it, and even more certain someone would steal it, I grabbed it and took it to the receptionist. No sooner I sat down he walked out and was obviously looking for his iPad. I got up and explained that I had found it. Did he thank me?

He was furious.

He began to berate me in a long rant chastising me for moving it. He felt unequivocally that I should've minded my own business. After all, he had left it there to save his seat.

I was stunned into silence. I could feel the tears welling up in my eyes. I hate any kind of confrontation and will do anything to avoid it. Besides that, I was trying to be helpful. The entire office came to a screeching halt. You could've heard a pin drop. Inquisitive eyes peered over magazines. I apologized profusely and tried to explain over and over that I was just trying to be helpful; to no avail. On my ride home, I told myself I would never try to help someone again. But, that's not who I am. That is not the heart of Jesus.

Why was he so hostile?

Not only was he unthankful, he was seething.

Why?

His actions were foolish. I revealed to him a fault, and he didn't like it.

I've seen the same hostile reaction to some hot topic issues recently.

If a Christian feels compelled to share a word of truth they are met with hostility. They may even be called names; intolerant, narrow-minded, hater, judgmental, or old fashioned.

Should this deter us from speaking?

Absolutely not! It should compel us!

James 4:17 Therefore, to him who knows to do good and does not do it, to him it is sin.

Christians cannot be swayed from speaking the truth. We cannot be silent. There is too much at stake. We have an obligation to raise up the next generation to know the truth and stand firm on it.

It doesn't matter what law is passed. Man's law will never supersede God's law.

1 Corinthians 6:9 Do you not know that the unrighteous will not inherit the kingdom of God? Do not be deceived. Neither fornicators, nor idolaters, nor adulterers, nor homosexuals, nor sodomites, nor thieves, nor covetous, nor drunkards, nor revilers, nor extortionist will inherit the kingdom of God.

The Bible is a mirror into the soul.

We don't always like what we see in the mirror.

When confronted with sin people become aggressive.

Lest anyone think I am judging I will tell you straight up I fit more than one of the above categories.

This mirror reflects my need for a Savior.

Romans 7:24 Oh, what a miserable person I am! Who will free me from this life that is dominated by sin and death?

God sent Jesus to free me.

This Savior came to earth and died a brutal death to take my punishment for sin. I will be eternally grateful for that.

What does He require in return?

Repentance.

Repent means to go in the other direction and follow God. Do things His way.

If you are actively involved in any of the above, Christian or not, you are in a very dangerous and vulnerable place. God is urging you to RUN in the other direction and don't look back. Live the rest of your life to please Him.

Is that judgmental? It is the most loving thing I can think of, since the penalty for all sin is hell.

Each person will spend eternity somewhere. There are only two choices: Heaven or Hell.

I love you enough to tell you the truth.

It's time to raise the white flag and surrender ALL to Him...He surrendered ALL for you.

January 28

Mark 6:31 And He said to them, "Come away by yourselves to a secluded place and rest a while." (For there were many people coming and going, and they did not even have time to eat.)

Jesus said, "come" and they went. Really simple; no need to complicate this.

Most of us have full plates. There isn't much more room on them. Why do we always do that? We overbook. When we have to let some things go, why is it "my time with the Lord" that always seems to go first? If you notice the end of this verse says they didn't even have time to eat. If we don't get our daily 'food' from the Lord, we will have nothing to give the people we come into contact with. Our time with the Lord must be non-negotiable. Leave it all behind. He has something to say. Don't miss it.

January 29

I love the romance of these verses.

Song of Solomon 1:4 Take me away with you—let us hurry! Let the king bring me into his chambers. Friends: We rejoice and delight in you; we will praise your love more than wine. She: How right they are to adore you!

Song of Solomon 2:3 I sat down in his shade with great delight and His fruit was so sweet to my taste. 4 He brought me to the banqueting house, and His banner over me was love. Sustain me with cakes of raisins, refresh me with apples. I am lovesick.

This brings to mind me and my love. When we first got together we anxiously awaited every meeting. Every phone call and date was longed for and anticipated with great desire and yearning. Remember when all you could think about was this guy? All you could think about was how you could please him. All you could daydream about is the next time you would be together.

I just want to get a glimpse of you.

I just can't wait to hear your voice.

I want to write you a love letter.

I'll stay up late to talk into the wee hours of the morning.

I'll get up extra early because I know he's calling before I go to work.

I am beaming because of his love and everyone can see it!

I will savor every moment with you.

I'll drive 100 miles out of my way just to spend 15 minutes with you.

I, I, I...all of these things I am willing to do for my love.

God wants us to have that same longing for Him. He wants us to continuously grow in our relationship with Him. He doesn't want our love for Him to cool. He wants us to be passionate about Him!

But...

Sometimes sitting down with the Lord can become checking a box. That is not His heart. He wants us to have a fervent desire for Him. Love is a choice. Fire must be stoked. We can't walk away and hope it kindles. We have to stick close and make a conscience effort to place wood on it. It will not happen by itself. We have to be proactive.

Song of Solomon 2:15 Catch us the foxes, the little foxes that spoil the vines, for our vines have tender grapes.

Foxes are crafty. You rarely will see one enter.

Fun stuff, sports, school, and even ministry can steal from our relationship with God. It's often a bunch of little things that add up. Each one carries off a chunk of time.

Maybe there was a time when you jumped out of bed to meet with God. Now you may be content to give him a nod at the start of the day.

God wants all of our hearts. Let's not be content with a mediocre spiritual life. Ask God to blow a fresh wind of His spirit upon your soul. Revive your heart! Fall in love with Him again. Take the time you so desperately need. Be with Him. Be all in. You deserve that.

January 30

Mary and Martha had a brother named Lazarus. He was sick. Lazarus was dying and they knew it. They were desperate. They needed help and they needed it now. They knew where they needed to go.

They sent for Jesus.

They knew Him. They knew He could heal their brother. Jesus didn't come right away.

In fact, Jesus waited two more days. Lazarus died.

It doesn't get much worse than that.

Mary says, "Lord, if You had been here, my brother wouldn't have died."

Jesus appeared to be indifferent. Why did He allow this to happen? Have you ever felt like Jesus could've done something, but didn't? Do you feel like He isn't listening? Perhaps you've been praying about something for a long time. Lord, where are you? Do you hear me? I know you can help me. I've come to the only One who can help. It's You Lord. It's You. But, You're not doing what I ask. You're not fixing this. You're not coming through.

Listen, Mary didn't know the rest of the story, nor do we. I am just like her. Lord, if only...

God was not finished yet.

He is not finished in your situation either.

Is God waiting "two more days?" Maybe its two more years later, and you're still praying the same exact prayer. Maybe its twenty years.

If only You would've done this...If only You would've done that.

If only I did this or I did that. I want to place the blame somewhere. I want to know WHY Jesus is not rushing in to save the day. I want to know how all of this is going to work out. Most of all I want to know that Jesus is hearing me. I want to know He is working. I want to know He hasn't abandoned me.

Two of the most important words in the whole Bible:

John 11:35 Jesus wept.

Jesus was not weeping over Lazarus. He was moved in His spirit over seeing Mary sobbing. Her tears broke His heart. I want to assure you that Jesus is deeply moved by your cries as well.

Psalm 56:8...You put my tears in your bottle; you record them in Your book.

You haven't shed one tear that Jesus isn't aware of. Nothing escapes Him. He is writing it all down and keeping track of every one of your struggles.

For Mary it was her brother. For you, maybe it's the state of your marriage. Lord, do you see? Is it your child? Lord, do you see? Maybe it's your health. Lord, do you know what I'm going through?

Jesus sees everything you are going through. He knows and He cares.

John 11:37 And some of them said, "Could not this Man, who opened the eyes of the blind, also have kept this man from dying?"

Couldn't He do something? You bet He could! But, it wasn't the right time.

Jesus said, "This is for the glory of God. I place you in circumstances where I will get the most glory."

Jesus is not necessarily as concerned about our comfort as He is about our spiritual state and that of those around us. He is placing us in circumstances where He will be glorified the most. Sometimes we don't understand. We second guess.

They asked for a healing. But, Jesus wanted to do so much more. He wanted a resurrection.

Ephesians 3:20 Now all glory to God, who is able, through his mighty power at work within us, to accomplish infinitely more than we might ask or think.

I'm not sure what you're waiting for today, but I do know God is able. God can raise the dead if He so chooses. I don't know what it's going to take, but He does! He is fighting for you. He is on your side. He has people in places that you know nothing about. His resources are endless.

The need is great, but He is greater.

January 31

Sometimes we come to a crossroads and we need direction. We need to know which road to take. We just want to do the right thing, but the right thing is just not clear.

Jeremiah 32:19 'You are great in counsel and mighty in work..."

The root word of "great," means to magnify.

What happens when we look through a magnifying glass? The thing we are looking at becomes large. It gets bigger. That's exactly what happens when we look to God for counsel.

Our problems may not cease. They may become bigger, but God is bigger still!

When we look to God for our counsel we silence every other voice. Yes, it's good to seek Godly counsel but not before seeking the Lord first.

For instance:

If you are struggling financially today, He wants you to know through His word that He sees your bank account.

He knows more than the financial advisors.

Philippians 4:19 My God shall supply all of my needs according to His glorious riches.

God can help us solve things that are way out of our league.

God has shown consistently: He is wiser than the doctors.

He'll give us wisdom we never had before.

I've seen it in every parent of a child with special needs; myself included, we give too much credence to the experts.

Yes doctors are good. We all go to them. But let's face it, there are things they just don't know about your child. No one knows him better than you. But greater still is the knowledge that God knows Him better than even you.

Psalm 139 O Lord, You have searched me and known me.

2 You know my sitting down and my rising up;

You understand my thoughts afar off.

3 You comprehend my path and my lying down,

And are acquainted with all my ways.

4 For there is not a word on my tongue,

But behold, O Lord, You know it altogether.

5 You have hedged me behind and before,

And laid Your hand upon me.

6 Such knowledge is too wonderful for me;

It is high, I cannot attain it.

7 Where can I go from Your Spirit?

Or where can I flee from Your presence?

8 If I ascend into heaven, You are there;

If I make my bed in hell, behold, You are there.

9 If I take the wings of the morning,

And dwell in the uttermost parts of the sea,

10 Even there Your hand shall lead me,

And Your right hand shall hold me.

11 If I say, "Surely the darkness shall fall on me,"

Even the night shall be light about me;

12 Indeed, the darkness shall not hide from You,

But the night shines as the day;

The darkness and the light are both alike to You.

13 For You formed my inward parts;

You covered me in my mother's womb.

14 I will praise You, for I am fearfully and wonderfully made;

Marvelous are Your works,

And that my soul knows very well.

15 My frame was not hidden from You,

When I was made in secret,

And skillfully wrought in the lowest parts of the earth.

16 Your eyes saw my substance, being yet unformed.

And in Your book they all were written,

The days fashioned for me,

When as yet there were none of them.

17 How precious also are Your thoughts to me, O God!

How great is the sum of them!

18 If I should count them, they would be more in number than the sand;

When I awake, I am still with You.

We make God too small.

He knows us inside and out.

Don't allow the wisdom of man to block your view of our great God. He holds the earth in the palm of His hand.

Nothing is too big for Him.

Oh how quickly we can forget He is with us. Our problems take over our field of vision.

Jeremiah 33:3 Call to Me and I will answer. I will show you great and mighty things which you do not know.

When I call upon the Lord, He diminishes the size of my problem. I can no longer see the problem. It's not that the problem went away; it's just that God has been brought to the center of my thoughts and becomes more prominent. God acts as a magnifying glass. Magnification allows you to see details that you won't see with the naked eye. He opens up our eyes to the things unseen.

There are secrets with God that cannot be seen with our natural eyes. They are only seen in the spiritual realm. And Satan will do anything to keep you from getting into that spiritual realm. If you're like me he's been working double time on me this week. It is NO surprise.

1 Peter 4:7 But the end of all things is at hand; therefore be serious and watchful in your prayers.

Satan doesn't want your eyes opened to these secret things of God.

He will do anything to destroy your relationship with the Lord.

Don't allow ANYTHING to come between you and your time with God.

Be on guard against little distractions.

God has something to say.

Jesus, open up my eyes to the things unseen. When things seem out of control, help me to remember You are still on the throne of my life. Be my magnifying glass. Come closer to me I pray. I need to see more of You and less of me; less of this problem. God be magnified I pray.

February

February 1

Proverbs 31:8 Open your mouth for the speechless, in the cause of all who are appointed to die.

These words "appointed to die" hold so much meaning for me today. In the old language they could mean "left behind." In the last few years I have come across many children who have been "left behind"; my own child being one of them. I'll never forget the teacher who very emphatically told me, "Mrs. Bollas I cannot slow down for Camden if he doesn't understand something. I have a set pace I must follow." At the time there was a lot he didn't understand...I was left speechless.

Left behind...

There is another very special boy I want to tell you about. He does not speak. He cannot use the potty. His mom was told they didn't have a place for him in the public school anymore. They said, "He is unteachable." They have completely written him off.

Left behind...

He has been coming to Zoe Life for a few months. He has begun to point to things. He has even been waving bye-bye. His mom said she has been waiting 8 years for him to do that.

Our God has NOT left him behind! He does not write anyone off. He never has and He never will. He can do anything at any time He chooses.

Isaiah 55:10 "For as the rain comes down, and the snow from heaven, And do not return there, But water the earth, And make it bring forth and bud, That it may give seed to the sower And bread to the eater, So shall My word be that goes forth from My mouth; It shall not return to Me void, But it shall accomplish what I please, And it shall prosper in the thing for which I sent it.

We don't always like the rain. We never want the storms of life to come our way. They are difficult. The snow and ice of long winter nights of uneasiness; we would rather avoid them. But they are necessary to feed our soul. Just like the Lord speaks about in these verses: The rain births new things in the earth. The storms in our lives birth new faith.

I could go on and on about this verse. How I love this verse. It was pivotal in my own life. But it is the end of this verse that we count on so much...God's word NEVER returns void. It never comes back empty. It never returns to Him without giving the hearer a gift...It always produces fruit.

A few months passed and now that child that couldn't talk can actually say a few words!

The power of God's word is MATCHLESS.

It is the power of this word infused and brought to life by the Spirit that has been accomplishing the things we are seeing in this very special boy. I praise God for what He is doing and can't wait to see what else He will do!

God's word has that same kind of power in your life as well!

February 2

John 5:6-7 When Jesus saw him lying there, and knew that he already had been in that condition a long time, He said to him, "Do you want to be made well?" The sick man answered Him, "Sir, I have no man to put me into the pool when the water is stirred up; but while I am coming, another steps down before me."

Jesus suggested that this man's healing was a choice. The choice was up to him.

Self- pity can leave us in a paralyzed state.

He was in that condition a long time. The Greek word that describes "a long time" is where we get our English word "chronic". Chronic means to persist or constantly recur.

Each of has something we've been dealing with for a long time.

Jesus saw him. Jesus sees what others don't. He sees underneath. He sees the root cause of our infirmity. He sees the condition of our heart. He knows how much it hurts. He knows what is keeping us from being whole and complete.

What this man was saying is something each of us has said, "I can't do this. I don't want to do this. This is not what I wanted to happen. This is not what I expected."

Sometimes we need Jesus to do something. We put demands on Him and when He does not perform like some circus pony we get angry. We begin to get hardened. When He declines our repeated requests we feel slighted. We think we know what is best. I remember well. When Camden was first diagnosed I was lying in this prostrate position. I was paralyzed; unable to move or do anything. It took everything I had to just get out of bed. I did not know if he would ever talk. One of his first words was Jesus. I specifically remember the Lord asking me this question:

"If he never speaks another word, will you still praise Me?"

I didn't answer His question for a long time.

I remained in my paralyzed state.

When I recognized that I am not a victim of my circumstances, things began to change.

God allowed this in my life for a very specific purpose. His ways are not my ways. Nor are His thoughts mine. I would never choose this for my life. Never. But God who loves me would.

Why did this happen?

John 9:2-3 And His disciples asked Him, saying, "Rabbi, who sinned, this man or his parents, that he was born blind?" Jesus answered, "Neither this man nor his parents sinned, but that the works of God should be revealed in him.

God wanted to reveal Himself through this situation. If I try to figure out any other reason it leads me to take my eyes off of Jesus and put them on myself.

I look at what I don't have instead of being thankful for what I do have. An ungrateful heart is so ugly. It mars the reputation of Jesus. People look at my downtrodden countenance and conclude my Jesus is not good.

But He is good!

Jesus asked him a piercing question. "Will you choose to be made whole?" The choice is yours. I won't force you. No one can do this for you. You have to do it yourself.

This man seemed to say, "I can't." Jesus replies, "Rise up. Get up. Quit laying around feeling sorry for yourself." I do take note that Jesus did not coddle him. When I'm feeling sorry for myself there are times Jesus says, "Stop it. Get up and move on. If you don't, you won't grow spiritually."

Self-pity stunts our spiritual growth. Whatever it is that happened, there is a lesson to be learned. If you don't learn it, God will have to reteach it in another way; perhaps another trial.

Will you be determined to take your eyes off of yourself? Will you purpose to live a life of praise? Will you resolve to be thankful?

Get up and walk. You are free!

Rise up! Live life again!

February 3

I was talking with my friend the other day when Camden let out this shrieking scream. It was startling. I did a quick "Mommy check"...no tears, nothing broken, no blood. It appeared to be a random scream. My friend, who has a special needs child as well, exclaimed that her son does the exact same thing. She wondered why he does this. I explained that his screams are not random at all. In fact, every scream has purpose. He cannot verbally express himself, so he tries to convey a message by his behavior. When he is angry or upset, scared or anxious, he will scream.

Somewhere along the line, he picked up this rogue behavior. I try not to get angry or upset when he does it, but I must admit it is very unnerving. Instead, I am trying to look beyond the scream. What's going on inside his heart? Every scream has purpose. If I take him by the hand and look him in the eye, I can see fear. It melts my heart. Although he cannot express himself verbally, his need is obvious and apparent. He needs love. And some reassurance.

Instantly, the Lord brought a few faces to my mind. One person in my family had a mysterious illness that she seemed to be making up. The doctors confirmed it was indeed "nothing physically wrong". Another person, seemingly has everything, decides to enter "the party scene" of drinking and drugs. Another guy, he is gruff, harsh and offensive. Another gives herself away. Why? Each one is screaming out. The screams appear to be random. Outwardly, they appear to have no purpose. But, I'm brought back to Camden; every scream has purpose. Do you know someone who is screaming out? Maybe the world has told them that who they are is not enough. The enemy has whispered they don't fit in. Maybe something in the past keeps flooding back, and they are trying to silence the pain. Eventually the pain causes a withdrawal into isolation. They become numb. The fire that once was, is just an ember, smoldering way down in a cold heart.

You have a chance to change the course of their whole life!

Romans 5:8 God demonstrates His own love toward us, in that while we were still sinners, Christ died for us.

This person's circumstances may even be a result of their own doing, or their own sin. It doesn't matter; they're still a child of God. They are still deserving of His love. We didn't love God first. He loved us first. He proved His love with action.

1 John 3:16 By this we know love, He laid down His life for us and we ought to lay down our lives for the brethren.

How? How do we put this into action in a practical sense?

Matthew 18:5 Whoever receives one little child like this in My name receives Me.

Will you take that person by that hand? Will you write that note of encouragement? Will you make that phone call? Will you extend that invitation? How about a smile and friendly "hello"? Sometimes it will take humility, selflessness, and kindness.

1 John 5:3 His commandments are not burdensome.

Change the course of someone's life today. Reach out to them with sincere love.

John 14:8...show us the Father, and it is sufficient for us.

What do we do when all of our attempts are rebuffed, ignored and spit upon? Just what Jesus did...He prayed for them..."Father, forgive them, they know not what they do".

Jesus will supply all that you need. You just have to give Him a willing heart.

February 4

God did not call me to raise a great football player or a beautiful ballerina. He called me to raise a soul for the kingdom of God. At the end of my life if my child goes to hell, my life will have been a failure. I don't want to play any part in leading these precious children astray. I don't want to give place to anything that may even suggest it is more important than Jesus. This world has nothing to offer my child. Is there anything wrong with playing football? Absolutely not, but when the team insists on having a game on Sunday at the same time as our church service I have to teach my child when he is young that nothing trumps God. Do you know why? One compromise leads to another. There will always be something that competes. When they go to high school, practice and games will be held on Sunday. Same thing when they go to college. Jesus becomes like leftover meatloaf in the back of the refrigerator. If there's nothing better to eat, I guess I'll eat that. He deserves so much more that.

John 8:37 My word has no place in you.

The world insists on endless activity and busyness; leaving no room in our hearts for the things the Lord has called us to do. No time for His word. No desire.

We can't yield to the pressure of the world.

Matthew 16:26 "For what profit is it to a man if he gains the whole world, and loses his own soul?

God we want you to be first in our lives. Not second and certainly not last. Help us not to compromise. Nothing supersedes You. The world has pushed You out enough. We invite you back in. Take over our schedules. Help us to take a stand for you. You took a stand for us.

February 5

The boy is usually never in worship with us. He is in Sunday School class. This day was special. With our mission team gearing up to leave in just a few days, the church was going to pray for us corporately after worship and before the message. My own worship was interrupted by the most beautiful sound.

"How great is our God...sing with me how great is our God...all will see...How great is our God..."

Sweet music to this mama's ears. Sweetest I ever did hear.

I tuned in.

He was just putting it out there! All out of tune and everything else. Wasn't concerned about that in the least. Just singing with all his heart. He didn't know all the words either, but he was sure trying. Trying his very best. Giving it all he had.

That is truly the heart of worship. It's the heart behind it.

That's what God sees. He sees the heart. Our motives. He sees our feeble attempts. They make His heart happy. He's not looking for perfection. Doesn't care about that at all.

The boy doesn't have a theology degree. It's not about what we know. It's more about Who we know.

Whatever "song" you're trying to sing today, sing as though you're singing for an audience of One. There are so many things we might attempt to do or say, if only we didn't care what people thought. God doesn't care if we're all out of tune. We may have no idea what we're doing, but we're doing it anyway!

We're doing it for Him!

That's all that matters.

We don't have to "know all the words." We just want to give Him something that's of worth. It doesn't matter if it's the best. Or the greatest. What could we give God?

We're doing it for Him!

1 Samuel 16:7... For the LORD does not see as man sees; for man looks at the outward appearance, but the LORD looks at the heart."

Our hearts. That's what comes along with our "song." Our work. Our effort. Our stepping out. Whether it's a new ministry, a book, a kind word or anything else you want to do, God sees the heart behind it.

I think all of heaven shut down for a few moments at the boy's singing. His heavenly Daddy shushing everyone so they could hear his sweet song...

"How great is our God..."

Sing your song today. Sing with all your heart. Give it your all. Just put it out there.

It blesses your God's heart. That really is all that matters.

February 6

Proverbs 22:3 A prudent [wo]man foresees evil and hides h[er]self...

How can a woman foresee evil?

To answer that question we would have to define prudent first.

What makes a woman prudent? Spending time with the Lord gives her supernatural insight into a problem or situation. The Lord will provide certain indicators which will allow her a better perspective. Since He gives wisdom, it is Him who will allow her to make good decisions. God has superior knowledge of a woman's heart. Therefore, seeking Him when making a decision allows Him to convey foresight we wouldn't otherwise have.

How do we know if our decision is from the Lord?

There will be a peace in our heart. If it isn't from the Lord it will be a continuous nagging thought that you shouldn't do it or say it. Once you feel the restraint of God, don't do it.

Godly counsel is very important. But, always seek the Lord before you seek anyone else. All of the circumstances may look favorable. God may see something they can't. God sees, but He also foresees. He may be trying to protect you from something.

John 10:4 And when He brings out his own sheep, he goes before them; and the sheep follow him, for they know his voice

We have to spend time with Him before we'll discern if it's His voice or ours.

When in doubt, don't.

Don't do it. Don't say it. Don't go there.

Lord God, I want to please You in all things. I don't want to take one step without your nod of approval. I am seeking Your voice to speak to my heart. Give me wisdom I pray.

February 7

Ray and I went on a little getaway to Pennsylvania recently. While the accommodations were beyond beautiful and the conversations delightful; it was a little donkey that resided on the side of their home that spoke to me most. After settling in and unpacking the car I strolled down to the barn. This donkey immediately garnered my attention. I walked to the other side of the fence, he came along. I went to see Mr. Horse and there he was tagging along. Everywhere I went, there he was. I couldn't help but think of a story in Numbers 22.

Balaam sets out on his donkey. He is going where God has already told him not to go. I have done this many times in my life.

It has never ended well. Never.

Balaam finds out he can't get down this path he's chosen. Every attempt is impassable. The Lord was blocking the way. He just couldn't see it.

Why do we always second guess God? When He says, "Don't do it," why do we always think it will be different this time. Or we think the age old question, "Did He reeeally say that?" And even, "I can make this work."

It was Balaam's donkey who saw that it was the Lord standing in the way. Why could the donkey see and not Balaam? He was too determined to go his own way. Why is it that everyone else can see what is so obvious, but we can't? It's because we are so focused on going our own way and making our own plans, we can't see that God is actually blocking the way. We want that job so bad we keep compromising to make it work. Or we want that guy so bad we can't see anything else. Even ministries can be that way. We jump through hoops to make it happen but yet it keeps falling apart. We think to ourselves, 'But this is such a good thing.' And it may be, but it's not Gods best.

He is blocking the way. When God blocks the way we shouldn't try to push through the roadblock.

His eyes see further than ours.

He knows what lies ahead. He is trying to protect you.

In our story with Balaam, he tries to push his way through and actually gets his foot crushed. Sometimes the roadblock brings pain.

Why?

A little pain now is better than a lot of pain later.

God knows what is best.

It's not too late. Turn back and get on the right path. There is nothing safer than being in God's will; and nothing more dangerous than being out of His will.

God I want to be in your will more than anything. Help me to accept your will with grace. Help me to overcome the pain. Sing to me Lord. It hurts. Give me a song in my heart again. I trust You. Forgive me for going my own way. I want to do Your will God.

February 8

Exodus 14:2 "Speak to the children of Israel, that they turn and camp...between Migdol and the sea...

They found themselves in a precarious position; that in-between place. Ever been there?

Can't go back. There's nothing there.

Going forward doesn't seem possible.

Sometimes we feel closed in. Even imprisoned. Or trapped.

Confusion sets in, and we don't know what to do.

Exodus 14:3 "For Pharaoh will say of the children of Israel, 'They are bewildered by the land; the wilderness has closed them in.'

The enemy makes us feel like we are out of options. Backed up against a wall. We may feel forced to make something happen. Pressured. As though the clock is ticking. It's in this very place he brings his A game. He chases after us with a vengeance. Whispering lies, he gets us to panic.

Pressure always leads to a bad decision. We can feel it growing. The clock is ticking. We can begin to think we have to make some things happen. If we don't, they never will. We're not getting any younger.

Exodus 14:13 Stand still...

In this place?

This word "still" is a verb. A verb is an action word. At first that seems contradictory. But let's take a look at some of the definitions of the word "still". It means: to relax, refrain, let go of it, to be quiet and take your hands off. To be still requires great faith. We naturally want to do something, anything, just so were not doing nothing at all. Sometimes when we take our hands off that's when God can put His hands on. Be still. You can trust Him.

Don't give in to fear.

See the salvation of the Lord. He will accomplish all things for you. He can pull this off. Let Him deal with it. This is His job, not yours.

February 9

Acts 4:12 And there is salvation in no one else, for there is no other name under heaven given among men by which we must be saved."

Who else can help us? When all of our attempts fail and we don't know what to do or where to go there is One who has the answer. Jesus. When you have no idea even how to pray, sing His name over the situation. Jesus.

His Name can move mountains.

His Name can raise the dead.

His Name can make a heart whole.

Is it any wonder the enemy doesn't want the Name of Jesus spoken?

February 10

One evening I went outside and was completely captivated by what I saw.

Breathless.

God literally took my breath away. I looked up and it was as though I had been transported somewhere else; perhaps a glimpse of heaven. It had just finished snowing. What I saw is so difficult to express. My words are inadequate. It was a serene moment in time. All was still; even my heart. I was trying to take it all in. Soft white snow blanketed everything. It was thick in the trees and its beauty indescribable. What I noticed most was its brightness. It was nighttime and it is typically so dark I cannot see a foot in front of me.

This night was different.

It was as bright as a morning dawn. Even the sky was a light blue backdrop to the clouds.

Revelation 22:5 There shall be no night there...

When I was little I was afraid of the dark. Soon enough I became afraid of everything. Darkness terrified me. I was always afraid of the unknown. I didn't have a dad. I wanted reassurance. I remember lying in bed and if I could just feel my mom near, I would be fine. I felt secure. She would protect me.

Some days I still long for reassurance like that. I want to know all is well.

In heaven there will be no night.

I find such comfort in that.

I won't have any fears because my Heavenly Dad will always be with me. I'll get to hold His hand.

He will never leave me.

Until that glorious day, He is our light shining in that dark place.

Psalm 139:11 Then I said to myself, "Oh, he even sees me in the dark!

At night I'm immersed in the light!"

It's a fact: darkness isn't dark to you;

night and day, darkness and light, they're all the same to you.

God you come down in our dark times. You see me even when I can't see You. You are my light and my salvation. Whom shall I fear? Take my fears Lord. Give me light. You are my only hope.

February 11

John 10:10 The thief does not come except to steal, and to kill, and to destroy. I have come that they may have life, and that they may have it more abundantly.

Satan is the father of lies. He whispers discouragement. He comes subtly and at an opportune time.

There are things the enemy tells us we will never do. Places we will never go and things we'll never overcome. The enemy is holding some of our children captive. He has some of our brothers and sisters deceived. He has blinded our parents and alienated our friends. There are jobs we are seeking, ministries to be established and yes church buildings to be had. Today finds some of us depressed and not sure if we can make it one more day.

Satan says: You can't get here. You won't be able to do that. You'll never be able to mend that friendship. You won't get that breakthrough. Your kid will never do that.

2 Corinthians 10:5 casting down arguments and every high thing that exalts itself against the knowledge of God, bringing every thought into captivity to the obedience of Christ...

We cannot brood on his lies! Cast them down. Violently! Kick him out of your thought process.

2 Samuel 22:29-30 You, LORD, are my lamp; the LORD turns my darkness into light. With your help I can advance against a troop; with my God I can scale a wall.

No fortress is too high.

Jeremiah 33:3 Call to Me and I will answer you; I will show you great and mighty things which you do not know

No goal unattainable.

No child out of reach.

...statistics can be stacked against us, the doctors may not be hopeful, and by our own estimation it does look impossible.

Luke 1:37 Nothing is impossible with God!

Meditate on this word of God.

You have to combat his lies with truth. Just like Jesus did. He tempted Jesus in the wilderness. He comes quite often when we are tired and worn out. When the checkbook is in the negative and a new job isn't on the horizon.

Philippians 4:8 And now, dear brothers and sisters, one final thing. Fix your thoughts on what is true, and honorable, and right, and pure, and lovely, and admirable. Think about things that are excellent and worthy of praise.

Think upon this:

God can do anything at any time!

Wait on the unexpected.

Lord I look to You. Surround my mind with Your truth. Send Your Holy Spirit into my thought process. Give me discernment to know truth from lies. I want to dwell on You. You are everything good, when nothing else is. You are for me. I stand on your truth. Nothing is impossible with You.

February 12

A good man out of the good treasure of his heart brings forth good.

Luke 10:34-35 "So he went to him and bandaged his wounds, pouring on oil and wine; and he set him on his own animal, brought him to an inn, and took care of him. "On the next day, when he departed, he took out two denarii, gave them to the innkeeper, and said to him, 'Take care of him; and whatever more you spend, when I come again, I will repay you.'

This man went to help a stranger. He could've crossed the street and walked on the other side. He could've chosen not to get involved. But he didn't. His heart wouldn't allow him to.

I think we can become so calloused to pain that we become unfeeling. We see so much of it, we aren't even fazed by it anymore. It doesn't even occur to us to try to help.

Let someone else do it.

Matthew 24:3,12 What sign will signal your return and the end of the world?... the love of many will grow cold.

We have to be on guard. Has our love and compassion grown cold? We need to do a heart check daily. It is so easy to just keep on going.

This man was moved with compassion to the point that he had to act. He had to do something about it.

Real love proves itself out in action.

No effort goes unnoticed. Every outreach will receive a reward.

He used his own resources.

He did it for a stranger.

It's not recorded that he received accolades from anyone. No one knew what he did. But it didn't escape the all-seeing eyes of God. He took note and it's recorded for all of time and eternity.

Luke 6:38 Give, and you will receive. Your gift will return to you in full— pressed down, shaken together to make room for more, running over, and poured into your lap. The amount you give will determine the amount you get back."

God open my eyes to the needs around me. Stir compassion in my heart. Remove any callus that has begun to form on my heart. Make me sensitive to the pain of others. Take away my indifference. Help me to act. Show me what to do. Give me tender words of mercy.

February 13

Valentine's Day is tomorrow. When I was in school I hated Valentine's Day. I never had a boyfriend. Everyone wanted to have a Valentine. They wanted to feel special. If you didn't have a Valentine, well you felt like you were lacking. A lot of my friends would stick with a boyfriend or girlfriend even if they knew it wasn't working out just because Valentine's Day was coming.

If a guy only treats you special one day of the year he is not worth having.

I didn't know how precious I was to Jesus and just how precious He would become to me. I did a lot of stupid things trying to impress people; people that didn't matter.

What is love?

Real men love Jesus.

Real women love Jesus.

Genesis 2:7 Then the LORD God formed the man from the dust of the ground. He breathed the breath of life into the man's nostrils, and the man became a living person.

Until a guy or girl becomes a Christian they cannot be considered a candidate.

So let's define what it means to be a Christian. We need to go to the Bible to get that definition. We cannot look to the world around us to see what that looks like. There are Christians everywhere who don't act like Christians. That sheds a bad light on Jesus.

A Christian can be defined as "a mini-Jesus". You've heard of a mini-me. Well a Christian is a little Christ person. A Christian is not in name only, but has truly become a member of the family of God. What do I mean by that?

Have you surrendered your whole heart to God? He is worthy of that surrender. He died on the cross for your sins. That is a love that is worthy of completely giving your heart. Jesus was sinless. He never sinned. He never did anything to deserve the death of a criminal. That is the death He died. He did it willingly for you and me. All of us sin. There is a penalty for sin. Hell is the penalty for sin. In hell there is eternal separation from God and everything good.

But, the Bible tells us if we repent of our sins we will not go to hell. What does it mean to repent? The simplest definition means to go in the other direction. I was going this way and now I'm going that way. I was doing this, but not anymore! Now I'm doing it God's way.

A lot of people say they are Christians. When my youth group kids say, 'I have a new boyfriend,' the first thing I ask, "Is he a Christian?"

'Well I don't know. It says he is on Facebook.' Well that's a good start. But don't go by that. Get to know him enough and find out. Actions speak louder than words.

If a person is truly a Christian his/her life will reflect it.

1 Corinthians 5:17 if anyone is in Christ he is a new creation; old things have passed away behold ALL things become new.

He will have a new life, new mind, and new heart.

Here is a good Christian litmus test...have all things become new in their life? Are they still hanging out with the same bad news people doing the same bad stuff? If they are, you need to stay away.

Do you have a new way of thinking? Do you have a new way of looking at things?

If a man does not love Jesus, he will not know how to love you or anyone else. He will have a selfish self-centered love.

If a girl does not love Jesus she will not know how to love you or anyone else.

John 14:15 if you love me obey my commands...

Do you obey what Jesus says? Does what you say match up to what you do?

I know we all sin, but is sin dominating your life? It's time to repent and go the other way. In our culture we want to say we are Christians but we want to pick and choose what to follow and what part of the Bible we will believe.

Every word of God is truth. Every word is worthy of our obedience.

Jesus is all or He is nothing.

He gave His all and He is worthy of our all.

So this Valentine's day I pray you will consider yourselves so blessed to have the greatest love of all; the love of Jesus. You are special. Each and every one of you is so very precious to Him. Jesus is the only love that can fully and completely satisfy the longing deep inside of your heart. No other love can fill that void. No other love died for you.

February 14

I was so overwhelmed. I went to Chick-Fil-A to buy a bag of their amazing chocolate chip cookies. Can't tell you how excited I was about these cookies. I also got a free gift card to go along with it for a future meal. On top of all that, the person in front of me paid what I owed and said, "Happy Valentines Day!"

As I drove away, I was elated. Smiling, and on the verge of tears. I tried to reason within.

Who would do this?

They don't even know me.

I didn't do anything to deserve this.

I was just so grateful.

That was so awesome, and such a snapshot of God and His love...

God is love.

I did nothing to earn His love.

1 John 4:19 We love Him, because He loved us first.

I definitely didn't deserve it.

John 3:16 For God so loved the world that He gave His only Son that whoever believes in Him will not perish but have everlasting life.

The gift of eternal life is for all who choose to receive it.

I didn't have to accept my free gift. Most certainly, I could've rejected it. If I rejected it, the burden of payment would lay on me. It's the same way in my life. There is a penalty for my sin: Hell and eternal separation from God. I actually love this aspect of God.

He is just.

God is a God of love. And therefore, He is a God of justice. If someone murdered my child, I would want justice. Someone to pay. My sin murdered Jesus. Someone must pay that penalty. If I accept Jesus paid the penalty for my sin by dying on the cross, I am free. I am no longer under a damnatory sentence.

That is real love. True love. A Man would give His life for me.

Ephesians 2:8 God saved you by His grace when you believed. And you can't take credit for this. It is a gift from God.

That is a gift to be celebrated!

Happy Valentines Day! You are loved!

February 15

Acts 9:17 So Ananias went and found Saul. He laid his hands on him and said, "Brother Saul, the Lord Jesus, who appeared to you on the road, has sent me so that you might regain your sight and be filled with the Holy Spirit."

We see three things that Ananias did:

He went to Saul.

He laid his hands on him.

He called him brother.

Ananias means to be gracious.

The Lord appeared to him in a vision and Ananias said, "Here I am Lord."

Oh God, may we say that to You.

There are many things that could've hindered Ananias from going to Saul. He had very valid reasons to hesitate. He didn't though. He trusted the Lord and went. When we know someone's background it can really cause us to question God. We reason within ourselves that this person could never change.

We think, "God send someone else." We look down at this person and say, "No way."

But, God says, "I will make a way."

John 14:6 I am the way the truth and the life and no man comes to the Father except through me.

And how will this man get there unless someone shows him the way.

Is there someone in your life that needs you to go to them? Some with a past? Others may not be willing to give them a chance, but the Lord gives all of us a second chance. And a third. And a fourth.

Go put your hand on him. When you do he will receive his sight. So many among us are walking around blind. They are so lost in this dark world. Deceived and broken down, they wander into our churches. We can't ignore them. We can't push them aside. They are too important in the eyes of God. God sent them here for a reason. He knows you will embrace them.

God I need Your grace. Remind my heart what You have done for me. Where would I be without a second chance from You? You cast my sin as far as the east is from the west. You don't remember it anymore. You never throw it in my face. I want to do what You are asking me to do.

February 16

"Mom I blew your candle out!" Camden sheepishly exclaimed; half smiling with eyebrows raised. He knows how much I hate the smell released from a burnt out candle. He wanted to see my reaction. I always overreact because that stench permeates the whole house. It's so difficult to get rid of. It actually makes me want to leave my house. I dislike it that much.

I think God hates a blown out candle that much as well.

A Christian whose candle is burnt out is an offense to God. She is critical. Why isn't anyone helping me? Why aren't they doing what I'm doing? She is unhappy about just about everything. She complains. She gossips. Gossip destroys friendships, marriages and even churches.

How do I know its gossip? If you aren't lifting that person up, then you're gossiping.

If it is not kind, don't say it. If it is not uplifting, don't say it. If it is not encouraging, don't say it. If it is not shedding a good light on the other person, don't say it. If you wouldn't want it said about you, don't say it.

Psalm 141:3 Set a guard over my mouth, LORD...

This is most difficult when a friend has said something to hurt us.

Psalm 55:12-13 It is not an enemy who taunts me—I could bear that. It is not my foes who so arrogantly insult me—I could have hidden from them. Instead, it is you—my equal, my companion and close friend.

Even when a close friend hurts us, we need to guard what we say. We don't need to defend ourselves. The Lord is our defense. We can't let everyone around us know either. That only serves to further the problem. It causes more damage. It douses our flame.

Is your candle smoldering?

It's your job to light it back up!

Psalm 55:22 Give your burdens to the LORD, and he will take care of you. He will not permit the godly to slip and fall.

God, I want to be burning for you. Help me to rise above these insults. You know the situations I am in today. I'm just willing to do anything you ask. Put a guard on my mouth. Be my defense. Heal my heart Lord. Mend the places that are broken. Restore the trust that has been lost. Show me how to proceed.

February 17

Exodus 4:21 And the LORD told Moses, "When you arrive back in Egypt, go to Pharaoh and perform all the miracles I have empowered you to do. But I will harden his heart so he will refuse to let the people go."

You may be doing everything God called you to do and see no visible results. No worries. Lack of "success" is not a sign that we are off track. God has His own ideas of "success".

Don't judge your work.

Exodus 4:11-12 So the LORD said to him, "Who has made man's mouth? Or who makes the mute, the deaf, the seeing, or the blind? Have not I, the LORD?... GO and I will be with your mouth and teach you what you shall say.

The conversation really should've ended right there, but Moses didn't trust the Lord. He argued with God, "I'm not good with words. I never was and I'm not now. I know you spoke to me but I'm still not feeling up to it." He should've obeyed the Lord and went out at the bare word of God. We do the same thing. We see the magnitude of the task and we think, "I can't do that! I'm not equipped to do that! God, you've got to be kidding! That's just a little too much and a little too far."

For me, there are times that I think I cannot, but there are other times I will not. I just don't want to do what God is asking.

God told Moses He would teach him what to say. This word "teach" is a word used in the old language for an arrow. When you step out of your comfort zone, God will make you an arrow in His quiver. You cannot miss your mark when He is the one guiding. He will give you the words to say. He will teach you the skills needed to accomplish your task.

Luke 12:12 "For the Holy Spirit will teach you in that very hour what you ought to say."

Don't miss an opportunity.

Lord Jesus, please help me to take my eyes off of all of my inabilities. I want to trust you. Help me to step out on Your bare word. My confidence lies in You. Not me. I know You will give me what I need to do what You called me to do. My heart is Yours.

February 18

Children need two parents.

Ecclesiastes 4:9 Two are better than one

I pass this family of ducks every morning. I love how they love. They stay close. When I come near they both perceive the threat. They go on high alert. Necks craning. Mom is looking one way; Dad another. They're protecting the children, but in the process they have each other's back. Each one could've flown away.

But they didn't.

They stayed.

Each one made a choice.

I will stay. I will die for you, if need be.

Marriage is much the same.

Each one makes a choice.

I will stay.

Even if:

I have to die to my plan, my way, my pride.

I don't feel like loving.

I don't feel happy.

Marriage is not always about being happy, but holy.

What does that mean?

Choosing to be a peacemaker, not because he deserves it, but in your desire to honor God. It's about choosing the hard.

For better or worse. There's a lot of worse that happens. But it's often making it through the worse that you get to the best.

It's about staying when everything in you says go.

What about all this insecurity?

Love makes itself vulnerable. Love finds security in Christ and Him alone. Love sees the future and can smile. It knows Who holds the future. No matter what may come, Jesus Christ will be there.

Commitment to Him is essential.

What does that mean?

Surrendering your life to Him.

Placing your man is His hands.

Raising your children to know Him.

Ecclesiastes 4:12...A threefold cord is not quickly broken.

He is the stability.

The one constant variable that never changes.

Everything changes in marriage.

Jesus never changes.

You can trust Him with your life.

Your man.

Your children.

Place your phone aside. Find something fun for your family to do together today. Something that doesn't cost money. Somewhere to connect. Be together.

February 19

2 Kings 2:9 And so it was, when they had crossed over, that Elijah said to Elisha, "Ask! What may I do for you, before I am taken away from you?" Elisha said, "Please let a double portion of your spirit be upon me."

Elisha could've asked for anything.

He asked for something profoundly simple.

"God use me," was the cry of his heart.

Elisha saw all that Elijah did.

Essentially saying, "I want to do what he did. I want to work for You Lord. Use me Lord."

Elisha had to stay right by Elijah's side in order to do the things that he did. So it is with us, we have to be so close to the Lord, right by His side, in order to do the things that He wants us to do..

He will give us His Spirit to accomplish what He has called us to do. We have to keep our eyes focused on Him. We don't have to worry about what everyone else is doing. He'll lead us in the way He wants us to go which isn't necessarily the way He wants others to go.

By the power of His Spirit we can accomplish the impossible!

But the key is keeping our eyes fixed on Him!

How about you?

Make every day count for God.

Be His hands and feet. Be His mouthpiece. Do it for the one. Make a difference in one person's life at a time. It will have a ripple effect. Make a change where you're at. You can't change where you're not at. Do it now.

God has placed you in a strategic location. You can reach people that others can't. Don't say, "When I get to that next destination, I'll do this or that." You're not at that next location. You are here. Don't say, "When things get better financially." They may not get better. And still God wants to use you just as you are. Don't say, "When I'm healed, I'll do it." God still uses us in our weakness.

We sometimes think God's great plan for us is prosperity, and it is. But His idea of prosperity and ours are completely different. Elijah was one of the greatest men that walked this earth. But he was also homeless and dead broke. In today's economy, he didn't have a dollar to buy a burger off the Dollar menu. By the world's standards, he was a failure. Yet God used him in a very special way.

Often we think God wants to use us to reach a multitude, and sometimes He does. But His great plan may be to reach one. He may send you to some obscure little spot that no one sees; but He sees. It may be to reach a frail forgotten widow who needs a prayer for her son. It isn't a place you would choose. But it's exactly where God wants you.

Don't despise where you're at. Embrace it! Are you broke? You're in good company. Are you sick? God is using you.

Success is not found in numbers; it is found in faithfulness. God could care less about our bank account. He doesn't take attendance at our church. Nor is He interested in our Coach bag.

How well are we using what He has given us?

Our time?

Our finances?

Our children?

Our struggles?

1 Corinthians 10:31...Whatever you do, do it all for the glory of God.

February 20

2 Samuel 5:19 So David inquired of the LORD, saying, "Shall I go up against the Philistines? Will You deliver them into my hand?" And the LORD said to David, "Go up, for I will doubtless deliver the Philistines into your hand." So David went to Mt. Perazim, and David defeated them there; and he said, "The LORD has broken through my enemies before me, like a breakthrough of water.

Look at the name of this place: Mt Perazim means "Lord of the breaks." There are times we need the Lord to breakthrough!

We need something to happen; something drastic. We need God.

Sometimes we need to know what to do or how to do it.

God is able to make a break in that seemingly impossible situation.

He can supernaturally make things happen. He rushes in like a mighty flood.

He caused the break for David. He will cause the break for you too.

2 Samuel 5:22 But after a while the Philistines returned and again spread out across the valley of Rephaim.

23-24 This time God said, "Don't attack them head-on. Instead, circle around behind them and ambush them from the grove of sacred trees.

When you hear the sound of shuffling in the trees, get ready to move out. It's a signal that God is going ahead of you to smash the Philistine camp."

25 David did exactly what God told him.

When David made this inquiry he had just fought the Philistines, and gained a single victory. The Philistines came up in great hosts but, by the help of God, David had easily put them to flight. Note however, that when they came a second time, David did not go up to fight them without inquiring of the Lord.

Learn from David to take no step without God... Charles Spurgeon

Lord we look to you for our breakthroughs. Where else can we go? You can do anything, at any time! Let us not look around, but up to You. You are our only hope. You saved David and you will save us too. Tell us decisively what we should do. Make it black and white for us. Help us not to take one step without You.

February 21

As we desire to trust God, sometimes we are assailed with doubts. Well-meaning family, friends and even strangers who desire to share their wisdom with us sometimes confirm these doubts. Sometimes we just need to get out of the boat. Staying where it seems safe gets us nowhere.

We must be willing to step out on the bare word of God.

Naaman was told to go wash in the Jordan and he would be healed. Seemed ridiculous. How could washing in the Jordan heal a man? What would people think of him? He was a commander in the army.

But he obeyed and he was healed.

Nehemiah heard the call of God and responded.

As soon as he stepped out he was met with opposition.

Sanballat and Tobiah were right there to criticize him. The names of these guys are interesting to note. Sanballat means "strength" and Tobiah means "Jehovah is good." This implies they were fellow Christians. Christians are sometimes our biggest critics. Remember, if it is God who called you to the work, man's opinion is irrelevant.

Every work of God will encounter resistance.

Nehemiah 2:2 The God of heaven Himself will prosper us. We will arise and build!

Don't respond to the critics. They are just being used as pawns to distract you from your work. If attacks are coming, be encouraged. You know the enemy feels threatened. So get to work with an even greater determination!

Don't look at your qualifications. If you're like me, you have none! But, that may be exactly why God called you.

Don't look at the enormity of the task. If God called you, He'll equip you.

If we look at the obstacles they'll seem too big to overcome.

Matthew 17:20 If you have faith as a mustard seed, you will say to this mountain, 'Move from here to there,' and it will move; and nothing will be impossible for you.

Prayer is our energizer. It is the power behind our work. We can't succeed without it.

We can't look around and wonder what people will think. We must look up.

2 Kings 3:16-18 And he said, "Thus says the LORD: 'Make this valley full of ditches.' "For thus says the LORD: 'You shall not see wind, nor shall you see rain; yet that valley shall be filled with water, so that you, your cattle, and your animals may drink.' "And this is a simple matter in the sight of the LORD...

What God was promising seemed impossible. But sure enough, that valley was filled with water the next day.

God made full every single one of His promises. He will do the same for you.

God grant me the faith that moves mountains. Silence the voice of my critics. Let not fear have dominion over me. I trust in Your word. Your Promises are greater than my doubts. Keep a guard on my mouth. Prosper my work I pray.

February 22

Camden used to wake us up all hours of the night. Even in all his cuteness, we needed sleep. Ray and I would take turns staying up with him. It didn't make sense for both of us to be up. I think the Lord was trying to convey this same message to my heart last night. I was lying awake worrying. As I thought over all of the scenarios of my problem, I became more anxious. And in turn my sleep became more elusive.

Psalm 121:4 Indeed, He [God] who watches over Israel [you], never slumbers or sleeps.

I am His precious child. He isn't falling asleep on His baby watch.

He whispered to me last night.

"I'm not slumbering. You can go back to sleep. I'm taking care of this. It isn't necessary for you to lay in bed at night worrying. You won't think of anything I've forgotten. I don't forget anything. I never have and I never will. I certainly haven't forgotten about you.

Isaiah 49:15 Can a mother forget her nursing child? Can she feel no love for the child she has borne? But even if that were possible, I would not forget you!

I don't know why doubts and fears assault us at night, but when they do we can remind ourselves that our Dad is holding onto us tightly. He is going to provide for every need. We don't have to lie awake wondering how, just know that He will.

February 23

Esther 2:15...she asked for nothing other than what Hegai, the king's eunuch in charge of the harem, had recommended. Esther, just as she was, won the admiration of everyone who saw her.

We need not do anything to impress the Lord. We don't need to jump through hoops. We don't need to put on the jewelry of the world. We just need to be ourselves. Humble. He will bring us favor with our audience. He will make His arrows hit their mark.

17-18 The king fell in love with Esther far more than with any of his other women or any of the other virgins—he was totally smitten by her.

Because she was NOT like the other women of the world he fell in love with her. Esther loved the Lord with all her heart. She trusted Him completely and there is an air that comes about a woman who is sold out for the Lord. It is unmatched beauty that wins the heart of her Prince.

You just be you. You don't have to write like others, just write a simple message from the King. You don't have to sing like others, just make a beautiful melody to the Lord. He will use it. If we try to be like others, we can't be used for God's purpose. You don't have to look like others. God made you perfect just as you are.

Women are not defined by a number on the scale. It's the world that gives women numbers. We don't have to measure up or down to those numbers.

Ephesians 3:18-19 [that you] may be able to comprehend with all the saints what is the width and length and depth and height—to know the love of Christ which passes knowledge; that you may be filled with all the fullness of God.

Paul's prayer is that we would fully understand how much God loves us. This word "comprehend" has the meaning of seizing hold. Taking possession. Fully grasping. Laying hold and not letting go of God's love. God wants us to be defined by His love! His love frees us!

We are free!

Free to be whom He created us to be. We don't have to pretend to be someone we're not. No more putting on masks. We can be done with trying to be like or look like everyone else. We were not designed for that. God made us each unique in our own special way. His love makes us full.

He completes us.

We are not complete when we reach that certain number on a scale. Nor when we get married. Nor when we have a baby. Get that perfect job. Or anything else that we try to "fill" ourselves with.

He completes us.

This world has nothing for us. Jesus has everything we need.

The next time Satan comes with his lies, take them captive.

2 Corinthians 10:4 For the weapons of our warfare are not carnal but mighty in God for pulling down strongholds, casting down arguments and every high thing that exalts itself against the knowledge of God, bringing every thought into captivity to the obedience of Christ...

He loves us. Just. As. We. Are.

Jesus, I pray for You to send Your Holy Spirit to help me to grasp how much You love me. I don't fully understand. Give me just a glimpse. Help me to base all of my actions on Your love. I don't want to put myself down anymore. Build me up in You. Take my eyes off of the world. Remove the lies I've been believing for so long. Fill me with truth.

February 24

Esther 4:11 "All the king's servants and the people of the king's provinces know that any man or woman who goes into the inner court to the king, who has not been called, he has but one law: put all to death, except the one to whom the king holds out the golden scepter, that he may live. Yet I myself have not been called to go in to the king these thirty days."

Esther knew what had to be done. She knew she had to speak to the king. But she also knew what was at risk. She may lose her life. But she considered the lives of others of more value than her own. The entire Jewish population was at stake. I'm sure she was terrified. It's not easy being placed in that position. While we aren't being called to speak to a king, we are being called to speak for the King. This can be risky business. I was challenged by Esther's willingness to risk her life.

What am I willing to risk?

Sometimes we are called to go in the mission field. We may be asked to give up our worldly possessions.

We may be asked to become nothing. To go into isolation. The desert. Become forgotten about.

Our reputation is at risk. It is not exactly the most popular time to be a Christian.

God is asking something different from all of us. But our reply should be the same:

Esther 4:16...I will... If I die, I die.

Esther 4:14 For if you remain completely silent at this time, relief and deliverance will arise for the Jews from another place... Yet who knows whether you have come to the kingdom for such a time as this?

God had Esther in that specific place for a very specific reason. Her cousin was quick to point out, while God wants to use you, He doesn't need you. He can just as easily use someone else. God only offers us opportunities. We don't want to miss any!

Luke 17:33 If you grasp and cling to life on your terms, you'll lose it, but if you let that life go, you'll get life on God's terms.

Lord Jesus, help me to die to myself. I want to be willing to give up all for you. You are worthy of all.

February 25

This particular morning found my thoughts being monopolized by a certain difficult situation. Try as I might I couldn't focus on anything else. Darkness seemed to be looming. Not just outside, but in my spirit. There didn't seem to be a good viable solution to the matter. My mind was reeling. I was supposed to be praying. But I couldn't focus on anything else; I was exasperated and joyless.

I looked up and there was God painting the sky. My view was somewhat limited though. There were houses and trees blocking me. I tried to crane my neck to get a better view, but to no avail. Just then this airplane flew straight into that view; completely unobstructed.

I want that view. From the sky.

God whispered, "I can give you that view."

If you come to Me, I will take you above the problem. I want you to see things from My perspective.

God wanted to open up my eyes to the unseen.

He wanted me to take my eyes off of the situation just for a moment. Even that was a struggle. While I was supposed to be "praying", I was really going over all the details with myself. Recollecting every word that was said; examining and reexamining.

John 16:24 "Until now you have asked nothing... Ask, and you will receive, that your joy may be full."

I have a better understanding of what this verse means now. I wasn't asking the Lord for anything. I was reminding myself how bad the situation was. I wasn't praying at all; just spinning in a vicious cycle. The more I mulled over the problem, the madder I got. It hurt and that's all I could think about. It was wearing me out.

My view was so limited, and what I could see was exhausting me.

Matthew 11:28 "Come to Me... I will give you rest."

He seemed to be shouting, "Come now! Stop what you're doing."

When I did finally go to Him, the situation didn't change. My thinking did though.

God took me above the obstacles so I could have a better view.

Coming to Jesus and sharing my heart with Him altered my perspective. He revived me and thus gave me peace.

Our feelings can be so deceiving. It's important not to speak or act when we're in the state that I was in. We might say the wrong thing in the wrong way, or make a bad decision. Hold off until you can hear the Lord speak clearly.

Isaiah 40:31 But those who wait on the LORD shall renew their strength; They shall mount up with wings like eagles, They shall run and not be weary, They shall walk and not faint.

For me, He said, "Wait." I did, and the situation resolved itself within the day. It may not be that quick for you, but it will be worth the wait.

February 26

We've all heard the expression "the truth hurts," but it doesn't have to.

Ephesians 4:15 NLT...Speak the truth in love.

We can speak kind and encouraging words all day long. Something I've noticed is that we don't like to give compliments.

Why don't we?

A compliment would lift the other person up and someone may think more of them than me.

That should not be!

You are an arrow in His quiver. He sends His arrow to hit a specific target. When God shows you something special about someone don't hesitate to tell them. Let them know how something touched you. Share how their efforts blessed you. Don't assume they know.

God will give us words to hit the mark. Don't miss the mark.

Do you admire someone's work, let them know.

Did a clerk give you good service at the store, tell them.

Catch your child doing something good and praise them for it. Catch them often.

Tell them you love them. Tell them often. They don't hear it enough.

Tell your husband how much you cherish him.

Do you have a friend you appreciate?

Tell them. Tell them now. Don't miss the opportunity.

February 27

I remember what the boy said. And I felt it deep in my heart.

All downtrodden, "I can't go to church. I'm a dummy."

I inquire, "Did something happen? Did someone call you a dummy? Who?"

He puts it like it is, "Satan."

So I probe a little more, "What does he say?"

"He says I'm a dummy. When I'm in my Sunday school class. He says I'm a dummy."

Satan does whisper lies.

If we aren't careful, we just may believe them.

Here are some of his subtle lies:

I am not enough. I wish I was better at that. If only I was smarter. Skinnier. Better. More like that person. Had that voice. That hair. A ministry like that one.

He instills fear. Fear that we won't live up to someone else's expectation of us.

Fear robs us.

Fear is not from God.

2 Timothy 1:7 For God has not given us a spirit of fear, but of power and of love and of a sound mind.

How can we discern truth from lies?

Go to the Word of God. It is truth.

John 14:6 I am the way, the truth, and the life...

Don't mull these thoughts over in your head.

Psalm 46:1 God is our refuge and strength, a very present help in trouble.

God is our refuge from these falsehoods.

The Word of God is truth. You can stand on it. Call upon it. Believe it. Grab hold of God's promises.

Psalm 139:14 I will praise You, for I am fearfully and wonderfully made; marvelous are Your works, and that my soul knows very well.

God made you perfect. Just. As. You. Are.

Others may be smarter, skinnier, prettier, or funnier. God made each one of us unique in every way.

You have everything you need to do the will of God in your life.

May I suggest you write this down? Put it in your pocket. When the lies come, and they will, pull it out and read it. Ask the Holy Spirit to come and fill you with His truth.

Psalm 46:5 God is in the midst of her, she shall not be moved...

February 28

Habakkuk 1:1 The burden which the prophet Habakkuk saw.

1:6 For indeed I am raising up the Chaldeans, A bitter and hasty nation Which marches through the breadth of the earth, To possess dwelling places [that are] not theirs. They are terrible and dreadful; Their judgment and their dignity proceed from themselves. Their horses also are swifter than leopards, And more fierce than evening wolves. Their chargers charge ahead; Their cavalry comes from afar; They fly as the eagle [that] hastens to eat.

Habakkuk was completely overwhelmed by the things that he saw. Destruction was everywhere he looked. Things were not getting better; they were getting worse.

Have you ever felt that way?

It didn't take a genius to see that his people were fighting a losing battle. He wondered how they would ever win. He felt the law was powerless. This law that was supposed to be so powerful seemed to be failing.

The enemy relentlessly pursued them.

His pursuit of us is the same. His hunt for our children is equal. We are clearly outnumbered. The enemy is faster, fiercer, and stronger than we are.

He is not stronger than our God!

Habakkuk 1:5 "Look among the nations and watch— Be utterly astounded! For I will work a work in your days which you would not believe, though it were told you."

God gave Habakkuk a promise. He said, "I am working. I will resolve this, but you're going to have to wait for it."

Waiting is sometimes more difficult than being in the heat of the battle. It takes more faith to wait than work. It can seem so long. When we're working, it's all about us accomplishing. But when we're waiting, it's all about God doing it.

Habakkuk means "embrace."

We need to embrace where God has us.

Habakkuk didn't find himself there by some accident.

He was in that place at that time for a reason. It was not coincidence.

Our God knows what He's doing. God showed him these things so that he could intercede.

He set a watch.

Habakkuk 2:1 I will stand my watch, and set myself on the rampart, and watch to see what He will say to me, and what I will answer when I am corrected.

While he was helpless to do anything in the physical, his real power came in the spiritual realm.

If distance is separating you from a loved one, God is able to bridge that gap.

He can reach anyone at any time. He is not limited by miles.

If time seems to be running out, remember God is not under our time constraints. He is able to make time stand still if need be.

If finances are dwindling He is able to supply all of our needs according to His riches, not ours.

When we are outnumbered and the odds are stacked against us, the greater the victory for God!

Romans 8:31...If God is for us who can be against us?

This enemy will not stop, nor can we.

Habakkuk gives us a great example of standing in prayer.

He climbed up there and stationed himself. He was removing himself from the equation. Doing so enabled him to get an accurate view of the situation. He had to set his feelings aside. Our feelings can often deceive us. We can make wrong assumptions. Climbing that "tower" to pray will give a wider view; a more correct assessment of what is happening.

Without prayer our view is so limited. We can't see the big picture. When we don't know what God is doing we can quickly lose heart. Our heart faints when we see what the enemy is doing. In prayer, Habakkuk recognized his doubting attitude was wrong. He was open to hearing what the Lord would say to him.

Habakkuk 2:3 For the vision is yet for an appointed time; But at the end it will speak, and it will not lie. Though it tarries, wait for it; because it will surely come, it will not tarry.

Prayer changes everything...

We can be waiting but not worrying.

We can be tarrying but not despairing.

We can be staying but not sleeping.

We need to be on watch for that thing we asked for! Did you ask for a revival, healing, financial provision, wisdom, words to speak, or a breakthrough? Anxiously await His answer! Be on the lookout for God to move, work and provide. When He does, give Him the glory! Not one promise of God's has ever failed. No not one. The promise He gave you will not be the exception.

February 29

"When I work, I work. When I pray, God works."

I've heard this quote three times in one week. I think Someone is trying to tell me something.

Ten thousand of our words can't come close to one word from God. So before we go speak to that person, we should speak to God first.

March

March 1

This morning is lovely. Winter seems to be evaporating; even if only temporarily. I only wish the things I'm mulling over in my head would melt away as well. The sunshine and fresh air were a cheerful respite. As I was walking I came to the spot of where an accident had obviously occurred. Someone hit a tree. There was broken glass. A bumper. And a license plate was attached.

Every weekend you can count on it like clockwork; beer bottles, cans, and empty food containers litter the street.

Remnants of the wreckage of alcohol.

I wanted to call the police and make sure the person who hit the tree got their license plate back.

It's not an emergency, but it is important.

I dialed Eastern District.

After three rings, a recording: "You have reached Anne Arundel County 911. Due to heavy call volume we are unable to take your call at this time."

Are you serious?

God spoke very softly to my heart, "I'm not too busy. I always have time for you. Remember those struggles you were trying to figure out a few moments ago? I know they aren't emergencies, but they're important to you. If they're important to you, they're important to Me. You need help. You don't have to figure this out on your own."

What a relief.

The government, friends, and family may be too busy or unaware of our needs...God is never too busy.

God is always there for us. He cares about the big things, but he also cares for the trivial. We can always go to Him. We don't have to carry these heavy burdens around all day long by ourselves. He wants to help. We just need to ask.

Jeremiah 33:3 "This is God's Message... 'Call to me and I will answer you. I'll tell you marvelous and wondrous things that you could never figure out on your own.'

March 2

Nehemiah 8:8-11 They read from the Book of the Law of God, making it clear and giving the meaning so that the people understood what was being read... all the people wept, when they heard the words of the law. Then he said to them, "Go your way... Do not sorrow, for the joy of the LORD is your strength...So the[y] quieted all the people, saying, "Be still... do not be grieved."

They were crying their eyes out when they discovered they were living so contrary to God.

Some of them never heard these things before. It was like a newborn babe opening its eyes for the first time. Tender and fragile. Innocent. Humbled, they now knew they had offended their God. It genuinely hurt. The pain was real. It cut to the heart. They were deeply sorrowful for their sin.

Hearts so sensitive to sin.

Ashamed.

Wrecked.

The word is a mirror into the heart.

They were appalled by what they saw.

But here is God.

Our God.

Our Dad.

Scooping them up in His arms, He quiets them with His love. He shushes them. Essentially saying, "I'm not angry at you. I love you. Jesus died for you. His blood paid your penalty. You are free from guilt. My arms are open."

"Come to Me."

"No matter what you've done, I'll forgive you."

"There's nothing you can do to make Me stop loving you."

"You're Mine. I will never abandon you. The world may, but I never will."

Not only does He not condemn them, He sends them out to rejoice, make merry and celebrate.

I'm in awe of that kind of love.

He loves YOU that much.

God wreck me like that when I offend You even slightly. I want to be blameless before You. Make me sensitive to Your Holy Spirit. Convict my heart the moment it wanders. Thank You for loving me in spite of all of my sins. You amaze me.

March 3

1 Peter 5:5 Be clothed with humility, for "God resists the proud, but gives grace to the humble."

In the Greek, this word "clothed" gives us a picture of a white apron worn by a slave. It was the thing that distinguished them from men that were free. This was to be worn as an outward expression of their lowly position. It was an exceedingly humble garment.

It defined their position as a servant.

Clothed with humility.

Hmmm. Clothing is not something that we come with. Humility isn't either. Humility is something we have to put on. We have to consciously choose to wear it. It isn't our first outfit of choice. Let's face it when choosing an outfit we want something that's going to make us look better. We want something to make a statement. Sometimes we want to stand out. Ok let's face it; we want someone to tell us we look good.

Humility wants to make Jesus look good. No matter what the cost to you. Humility wants to lift up the name of Jesus, no matter what the cost to your reputation.

John 3:30 He [Jesus] needs to increase. I need to decrease.

Humility always takes the lower position.

Humility is giving Jesus the credit. I write to lift up the name of Jesus. The moment I take credit for any of it, I'm lifting up my name. If I'm lifting up my name, I'm bringing Him down.

Humility is willing to be nothing.

Humility is willing to turn the other cheek.

Do people see your apron?

Colossians 3:13 So, chosen by God for this new life of love, dress in the wardrobe God picked out for you: compassion, kindness, humility, quiet strength, discipline. Be even-tempered, content with second place, quick to forgive an offense. Forgive as quickly and completely as the Master forgave you. And regardless of what else you put on, wear love. It's your basic, all-purpose garment. Never be without it. It is not optional.

March 4

Camden and I were preparing to go on a mission trip to Cambodia. It was his first trip out of the country. He had a lot of hesitations.

He exclaimed, "I'm not going." This became his mantra several days in a row. I tried reasoning with him. Attempted to talk it out with him. Nothing changed. I took a different approach.

I asked, "Camden do remember what happened to Jonah when he refused to obey God?"

His eyes got wide, he asked anxiously, "Am I gonna get swallowed by a whale?"

Jonah 3:1 the Lord spoke to Jonah a second time. "Arise. Go..."

Speak what I told you to speak.

Do what I called you to do.

Sometimes we don't want to do what the Lord asks for a variety of reasons.

We think people won't listen. Rationalize, they don't want to hear what I have to say.

We may feel intimidated by the enormity of the task.

Maybe we question our resources. Or feel unequipped. We conclude we don't have what it takes to carry this out.

For Jonah, quite simply, he didn't want to. This wasn't his plan.

Jonah 1:3 But Jonah got up and went in the other direction to Tarshish, running away from God. He went down to the port of Joppa and found a ship headed for Tarshish. He paid the fare and went on board, joining those going to Tarshish—as far away from God as he could get.

He went down...in our attempts to skirt the Lord, we can sink to new levels.

Jonah 1:4-6 But God sent a huge storm at sea, the waves towering.

The Lord allowed him to go so far down so that the only place he could look was up; up to his God.

God will do that in our lives too. If you've been running from Him, stop. You cannot escape Him.

There is no better place to be than in the will of God.

Submit to Him.

Submit means to yield or surrender oneself to the will or authority of another.

Submit is an action word. It is not just knowing the right thing to do... it is actually doing it.

Everywhere you go and everything you do, submit to the Lord.

He is your authority.

We need to do what He says.

We need to follow through with what He called us to do; no matter what the cost.

Did He call you to speak?

Say what He tells you, not what you think people want to hear.

Did God call you to write?

Don't censor God.

You don't need to worry about who is going to believe you, or listen to what you have to say. They may even mock you.

You need to write. You need to write with all your heart.

Did God call you to teach? Teach with passion.

Did God call you to break off that relationship? You need to do that today. Don't wait another day.

Did God tell you to go? You need to go and you need to go right now.

Whatever God called you to do, do it with all your heart!

Colossians 4:17 "See to it that you complete the ministry you have received in the Lord."

Incidentally, Camden never again mentioned that he didn't want to go to Cambodia.

He went in the power of the Lord Jesus Christ!

March 5

Do you ever find yourself saying, "What's the use?" Why am doing this? This is way too hard. I have wasted all my energy for nothing. All this time has been invested and I've seen nothing good come from it. I keep trying and trying, but with nothing to show for it."

It can feel like that sometimes. Ministry. Marriage. Motherhood.

We are in good company. Isaiah felt that way.

Isaiah 49:3 He said to me, "You are my servant...and you will bring me glory." I replied, "But my work seems so useless! I have spent my strength for nothing and to no purpose. Yet I leave it all in the LORD's hand; I will trust God for my reward."

God told him he was His servant. That word "servant" has an interesting meaning. It means to dig, work, and labor.

Digging anything is hard work.

The hard ground you find yourself on is not a coincidence. It was chosen.

A laborer doesn't get to decide what his work is. The boss decides.

You are digging up hard ground for Jesus.

This isn't for you. It's for Him.

This isn't for you to decide if it's successful or not.

Jesus decides that.

A laborer may think to himself, 'but, I'd be so much more useful over here.'

Nevertheless that isn't where the boss wants him.

Our Lord knows where He wants us to work.

He knows all of the surrounding circumstances. Others may have walked away from this hard ground long ago. You have to keep tilling. Tilling and digging are the most difficult part of farming.

There WILL be a harvest.

Proverbs 14:23 In ALL labor there is profit...

You may see no results. Nothing looks remotely like fruit.

A garden takes a whole season.

Fruit doesn't spring up overnight.

Be patient.

Galatians 6:9 So let's not get tired of doing what is good. At just the right time we will reap a harvest of blessing if we don't give up.

March 6

A funny thing happened one morning. As I was driving down the road I reached in my purse to grab my lip gloss. I keep all of my makeup in the same side pocket. The pocket was empty. Maybe I was on the wrong side of the purse? I flipped to the other side; nope, no pocket on that side. I reached in the pocket again as if it had magically appeared. Of course, the pocket was still empty. Normally, I would've concluded I lost the lip gloss. But, I knew I had just put it in there. It had to be in there. I put my hand in there again. Low and behold I found a hole in the pocket. As I dug around you wouldn't believe what I discovered! Not only did I find my lip gloss, I found so much more. I found 3 powder brushes, 2 brand new mascara's (one had never been used), 3 other lip glosses, unopened (expensive) eye drops, and lots of money! What if I hadn't searched for that lip gloss? All of that good stuff would've gone undiscovered.

You know people are that way too. You have to dig a little deeper to discover what's underneath. But for some reason if they're a little different than us we tend to avoid them. Maybe it's an age difference and we think we can't possibly have anything in common. Or sometimes people are downright difficult to get along with. They wear you out. People by nature can be offensive. Let's face it; they can get on your last nerve. But, it's that very person that God wants you to reach out to. Insert yourself into their life. He brought them to you for a very specific purpose. Often He wants to teach you a little bit about the love He has for you.

Digging deeper into my purse allowed me to discover everything that was hidden. So it is with that difficult person in your life. There's always a story behind the story. You may find this person has been rejected everywhere they've ever gone. When you dig past the annoying behavior you may discover they've been abandoned. Life has treated them harshly. Discouragement may have put them on the sidelines. Perhaps they've been an outcast all of their lives, so they just decided to play the part. Underneath all of their quirks and idiosyncrasies, lies a treasure trove of gifts just waiting to be discovered.

God wants us to slow down. Take the time to dig a little deeper. A vast treasure is waiting to be discovered. It works that way with God too:

Jeremiah 29:13 And you will seek Me and find Me, when you search for Me with all your heart.

We don't get to know God by some brief encounter. We actually have to work at it. It takes time to cultivate our relationship with Him, and it will take time with this person as well.

But, how do we get there?

1 Peter 1:22...so now you must show sincere love to each other as brothers and sisters. Love each other deeply with all your heart.

It's this word "sincere" that God is really trying to drive home. Why didn't He just say "show love?" What did He mean by "sincere"?

God is saying, "Quit putting on an act!"

We can be good actresses, or so we think. But, God knows the inner depths of our hearts. He sees behind the pretense. He knows when we're not being real, and He's not going to let us get away with it. He doesn't love us like that. God said, "Take off the mask!" God doesn't require a good performance. He wants sincerity. If you're faking it, people will know. Sometimes we're just going through the motions. That's exactly when we have to slow down. Be real with God. Ask Him to give you His eyes for that person. When He does your heart will break for them. Real love will flow out. That's when all of those hidden treasures will be discovered. Once they're revealed, many will be made rich by them, especially you.

March 7

There is power in the name of Jesus.

When you don't know where to go or what to do...say His name.

There is power in the name of Jesus.

Get back to the basics.

Revelation 12:11 "And they overcame him by the blood of the Lamb and by the word of their testimony, and they did not love their lives to the death.

Overcome means succeed in dealing with a problem or difficulty, to defeat an opponent, to prevail or to carry off a victory.

What problem are you dealing with today?

What difficulty have you been unable to overcome?

There is power in the Name of Jesus Christ.

He gives us strength to walk one more day in these shoes. To be mom to these children. When we don't know if we can carry on one more day. Or go through one more routine or ritual or change one more diaper or deal with one more meltdown.

There is power in the Name of Jesus.

What would you like your child to overcome? You haven't been successful yet.

There is power in the name of Jesus.

Are you broken hearted over a new diagnosis or still trying to come to terms with your own diagnosis? Maybe it's been 5 years and you still haven't. You don't want to accept what comes along with it. Is your marriage struggling?

You know what comes along with the difficulty?

You get Jesus.

You get more of Him. You need more of Him.

He is enough for your problem today.

Do you need comfort?

He sees your broken heart. He came to heal it. He'll set you free today.

Do you need to be rescued?

He's our Life Guard. He is on guard. He guards our lives. Holds us in the palm of His hand.

When we feel the waves taking us out to sea and it feels like we are being swept away and we are longing just to be on firm ground...He knows. We aren't out there alone.

Call on His Name.

There is power in the Name of Jesus.

When we don't know what the next day holds, and we have no idea what to do, that's when we come to the end ourselves. And He can begin.

That's where He works best. When we give up all our efforts.

Jesus can do what we can't.

There is Power in the name of Jesus.

When I didn't know if my son would talk, all I wanted and longed for was for him to say the name of Jesus.

I love the name of Jesus.

When everything is failing, He NEVER fails.

And if I don't know what to do in a situation and I have been there so many times...

I say the name of Jesus... I pray over and over the name of Jesus...

Jesus Jesus Jesus. Jesus Jesus Jesus.

How about you? Cry out to Jesus.

How about your husband?

Is your husband where you would like him to be spiritually?

Sisters, remember it is God who draws all men to Himself...

1 Peter 3:1-2 Wives, likewise, be submissive to your own husbands, that even if some do not obey the word, they, without a word, may be won by the conduct of their wives, when they observe your chaste conduct accompanied by fear.

We can win them over without a word.

I had to learn...ok I'm still learning...I am not the Holy Spirit...

John 16:13 when the Holy Spirit comes He AND ONLY HE can reveal the truth...

Our husbands cannot be nagged into a stronger walk with the Lord. Nor can our children. Nor can our other family and friends.

Constant badgering cannot increase their faith or win them over...

1 Peter 3 says our silence can win them over...SILENCE?

That is so hard! But God does not need our help.

Pray the name of Jesus over them.

There is no greater name than Jesus.

There is power in the name of Jesus.

He is enough for me today.

He is enough for you.

He is enough for our children.

March 8

I was feeling a little out of sorts this morning.

"Go for a walk."

That's what I felt God pressing on my heart. Don't go through your regular routine. I know He wanted to speak something fresh. I went outside and God just lit the sky up for me. It was a crystal clear morning and the stars twinkled bright on the dark backdrop of the night. But there was one star in particular that garnered my attention. It stood out just a little brighter than the others.

As I began to ask God what He wanted to speak, I remembered a guy who was mentioned last night at our prayer meeting. He "stood out" a bit brighter than all the others.

Psalm 106:30 Then Phinehas stood up and intervened, and the plague was stopped.

Phinehas was in the midst of a perverse world. It broke his heart.

Instead of joining them he said, "Enough is enough."

He had the courage to go against the tide. One man made a difference.

How big of a difference?

He changed the destiny of a whole nation.

Did he know it at the time? I doubt it. He was moved in his heart to stand up for what was right. He cared so deeply about the people around him that he had to act.

Being silent was not an option.

His conscience wouldn't allow it. He saw people being destroyed. He knew why this plague was rampant so he did something about it.

He stepped out on a limb.

It takes great courage NOT to go along with the crowd. He didn't care what people thought of him. He didn't consider his reputation. Nor did he pay any attention to what others might say.

He threw caution to the wind.

God posed a question to me:

What would you write if you didn't care what anyone thought?

I don't always say exactly what I know I should. Of course, there is prudence in choosing our words carefully. But, I'm talking about doing what God called me to do and saying what He called me to say.

So now I'll pose a question to you:

What would you do if you didn't care what others thought? What would you say? Where would you go?

What ministry would you step into? What would you step out of?

Singles: Would you be willing to walk away from that guy/girl, those drugs and that alcohol?

How would it change if you didn't care what others thought?

Would you be bolder?

Would you try something new?

We cannot live a full vibrant life if we are always worried about what others think. We can't fulfill God's perfect plan if we aren't willing to take some risks.

Sometimes walking in God's will is very difficult. Sometimes He asks us to do things that don't make sense. You can be sure our God will give us what we need to accomplish what He called us to do.

Philippians 4:13 I can do all things through Christ who strengthens me.

March 9

Mark 6:35 When the day was now far spent, His disciples came to Him and said, "This is a deserted place, and already the hour is late. Send them away, that they may go into the surrounding country and villages and buy themselves bread; for they have nothing to eat."

Mar 6:38 But He said to them, "How many loaves do you have? Go and see."

This was a lonely deserted place. They were exhausted. They already invested so much.

They asked the Lord to send these people away.

Instead, Jesus asked them to invest more. He told them to go take a look at what they had.

It wasn't much. They would never have enough.

Never mind that, Jesus told them to invite the people in.

Give them what you got.

The disciples knew they didn't have enough, but they did it anyways.

Don't we do this all the time?

We look at the task before us and feel overwhelmed. We look at the ministry that's going nowhere. Or the person sitting in the chair next to us in church. The man we're married to or the sister on the other end of the phone and we think to ourselves, 'I don't have what they need. I cannot do this. Let them go somewhere else.'

Send them away.

If I dig deep into the depths of who I am, I still don't have what it takes.

Send them away.

But God has other plans.

He wants you to embrace them. Give them your best.

That's more than enough.

Jesus took what they had. He looked up to heaven.

Blessed it.

Broke it.

Gave it back to them.

Now they had enough. In fact, at the end of the day, they realized they had way more than they needed.

God will do the same in our lives.

Place this person in His hands. God's going to give you what you need to meet their needs. Whether its words of encouragement, a listening ear, a difficult decision or endurance to love.

He will give you what you need.

He'll multiply your little breadcrumbs. Even turn them into a feast.

Expect God to do the unexpected.

March 10

Psalm 121:2 My help comes from the LORD, who made heaven and earth.

Help and Lord are nouns in this verse. This homeschooling mom picked right up on these words this morning! Good thing we were learning about nouns in our second grade English class today or I may have missed it.

For those of you on a refresher course (like myself)...a noun is a person place or thing.

My help isn't some vague distant "maybe" that might show up, but a definite reliable Person. A big strong Dad who won't let His daughter go out of His sight for even a moment. He is fighting on my behalf, leading me in the best direction and giving me His wisdom to make difficult decisions. He will give me the strength to follow through and squeeze my hand tighter when I'm afraid. He made heaven and earth. He holds them in the palm of His hand. I think He can handle what comes my way today. We can do anything together!

March 11

Acts 27:7 When we had sailed slowly many days, and arrived with difficulty off Cnidus, the wind not permitting us to proceed, we sailed under the shelter of Crete off Salmone.

Paul sailed slowly.

The winds would not permit him to move on to his next destination.

Paul was in a holding pattern.

He wanted to get on with his trip, but the wind would not allow him to progress.

He was still moving, but extremely slowly.

I'm sure he just wanted to get this over with. This wasn't some vacation on a Carnival Cruise line. He was in a cargo ship.

He was desperate for change.

Things were not progressing as planned.

They weren't moving along as quickly as he would've liked.

He was coming against some difficulty.

Paul was handed off from one authority to the next. He found favor with most of them. It's important to remember, he was always in the hand of God.

He arrived off the coast of Cnidus. Cnidus is named after an herbaceous plant with jagged leaves. Its edges cut, and are covered with stinging hairs. Most likely not deadly, but very irritating.

Like its namesake, this place Paul found himself was not pleasant. We can find ourselves in a similar situation.

We aren't progressing as we had envisioned. In fact, it is just plain exasperating at this point.

We have expectations that we want fulfilled.

Our time frames are in place.

Nothing is going as planned. This is taking much longer than expected.

But we can be sure it's going exactly as God planned.

We see delays.

God sees opportunities.

Our lives are in the hands of God.

Be patient.

People don't progress at the speed we'd like. Some things aren't resolved overnight.

Acts 27:25...I believe God that it will be just as it was told me.

March 12

Luke 1:13 But the angel said to him, "Do not be afraid, Zacharias, for your prayer is heard; and your wife Elizabeth will bear you a son, and you shall call his name John.

Zacharias prayed for a child for many years.

Did he give up praying for this child long ago?

Did he keep praying?

I wonder if his faith wavered.

The Lord spoke: "Don't be afraid. I heard your prayer."

God answered that prayer.

It was in God's own timing though. He granted Zacharias a son named John.

God knew the exact time he wanted John to arrive on the scene.

The name John means "Jehovah is a gracious giver."

John preached a gospel of repentance from sin. True to his name, he shared with a nation of people that God is a gracious giver. He grants forgiveness to those who seek it.

He had to come at that specific time. To those specific people. Not before. Not after.

Zacharias was not waiting in vain.

The Christian life is one of waiting.

What are you waiting for?

Don't be afraid.

Your prayer is heard.

Luke 1:20 "But behold, you will be mute and not able to speak until the day these things take place, because you did not believe my words which will be fulfilled in their own time."

The prayer would be fulfilled; just not yet. Therefore God chose to make him unable to speak until that time. Why was that?

Zacharias immediately responded by presenting the impossibility of the situation.

I do it all the time. I look at the outward circumstances and doubt floods in.

Sometimes it's best for us to just be quiet.

Our doubt can cause others to doubt.

Discouragement is contagious.

Gabriel came from heaven and spoke to Zacharias. He told him straight up what was going to take place. He was a messenger of God. Yet Zacharias still questioned. And hey, I'm not down on Zacharias because I know I would've done the same thing. You know what else I would've done? I would've demanded all of the details.

I want to know when.

I want to know how.

And no matter how many details He gave I would've wanted more. That's just me.

Zacharias seemed to say, "Don't you see how old I am?"

He was calculating without God.

Age is not a dynamic that has any bearing on God's plan.

Time is not a factor of any relevance. God is not under our time constraints.

The doctor's prognosis has no merit. God defies doctors every day.

If you are waiting for a prayer to be answered, God is still working on it.

Don't give up.

Your prayer is heard.

God will answer.

It will be at just the right time. Not one day early. Not one day late.

God is always right on time.

Don't look at the impossibility of it happening. The surrounding circumstances are irrelevant to God.

Luke 1:45 *"Blessed is she who believed, for there will be a fulfillment of those things which were told her from the Lord."*

March 13

We got a new puppy! He became an immediate member of our family. After having him for about a week, I recollected what life was like for him just the week prior.

This little fella was living outside on a cold concrete block.

How different life is for him now.

One chapter doesn't define a book.

It reminded me of Joseph's story. Genesis 37 begins with him being thrown into a pit and left to die.

But he doesn't.

Why?

Because God's hand is upon him.

In the pit?

Yes, even in the pit.

It may not seem like God is with us in the pit. But He does allow bad things to happen in our lives. When they do. it's important that we remember He is with us through it all.

Every breath you breathe is held in the possession of God. You are untouchable until He says so.

Romans 8:28 And we know that all things work together for good to those who love God...

Even those times in the pit God will use.

The end of Genesis 37 finds Joseph out of the pit and in a palace.

God is a redeemer.

People we encounter often have evil intentions and hidden motives. There are circumstances that are out of our control. Illnesses strike out of nowhere. All of these things can leave us in the pit of despair. In these times it's important to remember our destiny is not in the hand of chance. There is a God in heaven who is in control of every detail. Every aspect of our lives is in the hand of God who is able to lift a soul up and out of the pit. He redeems all of the lost time, wasted years and restores life.

What a difference a day, week, or year can make! Life is not over when we find ourselves in the pit!

God is still revealing the next chapter. It is often just the beginning of a life set apart for Him.

Isaiah 61:3 [God will]...give them beauty for ashes...joy for mourning...praise for the spirit of heaviness...

March 14

I was lost in thought one afternoon; driving on autopilot. I was pondering the many things on my heart. Some of them light, most of them heavy.

Happy laughter spilled from the back seat. I was brought back to the moment.

My son could barely contain himself.

I looked in the rear view mirror into that toothless grin.

He exuberantly asked, "Mom did ya heared it? Did ya?"

I soaked up some more giggles. They enveloped me and I didn't want to let them go. The best part is that I didn't have to.

I had no idea what he was laughing at, but he just wanted me to share in it with him. It's not necessarily the 'what' but the fact that he wanted me to be in that moment with him. I think that's what Jesus wants to remind me of.

He whispers to me, "I am in this with you."

Jesus is our partner in the work. We are in this together. He is working with us, in us and for us.

2 Corinthians 6:1-2 Companions (partners) as we are in this work...God reminds us, I heard your call in the nick of time; the day you needed Me, I was there to help.

A partner is someone to come along side and celebrate the seemingly insignificant joys of this life. He shares the happy times with us; laughing and giggling as little boys do. He is there to cheer you on. He is your biggest fan. When we think we can't take another step, He's there to shout out, "Yes, you can!" It's His very presence that gives us the courage to attempt the impossible; the thrill shared together.

He is a companion on the lonely parts of the trail as well. He is that Someone to carry our bags when they become too heavy. When we need words of affirmation, there He is. There are times when we need to talk to someone and we're afraid. It's like the school boy who brings his big brother along, just in case. He won't leave your side. In the hard times He is there to soften the blow. When we're feeling beat down, it's His hand that will lift us up. When the work gets daunting, it's His gentle nudge that keeps us going. When we need to hear the truth, He'll speak it.

Two are better than one...

He is with you.

March 15

Deuteronomy 33:2 "The LORD came...and dawned on them...He shone forth..."

Sometimes it seems like those black clouds will never go away. Long dreary hours pass slowly by. Gloom covers the soul. Sadness permeates every ounce of your being. Each breath takes effort. Every step is like dragging a weight. It's a long night. We wonder if the morning will ever come.

Darkness always precedes the dawn.

God is birthing something new in you...a deeper relationship with His Son.

Sit tight and listen.

God has something to say.

When He speaks, you'll have a precious message to share with someone else who is going through a similar situation.

A new day is on the horizon.

The sun will shine again.

Remember the sun doesn't rise all at once.

It peeks its head.

Slowly.

It takes its time.

While you may still find yourself in a dark uncertain place, God will meet you there.

Lamentations 3:22,26 Because of the LORD's great love we are not consumed, for his compassions never fail. They are new every morning; great is your faithfulness...It is good that one should wait quietly for the salvation of the LORD.

He is coming...

March 16

Judges 1:36 Now the boundary of the Amorites was from the ascent of Akrabbim, from Sela and upward.

The Amorites were apparently the greatest and most powerful nation in Canaan.

Enemies to be feared.

Israel met with some real opposition. This enemy was strong and powerful. BUT, this was the Promised Land. This was God's possession. He gave them this land. All they had to do was dig in and fight.

They didn't.

They gave in.

They didn't fully possess all that God had for them. They never did fully drive out the enemy.

The enemy was determined.

How I feel a sense of disappointment in myself for not fully possessing all that God has for me. In that I mean fully doing what He called me to do. I definitely have some unfinished "business" so to speak.

Judges 1:27 says the enemy was determined and they won out.

There are things in our own lives that need to be driven out. Things that are enemies to our souls.

We need to be more determined than our enemy. Our enemy wants us to overlook these things. Let them go. We can't allow the enemy to set our boundary. The Lord is our standard.

We must stop crossing the line. The enemy moves the line and we continually cross it. He gains more territory each and every time. He possesses more and more of our hearts. We become more and more like the world.

We give away what is not ours to give.

The Amorite boundary was Akrabbim, which means "ascent of scorpions."

The enemy's boundary led to the "stinging place". Israel would be stung by their own actions or better said, their own inaction.

Judges 2:12,14...they forsook the Lord...they followed gods from among the gods of the people around them...they bowed down to them...

...they could no longer stand before their enemies.

This is where we stand as a nation today. How much longer can we stand before our enemies? I shudder to think. We need to place the Lord back in His proper place on the throne of our lives.

Lord forgive us. Show us where compromise has seeped into our own hearts. Inevitably into our homes. Clear it out. We want to be steadfast before You. Make us more determined than ever! We want you to possess all of our hearts; not just a portion. You are our standard. Not the world.

March 17

When I was a kid, we had a fire in the house. Granny inadvertently left some grease on the stove and it caught on fire. While the house was still standing, smoke permeated everything. From clothes to curtains, there was nothing in our home that it didn't affect.

That's just what smoke does.

Our circumstances can often do the same.

Daniel 3:17-18 If we are thrown into the blazing furnace, the God whom we serve is able to save us...But even if he doesn't...

These guys knew, trusted, and believed with all of their hearts that their God was able to rescue them...but they also knew it may not be His will for them to avoid the fire.

There are times we pray for healing...it doesn't come.

We plead on behalf of a child...change doesn't come.

We beg for a marriage to be saved...he walks away.

God doesn't always rescue us from the fire.

But, He is always with us in the fire.

If we can see Him, our whole perspective changes.

If you find yourself in the midst of a trial, you can be sure God is right there with you.

They didn't know the outcome, but they didn't fear. They were confident in their God.

You can be too.

God is in the fire with you; even when you can't see Him.

He is there.

He is holding your hand through it all.

Others will see Him through your trial and learn that they can trust Him too.

Daniel 3:27 Then the high officers, officials, governors, and advisers crowded around them and saw that the fire had not touched them. Not a hair on their heads was singed, and their clothing was not scorched. They didn't even smell of smoke!

When they came out of the fire there was not even a hint of the smell of smoke. Can I say the same thing? Am I angry with God for allowing this trial? Do my words reflect a good God? Or is my heart bitter? Am I wallowing in self-pity? Do I have an unpleasant attitude over this trial?

I have a choice.

I want to emanate a fragrance of joy. I want to leave people with a good impression of my God. Whatever fire the Lord has me in today, I want to choose an attitude that pleases Him.

I want no hint of the smell of smoke.

March 18

Philippians 4:19 My God shall supply all your need...

Many times we think of this verse as referring to our physical needs and sometimes it is. More often, God is concerned about our spiritual necessities...our soul needs. He wants to conform us into His image. He definitely uses suffering to bring that about.

He will use the physical to bring about the spiritual.

That is what He did with Hagar.

Genesis 16:13 She gave this name to the LORD who spoke to her: "You are the God who sees me," for she said, "I have now seen the One who sees me."

Hagar did nothing to deserve the things that were happening to her. She had no control over her situation. She decided to run away. She didn't get very far. God came. He found her where she was hiding out. She was so scared. Alone and feeling like she had been abandoned, she probably wondered if anyone knew what she was going through.

It was here in this place of desperate need that God revealed Himself to her.

It will be the same for you.

Our vision is so clouded by things that don't matter. When crisis comes those things are whittled away.

Sometimes we may not understand what He's doing or why. But we can trust His word. He was doing something big in Hagar's life. She just didn't know it yet.

If you're in a difficult situation right now, here are a few things God wants you to know:

He hears your heart.

He sees your need.

He has something to say.

Don't miss it. He will speak to you. Slow down. Pray. Take time to read His word...those are some ways He speaks to us.

Jeremiah 29:12-13 Then you will call upon Me and go and pray to Me, and I will listen to you. And you will seek Me and find Me, when you search for Me with all your heart.

March 19

Sometimes we think our circumstances have hedged us in. Holed us up.

In some ways that is correct.

I felt that way before. I couldn't do anything. I couldn't go anywhere. I was angry that I could no longer serve Him in the way that I used to. I was frustrated when I wasn't able to spend time with people. I love people.

I finally concluded that the only thing I could do was pray.

So that is what I did.

It was during that prayer time that I saw God. I heard from Him. He spoke softly to my heart. He put things into perspective. His eyes were upon me. Indeed I was fenced in. This fence kept me in His will. It also kept some things out.

Now He had me where He wanted me.

That "hedge" is what actually gives us the ability to do what God called us to do. If it wasn't for that "hedge" I would not have started Zoe Life. I would not have written a book, blog or anything else for that matter. Consider where God has you. Don't look at it as confinement. I did for the first few years. I mourned my loss of freedom. But it was somewhere in that prison that God actually showed me I was freer than I'd ever been in my life.

God you have me here for a reason. Show me what you want me to do. Use me right here. Right now. Help me to see this place as good. It feels confined. Teach me to be content Lord. I want to praise you here.

March 20

You are uniquely you. Our abilities and inabilities are vastly different. And thank God! He has made each one of us for a special task in His body.

Romans 12:6 Having then gifts differing according to the grace that is given to us, let us use them.

Perhaps you have an undiscovered gift. Many times God brings us to a dark place so this gift will be revealed.

God has given you a unique platform. Based on your circumstances, He has placed you in a position to speak to people that others can't or won't. How many would speak to people with special needs if they didn't have a child with special needs? How many would speak to cancer patients if they had never had cancer.

1 Samuel 10:7 NLT... do what must be done, for God is with you.

Do what God called you to do.

Do it now. Don't wait. Get started. Take that first step.

Procrastinate: to put off until opportunity is lost.

As soon as you take that first step to go in the direction that God called you, He will give you what you need.

Taking the first step is the most important. It takes you off the sidelines and puts you in the game. You won't see anything happen until then.

That first step will be met with incredible opposition.

There is a very real enemy that is trying to stop your work.

Remember Who you are working for.

When God gives you a message, Satan wants to silence it. He wants to destroy and nullify it. He will do whatever it takes to make sure you are busy doing other things. For me, he works through various avenues.

Stirring up my children.

Rousing the dog to make a mess.

Or me deciding to clean one small thing; which leads to the domino effect. Next thing I know an hour has gone by and I've done nothing I'm supposed to be doing.

Press on sisters!

God has something to say through you. Your testimony is powerful.

Use it.

March 21

"Jesus, help me to recognize when I am allowing something to come in between our relationship."

Luke 19:46 'My house shall be called a house of prayer, but you have made it a den of thieves.'

I think it would be safe to say we all have a desire to pray. We have such great intentions. But, if you are like me, many times the prayer never happens. Why is that? Well, I'll be quick to say, 'Satan hindered me'. But did he really? Well sometimes...but, that's not what I want to talk about today. Let's take a closer look at our verse. Jesus said, 'you have made it a den of thieves.' You have. What did I do now? You have made it a den of thieves. In the Greek, this word thieves gives us a picture of a bandit, one of a roving band. It's not just one. There are many roving bandits that have made my heart their home. One of them, if not all daily rob me of prayer time. You see my body is the temple of the Holy Spirit. It is a spiritual house that should only be occupied by things that are lovely and pure. If that is not so, I am sinning and my prayers will be hindered at best.

That really hit home with me. Am I guilty of bringing things into this "house" that are robbing my prayer life?

Jesus wants us to pray individually. Jesus wants us to pray corporately.

Are there things that I have allowed in that are ripping me off?

Misunderstandings...Are you irritated, annoyed or otherwise just plain mad at someone right now? They keep doing something or saying something that really gets to you. You know it's not that big of a deal. You've tried to ignore it. But, it's like a little fly that keeps buzzing around you while you're eating dinner. You shoo it away and it keeps coming back. It frustrates you, but you try to continue eating. You just want to enjoy your food and eat in peace. Back it comes. Now you're angry. You won't be able to enjoy your delicious meal until this pesky fly is gone.

These "misunderstandings" are part of this "band of bandits". They are trivial things that need to be dealt with before they cheat you out of an effective prayer time. We can't enjoy our time with the Lord until they are gone.

Matthew 5:23 Therefore, if you bring your gift to the altar, and there remember that your brother has something against you, leave your gift...First, be reconciled to your brother and then come...

Unforgiveness...at the heart of unforgiveness is usually pride. I want to be right, I know I'm right and I'm not going to forgive. This is not my fault. They should not have done that, said that, looked at me like that.

James 4:10 Humble yourself in the sight of the Lord and He shall lift you up.

It takes humility to forgive. I don't have to be right.

Mark 11:25-26 And whenever you stand praying, if you have anything against anyone, forgive him, that your Father in heaven may also forgive you your trespasses. But if you do not forgive, neither will your Father in heaven forgive your trespasses.

Pride is a bandit that will steal and rob us blind until it is apprehended and dealt with.

Matthew 7:1-2 Judge not, that you be not judged. For with what judgment you judge, you will be judged, and with the measure you use, it will be measured back to you.

This verse gets me every time! If you're like me I begin to pray for someone and suddenly I'm criticizing. I start critiquing all the things they are doing wrong. The Lord doesn't show us their flaws or sins so that we can be critical. He shows us for one reason and one reason only; and that is to intercede.

I know myself. I have to be extremely disciplined with my prayer time.

When all of these bandits unite, we are powerless. Let's be on guard and diligent not to invite them in to our "house of prayer".

"The very powers of darkness are paralyzed by prayer." O. Chambers

March 22

I thought spring had arrived. It said so on the calendar. The sun was warm on my face the last few days. I love springtime. Winter blues drift away. My flowers peek out of the garden. Like little babes opening their eyes for the first time; delightful and breathtaking. If spring was here, why was it snowing this morning? Even worse, the frigid air had returned.

It's like that in my life sometimes. I am certain God is working in one direction and something happens to completely contradict that.

He can be so unpredictable.

I don't like that. I like to know what He's doing. I like to be in control of the situation and when I'm not, I become anxious. God is teaching me to trust Him.

Exodus 34:9-10 "If now I have found grace in Your sight, O Lord, let my Lord, I pray, go among us...The LORD replied, "Listen...I will perform miracles that have never been performed anywhere in all the earth or in any nation. And all the people around you will see the power of the LORD—the awesome power I will display for you."

Check out this word "performed." It is the Hebrew word "bara." In the old language this word "bara" meant to create something out of nothing.

God was telling the people, "Indeed, you have found grace! My favor is with you! I am doing something extraordinary on your behalf. You just have to trust me."

Only God can create something out of nothing.

I know it looks like there is nothing there. God can create new conditions.

I know it's not going as you planned. But, it's going exactly as He planned. Are you willing to surrender your plan?

God is distinguishing Himself so that all will know it was Him that did this.

Sometimes He must sever the old before He can bring the new.

Will you allow Him to do that?

God doesn't work under our time constraints. When He doesn't, we can become disappointed. He seems to have let us down. Our heart can turn as hard as a stone very quickly.

Ezekiel 36:26 And I will give you a new heart, and I will put a new spirit in you. I will take out your stony, stubborn heart and give you a tender, responsive heart.

Will you allow Him to do that?

Hebrews 11:1 Faith is the confidence that what we hope for will actually happen; it gives us assurance about things we cannot see.

God is working on your behalf. You cannot live by what you see.

God is doing wonderful things. Consequently, His enemies hate it. They will stop at nothing. They want to destroy His work. The spiritual battle we face is fierce and ongoing. It may actually seem like they are succeeding. He will thrust out the opposition you are confronting. You trust God!

He still does miracles! If God has ordained it, who can stop it!

March 23

John 1:14...and that Word became flesh, and dwelt among us, and we beheld His glory, the glory as of the only begotten of the Father, full of grace and truth.

Jesus Christ came as a living breathing human being; an innocent baby. He allowed Himself to be vulnerable and fragile. He wanted us to know He experienced the depth of every emotion that we've experienced. He understands how we feel inside even when no one else does.

The Word became flesh, in like manner; we become His living breathing hands and feet. Serving these little gifts that we have been given. It is a high calling. Jesus was the epitome of self-less giving.

1 Corinthians 10:31 whatever you do, do it all for the glory of God.

Recently my husband recanted a beautiful story:

A man was visiting a large corporation. The manager said, "I'd like you to meet our Employee of the Year, five years running. As they walked, the man envisioned he was going to meet the Chief Financial Officer, or maybe the Lead Engineer. When they reached the bottom of the building, there was the janitor, sweeping the floor. He tried not to act surprised, and he greeted her. He said, "So, you're the Employee of the Year?" The woman answered confidently, "Yes I am!" I sweep the floor around here. I sweep from the top to the bottom of this building. I sweep from corner to corner, and then I sweep again." Then she said, "You know why I sweep so well?" The man answered, "No, why?" She replied enthusiastically, "Because I sweep for Jesus." Then she paused and said, "Who do you sweep for?"

The man was never the same again. The question remains, "Who do you sweep for?"

Lord, open my eyes to see that You find great value in doing menial tasks. Dirty jobs honor You. Everything I do today is for You. I pray that it will bring you glory. Help me not to get upset when I have to clean up messes or deal with unpleasant things. I do it all for You.

March 24

Genesis 8:1 But God remembered Noah... He sent a wind to blow across the earth, and the floodwaters began to recede.

Everything that meant something was removed.

God gives and He takes away.

He builds, and He destroys.

Many times he has to wipe out everything we are trusting in.

All that we find comfort in must be obliterated.

We can't hang on to any part of the past.

Luke 9:24 If you try to hang on to your life, you will lose it. But if you give up your life for my sake, you will save it.

When God called Noah, he came. He didn't hesitate. While he didn't know what the future held, he did know he could trust the Lord.

When He wants to begin something new, He must wipe out the old.

He does that through the flood of our circumstances. We are inundated with adversity. Overwhelmed by the struggle.

The water got deeper. First it covered the hills, then the mountains. It wiped everything out.

But Noah was safe.

God knew exactly where He was.

He planned for his protection in advance.

It's easy to think God has lost sight of us. When the waters don't seem to be receding, they seem to be getting deeper and deeper. It may feel like we can barely keep our head above the water.

1 Corinthians 10:13 And God is faithful. He will not allow the temptation to be more than you can stand. When you are tempted, he will show you a way out so that you can endure.

God will never give me more than I can handle, with Him. At just the right time God will come to my rescue. God is always right on time. He is never early; He is never late.

God is never in a hurry.

We just want this to end. Our end is sometimes God's beginning. God knows exactly what is necessary to conform us into His image. It's not comfortable, but comfortable isn't the goal.

After the flood, God sent a wind to pass over the earth.

The floods receded.

Indeed, Noah had lost everything...

Genesis 8:20 Then Noah built an altar to the LORD, and there he sacrificed as burnt offerings the animals and birds that had been approved for that purpose.

He worshiped God. In losing everything he gained all. When you go through the flood and everything is taken, you find out what is most important.

Noah still had his family.

More importantly, Noah still had the Lord.

Noah's life was preserved because he was willing to give everything up.

God, my precious Lord please make my heart willing to yield to you. Take my hands off of things that don't matter. You are what is most important. I yield my heart to you. I want to give you whatever it is you are asking of me. No holds barred. It's yours. Everything I have, I offer to You. Do with it whatever you wish. I pray it brings you glory.

March 25

"Jesus, You know how much she hurt me. I don't know if I can ever be her friend again. She doesn't understand. She thinks I don't discipline my son. But I do God, I do. She doesn't even know he was on his best behavior. I was so proud of him. She made me feel so bad. It hurts me so much."

"Renee let me show you forgiveness..."

Genesis 41:38 So Pharaoh asked his officials, "Can we find anyone else like this man so obviously filled with the Spirit of God?"

What a beautiful compliment! The Spirit of God was evident in Joseph's life. The depth of his relationship with God was clearly seen in his words and his actions. As Christian women our heart's desire is the same. We want to be so obviously filled with the Spirit of God that no matter what someone says we let it roll off. We want our relationship with God to be apparent. Joseph's whole way of life was an expression of his right relationship with God. We see His wisdom. He brought blessing to Potiphar's house and to the people in prison. He was a man of faith who expected God to work. Possibly one of his greatest achievements: He was enabled by God's grace to wipe out the pains and memories of the past and make a new beginning. It's a wonderful thing when we can come through times of trial with Joseph's attitude of forgiveness. He was able to bury past hurts and rejoice in his present blessings. It's a tragedy when a woman clings to the painful things others have done to her, and all her life carries bitterness that robs her of peace and joy. I needed to forgive my friend.

Just as Joseph laid aside his "prison clothes" and made a new beginning, so we frequently need to "take off" the old hurts and put on a new attitude of love. How was he able to be overflowing with all that love? Why was Joseph so willing and able to forgive? Where did his ability to be so patient come from?

It will benefit us to take a peek at what Joseph was clothed in.

Genesis 41:42 He dressed...in fine linen...

The source of this linen is quite intriguing...

This fine linen was a rare fabric obtained from the "byssus", otherwise known as a "mussel". The analogy here is not to be missed! A mussel attaches itself fast to a firm fixed surface by the silky threads it produces. The attachment can be temporary or permanent.

Joseph chose to be permanently attached to God. He lived with an acute awareness that he was in the presence of God. He was not hanging on by a thread. He had a hold on God and did not let go.

The "byssus" was distinguished for its whiteness. It was pure and bright. We need to be the same. Being tainted with bitterness and anger hinders a heart of forgiveness. It weighs us down. We can't allow even a hint of it.

I decided to ask God to help me to forgive my friend for hurting me. I couldn't do it on my own. I had to attach myself to God, and detach myself from bitterness. Doing so filled my heart with a love for her that can only come from God. This enabled me to forgive.

If there is someone in your life who has hurt you, ask God to fill your heart with His love for that person. Ask Him to show you how much you've been forgiven.

Remember the words of Jesus Himself:

Luke 23:34...”Father, forgive them, for they do not know what they do.”

He spoke these words about the people who hung Him on the cross.

Lord give me a heart of forgiveness. Help me to remember what you have done for me. Humble me. Remove pride and every other evil thing from my heart. I want to be like you. Restore my relationships that are broken. Heal and mend them like only You can.

March 26

Matthew 27:46 My God, My God, why have You forsaken Me?”

Friday came.

Death.

Saturday came. He was buried.

When my son was diagnosed with Autism I experienced the deepest darkness upon my soul.

It wouldn't go away.

My pain was overwhelming.

It was actually physical at times.

I couldn't understand why. Why did God allow this to happen? I didn't know how I would go on.

Feelings of helplessness permeated my being. I felt like all of the world was moving on. While I was left behind.

“Saturday” lasted a long time.

But Sunday was on its way.

Sunday always comes.

Jesus wasn't lying in the grave inactive.

At death the veil was torn, granting permanent access to the throne of God. Heaven was opened up.

He said, “after 3 days I will rise.”

What was it like for Mary on that Saturday?

Her mother's heart must've been broken. She was chosen to birth the Son of God physically.

We are called to do the same spiritually.

The birthing process is painful; the death process even more.

She was there at his crucifixion.

John 19:25 Now there stood by the cross of Jesus His mother,

Looking on, helpless to intervene. We sometimes find ourselves looking on, helpless. We want to do something. We'll do anything to stop the trial. If you're like me I want to fix it all. I don't like to see suffering.

Suffering is necessary.

Darkness came upon the life of Jesus. Why shouldn't it come upon mine?

Philippians 3:10 that I may know Him and the power of His resurrection, and the fellowship of His sufferings, being conformed to His death...

Suffering makes us more like our Savior.

Mary didn't know the end of the story. And you don't either. There was a metamorphosis going on that "Saturday"; a complete change for the better. The same thing is happening in your "Saturday" of waiting.

John 20:1 Now on the first day of the week Mary Magdalene went to the tomb early, while it was still dark, and saw that the stone had been taken away from the tomb.

If darkness is still hovering, be encouraged.

Sunday is coming.

There will be a resurrection story for you.

God You are able to resurrect every dead thing in my life. There is nothing you can't do. No one is out of Your reach. Go talk to that person. Open their eyes to see You. Show them who You are Lord. Show me. I want to see You. Keep my own eyes looking to You. Expectantly. Increase my faith; renew my hope.

March 27

1 Kings 2:2 take courage and be a man.

We must raise up boys who know how to be men.

How should a man act?

Who is our example?

Why Jesus, of course.

Qualities of a man:

He should fear God.

He should love the word.

He should be a servant.

He should be a soul winner.

He should be a leader.

We need men who will take the lead.

Therefore, we need to be women who know how to follow our men.

Give them confidence. Don't put them down and question every decision they make.

Little eyes are watching.

Don't allow your son to disrespect you. He can never be allowed to speak to you in a manner that does not honor you.

Teach them to obey you. Children learn to obey Jesus by first obeying their parents.

Chivalry is not dead! It is only dead if we allow it to die. Teach your son to open the door for ladies. Teach him to allow ladies first. This will trickle into every aspect of his becoming a man.

Teach them to love.

Teach them to be humble.

Live it out.

Invest in your marriage. Love your man lavishly.

Give your son an example. Good marriages do exist. Faithful women are out there.

Read your Bible. Do not let your child interrupt your time with the Lord. He will learn God comes first in his mommy's life. He will learn that life is NOT all about him. It's about loving Jesus.

Take him to church every week. Don't allow church to take a backseat to anything. Say no to anything that would interfere with the most important thing in his life: his relationship with the Lord.

Little things add up to big things.

God show me how to raise up my children to love you. Teach our boys to be men. Instill a love for you deep down in their souls. Burn a fire in their hearts for Your word. Let Your word dwell richly in their hearts. Make us passionate for You. We want our children to emulate our love for You. Show us when our love is lukewarm. Let us care enough to do something about it. Save our generation of boys God. Please set them apart for You.

March 28

Psalm 84:2 My soul longs, yes, even faints for the courts of the LORD; my heart and my flesh cry out (to overcome) for the living God.

Here is what happens when we are on fire and burning for our Lord...the quencher of our souls comes to steal.

John Bunyan says (in Grace Abounding) when he felt on fire for God 'Then hath the tempter come upon me, also with such discouragements as these: You are very hot for mercy, but I will cool you; this frame shall not last always; many have been as hot as you for a spirit, but I have quenched their zeal. And with this, such and such who were fallen off would be set before mine eyes. Then I should be afraid that I should do so too; but thought I, I am glad this comes into my mind. Well I will watch and take what heed I can. Though you do, said Satan I shall be too hard for you; I will cool you insensibly, by degrees, little by little. What care I, saith he, though I be seven years in chilling your heart if I can do it at last? Continual rocking will lull a crying child asleep. I will ply it close, but I will have my end accomplished. Though you be burning hot at present, yet, if I can pull you from this fire I shall have you cold before it be long.'

Revelation 3:16 "So then, because you are lukewarm, and neither cold nor hot, I will vomit you out of My mouth.

God hates lukewarm.

What do you do with coffee that's cooled off?

You dump it down the drain.

We don't want to raise a generation of children who become good for nothing.

Lukewarm Christianity is spreading like wildfire across this nation.

Revelation 3:17 "Because you say, 'I am rich, have become wealthy, and have need of nothing'—and do not know that you are wretched, miserable, poor, blind, and naked—

God has blessed us so much that we have need of nothing...even Him.

We are not desperate. We are not in dire straits.

We put Him on the shelf until something really bad happens to us. Then we pull him out like a magic genie. Rub his belly three times and beg for help. Help comes and we return Him to the shelf.

Revelation 3:18 "I counsel you to buy from Me gold refined in the fire, that you may be rich;

The Lord is our treasure!

Give everything you got to hold onto Him. He is what makes us rich. He is what makes our lives have value. He is the only good thing in it.

We are deluded to think our country can stand and endure the way things are.

Love God with all your heart, mind, soul and strength.

Fan those embers into flame.

March 29

One minute Elijah is speaking to the King.

He was being used mightily by God.

Next minute he is isolated and alone.

Did he feel like he was put on a shelf?

Useless?

Unimportant?

Worse yet, a failure?

I certainly did. I was no Elijah, but I enjoyed my ministries. I loved talking to people. People were my life. All of the sudden, I found myself a prisoner of my own home.

Isolated. Alone. Despairing.

Did I do something wrong?

1 Kings 17:3 "Get away from here and turn eastward, and hide by the Brook Cherith, which flows into the Jordan.

In the old language there is an obsolete word used before the word Jordan. It is the word that was used for the face of God. When God calls us away through difficult circumstances, it is right there in the midst of that despair that he descends down and we see His face.

Sometimes we wonder why?

Why do we have to struggle so much?

When we are so far down we have no other choice but to look up.

Our circumstances often bring us to a place of isolation.

If you're alone right now, take heart.

God wants to refresh your soul. He wants to place you under that constant flowing fountain of living water.

Notice the Kerith Brook flows into the Jordan River.

This place of separation flows down into the place you will see God Himself descend down. He'll feed your soul with the breadcrumbs of His word.

It is this place of greatest need that brings us face to face with God.

He was actually hiding Elijah. It was His place of protection.

God prepared for Elijah's need in advance.

God wants to take your life in a new direction.

He usually has to clear some things away first.

God wants to show you He is your sole provider.

Soul provider.

Enough for you.

He wants to make a new beginning.

The only way to do these things is to get you alone.

Once you encounter God in this way, you will be changed forever.

March 30

2 Corinthians 9:7 So let each one give as he purposes in his heart, not grudgingly or of necessity; for God loves a cheerful giver.

Sometimes you're running on empty, and someone wants something from you. They want your time or your money. They want you to do them a favor, and you literally have nothing left to give.

There are times we just feel drained.

When you give out of your poverty something happens.

God gives more.

He turns your nothing into something.

The more you give the more you have.

The less you give the less you have.

When you give in faith your heart becomes fuller. So although you may have less physically speaking, your heart will be brimming over.

We can't focus on our lack. If we fix our eyes on the problem we'll become overwhelmed. Fear and doubts will cause us to cling to what we have. Many times we think if only our situation were different. If only I had more. No matter what it is...time, money energy...If I had more, I would give.

Be willing to give out of your lack and watch what happens!

God will reward your generosity.

God will sustain you. He will not only supply your lack, but others as well. Your service to another will bring an abundance to your own household. Keep your eyes on the One who can do anything.

What God has done in the past He can do again.

Just give Him a willing heart.

Share from your lack. Don't horde it, hide it or give in a stingy manner.

God loves a cheerful giver.

God has given us everything we have. It is on loan. Why do we think it belongs to us? It is His. We're really just giving it back to Him.

None of our resources will be used up and dwindle away. But rather they will be multiplied. You will actually have an overabundance. Remember that God owns everything. He doesn't need your stuff. It is you He is after.

God never runs on empty.

Luke 6:38 "Give, and it will be given to you: good measure, pressed down, shaken together, and running over will be put into your bosom. For with the same measure that you use, it will be measured back to you."

March 31

Revelation 1:10-11 I, John, with you all the way in the trial and the Kingdom and the passion of patience in Jesus, was on the island called Patmos because of God's Word, the witness of Jesus. It was Sunday and I was in the Spirit, praying. I heard a loud voice behind me, trumpet-clear and piercing: "Write what you see into a book. Send it to the seven churches...

John was serving his prison sentence on the island of Patmos.

It was sweltering heat.

Horrendous conditions.

He was isolated.

Alone.

Abandoned.

The world would see that as failure.

God sees it as success.

God had a purpose for it.

John wrote the book of Revelation while he was there. It is a book that has been encouraging the church for more than 2000 years.

God needs to take us to a place we would never go.

Who would choose to go to a sweltering prison in a barren land? Not me that's for sure.

Who would choose Autism? Bankruptcy? Loss? Pain?

God has to get us away from everything familiar. He asks us to give up our plans for His.

It is a struggle.

Sometimes we don't know what to do next. Things didn't turn out the way we expected.

It feels like everything is wasted.

God wastes nothing.

God has you on His training ground.

He is preparing you.

The songbird learns to sing in the dark. At nighttime. When she is alone.

Don't take a rest from praising Him.

God wastes nothing.

Jesus showed up on the island of Patmos. In the barren place. He spoke to John.

He will do the same for you.

There are so many hidden treasures yet to be found in this dark place.

Search for them. Cry out for them. They are there.

April

April 1

I want to tell you about the Vaughn family. John and Brenda Vaughn. John is a Pastor. The family was preparing to move to a new home. They had three children at the time. John was doing some tidying up and for reasons unknown, he decided to bring a gas can that he found outside and place it inside the home in a utility closet off the kitchen. He told his wife Brenda it was in there. He exhorted her to take caution and not allow their toddler near that room. She was only two at the time. Brenda was very busy cooking dinner and doing chores. She became preoccupied. Suddenly she looked up to find gas running out into the kitchen and her daughter sitting in the midst of it. As she closed the oven door, there was an explosion. Her daughter was engulfed in flames. Instinctively, she picked her daughter up and ran for the back door. She also became engulfed in flames. They made it outside where neighbors came running. They spent months in the hospital and years recovering. Brenda had burns over about 80% of her body. Their daughter Becky had burns over 95% of her body. She lost both of her ears. Although she could still hear. And she lost both of her hands. Pastor John recounts that one evening Becky was sitting on the living room floor reading a picture book. Her older sister was playing the piano. He watched Becky struggle turning the pages of the book with what was left of her hands.

Becky looked up. She asked her mom Brenda, "Mommy when I grow up will I have hands like Debbie?"

Brenda didn't miss a beat. She said gently, "Becky, Debbie has the hands that God has given her to do her job, and you have the hands that God has allowed you to have to do your job. You have everything you need to do the will of God in your life."

While most of us haven't suffered the trauma the Vaughn family has, we do each have our own unique situations.

Maybe you're struggling. Some of you have illnesses that you're dealing with. While others may have a strong willed child or one that has learning disabilities. Perhaps a family member is weighing heavy on your heart; a distant husband or wayward child. Have you been met with new challenges in your ministry?

Each of our family's dynamics can be extremely trying and challenging.

Sometimes overwhelming.

Our God is not caught off guard by our situations.

Our needs don't surprise Him. He ordained them. Yes even the most trying ones are sent from Him. Nothing touches us that is not filtered through His loving hands.

The enemy assaults us with doubts. He plagues us with fear.

Psalm 56:3 Whenever I am afraid, I will trust in You.

In every season we can trust our God. He is faithful to the end. Whether in old age or just starting out, we can rely on Him. Sunrise or sunset, His word can be trusted.

He'll give us what we need. Body, soul, and spirit needs will all be met.

Today, I will trust You Lord. There is no challenge I cannot overcome. Silence every voice that tells me otherwise. Pour out Your grace on me. I have everything I need to do Your will in my life.

April 2

New things are often birthed in pain.

The birth of Jesus was no different.

It was difficult.

Matthew 1:24 Then Joseph, being aroused from sleep, did as the angel of the Lord commanded him.

God was asking Joseph to join Him. He needed a partner.

This was Joseph's new assignment for life.

His new beginning.

I am sure Joseph was planning his future. Looking ahead and beaming with excitement at the prospects it held. His lovely fiancé brought him so much joy. They were the perfect couple. They would get married. Maybe start a family in a few years. Perhaps have a house with a white picket fence.

His dreams were wrecked.

One night, one dream and everything changed. His plans came to a screeching halt. The Lord came to him with a new assignment.

God's assignments are not always pleasant. They are far from glamorous. More often than not, they are difficult, humbling, and embarrassing in the world's eyes.

Joseph took it head on.

It was a lot to absorb. How did Mary explain what happened?

As he pondered all the chaos that entered his life so unexpectedly, the Lord delivered a message to him.

"Don't be afraid."

Three simple words changed everything.

You don't have to fear this. I am still in control. I still have a perfect plan. It isn't exactly what you had in mind, but it's exactly what I had in mind.

Remember that prophecy I gave you?

This had to happen in order for my perfect plan to be filled.

I know it looks bad.

I am fulfilling My word.

Joseph had a choice to make. He could have taken the easy way out. No one would have blamed him. He could have told Mary she was on her own. God would have sent someone else to help Mary. He did not need Joseph. He does not need us. He wants to use us, but He does not depend on us to accomplish His will.

He was asking Joseph to go this alone. He would most likely lose the support of his entire family. I am sure all of his friends were snickering behind his back. Most, if not all, would think he was a fool. Joseph was willing to lose it all for the Lord. He chose to accept his new assignment. I know God rewarded him for it. He will reward you as well.

Matthew 10:39 NLT If you cling to your life, you will lose it; but if you give up your life for Me, you will find it.

April 3

It rained one morning. This greatly hindered Camden's big plans for the day. He was very disappointed, and it was written all over his face.

I tried to explain, "Sometimes things happen that are out of our control."

He didn't like that answer.

Pouting he whimpered, "I have my broken heart with me."

He moped around the house for a while. Reconciled to the fact that he couldn't go outside, he decided to play his Wii game. Don't you know the game broke and he couldn't play?

When it rains it pours.

Why does everything seem to happen at once?

There's a great story in the Old Testament in 2 Chronicles 20. The King finds himself in a similar situation, but much more severe. He was facing the battle of a lifetime. He heard it wasn't just one army coming against him, it was many. The king was terrified by this news and begged the LORD for guidance. In his prayer he acknowledged God's power and might.

God rules and He overrules.

He remembered what God did in the past.

What God did before, He can do again.

God sent word to him:

'Do not be afraid or discouraged because of this vast army. For the battle is not yours, but God's. You will not have to fight this battle. Take up your positions; stand firm and see the deliverance the LORD will give you.'

At this word he stopped everything. He worshipped God and ordered all the people to do the same. He didn't plan his attack. He didn't set up his defenses.

I love this! Right in the midst of the greatest battle of their lives they bowed their faces to the ground and worshipped the Lord.

An amazing thing happened when they did. At the very moment they began to sing, the Lord had the enemies turn against each other. They defeated each other.

If the sun is not shining in your life today and the clouds seem to be releasing torrential downpours upon your life you can still praise God. Here's why:

Praise will renew your strength. It fills us with a fearless confidence to face this battle.

Praise refocuses our eyes; it puts them back on Jesus.

Praise relaxes us. It removes the burden from our shoulders and places it back where it belongs: on His shoulders.

Praise restores our hope. Our God can do anything!

Camden and I prayed. I took him for a ride and we sang some worship songs together. Believe it or not, the sun came out!

"Oh look Camden, the sun is out. The Lord answered your prayer."

And he replied very matter-of-factly, "And Satan died because the Son came out."

April 4

Elisha crosses paths with a woman needing help. She lost her husband.

She was suffering.

Out of options.

She simply saw no way out.

Elisha says to her, "What can I do for you? Let's figure this out together. We'll use what you have... What do you have?"

She replies, "Nothing but a jar of oil."

Elisha tells her to go get some empty jars. In fact, go get a lot of them. Don't bring me a few.

Elisha believes big. He knew what Elijah did with a handful of flour and jar of oil.

Go. Bring me what is empty and I will fill it.

We have a big God.

Oil is always symbolic of the Holy Spirit. We may be facing the same situation as this woman.

We need help and we need it now. We have no resources. There is no one to rescue us.

We have nothing.

But we have God and His Holy Spirit.

Elisha exhorts her to expect big things from God. She had a bleak outlook.

Don't bring me your low expectations.

God changed everything.

If you want change, start right here in your own house.

2 Kings 4:2-3 So Elisha said to her, "What shall I do for you? Tell me..."

What do you need me to deal with?

Her reply: "This slave girl has nothing."

She addressed him in the highest form of humility.

A slave was completely at the mercy of her Master.

She had nothing, but knew her master possessed all. It was in his power to make it happen.

We may be feeling the same. Nothing in this house, body, family, church, on the inside...

Only God can make something out of nothing. He has been doing it since the beginning of time.

I have nothing but this jar of oil. It looked like nothing, but it was a start.

What she had, she gave.

It didn't look like much, but God used it.

He multiplied it.

She opened up her hands and surrendered all.

She didn't try to hold onto it.

She didn't look at what she didn't have. That surely causes doubt.

She looked at what she had and gave it all.

We may not have much either. Energy, ability, money, motivation, food, or whatever it is that you feel God is asking you to give.

He is really asking us to trust Him. He wants faith.

If we had everything we needed, we wouldn't need Him.

We need Him.

Philippians 4:19 And my God shall supply all your need according to His riches in glory by Christ Jesus.

April 5

"Oh, sir, what will we do now?" the young man cried to Elisha.

The mountainside was filled with the enemy.

Elisha was facing staggering odds and yet he was not phased a bit.

He was not moved. Elisha was not afraid.

What did he know?

He knew God gives power to the weak.

And exhausted.

And weary.

Running in every different direction and getting nowhere fast. Sometimes our prayers seem to be bouncing off of a brick wall. Answers aren't coming and we can feel like giving up.

Surrounded.

We just don't want to make the effort anymore. The struggle can be so exhausting. We can't see any way out.

Elisha's servant couldn't see any way out either.

2 Kings 6:15-17 And when the servant of the man of God arose early and went out, there was an army, surrounding the city with horses and chariots. And his servant said to him, "Alas, my master! What shall we do?" So he answered, "Do not fear, for those who are with us are more than those who are with them." And Elisha prayed, and said, "LORD, I pray, open his eyes that he may see." Then the LORD opened the eyes of the young man, and he saw. And behold, the mountain was full of horses and chariots of fire all around Elisha.

They were facing a whole army.

He could see they were outnumbered.

Odds were staggering.

The situation was impossible and he knew it.

Was he paralyzed with fear? I would've been.

Why wasn't Elisha afraid? Where did he get his boldness to face this great army?

What did he know?

God is surrounding us!

He is so for us!

If God is for us who can be against us!

Elisha smiled in the face of danger.

His confidence wasn't in the wisdom of man, but the Power of the Living God!

Don't panic.

God is always a step ahead of the enemy.

Our God is bigger, greater, and stronger.

He is enough.

God is more. So much more than we can imagine.

He is all we need.

Elisha prayed. God intervened.

God unveiled his servant's eyes. He was able to see the vast army that was fighting for him.

It changed everything.

When we can see what He sees, we can endure.

We can stand against anything!

He is with us!

Lord Jesus open our eyes to see that You are surrounding us. You are so for us. We are your children and You love us.

April 6

Matthew 14:12-14 Then they went and told Jesus. When Jesus heard it, He withdrew from there privately in a boat to a solitary place. But when the crowds heard of it, they followed Him [by land] on foot from the towns. When He went ashore and saw a great throng of people, He had compassion (pity and deep sympathy) for them and cured their sick.

The disciples just suffered a great loss. They lost John the Baptist.

They knew where to go when they were hurting. Overcome, they came to Jesus. He was overcome Himself, but He didn't see them as a burden. He didn't send them away. It says he was moved deeply inside with compassion and pity. That moved Him to action. They were not an inconvenience. He gave Himself. In times of suffering we may be tempted to push others away. We may think we have nothing to offer. Sometimes in our greatest times of need the best thing we can do is give of ourselves. Staying secluded can be more depressing. When you give of yourself it takes your mind off of you and puts it on others.

When evening came, the disciples came to Him and said, "This is a remote and barren place, and the day is now over; send the throngs away into the villages to buy food for themselves."

16 Jesus said, "They do not need to go away; you give them something to eat."

17 They said to Him, "We have nothing here but five loaves and two fish."

18 He said, "Bring them here to Me."

Jesus didn't have much to work with.

But He multiplied the little that they had. He will do the same in our lives as well.

Bring Him what you have.

If you're physically exhausted and you have some people to "feed" today, bring Him what you have.

Jesus will supernaturally multiply what you have.

Lord, I don't have much. What I do have, I give You. I offer it up to You. Multiply it. Remove the callous from my heart. Help me to be sensitive to the needs around me. Give me your heart for the people in my life. Teach me how to love like You love.

April 7

Acts 9:1-6 Then Saul, still breathing threats and murder against the disciples of the Lord, went to the high priest and asked letters from him to the synagogues of Damascus, so that if he found any who were of the Way, whether men or women, he might bring them bound to Jerusalem. As he journeyed he came near Damascus, and suddenly a light shone around him from heaven. Then he fell to the ground, and heard a voice saying to him, "Saul, Saul, why are you persecuting Me?" And he said, "Who are You, Lord?" Then the Lord said, "I am Jesus, whom you are persecuting. It is hard for you to kick against the goads." So he, trembling and astonished, said, "Lord, what do You want me to do?" Then the Lord said to him, "Arise and go into the city, and you will be told what you must do."

I always have to remind myself that Paul was a hardened murderer when God called out to him.

Why did He choose Paul?

He chose Paul for the same reason He chose you and me.

He loves us.

We are His children.

When the Lord appeared to Paul on the road to Damascus, Paul responded with two questions.

"Who are you, Lord?" and "Lord, what You want me to do?"

Your answer to the first question will directly affect how you respond to the second.

Every man and woman must answer this question: "Who are you, Lord?" I am no exception.

For me personally, I never had the love of a father. I don't know what it's like to have a daddy. Now, please don't feel sorry for me. I know it sounds sad, but God used this part of my life to show me what a real Father is like. I didn't have a skewed perception. I didn't have an abusive father to compare my heavenly Father with, and I am thankful for that. I just had a nonexistent father.

When I first gave my heart and life to Jesus, I longed to know Him; this far and distant God. The Bible said He loved me, but just like Paul I had never done anything worthy of love.

Why did He love me?

I longed to know.

Who is this that would love the unlovely me? Before I gave my life to Jesus, I was very mixed up inside. Many of my friends seemed to be happy and having a good time, but I could never feel completely content in any of those things. No one would have known. By all outward appearances I was the all American girl. I was always smiling and vibrant. But, on the inside, I was restless.

Hurting.

Searching. There had to be more to life. How can I truly be happy? I longed to know.

I knew the Bible was the only place I could find answers to my questions.

I began to read the Bible as much as possible. I needed to know more about God and who He was.

The more I learned about God, the more I found I could rely on Him. I began to take baby steps at trusting Him. I wanted to please Him. There were things in my life that I no longer felt comfortable doing and saying. Did they all come to a screeching halt? No. It was gradual, and I am still a work in progress. But, I wanted to please my new found Father.

1 John 4:19 We love Him because He first loved us.

When I was pregnant with my children I began to love them before I ever saw them. Once they were born I loved them even more. Although they did nothing to earn my love, I loved them with all my heart. I would do anything for them. I would give my life for them. It is the same with us. We don't have to do anything for God to love us. God loves us because love is the essence of who He is. He is our Father, and He loves us unconditionally.

This was very freeing for me. I do not need to find acceptance in what others think of me. I don't need men to find me beautiful. I only want to please my Father. Do I still struggle with this? Yes, but it has gotten easier. The voice of the enemy is constantly whispering lies to me. When this happens, I remember my Father's word:

"You're my girl. I love you."

You are God's girl; His special one of a kind daughter. You are the apple of His eye. There is not one time you have ever slipped His mind. No matter how far you have gone from Him, He will never let you go. He will search for you. He will go to the ends of the earth to bring you back home. He cherishes you. You are so precious to Him. Just as he appeared to Saul, He is making Himself known to you right now. I pray you will answer Him with, "Lord, what do you want me to do?"

April 8

Still alone?

Sigh.

Don't sigh! Celebrate!

Ruth 2:8... "Listen, my daughter. Stay right here with us when you gather grain; don't go to any other fields. Let your eyes be on the field which they reap, and go after them. Have I not commanded the young men not to touch you?"

This is Boaz speaking to Ruth...and it could very well be God speaking to us.

Ruth was alone.

You may feel alone.

The hand of God may be keeping it just this way. Perhaps He is keeping people away for a reason.

He tells Ruth to stay close. Super glue yourself here. I know it looks tempting to go off in search of something better. The grass always looks greener in another field.

If you stay in my field I can protect you.

I can keep my eyes on you.

You will be safe.

If you stray from here, you leave my protection.

You will be in danger.

It may look sparse here, but I will provide for you.

Whatever you're waiting for, don't go out on your own. You don't have to compromise. Hold fast to what you know is true.

God will provide.

You don't need a man to complete you.

Let Jesus be the One to fill in all the missing pieces of your life.

You don't want what God does not have for you. It can only go bad.

Come back under His wings of protection.

You can trust Him.

He is enough for you.

There are no coincidences in the life of a Christian.

There will never be a time like this again in your life!

Embrace it!

April 9

The gardener did some pruning in my neighborhood. He comes through every spring and does some trimming. This year was different. I would say he did a major hacking. Trees had major limbs missing. It hurt me to even look at them. What was he thinking? Why did he do that? As I got closer I noticed the bull's-eye ring at the trunk.

The cutting revealed what was underneath.

It was such a picture of the Christian walk. There are times in our lives when things are taken from us. Or things don't go as we planned.

We don't understand why.

We have an idea of what God is aiming for. But He has another.

We think we know what God is after; it seemed so clear He had us on this path. This mark we were aiming for. And suddenly everything changes.

We were certain of our destination. Positive. He gave us a word to stand on. And then out of nowhere everything changed.

Suddenly. And unexpectedly.

We start to question, "Was I not in God's will?"

You are exactly in God's will.

He got what he was aiming for.

It was you. He wanted you. He was aiming for you.

All that time that you invested was for Him.

He was the aim. You had to depend on Him. He showed you your need for Him. The time is not wasted. It is treasured time. There will never be another time like that. And it will never go to waste. God has used it. God will use it.

It is not lost. God is a redeemer.

I took a close look at that bull's-eye ring. Every ring represents growth.

Trees grow fuller and strike deeper roots through the storms. Because of the wind. Because of the rain. They go down deeper. And we do the same. Our lives become fuller and we grow spiritually mature because of the hurt, the disappointments and challenges of life.

Every let down, every heartache matures us. It helps us to grow more like Christ.

If things have not gone as you hoped, don't be discouraged. Don't allow the enemy to steal your joy. Jesus came to give you life more abundantly. He wants more for you. He has more for you.

There is no better place to be than in the will of God.

Look at Jacob. While Rachel was his aim he ended up with Leah first. Not at all what he wanted. Not at all what he was aiming for. But you see, it was through Leah and her son Judah that the Messiah came. Jesus Christ was birthed through that union generations later. No detour, no Messiah. I have no doubt the same is true in your life. The places you've been, the people you've met have encountered Jesus through your life. You were able to plant seeds where He had you. Seeds of life. And the next place He sends you will be exactly the same. That is the exciting Christian life.

April 10

It was real early one morning.

I had gone upstairs; unbeknownst to my pup.

Most of the house was still quiet. No one was stirring.

Even still, the pup didn't know where I was.

As I headed out of the bedroom, I heard him coming in. His collar jingling the familiar.

I flipped the light off.

Everything went black.

He had just come in the door.

But he couldn't see me. He didn't know I was in there.

He lunged towards the door in fear.

Trying to escape, he ran right into the door.

That made him all the more afraid.

He darted out and ran. Even began to growl.

As if I was a stranger.

In the dark I was a stranger.

He didn't know it was me. Didn't recognize me.

God can appear that way to us sometimes.

When it's dark, we don't recognize Him. Things aren't going our way. Everything seems so unfamiliar.

It makes us feel afraid. We don't realize it's Him. He is right there.

In this with us. The whole time.

When He acts in a way that is unfamiliar, we get fearful. Often wanting to run in the other direction.

As soon as the pup turned and looked up he saw it was me.

Sometimes we're so consumed with our circumstances we forget to look up.

I gave him a big hug. He was actually shaking.

Poor guy. With a big sigh of relief, he laid down at my feet.

I reassured him, "It's me. Don't be afraid."

Lord Jesus, help me to know You are with me today. Even if it is very dark, help me to know You will not leave me. Keep my eyes fixed on Yours. Your eyes reassure me. They strengthen me when I am weak. I am weak and I need you every second of this day. I want to lie down at your feet.

April 11

Birth is painful.

That's all there is to it. Let's not sugar coat it.

It hurts.

When God desires to birth something new in our lives, it is painful.

Luke 1:30-31... "Mary, you have nothing to fear. God has a surprise for you: You will become pregnant and give birth to a son and call his name Jesus.

God is pleased with you! You are blessed.

The Lord is with you.

I don't think I would feel very blessed by those words.

I would feel the Lord was against me.

And I did.

God interrupted my comfortable little life, just like He did with Mary.

He came with very difficult news. My son had Autism.

Immediately, I asked God what I had done. I couldn't see anything good coming from it. It was so painful I thought I would die.

How wrong I was.

Mary questioned, "How can this be?" She had never been with a man.

It was an impossibility.

We can ask the same.

How will I ever handle this?

How are you going to do this Lord?

The Holy Spirit will come upon you.

Luke 1:37 Nothing is impossible with God.

In the old language there is another word that's used in this verse. The Greek word "Rhema" is translated "word". In other words, this verse reads, "Nothing is impossible with God's word."

"Rhema" birthed the Son of God.

Is there anything too hard for the Lord?

The Word of God alone births life. It will birth the life of the Son of God in your heart and those around you too. This impossible situation you face will birth the Son anew in your life.

It will be painful.

Most often, pain is thought of as a bad thing.

Mary must've wondered if she had done something wrong. The answer is an emphatic "NO"; in fact, it was just the opposite. And the angel told her she found favor with God.

God is pleased with you too.

Mary was just a young girl. She had no formal education. She had no means of taking care of this child. But she set out to do her best. That is all God requires of us.

Give God your best.

Mary had a helper. She was not alone; nor are you.

The Holy Spirit endued her with Power. He was her teacher. He was her comforter when she had to stand by as other children mocked her Son. He was despised and rejected. There is nothing more painful than to see your child be made fun of. The pain is unbearable.

A sword would pierce her soul.

As these situations come upon our lives, God will use each and every one for His glory.

Genesis 50:20 You intended to harm me, but God intended it all for good. He brought me to this position so I could save the lives of many people.

God is doing something we can't imagine through our pain. Keep trusting Him. He is birthing something new in your life. Something that will be for your good and His glory.

Father, what I have I give You. Send Your Holy Spirit to invade every aspect of my life. Change the way I think. Empower me to go beyond myself. Lead me through this difficult time. Strengthen me I pray. Comfort my heart like only You can.

April 12

Nehemiah 1:3 And they said to me, "The survivors who are left from the captivity in the province are there in great distress and reproach. The wall of Jerusalem is also broken down, and its gates are burned with fire." So it was, when I heard these words that I sat down and wept, and mourned for many days; I was fasting and praying before the God of heaven.

Nehemiah heard the state of these people and he was heartbroken.

How did he have such compassion?

More importantly, how can we get such compassion?

Nehemiah was fasting and praying.

It's in our prayer time that we receive God's heart for people.

These were mostly people he didn't even know.

When fasting, God detaches us from thinking about ourselves. He attaches us to Himself.

He gives us His heart for the people He desires for us to serve.

We become one with Him.

A woman who is one with Jesus will have His eyes for the lost. The prodigal. The destitute. She will extend His hands to help. Give His heart. She won't be conservative. But liberal.

If you've lost the love for those you're serving, they will know it. It will be evident in your words. It will be written all over your face.

People know who loves them. People know when you're just going through the motions.

It's obvious.

There is a danger when we've been doing a ministry for so long or married for a number of years.

We have a tendency to coast. We forget to pray for them. We don't pay attention. We lose focus. We don't put as much thought into them as we used to.

We need a heart check.

Go before the Lord.

Nehemiah means comfort.

God chose Nehemiah to be a comforter to the people.

God chose Nehemiah. He rose up and went. He told no one what God put in his heart to do. He didn't need the approval of man.

The opinions of man are irrelevant.

1 Corinthians 2:5 your faith is not in the wisdom of men but the Power of God.

He wasn't asking for accolades.

He only wanted to please his God.

He went and scoped out the broken down walls. He surveyed the damage.

That's what we need to do. Go take a good look at what the people are dealing with.

We can become desensitized to what is happening around us. We hear so much violence and brutality that it doesn't even faze us. Sometimes it's so bad, we want to put blinders on. We reason it's not our problem. I have enough problems of my own. We become oblivious to pain. Our needs supersede theirs.

We can be so overwhelmed by the needs that we think 'what's the use'. I can't possibly change all this.

God isn't asking you to change all of it; just some of it.

Change begins with one heart.

One spark can kindle a forest fire.

Nehemiah purposed in his heart to be that spark.

He chose to be sensitive to the needs. It was a decision we all must make.

Opening our eyes is a choice.

Nehemiah 2:2 the God of heaven Himself will prosper us. We will rise and build!

Don't look at the enormity of the task.

Look at how big your God is!

Don't look at the obstacles. They'll seem too big to overcome.

Matthew 7:19...faith can move mountains

God called you. He will equip you.

April 13

Hebrews 7:25 He [Jesus] is able to save to the uttermost those who come to God through Him, since He always lives to make intercession for them.

Take risks on this. Stake your all on it. ~Mrs. C. Cowman

Believing this will change your whole life.

Let's define uttermost: it means all the way, fully, completely, lacking nothing, finally, at all times and in all seasons.

Where does today find you?

Are you dealing with an impossible person?

God can save anyone at any time.

Are they out of your reach?

No one is beyond His reach. Distance is no matter for Him. When we call upon His name, He acts.

He intercedes. They may not be speaking to you. No worries.

Romans 8:27 And he who searches our hearts knows the mind of the Spirit, because the Spirit intercedes for God's people in accordance with the will of God.

The Spirit intercedes on our behalf. His voice is unavoidable.

Do you think they will never change?

Jesus doesn't come for good people.

Mark 2:17 Healthy people don't need a doctor, sick people do. I have come to call not those who think they are righteous, but those who know they are sinners.

No one has gone too far.

Nothing is off limits for Him.

There is not a marriage that He cannot restore. No drug addict He can't redeem. No child He can't return. No struggle we can't face.

He is able.

I am not.

Jesus Christ has the power to change a man on the inside. To give a new heart. Melt a hard heart of stone. Renew a depraved mind.

He is capable of all that I am incapable of. All that I can't handle.

He can break any stronghold.

There really is nothing our God cannot do.

He never fails.

He is all knowing. All wise. All sovereign. All good. All in all, He is all that I am not.

He saves. He keeps safe and sound. He can rescue from danger. Heal. And restore.

Saving is His job. Not mine. My job is to trust that He can. And proceed accordingly.

1 Timothy 1:15 This is a faithful saying and worthy of all acceptance that Jesus Christ came into the world to save sinners, of whom I am chief.

He can bring life in the most unexpected places.

April 14

Soft delicate hands rested easily on the crisp white sheet. I was immediately struck by her beauty; captivated by the sparkle in her eyes. Quite certain her face was a reflection of her heart. Our delightful conversations confirmed, her heart was at peace. Though cancer was ravaging her body, it couldn't touch her soul.

A candle flickered on the bedside table, sending a gentle fragrance throughout the room.

Fragrance is like light. It cannot be hidden. It is like love: intangible, invisible, but always at once recognized. Amy Carmichael

Love emanated from the deepest recesses of her soul. It was her love for Jesus that permeated my very being. Her love for Him so apparent. We talked of Him often. Although I only had a few short visits, I fell in love with her. We made an instant heart connection, she and I. Camden too. He came with me on every visit.

She loved Psalm 23. It was clear, though she was walking through the valley of the shadow of death, she feared no evil. Her God was with her. Firm to the end. She never despaired; she was so confident in her Shepherd.

Upon learning of her death, Camden pondered my words; deep in thought. He asked me three things:

"Mama, can Miss Betty walk now?"

It hadn't occurred to me until just then, he had only seen her lying in bed. He never saw her walk.

He paused again.

"Is Miss Betty healed?"

Another longer pause.

"Is Miss Betty with Jesus?"

What a sight! Tears welled up in my eyes. My throat got so tight as I envisioned her taking a stroll with Jesus; walking on streets paved with gold. No more cancer. Everything she believed became reality.

She was certain she would rise again. Her last breath on earth would usher in her first breath in heaven. She was more alive than ever.

As we face adversity of every kind, we can have this same blessed assurance.

Heaven is our hope.

Revelation 21:4 God will wipe away every tear from their eyes; and death shall be no more, neither shall there be anguish (sorrow and mourning) nor grief nor pain any more, for the old conditions and the former order of things have passed away.

April 15

Genesis 6:22 So Noah did everything exactly as God had commanded him.

Noah set out to accomplish all that God told him to do. It may have sounded outlandish. It didn't make much sense. There had never been rain on the earth before.

Why should he build a boat?

Sometimes God asks us to do things that don't make sense.

Noah got to work right away. He didn't wait. He didn't ask his friends what they thought.

Man's approval is irrelevant.

He didn't deviate from God's specific instructions.

He didn't take shortcuts.

Noah worked with all his heart. He didn't debate with God. He didn't say, 'I don't have the right tools.' Nor did he say, 'I don't have what it takes.' God called him to do an astronomical task. It would require perseverance, diligence and I'm sure it would exceed his physical capabilities. He didn't tell God that he was too busy. He didn't take a look at his schedule and decide making a boat wasn't going to fit in. It could've taken him 120 years to build the ark. He didn't take into consideration this task would require him to sacrifice a good part of his life. Even his financial resources would've been exhausted.

Philippians 4:19 And my God shall supply all your need according to His riches in glory by Christ Jesus.

God loves a cheerful giver.

New ministries can be daunting. Day in and day out. Sometimes sheer monotony can be our biggest enemy.

Keep it simple. Do what God called you to do.

Do it right away. Do it all the way.

It's that "right away" part that causes me the most difficulty. Things don't usually work that way in my life. I'm a planner. I like to calculate what such a request might require. How much of 'my' time is this going to cost me? Am I qualified for this? Who is going to help me? What will people think?

When people ask you questions about why you're doing it, you can give a simple reply:

Because God said so. God told me to do it.

That's why.

There is protection in obedience.

Noah and his family were saved because he obeyed.

April 16

The Storm Thrush is a little bird that sits perched in the highest branches of the tallest trees.

She is peculiar though.

She loves storms. The wilder the storm the louder she sings.

She perches high in a treetop, waving in the wind and singing for joy!

The stormy winds give her the joyful songs.

If the winds are contrary in your life, go up higher.

Seat yourself before the throne and sing. Sing with all your heart.

Your God is faithful.

Let the tempest lift you up and increase your faith.

God will work in the most effective and efficient way.

Luke 8:23 but as they sailed He fell asleep; and there came down a storm of wind on the lake; and they were filled with water, and were in jeopardy.

The danger was real. It may look like we're about to go under, but God won't intercede until the most effective time. Often, His timing makes me uncomfortable. When He seems indifferent, He isn't. Just because He's quiet, it doesn't mean He doesn't hear our cries.

He sees everything.

He is in control.

When they called, He came. He rebuked the wind and the raging water.

There was a calm.

He'll do the same for you. Call to Him.

It may be dark, but we can still sing. Winds may be howling, sing a little louder.

Calm seas are headed your way. Remain confident in the One who is still in the boat with you.

April 17

Acts 16:6-7 Now when they had gone through Phrygia and the region of Galatia, they were forbidden by the Holy Spirit to preach the word in Asia. After they had come to Mysia, they tried to go into Bithynia, but the Spirit did not permit them.

It may seem odd that the Holy Spirit forbid Paul to go into Asia and also Bithynia.

God has a reason for everything. God wanted to send Paul to a little gathering of people in Philippi to meet Lydia.

God had one woman on His mind.

Paul traveled hundreds of painstaking miles, by ship, to get to this one woman.

God will send you hundreds of miles out of your way for one person.

God considered her worth it.

If God seems to be closing some doors, it may be because he is opening others.

Psalm 84:11 No good thing will He withhold from those who walk upright-ly.

April 18

John 14:8 Philip said to Him, "Lord, show us the Father, and it is sufficient for us."

Philip seemed to be saying, "God unveil our eyes. We want to see You."

Seeing my Dad will be enough.

Jesus is enough for us.

There are situations in our lives that can cause us to question God. In those times, Jesus is enough to sustain us.

We wonder why bad things happen.

When we have questions, we only need to take a look at what our Heavenly Father did for us and we will never doubt His love ever again.

He allowed His Son Jesus to come into this dark world as a little baby. For our sake. So we could never say, "Jesus doesn't understand me. He doesn't know what I'm going through. He doesn't know how hard this is."

He absolutely knows. He does care. Deeply.

I pray God reminds you of His love. He whispers, "I am with you. I understand your struggle. You can trust me. I know what you're going through."

Sometimes our circumstances blind us to the truth. All we can see is the struggle. We see our failures. Past mistakes. We see our children in pain. We are separated from people we love and long to be united with. Our financial situations are not always good. When we long to understand why, God reminds us of His love.

That is enough.

The Father was willing to give His only Son to come as a tiny vulnerable baby into a hostile world.

That is love.

Love proves itself out in action.

Slow down today. Remind your heart that God loves you. He sees. He understands. Your heart will overflow with delight.

No matter how bleak your circumstances, God isn't done yet.

Give Him time to work.

April 19

Luke 8:22-24 One day He and his disciples got in a boat. "Let's cross the lake," He said. And off they went. It was smooth sailing, and He fell asleep. A terrific storm came up suddenly on the lake. Water poured in, and they were about to capsize. They woke Jesus: "Master, Master, we're going to drown!"

Getting to his feet, he told the wind, "Silence!" and the waves, "Quiet down!" They did it. The lake became smooth as glass.

Smooth sailing one moment, sinking the next.

Sounds like my life.

I can go from firmly trusting to seriously doubting in about a half a second.

Why is that?

I put my eyes on what I can see.

It doesn't look good.

If you've ever been out on a lake and a storm blows in from nowhere, you know fully well it's scary. The storm caught them by surprise. And this wasn't just a little shower. It was a torrential downpour. They were out in the middle of nowhere with no help in sight. Water was rushing in faster than they could get it out. The situation was going from bad to worse. They began to sink. They had every reason to be alarmed.

Death seemed imminent and they were terrified.

They took their eyes off of Jesus.

They didn't need to panic.

Jesus was in the boat with them.

When I take my eyes off of Him and really evaluate the severity of my situation, I start to fret. I begin to wonder if He is still with me.

Can I still trust Him?

We see in this story, Jesus is resting comfortably. He isn't panicking. I don't have to either.

He still has full control.

If you notice it was Jesus who chose to go to the other side of the lake. When He chooses your destination, you can be certain you'll get there. He'll be with you every step of the way. When the storms come, there's no need to fear.

Jesus is still with you.

Keep your eyes on Him.

Psalm 121:1-2 I lift up my eyes to the mountains— where does my help come from? My help comes from the LORD, the Maker of heaven and earth.

April 20

Who do you think you are?

People questioned David when he stepped up to go against Goliath.

He promptly gave them his resume.

They were not impressed.

His own brothers ridiculed him.

He was not ashamed that he was a mere shepherd. That's right, he fed sheep and he was proud of it. He cleaned up sheep poop too. He took pride in it. It was insignificant in the eyes of the world, but very important to God. Along the way he also protected those sheep. And God would use that insignificant part of his life, that seeming waste of time, to qualify him for another job. He would soon take on a giant.

God wastes nothing.

It was a job no one wanted. People ran from it. But David felt confident he could do it. He learned a thing or two as a shepherd. If he could take on a bear, he could do anything. He knew if God was for him, there was nothing he couldn't overcome. His confidence wasn't in his own strength. He knew he was weak. But he was bold in his God.

God wastes nothing.

When the time was right, God used that seemingly trivial thing in his life. He will do the same in our lives too. So if you've recently taken a class and failed or worked a job for only a few weeks and got laid off or whatever you deem a waste, just know God will use it. I'm a stay at home mom. Some people think that's a waste. God doesn't think raising the next generation to walk with Him is a waste at all.

God wastes nothing.

God is sending us out to conquer giants. We can stand and face them with confidence. It's God Himself who has qualified us for the task.

1 Samuel 17:49-50 David reached into his pocket for a stone, slung it, and hit the Philistine hard in the forehead, embedding the stone deeply. The Philistine crashed, face down in the dirt. That's how David beat the Philistine—with a sling and a stone.

A simple stone in the hands of a simple shepherd.

Our God wastes nothing.

April 21

Has God called you to an impossible task?

Often we feel like Moses when God called him to go speak to Pharaoh. He did not feel equipped. He didn't feel he had the skills to pull it off.

He said, "Who am I that you are calling me to do this?"

Maybe you feel that way. How am I ever going to do this? I have no idea what I'm doing! How will I make this work?

Moses questioned himself. What will I say if they question me?

God so graciously said to Moses, "Tell them I AM has sent you!"

It is not about who you are Moses, it's about who I AM.

I AM all that you are not. I will become to you all that you need.

God says the same thing to us.

I called you to do this.

You have everything you need to do the will of God in your life.

Psalm 138:8 The Lord will perfect that which concerns me.

He will complete what He called me to do. He will finish it. He will bring me to the end.

Philippians 1:6 *being confident of this very thing, He who has begun a good work in you will complete it until the day of Jesus Christ...*

God called you. He will equip you.

Something I want to point out.

Things didn't go exactly as Moses planned. Pharaoh didn't let the children of Israel go right away.

Things may not go exactly as we have planned either.

Isaiah 55:8-9 *"For My thoughts are not your thoughts, nor are your ways My ways," says the LORD. "For as the heavens are higher than the earth, so are My ways higher than your ways, And My thoughts than your thoughts.*

If you're like me you have your calendars. Your time frames. Your agendas.

But God has His. More often than not, God deviates from my plan.

Delays happen. Delays are part of His plan. Don't be discouraged.

Don't compare yourself to other women. Comparisons create pressure. Pressure creates unrealistic expectations.

Pressure steals your joy.

Maybe you feel underequipped and lacking in every area...

2 Corinthians 12:9 *My grace is sufficient for you my power is made perfect in weakness.*

God's grace is enough for you.

Don't be afraid.

Fear is not from the Lord.

2 Timothy 1:7 *God has not given us a spirit of fear but of power, love and a sound mind.*

God called you. You have His power.

Will there be trials? Absolutely!

James 1:2-4 *My brethren, count it all joy when you fall into various trials, knowing that the testing of your faith produces patience.*

There are two Greek words that make up this word patience.

Combined they mean to remain under.

Remain under the pressure. Don't quit.

1 Peter 4:12-13 *Dear friends, don't be surprised at the fiery trials you are going through, as if something strange were happening to you. Instead, be*

very glad—for these trials make you partners with Christ in his suffering, so that you will have the wonderful joy of seeing his glory when it is revealed to all the world.

There is a reward.

1 Thessolonians 2:19 For what is our hope, or joy, or crown of rejoicing? Is it not even you in the presence of our Lord Jesus Christ at His coming?

Our reward is ushering people into the kingdom of God.

Yes it is costly. It will cost you your time. Your energy.

2 Samuel 24:24...I will not offer burnt offerings to the LORD my God that cost me nothing."

Costly but worth it!

You have everything you need to do the will of God in your life.

April 22

1 Thessalonians 4:10... you already show your love... Even so, dear brothers and sisters, we urge you to love them even more.

It is not easy to love everyone. It's not.

Sometimes we just go through the motions. God wants us to give it our all.

He wants our love to abound.

What does this look like? The old language gives us a great picture. It is that of a rose going from a bud to full bloom. The bud is lovely, but when it opens up it's even more beautiful.

He wants it to overflow...

Luke 6:38 "Give, and it will be given to you: good measure, pressed down, shaken together, and running over will be put into your bosom. For with the same measure that you use, it will be measured back to you."

I recently read a book by Amy Carmichael. In it she shares how the Indian grain merchant or buyer of grain never requires the above verse to be explained to him. Seller sells, and buyer buys, according to this rule, 'good measure, pressed down, shaken together, and running over.' This is the measure expected. If what is called 'flat' measure is wanted, it is so stated, otherwise the running over kind is taken for granted all round. Our God gives like that... There is no 'flat' measure with Him.

God gives largely.

And maybe you have been loving. Go a little further than what you've been doing.

Love should extend out beyond our limits. It is truly not in us to do that on our own.

We need Jesus.

Go to Him in prayer and ask Him to give you what you need to love that person; despite what they may have said and done.

He'll give you what you need to exceed the limits you've put on yourself.

Love makes itself vulnerable. Love keeps no record of wrongs. Love never fails.

Love changes everything.

Put yourself out there.

Give it all you got!

You'll be glad you did.

April 23

Genesis 22:1 God tested Abraham

It was a proving. Every relationship will require a proving.

True love is willing to sacrifice everything...even what is most precious.

God tells Abraham to "go to the place I tell you and offer him."

We don't get to choose the place of our sacrifice. We often tell the Lord, "I'm doing this. I'm doing that. I feed the poor. I go to prayer." But God says, "Those things are great. But that's not what I asked you to do."

God requires obedience.

God requires our will to be sacrificed. Kill it and burn it until there is nothing left.

When Abraham set out to do what God asked, he left his servants and went forward.

No one else can go with us to our place of sacrifice. The transaction of the will must be between us and the Lord. We cannot be concerned about how it will affect other people. We must leave them in the hands of the Lord. Concede that His way is the best way and go.

Abraham seems to say, "I know you called us here. We obeyed right away. You called and we answered. We have everything ready to do what You called us to do."

Ready mind and willing heart are all that is required of you. God will provide the rest.

Genesis 22:7...My Father... where is the Lamb?

My son God will provide Himself.

God sees what the need is.

God will provide; Him and Him alone.

He is enough.

God will not move you on until you get to that point of acknowledging that He is enough.

Until then, He will continuously bring you back to that same point of surrender.

Then they came to the place God told him...

Isaac couldn't see how God would provide. But he conceded that his father knew best. He trusted him. He trusted the Lord. We can trust the Lord with our lives. When we surrender our will, we place our lives in His hands to do as He pleases.

There is no better place to be than in the will of God.

April 24

John 15:2 He cuts off every branch of mine that doesn't produce fruit, and he prunes the branches that do bear fruit so they will produce even more.

Warm sunshine and golden yellow daffodils swaying in the breezy air; spring has arrived! It is my favorite time of year. But, with the arrival of a new season comes lots of extra work. Inside and outside I find chores calling my name. I've been putting them off long enough. I decide to start outside. Yard work is daunting, but it must be done. My top priority is the hydrangea bush that resides next to the entryway into my home. I refer to this bush as my baby. I love it so much. I got it when it was just a sapling; it was no more than 18 inches high. I am amazed at how much it's grown in such a short time. In fact, at the end of the season last year I noted that it needed to be cut back. I never thought I'd say that, but it grew too much. The branches could no longer sustain the flowers. When a storm came along the flowers filled with rain. The sheer weight bent the branches over and the flowers fell to the ground. My bush needed to be pruned.

It is like that in my life sometimes too. I'm no longer blossoming, but I'm weighed down and bowed over. We as women think we can do it all, don't we? We have good intentions. But somewhere along the line we take on too much. There are things that need to be cut off. It is time to let some things go. If you're like me you need to decide what stays and what goes. Ask yourself these three questions: Is it producing fruit? Is it bringing praise to God? Is it what God called me to do?

Is it producing fruit?

If it is not producing fruit then cut it off. Often God must completely remove the old before He can begin the new. Sometimes there are things we try to keep going that are on artificial life support. Perhaps they had their fruitful season, but it is time to let them go.

Is it bringing praise to God?

The goal of every ministry, relationship and responsibility we take on should be to bring praise to God. It should be a joy. It should not be a burden.

John 15:4 Remain in Me, and I will remain in you. For a branch cannot produce fruit if it is severed from the vine, and you cannot be fruitful unless you remain in Me.

At times I've run off on my own. I've pushed Jesus to the backburner. The power to sustain what I've taken on is gone. I cannot do anything without Him. If there is anything in your life getting in the way of your relationship with the Lord, cut it off. It must go. He is the power behind everything we do. We have to maintain a strong relationship with Him. If that suffers, everything in our lives will be chaotic and fruitless. Protect your time with Him. Don't let anything else take first place. If it does, cut it off.

Is it what God called me to do?

Set priorities and keep them.

My first priority is my husband and children. Nothing is more important. Everything will compete with your time with them. Don't allow yourself to compromise. Guard it fiercely. If anything is interfering:

Cut it off.

What else did God call you to do? Are you doing it?

Do what God called you to do, even if that means cutting some good things off. Don't worry about the consequences. Let the chips fall where they may. Don't worry about who will do it if you don't. Don't worry about what will happen as a result. Don't worry about what others will say.

God holds the whole world in His hands. He will surely work something out.

Go ahead and do some spring pruning. You will be blooming and blossoming again before you know it. When you see the end result, you may ask yourself, "Why didn't I do that sooner?"

April 25

I was meandering around the house; a little lost. I knew I was supposed to be working on something but I couldn't seem to find the words. My to-do list was made, but none of it was getting scratched off. I couldn't get anything accomplished.

I sat down at my computer. There was a message waiting for me.

The message said: Your network has lost connection.

I realized the same thing could be said of me.

I had lost my spiritual connection to God.

If we want to do God's work we have to stay connected to Him.

He is the power behind all of our efforts.

We can't step out without Him or we would be getting ahead of Him.

If we stay back, we start lagging behind where He wants us to be.

One step without Him and we'll be lost.

We can't give people what we don't have.

Go to the Source of all your strength. It's there you'll find the right words. Get the direction you so desperately need. He'll give you step 2. But step one has to be first.

Step 1 is seeking Him.

Isaiah 26:20 Come, my people, enter your chambers shut your door behind you; hide yourself for a little moment...

God wants us to slow down. Withdraw ourselves from everything and everyone...not forever...just hide yourself for a little moment.

God is not in a hurry.

Reconnect with Him.

Matthew 6:33 "But seek first the kingdom of God and His righteousness, and all these things shall be added to you.

Jesus help me to slow down. I know if I put you first, everything else will fall into place. Reveal the distractions of the day, so I can put them at bay. My greatest need today is for You. To be near You. And make a real connection. Slow me way down today.

April 26

Hebrews 7:24...unchangeable

So many things in life change.

Trends come and go. Our health wavers. The economy is up and down. Retirement may or may not happen. Family is for us and then against. People enter and exit like a revolving door.

Through it all God remains the same.

He is the One constant thing in my life.

He never changes.

My circumstances don't dictate, define or change who God is.

God is still God.

He is still on the throne.

He still reigns.

Hebrews 6:19 We have this hope as an anchor for the soul, firm and secure.

Winds of doubt may swirl. Waves of disappointment can be crashing all around. Heavy rain may be falling.

God stays the same. He is still in control of every detail of my life. There is not one thing He doesn't know about. Nothing has caught Him off guard.

He is working all things together for good for those that love Him.

I can count on that.

Our God...unchangeable.

April 27

Zechariah 2:5 'For I,' says the LORD, 'will be a wall of fire all around her...'

Fire is often used as a means of protection.

We need to call upon the Lord to be that wall of fire around our marriage.

A few aspects of fire:

Fire must be kindled.

Fire must have oxygen.

Fire must be maintained. If you neglect it, it will go out.

We don't want to be a statistic.

Be passionate about your marriage.

Passion is a state of mind. You become passionate about what you spend your time thinking about.

Ponder this: when you are going on a vacation, you get excited. You spend lots of time thinking about it. Planning and mapping out what you'll do. Thinking about it makes you excited. It's the same thing in your marriage.

Feed the fire! Ok, so maybe it's a little smoldering ember? Just a little stirring can stoke it again. You'll be surprised.

Sometimes we can get in a rut.

STIR IT UP!

Do something fun together. Plan a little getaway with just the two of you...even if it's just for a few hours.

Marriage that is lackluster can be open and vulnerable to attack.

Let's face it, we have maxed out schedules. Little mouths need to be fed. Laundry never stops piling up. Nor do our obligations to Bible study, play groups, practices and everything in between.

We make time for what's important.

Your husband is important.

Find ways to let him know he is still the one.

Stick a love note in his pocket as he's heading out the door. Send him a little text. Make his favorite dinner.

A certain look, a gentle touch or an unexpected compliment can speak volumes.

I know your husband recognizes you're maxed out. You're giving your all and then some. When you just take that little initiative, he'll recognize the effort.

Pray for your husband.

Pray.

Pray hard.

Be that wall of fire round about him. He needs you. Satan desires your husband. Plain and simple.

Pray with him. Praying with him brings you into such a vulnerable place. It brings an unmatched intimacy.

A wall of fire.

Impenetrable.

No one's getting in. No one's getting out.

The more you feed a fire, the hotter it gets...

April 28

Leviticus 24:2 "Command the people of Israel to bring you pure oil from beaten olives for the lamp, that a light may be kept burning continually."

Typically olives were put in a press to exude oil. But the method spoken of in this verse called for something different. The olives were to be beaten and crushed in a mortar instead. It wasn't the conventional way. While this way was much more time consuming, difficult and labor intensive, ultimately it produced the finest oil.

This is often the way our lives are.

We want to be like everyone else.

When we look around it seems like everything they do works out well. Prosperous, with very little effort. Great marriage, perfect kids, good health...perfect life.

We want easy.

But easy never increases faith.

It's the hard that keeps the oil flowing. Hard things set us apart.

We're in a hurry to get them over with.

Sometimes God takes us the long way.

It is more difficult. It can feel overwhelming.

The crushing upon the olives is what produced the oil.

It was the only way.

It still is.

It's the crushing things that keep us needing Jesus. They supply the oil that keep our lamps burning for others to see how great our God is. If He took us the usual way, there would be no glory in that.

In this dark world that we live in, God has chosen for our lamps to shine and shine bright.

Blending in isn't standing out.

Psalm 86:8 Among the gods there is none like You, O Lord; Nor are there any works like Your works.

He wants the world to know that He can do anything!

He does what we can't.

He is able to work in ways we can't fathom.

He is going to use this time to give someone else hope.

Keep your eyes on Him.

Praise Him!

He isn't finished yet...

April 29

I stumbled upon the most beautiful Cherry Tree. She was in full bloom.

Last month this tree was lifeless and dead. By all outward appearances there was no hope for this tree.

Everything was barren.

If you could see her now? Spectacular. One might think she was showing off. She had radiant new blossoms all over.

She was vibrant. Alive and producing fruit. Bringing joy to everyone who came into contact with her.

This change didn't happen overnight.

Change doesn't come all at once in our Christian walk either.

If you've had a setback, said something you shouldn't have, done something you shouldn't have, ask for forgiveness and move on. You may be thinking, "Well you don't know what I've done. You don't know how far I've gone." That would be correct, I don't know. But God does. It's Him who we stand or fall before. If you've fallen, He'll be there to pick you up; when you're ready. When you're done running, it's His arms that will be open wide.

We are a work in progress. God is still making us who He wants us to be.

2 Corinthians 4:16 That is why we never give up. Though our bodies are dying, our spirits are being renewed day by day.

Moment by moment. Change happens gradually.

When you do fully surrender your life, heart, mind and will to Him, there's no need to keep reminding yourself of your sin.

Philippians 3:12-14 I'm not saying that I have this all together, that I have it made. But I am well on my way, reaching out for Christ, who has so wondrously reached out for me. Friends, don't get me wrong: By no means do I count myself an expert in all of this, but I've got my eye on the goal, where God is beckoning us onward—to Jesus. I'm off and running, and I'm not turning back.

You are a wonderful work in progress. Take your eyes off of the past and put them on Jesus the author and finisher of your faith.

April 30

2 Samuel 5:6 David and his men immediately set out for Jerusalem to take on the Jebusites, who lived in that country. But they said, "You might as well go home! Even the blind and the lame could keep you out. You can't get in here!" They had convinced themselves that David couldn't break through.

David is just anointed King. He is new at all of this. He was used to some battles, but he was brand new in his position. The Jebusites know it and they taunt him.

We may find ourselves as David did; in unfamiliar territory. We may be facing a new diagnosis. Or we may be up against some new challenges. Or perhaps the same old problems keep coming back.

The enemy was taunting David.

They knew he was inexperienced. He was weak. Maybe he felt like he was in over his head.

David's first enemy in 2 Samuel 5 is the Jebusites.

Jebusite means "downtrodden, beat down, worn out". Maybe that describes you today.

The challenges you're facing have left you feeling worn out.

The enemy always kicks us when we're down. He assaults us with our inadequacies. He causes doubts to arise. He always presents the glass half empty. He is always quick to point out the hopelessness of the situation.

David was young. He didn't have all of this down. He was weak.

2 Corinthians 12:9... I was given the gift of a handicap to keep me in constant touch with my limitations. Satan's angel did his best to get me down; what he in fact did was push me to my knees. No danger then of walking around high and mighty! At first I didn't think of it as a gift, and begged God to remove it. Three times I did that, and then he told me, My grace is enough; it's all you need. My strength comes into its own in your weakness. Once I heard that, I was glad to let it happen. I quit focusing on the handicap and began appreciating the gift.

We are exhorted to appreciate the gift of weakness.

We should view limitations and lack of knowledge as a gift from God.

So much worry, anxiety, and unanswered questions have left us feeling like we cannot beat this, do this, and take this.

Worry depletes everything. It brings hopelessness.

We despair that things will ever change.

I want you to see David gets his first victory in that downtrodden place. The place the enemy taunted him and said he would never win.

He did win. He did overcome. He did break through.

David came before God to get his victory. He asked the Lord for help against this mighty army.

Ask and you shall receive.

He didn't go out on his own. A lot of things can seem like good ideas. It doesn't necessarily mean we should do them.

David inquires of the Lord.

This is something I love about David. We always see him seeking the Lord. He doesn't take matters into his own hands.

We need to do the same thing. We need to seek the Lord on big things and small things. We shouldn't presume we know what to do.

Psalm 119:105 Your word is a lamp to my feet, And a light to my path.

God is going to give us the help we need to overcome.

We will get the victory.

He never fails.

Lord our eyes are on You. Where else can we go? Be the lifter of my head today. Even in this place. Give me wisdom to make the best choices. I will overcome because You first overcame. Be my strength. I am weak. I am leaning on you hard. Pressing closer today. Give me victory in this downtrodden place.

May

May 1

This morning I passed by a rose bush. Everyone knows I am enamored by flowers. But this particular rose bush is very significant in my life. It held a very precious message for me a few years ago and I know it can't be a coincidence that I passed by it today of all days. Today I will complete my first full year of homeschooling my youngest son.

I couldn't help but recollect his last day in public school. Please allow me to set the scene: Big round table with teacher, Child Psychologist, Special Ed Director, Vice Principal and me. I'm pretty certain everyone in that room had a Master's degree or above, except me of course. I barely made it through high school. Camden's behaviors and fears had hit crisis level. He was crying before school refusing to go. He was refusing to eat. And most days after school there was hours of crying. I made it clear I was open to any and all of their suggestions. After all, they were the experts in the field.

The reply was dead silence and empty stares.

However they did make some recommendations: They suggested he see a Behavior Psychologist for his behavior, a Gastroenterologist/Nutritionist for his eating issues, a Psychiatrist for his anxiety, Speech Therapist for his communication delay and an Occupational Therapist for his fine motor skill delay.

At the conclusion of our meeting I smiled politely, wished them well and walked out the door. I never looked back.

I knew at that moment God wanted me to homeschool. I had no idea how I would do it. I only knew that God was calling me to get out of the boat and walk in the middle of the sea. I did and He has kept me from sinking ever since. He led me every step of the way.

Just for the record, my son has never been to the experts they recommended.

I sought His Creator. He knows Him inside and out.

Psalm 139:15-16 You know me inside and out,

you know every bone in my body;

You know exactly how I was made, bit by bit,

how I was sculpted from nothing into something.

Like an open book, you watched me grow from conception to birth;

all the stages of my life were spread out before you,

The days of my life all prepared

before I'd even lived one day.

Having a child with special needs is much like a beautiful rose bush. There are thorns, but many more vibrant blossoms.

If today finds you in a difficult situation, keep your eyes on the beautiful blossoms. God will lead you every step of the way.

John 16:33 Here on earth you will have many trials and sorrows. But take heart, because I have overcome the world."

May 2

Matthew 14:28-30 And Peter answered Him and said, "Lord, if it is You, command me to come to You on the water." So He said, "Come." And when Peter had come down out of the boat, he walked on the water to go to Jesus. *But when he saw that the wind was boisterous, he was afraid; and beginning to sink he cried out, saying, "Lord, save me!"*

Peter was testing the waters. He is the one that asked the Lord to perform the miracle.

"Lord call me to come."

Show me that I can do this.

Sometimes God calls us to do something, but it's risky.

Peter took that step. He came out of the boat. He did walk on water.

When Jesus calls you to do something it will get accomplished. But sometimes there are complications in between the call and the completion.

Peter looked at the boisterous wind and began to sink.

Are your eyes on the "wind"?

A complication.

Something unexpected?

Are doubts flooding in? Becoming louder and louder; so loud they drown out the voice of the Lord? Maybe you're wondering if He even called you. Questioning if you'll even make it through this.

Psalm 56:4 In God (I will praise His word), in God I have put my trust; I will not fear. What can flesh do to me?

Just the bare word of the Lord alone gives us the power to do miracles.

His word empowers us to do the impossible.

Step out of the boat.

God wants to show you that you can do it.

Peter had to step down.

Notice he didn't step up into safety. He stepped down into the unknown. Out of his place of security.

His comfort zone was gone. There was nothing to hold onto.

The sheer word of Jesus sustained him.

Peter didn't know he could walk on water until he took the first step.

Take that step and keep on walking. Don't look at the waves. Keep your eyes fixed on Jesus. He is sure in the storm. No matter what may come, keep on walking. He called you to come. He is faithful. You won't fail.

Zephaniah 3:5...He never fails...

May 3

Sometimes we just need a little help...

Derek Redmond arrived at the 1992 Olympic Summer Games in Barcelona determined to win a medal in the 400. Derek's father Jim had accompanied him to Barcelona, just as he did for all world competitions. ESPN reporter Rick Weinberg reports they were as close as a father and son could be. Inseparable, really. The best of friends. When Derek ran, it was as if his father were running right next to him.

The day of the race arrives. Father and son reminisce about what it took for Derek to get to this point. They talk about ignoring past heartbreak and past failures. They agree that if anything bad happens, no matter what it is, Derek has to finish the race, period.

The stadium is packed with 65,000 fans, bracing themselves for one of sport's greatest and most exciting spectacles. The race begins and Redmond breaks from the pack and quickly seizes the lead. "Keep it up, keep it up," Jim says to himself.

Down the backstretch, only 175 meters away from finishing, suddenly, he hears a pop in his right hamstring. He pulls up lame, as if he had been shot.

"Oh, no," Jim says to himself. His face pales. His leg quivering, Redmond begins hopping on one leg, then slows down and falls to the track. As he lays on the track, clutching his right hamstring, a medical personnel unit runs toward him. At the same time, Jim Redmond, seeing his son in trouble, races down from the top row of the stands, sidestepping people, bumping into others. He has no credential to be on the track, but all he thinks about is getting to his son, to help him up. "I wasn't going to be stopped by anyone," he later told the media.

On the track, Redmond realizes his dream of an Olympic medal is gone. Tears run down his face. "All I could think was, 'I'm out of the Olympics — again,'" he would say.

As the medical crew arrives with a stretcher, Redmond tells them, "No, there's no way I'm getting on that stretcher. I'm going to finish my race."

Then, in a moment that will live forever in the minds of millions, Redmond lifts himself to his feet, ever so slowly, and starts hobbling down the track.

Slowly, the crowd, in total disbelief, rises and begins to roar. The roar gets louder and louder.

"Whether people thought I was an idiot or a hero, I wanted to finish the race."

Suddenly, Jim Redmond finally gets to the bottom of the stands, leaps over the railing, avoids a security guard, and runs out to his son, with two security people chasing after him. "That's my son out there," he yells back to security, "and I'm going to help him."

Finally, with Derek refusing to surrender and painfully limping along the track, Jim reaches his son at the final curve, about 120 meters from the finish, and wraps his arm around his waist.

"I'm here, son," Jim says softly, hugging his boy. "We'll finish together." Derek puts his arms around his father's shoulders and sobs. Together, arm in arm, father and son, with 65,000 people cheering, clapping and crying, finish the race, just as they vowed they would.

There are times we fear we don't have what it takes to finish this race.

Sometimes we just need help.

Hebrews 13:5-6... For He Himself has said, "I will never leave you nor forsake you." So we may boldly say: "The LORD is my helper (to run); I will not fear.

It seems like it would be so much easier to quit.

It's so hard to keep going.

The pain can be overwhelming.

In those times you have a Helper. Your Father. Nothing will stop Him from getting to you.

Your Daddy is running in step with you.

Hear Him cheering you on.

Whispering in your ear, "Keep going. Don't quit."

When you fall down, He is right there to lift you back up.

You will finish this race.

Albeit you just may limp across the finish line, but you will finish.

Feel His hand upon you. Speaking softly, "Don't be afraid. I'm not going to leave you."

Isaiah 30:21 Whether you turn to the right or to the left, your ears will hear a voice behind you, saying, "This is the way; walk in it."

You will finish this race.

Let Him fill you with courage to take the next step. His strength will help you endure.

No matter what happens, you will finish this race.

Your Father will make sure of it.

May 4

"Excuse me, is that a church over there?"

I was a bit startled. I put down the load I was carrying to my trunk.

A young man, who looked to be a junior or senior in high school, was inquiring from across the parking lot.

I replied, "It sure is. We meet every Sunday morning at 10:00 a.m. We also have a youth group. We would love for you to come join us."

He looked down and said softly, "We have a church, but my parents don't go as often as I like."

I cannot stop thinking about this boy.

His heart cry is to know God more.

It is the cry of this generation.

When everything falls apart in their world, they need to know there is Someone bigger than they are to help them pick up the pieces. When a classmate rejects them, they have a God in heaven who welcomes them with open arms. He loves them more than anyone on this earth ever could. When they are let down, and they will be, they have a God who will never fail them. He will be the lifter of their head. When their friends abandon them and talk about them behind their back, their God will never leave them.

Each one of our children has a longing in his heart that nothing in this world can fill.

Only a true relationship with Jesus can fill it.

Not religion. Not more clothes. Not more activities. Not more of anything.

But less. Less of all of that.

More of Him.

When the scoreboard is turned off and they lay their head on the pillow and ponder the meaning of life, only one thing counts. Only One Person counts.

Jesus.

There is nothing greater we can give them.

There is a famine in the land.

A famine for the word of God.

Our children are starving. And it shows. Look around.

Depression is rampant.

This world has nothing to offer them.

Noting can match drawing nearer to our God.

Hear the cry of your children.

They want more of Him.

Colossians 1:17 He is before all things, and in him all things hold together.

If Jesus is not holding it all together, it will fall apart.

In those areas we may have gotten distracted and drifted, let's make it right.

Give our children the desire of their hearts.

Make them full.

May 5

It had rained all morning. I found my little rose bush slumped over and hanging down. She had lost her joy.

Last week she was stunning. Vibrant. Radiant.

A storm blew in.

This day she couldn't seem to lift her head.

The weight of the rain was holding her down.

This same thing can happen to us...

We try to carry things that are too heavy for us.

Things that our God is supposed to be carrying.

Instead of singing, our song is silenced.

It so difficult to lift up His name when we are so heavily burdened.

Instead of allowing the rain of adversity to roll off, we absorb it.

The very fiber of our being becomes so overburdened we render ourselves useless.

John 3:35 The Father loves His Son and has put everything into His hands.

Problems arise when we try to take things out of His hands and place them into ours.

We don't make it very far before we begin to be worn out under the weight.

It is not our job to change people.

Our job is to bring them to Jesus.

Place them in His hands.

His hands are so much stronger than ours.

Ministries don't belong to us.

They belong to God. Power belongs to God.

It is His responsibility to supply all their need. Not ours.

Matthew 11:28-30 "Are you tired? Worn out? Burned out on religion?

Come to Me.

Get away with Me and you'll recover your life. I'll show you how to take a real rest. Walk with me and work with me—watch how I do it. Learn the unforced rhythms of grace. I won't lay anything heavy or ill-fitting on you. Keep company with Me and you'll learn to live freely and lightly."

Here's praying you allow Him to do all the laboring.

And you do all the resting.

May 6

Isaiah 49:25 But this is what the LORD says: "Yes, captives will be taken from warriors, and plunder retrieved from the fierce; I will contend with those who contend with you, and your children I will save."

In the original language this word "contend" was used for grabbing someone by the hair. In other places it means taking hold of and striking with blows.

God is not playing around. He is going after the enemy to retrieve His children.

He is not talking about a little chat here.

It's more like a throw down.

He means business.

If Satan happens to be holding your child hostage right now, take comfort. If your husband is in the grips of the enemy, be encouraged. If your brother is being held captive, be of good cheer. God is fighting for them. Sometimes the grip is strong. They are held tightly as in a vice.

God's hand is stronger still.

Do you have some obstacle that has become impossible for you to overcome?

He is fighting for you; on your behalf.

We wonder, "Even this...Even that?"

Even the most powerful strongholds can be broken.

We aren't calling on a weak passive indifferent bystander. Our God cares. He has a vested interest.

This is His child; the love of His life. The apple of His eye.

We are calling on our Mighty God. The God who can move mountains.

He is our Savior. He is able to take back the captives.

God I lift up the people in my life who are being held captive by the enemy of their souls. Go get them. Lord I am helpless. I need You to do this. Let your will be done in their lives. Do whatever it takes. Set them free from this bondage. Empower them to walk away from the sin that is ensnaring them. I come boldly before Your throne asking that they will serve You the Living God.

May 7

Mark 6:32-37 So they departed to a deserted place in the boat by themselves. But the multitudes saw them departing, and many knew Him and ran there on foot from all the cities. They arrived before them and came together to Him. And Jesus, when He came out, saw a great multitude and was moved with compassion for them, because they were like sheep not having a shepherd. So He began to teach them many things. When the day was now far spent, His disciples came to Him and said, "This is a deserted place, and already the hour is late. Send them away, that they may go into the surrounding country and villages and buy themselves bread; for they have nothing to eat." But He answered and said to them, "You give them something to eat." And they said to Him, "Shall we go and buy two hundred denarii worth of bread and give them something to eat?"

This was a lonely deserted place. The disciples were exhausted. They already had so much invested. Feeling spent, they asked the Lord to send the people away.

Instead, Jesus asked them to go look at what they had.

It wasn't much. They would never have enough.

Never mind that, Jesus told them to invite the people in.

Give them what you got.

The disciples knew they didn't have enough.

Amy Carmichael: 'Send them away.' They wanted to arrange for an orderly failure...

Don't we do this all the time?

We look at the task before us and feel overwhelmed. We look at the ministry that's going nowhere. Or the person sitting in the chair next to us in church. The man I'm married to or the sister on the other end of the phone and we think to ourselves, 'I don't have what they need. I cannot do this. Let them go somewhere else.'

Send them away.

If I dig deep into the depths of who I am, I still don't have what it takes.

Send them away.

Jesus had other plans. He commanded them to make the people sit down.

Prepare for the miracle.

He took what they had, looked up to heaven.

He blessed it.

Broke it.

Gave it back to them.

Now they had enough.

In fact, at the end of the day, they realized they had way more than they needed.

God will do the same in our lives.

Place this person in His hands.

Prepare for the miracle.

God will multiply what we have. Even if it's just a little bit. He's going to give you what you need to meet their needs. Whether its words of encouragement, a listening ear, a difficult decision or endurance to love.

He will give you what you need.

He'll multiply your little breadcrumbs. Even turn them into a feast.

Expect God to do the unexpected.

Give them what you have. See what happens.

The disciples looked at what they had.

They didn't have enough. They knew it.

The obvious solution was to send them away.

The difficult decision was to ask them to stay.

When they did, that's when the miracle happened.

Mark 6:41-43 And when He had taken the five loaves and the two fish, He looked up to heaven, blessed and broke the loaves, and gave them to His disciples to set before them; and the two fish He divided among them all. So they all ate and were filled. And they took up twelve baskets full of fragments and of the fish.

There was even leftovers!

How you amaze me Lord! I place all that I am in Your hands. Father, multiply my little bread crumbs. Use my words to feed hungry souls today. Increase my energy. Give me a willing heart to extend myself. Fill me with your Holy Spirit. Lord all I have is You. You are enough for me. You are enough for them.

May 8

Jesus pointed out the actions of Paul's friends. He took note, and so should we.

Acts 14:19...they stoned Paul and dragged him out of the city, supposing him to be dead. However, when the disciples gathered around him, he rose up and went into the city. And the next day he departed with Barnabas to Derbe. And when they had preached the gospel to that city and made many disciples, they returned to Lystra, Iconiium, and Antioch, strengthening the souls of the disciples, exhorting them to continue in the faith, and saying, "We must through many tribulations enter the kingdom of God."

One minute Paul is out serving the Lord. He is healing a man in the name of Jesus. Then next, he is pummeled to near death with stones. He is left for dead on the side of the road. Paul is an extraordinary man of God. But, that's not who I want to draw your attention to today. Let's take a look at the overlooked in these verses: the disciples; the friends of Jesus. After they gathered around Paul, he "rose up and went into the city." He was nearly stoned to death, and the very next day Paul was on his way to preach the gospel in another city. That is astounding. Stoning is a barbaric cruel punishment. He wasn't just slapped around a little bit. What he went through, most didn't survive let alone walk away and continue to minister, undaunted. What made the difference? Paul appeared dead. They could've just said, "What's the use?" But they didn't. They went the distance for him. His friends were willing to go out of their way to get to him. His friends gathered around him. I am certain they prayed for him. Those prayers are what empowered Paul. Those friends aren't named here and I think that is intentional. We may think their actions are overlooked...

But, there is One who sees...

Maybe someone you know is feeling beat down and half dead. You may not even know it. They may put on a happy face every day; disguising the pain.

Many master the happy face.

Do what the Lord has put on your heart to do.

Send a kind word, pray for them or simply sit and listen. It may seem like an insignificant gesture at the time, but it will be water to the soul. It can revive and keep them going one more day.

Matthew 6:4 your Father who sees what is done in secret will reward you openly.

May 9

As I went out to walk the pup one morning, a little birdie flew right into my legs. She was tiny and quickly fell to the ground. She scurried to get out of my path. Mostly because I had my pup with me. She tried to fly away. She couldn't. She was flapping her wings so hard. Trying so hard. But she was getting nowhere quick. After she had exhausted herself, she let down her wings. I was able to see her there. All alone on the grass. My yard is large. It looked threatening and scary; as if it may swallow her up. She was extremely vulnerable. I wanted desperately to help her. I wanted to change her situation. To lift her up and help her spread her wings and fly.

I was helpless. I prayed for that little girl. And the Lord assured my heart of one thing:

That little girl is mine.

She is mine and I am going to take care of her.

When I got back from my short walk, she was gone. I was so happy for her.

But guess who showed up again the next day?

You guessed it. She returned. This time she was in back yard. My back yard is large. It is completely closed in; surrounded by a six foot fence.

I heard shrieks and screams emanating from the back yard. Screams a momma hears and takes off running.

Camden breathless, "Mom come quick!"

I rushed outside.

Our pup was trying his best to play with this little bird. If left to himself he would've hurt her; more than likely she would not have survived.

I found her quivering under a bush. Completely helpless.

Do you ever feel like that little birdie? I sure do.

She found herself out front first. She was in a precarious position. A very bad place. She got out that. She learned to fly. Next thing you know, she finds herself in a position worse than the first.

Our lives look like that sometimes.

We go from one predicament to the next. We overcome a major obstacle. We're feeling good. Next thing you know, we are down again. Struggling again. In a scary place. Helpless. Vulnerable. Really no way out.

Luke 12:6 Are not five sparrows sold for two pennies? Yet not one of them is forgotten by God.

If God knows where each one of his little birds are, how much more does He know where you are?

That little bird didn't end up in my back yard by coincidence. There are no coincidences with God. He is in every single detail of our lives.

God doesn't make mistakes.

1 Peter 1:5... who are kept by the power of God

We are kept by the power of God. What exactly does that mean? That word kept, in the old language, meant to be guarded by a garrison of troops. These troops were to protect a town. Defending it from hostile invasion. It was also to keep the people of the town exactly where they were.

Soon enough that little bird was trying to fly away. She actually got some height. She was flapping her wings as hard as she knew how. She crashed right into the fence. Down she went.

Poor little girl. So I thought.

The fence she was trying to make it over was there for a reason.

She doesn't realize it. She just wants out.

God has her fenced in for a reason. There is protection in that fence. He is protecting her from unseen predators. He is guarding her. Keeping her safe. She doesn't know what's on the other side.

She wants to spread her wings and fly.

God wants her to let down her wings and rest.

Ezekiel 1:24-25 When they went, I heard the noise of their wings, like the noise of many waters, like the voice of the Almighty, a tumult like the noise of an army; and when they stood still, they let down their wings. A voice came from above the firmament that was over their heads; whenever they stood, they let down their wings.

When they let down their wings, they heard the Voice of God.

God has us where he wants us. He wants us to let down our wings for a while. Relax. He has something to say. Right here in this place you find yourself in.

God is revealing Himself through these trials.

What is He revealing?

1 Peter 1:5 that the genuineness of your faith, being much more precious than gold that perishes, though it is tested by fire, may be found to praise, honor, and glory at the revelation of Jesus Christ...

God wants to reveal our faith. He wants to show us the motives our hearts. Our plans, but maybe not his plans.

If things don't go as you planned, will you still trust Him?

It's time to stop flapping. Take a breather. Hear what your God has to say to you.

May 10

John 14:5... "Lord, we do not know where You are going, and how can we know the way?"

Perhaps today finds you in the dark. You can't see the road ahead. Blackness and a sense of foreboding fill the air. Thomas had some questions. He was honest with Jesus. I like that. Sometimes we have the same sense of bewilderment. We wonder, "Why are you allowing this God? Where are you taking me? How is this all gonna turn out?" All we can see is the problem.

The here and now.

Our own failures often haunt us. Past mistakes flood our mind. Some have children that are separated from them. Others are estranged from their husbands. Many are swamped with financial burdens; while others are plagued with illness. Where is this broken road leading?

We feel helpless.

How can we know the way?

John 14:6 Jesus told him, "I am the way, the truth, and the life..."

I am the way.

The only way.

Jesus doesn't always take us out of a bad situation, but He always walks through it with us. We may feel completely lost, but we can rest assured He will guide us. He will give us wisdom to make sound decisions. He's not surprised by where we are. He is not caught off guard. He'll pave the way; one stepping stone at a time. Grab hold of His hand, and don't let go.

I am the truth.

The opposite of truth is a lie. During these tough times we may feel like we can't make it. It may seem as though the situation will never change.

Overwhelmed, we may feel like giving up. It's important to recognize where those thoughts come from. They are lies that come from the enemy of your soul. Satan is the father of lies. He subtly whispers these lies and we begin to believe that God cannot be trusted. He implies God doesn't love us or that He has forgotten about us.

God wants you to know through His word that He hasn't lost sight of you.

God is working behind the scenes; even when we can't see it.

Romans 8:28 And we know that all things work together for good to those who love God and are called according to His purpose.

I am life.

Do you feel like life is being zapped from you? Is all of your energy being drained away? Worries and anxiety steal your joy. No matter how impossible your situation may appear, remember God is not done yet. Give Him time to work. Worry stems from lack of trust.

You can trust God.

But, how do you know? I like Philips reply to Jesus,

John 14:8... "Lord, show us the Father, and it is sufficient for us."

Philip seems to be saying, "Lord, unveil my eyes. I want to see You. That will be enough. I want to know that You understand. I want to know that You aren't going to leave me alone. Help me to see beyond my circumstances."

When we don't understand what Jesus is doing in our lives, we need to keep our eyes fixed on Him. Don't take them off for a second. He will be enough for your every need.

Jesus was enough for Philip.

He will always be enough for you.

May 11

It's so easy to love people when it's springtime: flowers are blooming, nice breeze in the air, your health is good, friends are understanding and responsive, your husband is sweet and loving you well. It's not so easy when its wintertime: the cold wind is blowing, your health is poor, your friends are indifferent, and your husband just isn't all you think he should be.

We can learn a lot about true love from Ruth. As the book of Ruth opens up it certainly is "wintertime." Ruth had lost her husband. Naomi (Ruth's mother-in-law) lost her husband and her sons. The devastation was mounting, and Naomi just wanted to push everyone away.

Ruth 1:14 Then they lifted up their voices and wept again, and Orpah kissed her mother in law, but Ruth clung to her.

When Naomi pushed away, Ruth clung to her. This word "clung" in the Hebrew gives us a vivid word picture. It has a meaning of glue, such as Superglue. Ruth Super-glued herself to Naomi. Once something is Super-glued, it cannot be pulled away. Nothing can tear it away. Naomi is not the most lovable person. In fact, by her own mouth she says she is bitter. She was angry. She did her best to push Ruth away. No matter how hard she tried, Ruth was going to stick by her side. She was going to love her through this difficult time. What a beautiful example she provides for us. Ruth's love was excessive, extreme, and extravagant.

Ruth's love was excessive. She went over the top. She could've chosen to just keep her distance. But, she didn't. No matter how much Naomi may have offended her she was going to go the distance with her. She didn't lash out with words. When I consider the same scenario happening in my life, I think of the many words I may have chosen to speak. Ruth chose her words carefully, and many times she was silent. Her actions spoke louder than any words could have.

1 Peter 3:1-2 Wives, likewise, be submissive to your own husbands, that even if some do not obey the word, they, without a word, may be won by the conduct of their wives, when they observe your chaste conduct accompanied by fear.

Husbands, friends and family alike can be won over without you saying a word; even if they are not obeying God, love them in spite of it. Love is a choice. You have to determine in your mind that no matter how bad things get, you are not leaving. Love proves itself out in action. Words are empty and meaningless unless they are followed with actions.

Do the unexpected. Make the nice dinner. Write a heartfelt letter. Sit close and listen.

Ruth's love was extreme. In this day and age everything shouts, "It's not worth it, just leave!"

Ruth stayed.

Ruth did a lot of overlooking. We have to do a lot of overlooking as Christians. We have to turn the other cheek. We have to remember when people offend us that the foundation of the Christian life is forgiveness. When we remember how much we've been forgiven, we can more easily and readily forgive and overlook offenses that have been done to us.

Ruth's love was extravagant. Her love was completely selfless. She wasn't looking out for herself at all. She was only concerned about Naomi. Jesus did the same. When He went to the cross, He had you and me on His mind. He had your husband on His mind. He had that unlovable person on His mind, and He did it anyway. It was not because we deserve it. God is love. He loves the unlovable. It is a sacrificial love that is not based on a feeling, but a determined act of the will. When we wanted nothing to do with Jesus, He pursued us. It wasn't a half-hearted pursuit. He gave us His all. He never gave up on us. When we pushed Him away, He stood with His arms wide open waiting for us to respond. He never quit on us.

Is there someone in your life that you're ready to quit on?

1 Corinthians 13:4-8 Love is patient and kind. Love is not jealous or boastful or proud or rude. Love does not demand its own way. Love is not irritable, and it keeps no record of when it has been wronged...Love never gives up, never loses faith, is always hopeful, and endures through every circumstance.

Lord Jesus, fill me with a desire to love like You love. I cannot do it on my own. Remind me of the enemy's plot to destroy my relationship. Please overflow my heart with enduring love. I know You are able to do exceedingly abundantly above anything I can ask or imagine. Please do a mighty work in my heart. Change me first. Amen

May 12

What does God think of me?

Have you ever asked yourself that question?

Most often, I ask that when I think I have somehow disappointed God. Or failed Him.

There have been many times when I've completely blown it.

What does God think of me?

Psalm 139:16-17 You saw me before I was born. Every day of my life was recorded in your book. Every moment was laid out before a single day had passed. How precious are your thoughts about me...

As an artist, when I set out to make a painting, I envision what my picture will look like before I begin. I put a lot of thought into it. I know precisely what it will look like when it is finished, and I plan accordingly. I choose the size of the canvas. I decide which brushes will work best. I carefully select the colors of the paint. I even know exactly where I'm going to display it. When I am inspired by a new idea, I get so excited. It consumes my thoughts. Sometimes it may take me awhile to complete my painting, but I will finish. And when it is brought to completion, I am all the more exuberant. Every one of my paintings has deep meaning to me. They are precious to me. You see they may not have much value to anyone else, but they are priceless to me.

In the same way, you are precious to God. You are His prized possession. He has planned out every detail of your life. You are a beautiful portrait in the making. Before you were born, He decided what you would look like. He knew your name. He knew your strengths, and He was also well aware of your weaknesses. He even knew every time you would slip up. He knows every bad choice you are going to make. There may be black splotches on your canvas. He loves you anyway.

My painting may find its way to the garage. Some dirty old cloth may inadvertently cover it up. But, the old cloth doesn't change the value of my painting. But it will hide the painting. In like manner, our bad choices act like that old dirty cloth. They hide our eyes from seeing God fully. They separate us from seeing God and His plan. They blind us to the truth. But, they can never separate us from God's love.

Nothing can separate us from God's love.

Psalm 139:8 If I go to the pit of hell, You are there.

We are not defined by our bad decisions. We are not the sum total of our mistakes. We are so much more than that. God said so! It doesn't matter what others think of us. Their perception of who we are is irrelevant and unimportant. We are only defined by what God thinks of us. Here is what God thinks of you:

Psalm 139:14...for I am fearfully and wonderfully made; marvelous are Your works, and that my soul knows very well.

To fully grasp how God feels about you, we need to look at the Hebrew meaning of the words "fearfully" and "wonderfully". They mean: stupendous, illustrious, awe inspiring. In other words, you take God's breath away! He can't stop thinking about you. He is astounded by you! In spite of your faults, He loves you. You are so precious to Him. He loves you so much that He gave His Son as a sacrifice for you.

If you are looking at the canvas of your life today and thinking your life looks really messed up...remember the picture is not complete. The Creator is not finished with you yet. He sees the beginning and the end. You can't see what the future holds, but He can. Maybe you've taken the brush out of the Creator's hands and decided to do things your way. Put the brush back in His hands. He will perfectly complete what He began. In fact, He will even use the times we messed up, and totally blown it.

Romans 8:28 We know all things work together for good to those who love God and are called according to His purpose.

Think of the Monarch butterfly. It is the black lines throughout her wings that bring out her true beauty.

Psalm 139:23-24 Search me, O God, and know my heart; test me and know my anxious thoughts. Point out anything in me that offends you, and lead me along the path of everlasting life.

If you find yourself going in the wrong direction, stop.

1 Peter 5:6 Humble yourself under the mighty power of God, and He will lift you up.

One of the best things about being an artist is the fact that if you mess up, you can begin again. If you want a new start, tell God you're sorry for the things you've done. He will know you truly mean it if you turn your back on those things and go in the opposite direction. It's not too late! Back away. Be who you were made to be.

Don't wait another day.

God has a masterpiece He wants to display: you!

Dear God, thank You that You are the God of second chances! Help me to truly grasp what you think of me today. Bring to the forefront of my mind how precious I am to You. I am Your daughter and You will never stop loving me. Thank You for Your unconditional love.

May 13

Imagine driving down the interstate. You suddenly come upon the worst accident you've ever seen. You slam on the brakes. Jumping out of your car, you rush over to the mangled vehicles. What you see stops you dead in your tracks. You think to yourself 'no one could survive this.' You realize there is no way you will be able to reach the victims.

Instinct says you must call for help immediately. You dial 911 as fast as your hands can move. A sense of helplessness engulfs you. It seems like forever, but the EMT's arrive on the scene with authority. They try feverishly to extricate the victims. But, they are trapped by immovable bars of steel. Undaunted, the EMT's go for the proven instrument that never fails...the "Jaws of Life".

I don't know about you, but I have some people in my life who are examples of this crash scene. Their lives are wrecked. Every aspect of their lives is in ruins. Heading down a path of destruction, if they aren't rescued, the result will be death. Spiritual death and possibly physical death loom. Even being a Christian, knowing what we know, we think to ourselves there's no way can they be saved. This situation is hopeless. I will never reach them.

EMT's are a perfect example of perseverance. Despite the outward appearance of the scene, they give it their all. Prayer is essentially the 'Jaws of Life' we use to extricate the crash victim out of the mangled mess. They are unable to get out on their own. The cause is irrelevant. Whether it was an accident through no fault of their own or it was caused by their own negligence, bad decision or stupidity, the rescue mission remains the same.

They must get the victim out. The victim may appear lifeless. That doesn't stop them though. Aren't you glad?

James 5:16...The effective fervent prayer of a righteous [wo]man avails much.

In the Greek, the combination of the words "effective fervent" is where we get our English words 'to be at work'. What is the 'work' that God calls us to do?

Pray.

Prayer sounds kind of simple doesn't it?

Well it is, until we don't see any results. It's simple until we come to a mangled crash scene where everything looks hopeless. It's simple, until we're doing it for a while and things don't seem to change. It's simple, until we've done everything we know how to do and still, nothing.

Then it becomes work.

Prayer is hard work. Prayer is work that demands all of your energy.

1 Thessalonians 5:17...pray without ceasing...

Pray without an intermission. When you're on a rescue mission you don't take a break. You don't sit down and rest. You work incessantly. You have one task and one goal: Save the victim. Pray without ceasing.

James 5:16...The effective fervent prayer of a righteous [wo]man avails much.

The words "avails much" means to "have strength to overcome."

When we pray there is a dual result. The prayer strengthens the other person or situation. It enables them to overcome insurmountable obstacles.

The prayer strengthens you. It keeps your heart strong. It quickens your mind. You have an abundance of spiritual energy that you didn't have before you began praying. That energy is then exerted into the life of the one that is being held captive by the enemy. Prayer gives you the ability to do extraordinary things. It builds your confidence and guards you from the temptation to give up on that person. You realize nothing is impossible with God! Prayer removes fear.

Daniel 10:12 Don't be afraid Daniel, from the very first day you began to pray...you were heard...I came because of your words...I came because you prayed.

"Your words were heard. I came because of your words!"

My sister every time you pray your words are heard!

With prayer comes power! The power of Almighty God is acting on our behalf.

What keeps me from being victorious and prevailing in prayer?

Unbelief.

An EMT works with the absolute certainty that they will remove the victim. The appearance of things is irrelevant. We need to work in the same manner.

Jesus Christ is able to bring the dead back to life if necessary.

What did God say? Did He give you a promise? Don't waver on that promise.

Stand firm on that promise. Don't let it go just because it hasn't come to pass yet. No, rather work all the harder. You're that much closer to seeing it come to pass.

In Psalm 40 David cried out to the Lord in prayer.

Psalm 40:1-3 I waited patiently for the LORD to help me, and he turned to me and heard my cry. He lifted me out of the pit of despair, out of the mud and the mire. He set my feet on solid ground and steadied me as I walked along. He has given me a new song to sing, a hymn of praise to our God. Many will see what he has done and be astounded. They will put their trust in the LORD.

We must be patient. God is working.

Matthew 20:32 What do you want me to do for you?

Ask. Be specific. Don't look at the mountain. Keep your eyes on the mountain mover.

EMT's have chosen an incredibly rewarding occupation. When they extricate that victim, there is nothing like it! There is a rejoicing in their heart that is unexplainable.

Luke 15:7 I say to you that likewise there will be more joy in heaven over one sinner who repents than over ninety-nine just persons who need no repentance.

I want you to experience that joy. You can begin by celebrating the victory right now. Sing to God. He will answer in His timing. He is mighty to save.

May 14

Have you ever found yourself in a state of turmoil; wondering what else you could possibly do for a loved one or friend who is struggling? Are you questioning yourself? Maybe you could've said this or that differently? If only you would've done this instead of that? Maybe it's time for you to put on the brakes and remove yourself from the equation. Sitting back and doing nothing is sometimes more difficult than climbing a mountain. But that's exactly what we have to do sometimes.

Psalm 56:3 When I am afraid I will trust in You.

Yesterday was a sweltering hot day. Reluctantly I went out to water my garden. My flowers were drooping, and the ground was cracking from the heat. The humidity took my breath away. Over to the left of my daisies I was surprised to see a little baby bird. I didn't know what to do. He was all alone. My heart broke for him. My first thought was to pick this little helpless thing up and take him in my nice cool house. But on second thought I remembered hearing if you touch a bird his mama would smell you and thus reject the baby. I didn't know what to do? I did the only thing I could think of. I prayed to God that He would take care of this little helpless bird. I begged Him to get His sweet little baby out of the sun. I knew he must be hungry, so I asked God to provide food and water for it. Everything looked hopeless; certainly death awaited this bird. But, I could do nothing for it. Tears stung my eyes as I had no other choice but to leave that bird exactly where he was; helpless and alone. I had to walk away and trust God. In doing so, God spoke to my heart. It was then that God reminded me of this scripture:

Matthew 6:26 Look at the birds. They don't plant or harvest or store food in barns, for your heavenly Father feeds them.

God said, "That little bird is Mine. I know exactly what it needs. I made it. I certainly know how to provide for it."

I have a little birdie in my life. Maybe you do too; a friend who is hurting or a child who has gone astray. I know she is in the heat of the day. From the appearance of things, all looks very grim. I've done everything for her that I can possibly do. I've said everything I can possibly say, and yet it hasn't changed the situation. She only seems to get worse. If there is one thing I am certain of it is this:

God can do what I cannot.

God can move and remove what I cannot.

Ephesians 3:20 Now all glory to God, who is able, through His mighty power at work within us, to accomplish infinitely more than we might ask or think.

If you're like me you don't like to see people suffer. I just want everyone to be happy and joyful; especially my children. It tugs on my heart to see them struggling. But our intervention can actually block their view of God. We can get in the way of what He wants to do in their lives. The only person they can see is you. They may never see their need for Jesus if we keep stepping in and saving the day. By continuously listening to us, it is difficult for them to hear the still small voice of God.

Yes, there is a time to step in and help. But, there is also a time to step back and allow God to be God. The greatest times of my own spiritual growth were those times I've found myself being in the place of this baby bird. Only God could supply what I truly needed. I wasn't alone; He was always there to pick me up. Only He had what I needed. But, I had to find out for myself.

You will be thrilled to know when I went out to check on that little bird, he was gone!

I don't know if God taught that little bird to fly that day or if God picked him up and carried him in His arms. But, he was safe and sound nonetheless. I knew that was a message straight from God to my heart. God was able to do what I could not.

May 15

Proverbs 31:10 Who can find a virtuous woman?

You may ask what exactly a virtuous woman is, and why is she so hard to find? Why does the author of Proverbs place such great value on her? Let's define virtuous. The Hebrew word for virtuous may surprise you. It paints a picture of a strong woman with warlike qualities. Powerful, mighty and courageous are just a few words used to describe her. A strong woman is very hard to find; they are few and far between.

Anything worth having will take work. It is extremely difficult to be a strong woman in this day and age. But, we must!

God places a high value on strong women.

How can I become a virtuous woman? These warlike qualities are only acquired in prayer.

Matthew 7:7 "Ask, and it will be given to you; seek, and you will find; knock, and it will be opened to you.

Ask:

Hearing from the Lord must be a daily necessity. We don't want to make decisions on our own. Starting our day without first asking the Lord to speak to us is disastrous. What if we go and He wants us to stay? What if we speak and He wants us to be silent?

Satan wants to deceive us into thinking it's really not all that important to pray and read God's word. After all, things are going relatively well. I got this. God's law is the same yesterday, today and forever.

If you sow sparingly, you reap sparingly. If I don't put much time and effort into prayer, I will not have very much fruit. I will be spiritually weak. But, on the other hand, if I invest time into my spiritual growth, I will be spiritually strong.

A woman who knows who she is in Christ is a powerful force to be reckoned with!

Most women today do not possess self-esteem. They are extremely insecure. It is evident in all aspects of their lives. They are not to be faulted for this; they are simply a product of their environment. They don't know what Jesus thinks of them. They don't know how valuable they are to Him. A woman is a treasure to the Lord. She is His precious daughter. A virtuous woman can grab hold of this and be an example to the younger women. She cannot be persuaded to compromise. No matter what the cultural shift is in this country, she can maintain moral excellence. The way that she dresses, what she watches on television, and the way that she talks are a reflection of the value she places on her identity in Christ. She does not seek the approval of friends, family or anyone else for that matter. A virtuous woman seeks the favor of God. His approval is of the utmost importance to her.

Seek:

Jeremiah 29:13 you will seek Me and find Me when you search for Me with all your heart.

Sometimes we only have 5 minutes to spend with the Lord. If we only have 5 minutes, then hey, we only have 5 minutes. But, how much more time could we have if we went to bed earlier? If we turn the television off, put the phone on silent and we get some good sleep we'll be excited to get up early and meet with the Lord. We'll have that quality time to invest with Him. The payoffs are astounding. You will be so glad you did it. Instead of the meager bread crumbs you've been settling for, God will reward you with a wonderful banquet!

Hebrews 11:6...He rewards those who sincerely seek Him.

Knock:

We have to knock with heavy blows. Pound on that door! A virtuous woman must persevere in prayer. In doing so, she gains entrance into the heart of God. Thus, He will allow her entrance into the soul of others. She has the power to influence others decisions, thoughts and actions. When everyone around her seems to be falling apart, she is able to mend them back together. God will give her comforting words to speak to others. Instead of being ministered to, she will have the power to minister. A strong woman will have a word in due season; even when it is inconvenient.

When uncertainties and trials abound in her own life, a virtuous woman is able to face them with grace. Her trust is solely in the Lord. She may be uncertain about many things, but she can be certain of her God. Consequently, a peace that passes understanding guards her heart. She can sing when hard times come. Pain and joy can reside together.

She cultivates a life of joy; accentuating the positive and not dwelling on the negative.

A virtuous woman knows full well:

Romans 8:28... all things work together for good to those who love God, to those who are the called according to His purpose.

Dear Jesus, I desperately need you. Please teach me how to be a virtuous woman. You need leaders, and I want to be one. Help me to be an example to this generation of girls. Let the opinion of others be meaningless to me. Remind me of how much you love me and care for me. Help me to put everything aside so that I can spend time with you. Speak to me Lord. I need to hear from you. Give me words of hope for my hurting sisters; I long to be faithful to your calling. Speak Lord, I am listening.

May 16

FaceTime with God...what is the requirement?

Exodus 30:20 "When they go into the tabernacle of meeting, or when they come near the altar to minister... they shall wash with water, lest they die.

The Old Testament gives us a picture of what was required when going into the tabernacle of meeting to meet with God; to pray, to minister and serve Him. One had to wash the body, and if you didn't you would die. Seems pretty harsh don't you think? Well, yes at first glance. Not washing brought death? God's ways are strict, but for good reason. When we request FaceTime with God, it is not to be taken lightly. Our hearts need to pure. If they aren't, the consequences can be devastating. They bring about separation from God; and eventually can lead to spiritual death.

James 5:16 Confess [your] trespasses to one another, and pray for one another, that you may be healed. The effective, fervent prayer of a righteous [wo]man avails much.

It is the prayer of a righteous [wo]man that moves the heart of God. Our sin separates us from God. It taints us, and our prayers. We may physically show up to a prayer meeting, but if we come with an obstinate heart, our prayers will not be heard. If the Lord has put His finger on something in your life and said, "I want that", obey immediately. If not, your prayers will, at best, be weak. They will be hindered. Until we are honest with God, we can't look Him in the eyes.

Matthew 5:8 The pure in heart shall see God.

I'll give you an example. When a child knows he's lying, he cannot look his mother in the eyes. Try as he might, he avoids eye contact. He looks down. He looks around, but he cannot look her directly in the eyes. He knows he's guilty, so his conscience continually draws his mind to the sin which makes him avoid her. Our sin does the same with God.

Acts 3:19 "Repent therefore and be converted, that your sins may be blotted out, so that times of refreshing may come from the presence of the Lord."

Repenting is a change of mind. Conversion is the turning to a better way; obedience to God. When we obey God, then and only then can our sins be blotted out. The barrier that was separating us is removed. Joyfully, we are ushered into the presence of the Lord.

When we are able to truly enter into the presence of the Lord and look Him in the eye, the world around us fades away. The only voice we hear is His. All other voices are silenced. The only thing we see is His face. His eyes speak affirmation. His look brings with it assurance. His assurance brings strength. Now we are ready for Kingdom business.

Once we are acceptable to the Lord, there is no limit to the things God will do!

May 17

It's no secret that I love to bake. Recently I made some wonderful maple nut scones. They turned out perfect. One of the best parts of baking is sharing what I've made. Food makes people happy. I love when people enjoy my desserts. When they do, they usually ask me for the recipe. I gladly give them the list of ingredients. When followed, they turn out just right.

The same thing could be said of our prayer life. There is a recipe to a vibrant prayer life.

Exodus 30:34 And the LORD said to Moses: "Take sweet spices, stacte and onycha and galbanum, and pure frankincense with [these] sweet spices; there shall be equal amounts of each. "You shall make of these an incense, a compound according to the art of the perfumer, salted, pure, and holy."

Throughout scripture incense is used to give us a picture of prayer. It is fascinating to take a look at the list of "ingredients" the Lord gave in his "recipe" for prayer. When followed, our prayers will be sweet and make His heart happy as well.

The first ingredient is stacte. I've never heard of this before. Stacte means "a flowing forth." I found it to be very interesting that the root of this word is where we get our word for "prophet". Very simply, a prophet receives a message flowing forth from the heart of God.

1 Corinthians 14:1 Pursue love, and desire spiritual gifts, but especially that you may prophesy.

This verse exhorts us to have a passionate desire for the gift of prophesy. It's a powerful gift that is often overlooked.

It's imperative that we not leave prayer until we receive that prophetic message the Lord has for us. The message He conveys to us is often one that He wants us to deliver to someone else. The message may be used to encourage, warn or praise.

If I'm certain I have received a message straight from God's heart, I can stand firm. I can be confident. Speak boldly. I can overcome anything I'm facing in my life.

Onycha is the second ingredient. It was derived from the hard outer shell of a muscle. The root of the word means "bold lion." What a fitting ingredient for prayer; the boldness of a lion. It honors God to ask big things from Him!

James 4:2...you have not because you ask not.

I have asked for a cupful, while He owns the entire ocean! J H Jowett

Don't sell yourself or those you love short. We don't just want our children to be saved, we want them to be radically saved! We desire them to be strong in their faith, and very useful for their Master. Don't settle for just being married! Ask for a vibrant marriage overflowing with love. One that magnifies God and brings Him praise; just ask!

Galbanum is the third ingredient. It grows in soft transparent clumps on the slopes of mountains. What a good reminder for us. Being transparent in prayer is vital. Lay aside all pretenses and eloquence. Fancy words don't impress God. Come with the innocence of child. Speak to Him honestly.

Galbanum is one of the oldest drugs known. Hippocrates employed it as medicine and ascribed to it extraordinary curative powers. We can assert the same to our prayers. The power of prayer can cure any sickness, heal any marriage, and revive any dead thing in your life! It is greater than anything this world has to offer.

Hippocrates concluded his account with the assertion that the very touch of it mixed with oil is sufficient to kill a serpent. Likewise, prayer is all we need to kill the schemes of Satan!

Psalm 18:16-17 He reached down from heaven and rescued me; he drew me out of deep waters. He rescued me from my powerful enemies, from those who hated me and were too strong for me.

Frankincense is the last ingredient. Frankincense trees are known for their ability to grow in environments so unforgiving that they sometimes grow directly out of solid rock. The growth at the base of the trunk prevents it from being torn away from the rock during violent storms that frequently come. Prayer attaches us to the solid Rock of Jesus Christ. Even during the fiercest storms of life we can continue to grow if we are solidly attached. It's impossible to grow in our faith without prayer.

Dear Jesus, revive every dead area in our lives! Where we have been complacent in prayer God, stir us up! Light our hearts on fire for you! Teach us how to pray. We want to hear from You. We are lost without you. Use us in this time and this season. Give us words to speak to the fragile ones in our lives. Fill our hearts to overflowing with your love for them. Revive our families. Breathe new life into them Jesus. Empower Your church with great boldness to speak truth. Knit our hearts together with yours. When the storm rages, let us stand firmly on the Rock. We pray in your name, Jesus, the name above all names.

May 18

Exodus 1:17 But the midwives feared God, and did not do as the king of Egypt commanded them, but saved the male children alive...Therefore God dealt well with the midwives...

Egypt[ians] means "dire straits". The king of Egypt placed an incredible burden upon the Hebrew women. This was no small predicament. It was a really bad situation with dire consequences. Life and death hung in the balance. When we find ourselves in a similar situation, facing impossible circumstances, we have a choice. We can believe Satan or we can believe God.

It's our choice.

When a trial of our faith comes we're brought to a crossroads.

Which way should I go? It demands a decision. Who will I believe?

One road leads to despair. On it, you will meet with the Father of lies. He will continuously fill your mind with half-truths. Doubts will assail you from every side. As your energy is zapped there will be no rest for your head. Fear will be your guide; fear involves torment. Anxiety will bring instability to every aspect of the journey. Every ounce of happiness will be stolen from you.

Proverbs 12:25 Anxiety in the heart of [wo]man causes depression, but a good word makes it glad.

Believe the word of God!

1 John 4:18... perfect love casts out fear

The other road leads to joy. When we go against common sense we find faith sustaining us. The Holy Spirit opens our eyes to see God will provide for us! He always has and He always will. The Hebrew women chose to believe God. Their choice was not an easy one. They chose the difficult road, and they were blessed beyond measure.

Ephesians 3:20 Now all glory to God, who is able, through his mighty power at work within us, to accomplish infinitely more than we might ask or think.

May 19

Lamentations 3:51 My eyes bring suffering to my soul because of all the daughters of my city.

We don't have to look very far to feel heartbroken over the state of our children. Many are so young, and yet so depressed. They have a bright future, but can't seem to see it. They are wandering around aimlessly; groping for hope. What is happening, and what can you do about it?

2 Kings 2:19 Then the men of the city said to Elisha, "Please notice, the situation of this city is pleasant, as my lord sees; but the water is bad, and the ground barren."

This word "**barren**" really caught my attention. In the original language it was defined as: to make childless, to miscarry, to cause abortion...

We are losing our children at epidemic proportions. Some are raised in a Christian home, but they begin to drink from the stagnant cesspool of the world.

The opposite of barren is life; to be fruitful and multiply.

Water is the basic necessity of life. You cannot go without clean water for very long. Everyone needs a clean water supply to sustain life. There are no exceptions. If the source of your water supply is polluted it can make you very sick. All sorts of water borne illnesses can come from a bad water supply. Many of these illnesses can lead to death.

The water of this world is polluted; it is killing our children.

The greatest need they have is the pure water of life that only Jesus has to offer.

This poisonous water is spreading rapidly. It knows no bounds. It is aborting this generation. Our children are dying spiritually. The bacteria begins to fester, and spreads rapidly to those around them. The world and its ways are wooing them to drink in more. But the more they drink the sicker they become. They drink to quench their souls. The very thing they're doing to try to heal their brokenness is deceiving them. They drink in more and more of the world. The void they seek to fill grows larger. It's so painful to watch. They are becoming sicker and sicker, and we are losing our children. Genuine life is being aborted.

Problem: The water is bad.

Solution: *Salt*

2 Kings 2:20 And he said, "Bring me a new bowl, and put salt in it." So they brought it to him. Then he went out to the source of the water, and cast in the salt there...

Matthew 5:13 You are the salt of the earth.

Go to the source! Put yourself out there!

You have the solution.

Jesus is the answer.

For some reason God chooses to use us. He wants to send us into the world. He often sends us where our children aren't the ones we minister to. But, in like manner He may send someone to nurture my child in ways that I can't.

Drastic measures have to be taken, and they have to be taken immediately. We can't sit on the sidelines. Someone has to take action. The situation seems so dire and so widespread we often think it's hopeless. We may question ourselves. What can we do? I am only one person. Doing nothing is not an option. You know the truth. You cannot keep it to yourself. You have the words of life. Get out there and share this life! Bring real hope!

2 Kings 2:21 "Thus says the LORD: 'I have healed this water; from it there shall be no more death or barrenness.' "

It's important to note that the LORD healed the water. The power wasn't in the new bowl, nor the salt. The power was in God. God chose to use the salt as His means to heal.

You have the power to do something. It would be such a shame for you to believe the lie that says you can't make a difference. Just as the source of this pollution spreads like a cancer, so can the cure!

Where the word of the Lord is, there is power!

Luke 1:37 Nothing is impossible with God!

We cannot underestimate Him. He can do anything.

Go!

Don't wait. Don't put it off. Don't say, "Send someone else." God is calling you!

We can't stand on the sidelines and shake our heads. Look at these children. They are so deceived. They are so mislead. They are buying into the lies of the world. They are drinking in the water of the world, not knowing it will lead to a slow death. It will leave them thirsting. A deep void penetrates their soul; so desperate for a cure, but not knowing where to find it.

If these children truly grasped how much God loves them, they would not be doing what they're doing. If they really knew how precious they are to God, they wouldn't go near anything the world has to offer. We need to look beyond the behavior and see them for who they really are. They are sons and daughters of the Living God. He created them for a purpose, but something has happened along the way to lead them astray. Quite often it is something tragic. Someone or something may have hurt them. You never know what is hiding behind the façade. A tender soft heart is waiting to be discovered. They only want to be noticed. They don't believe they are important. They don't know Someone truly cares for them. Jesus commands us to "go" tell them.

Father, we are so desperate for You. We beg you to heal the hearts of our children. We don't want to watch another slow death. Lord we need you. They are so broken. Sew and mend them back together. We know the enemy has poisoned their minds. Jesus, touch them. One touch from You can restore them back to perfect health. Saturate their souls with Living water. Only the water of life can truly satisfy. We pray to You, the Lord of the harvest, send out workers. Truly the harvest is great! Lord I ask You to show me where You want me to go. Do you want me to teach Sunday school? Do you want me to help with youth group? Should I help at the YMCA? Speak to me Lord. Show me the way. Bring these children back to You! Bring a revival into this generation! Fill their hearts with a passion for You!

Jesus, it is in Your Name we pray

May 20

Ephesians 2:14 For He Himself is our peace, who has made both one, and has broken down the middle wall of separation

There is no longer a "wall of separation" between me and Jesus. He has broken down that wall that kept me from going to heaven. He broke down that wall through His death on the cross.

Walls serve one purpose: to divide.

There are various "walls" in our lives: pride, jealousy, unforgiveness, lust, the need to be right...just to name a few.

Walls keep us at a distance. They even distance us from Jesus. We can't enjoy fellowship. They steal our joy. We can't produce fruit for the kingdom.

Walls build because someone is unwilling to die. They have a spirit that is unwilling to yield. They are unwilling to waive their rights. They actually may be right; dead right. One wall can separate a husband and wife, a mother and child, or two longtime friends. In their determination to prove they're right, they cause division.

Matthew 12:25 [a] house divided against itself will not stand.

Division in a marriage, division in a church or division in a nation leads to destruction.

Ephesians 2:15...[Jesus] abolished in His flesh the enmity

In other words Jesus did away with the law that had become so clogged with fine print and footnotes that it hindered more than helped. We would be wise to use this example. Whatever is fueling this division needs to end. The animosity and suspicions must go. Stop keeping a record of all their faults. Don't keep track of all that you have done for them. You have to sever this completely. Doing so will deprive the enemy of influence and power in your life.

You may desire reconciliation, but you may not know where to begin.

Go to the cross.

At the cross we see two beams intersecting. They intersect at the heart of Jesus.

The heart of Jesus is love. He died because He loved us.

1 John 4:19 We love Him because He first loved us

The heart of Jesus is humble.

Philippians 2:8 Jesus was humble to the point of death.

Lay down your pride.

The heart of Jesus is forgiving.

Ezekiel 36:26 And I will give you a new heart, and I will put a new spirit in you. I will take out your stony, stubborn heart and give you a tender, responsive heart.

The heart of Jesus is our example.

1 John 3:16 By this we know love, because He laid down His life for us. And we also ought to lay down our lives for the brethren.

Jesus gave His life. Is there anything that we cannot be willing to give up?

Death brings life! New life begins at the cross.

Do you want a new marriage?

Do you want a new friendship?

Do you want a new ministry?

Do you want to win new converts?

Do you want new spiritual vigor?

Go to the cross. Go back to where the beams intersect...the heart of Jesus.

Dear Jesus, some of these walls have been years in the making. They look impossible to tear down. Lord God, with You they are as nothing. You can do anything. You overcame death! Give me Your heart of sacrifice. I ask You to tear down this wall of separation. I can't do it, but You can. Show me what to do next. Make me desperate for reconciliation. Give me a heart that is willing to do anything that You ask me to do. I acknowledge that I am prideful. Give me a humility that I could never know without You. Birth something new in my life. I humbly ask this in the precious Name of Jesus. Amen

May 21

Matthew 14:14-15 And when Jesus went out He saw a great multitude; and He was moved with compassion for them, and healed their sick. When it was evening, His disciples came to Him, saying, "This is a deserted place, and the hour is already late. Send the multitudes away, that they may go into the villages and buy themselves food." But Jesus said to them, "They do not need to go away. You give them something to eat."

17"But we only have five loaves and two fish here," they said to Him.

18 He said, "Bring them here to Me."

This word "bring" is interesting. In the Greek it means "to carry a burden."

Sometimes we look at what is before us, the physical needs alone are staggering. And then the desire to feed the people spiritually. All of it can be a very heavy burden.

The morning before I left for Cambodia, this verse just became so dear to my heart. I just wanted to give the Lord something that would bless His heart while I was there. I wanted His name to be lifted up. Just wanted to bless His soul. I wanted to have more, give more, do more. It was that desire alone that the Lord said:

Bring that to me.

I know you have that strong desire in your heart to feed the beautiful people that the Lord has brought into your life as well. He says, 'Give Me that desire. Carry that burden to me.'

Sometimes we just don't have the energy. Or other times, we desire to 'feed' our children the word of God and it seems they aren't hearing a word we're saying.

Hear God whispering, "I see your heart."

Matthew 14:19 Then He commanded the multitudes to sit down on the grass. And He took the five loaves and the two fish, and looking up to heaven, He blessed and broke and gave the loaves to the disciples; and the disciples gave to the multitudes.

Matthew 14:20 So they all ate and were filled, and they took up twelve baskets full of the fragments that remained.

They ate and were filled. They were fully satisfied. So much so that they had tons left over...perhaps to give to others.

God takes the little bit we give Him and multiplies it exceedingly.

God multiplies and uses what we have. Even our desires.

May 22

Have you ever prayed for something or someone and God told you He was taking care of the situation? He didn't tell you what He was going to do, but He did tell you He was working on it. He gave you a promise or a word to stand on, but it hasn't come to pass yet.

Are you getting impatient?

Exodus 14:16 Pick up your staff and raise your hand over the sea. Divide the water so they can walk on dry ground

This is such a familiar story we can tend to graze over it...but today I want to grasp hold of this scripture. I want us to emulate it. Doing so will increase our faith, and encourage us to move forward despite the outward appearance of things.

This story seems to capture Moses between a rock and a hard place. God tells him where to go and he goes. He is leading the people out of Egypt to the Promised Land. They are being saved from slavery and the grip of the enemy. God speaks directly to him. He tells Moses exactly what is going to happen; even the fact that the enemy is going to pursue them. Moses relates God's plan to the people: turn and camp by the sea. They're all for it. In fact, they are filled with boldness! But, it's not very long before they find themselves in quite the predicament. They've obeyed God. But when the enemy overtakes them, they begin to panic. They are left with nowhere to run. The sea is before them and the enemy is closing in from behind. They quickly forgot the word the Lord spoke to them. They began to panic. The same can happen to us. We find ourselves in a hopeless situation. We are facing a staggering obstacle or we're left to deal with a difficult person or impossible situation. God gives us a promise. Suddenly our hearts overflow with hope. A newfound confidence fills our heart. Boldness enters and we are no longer discouraged...we start to move forward and without warning we find ourselves facing the same situation/person; back at square one. Instead of standing on God's word, we waver. Anxiety rushes in. Fear takes over, and we start cowering in a corner again. We start second guessing God. Did He really say that? Is He really going to make this happen? Sometimes that can lead to us taking matters into our own hands. We decide God isn't working fast enough so we must act. All of our efforts end up being futile, and we are more frustrated and discouraged than ever. We may find ourselves complaining and grumbling against God. We may accuse God of being unfair. "Why are you doing this to me? What have I done to deserve this?" It's important to note that from the very beginning of chapter 14 we see that God brought them to this place. It was His plan. We can be smack dab in the middle of God's will and face tremendous adversity. Why?

Exodus 14:18...[so that] all will see and know that I am the Lord.

That means even God's enemies. For us, we are surrounded by doubters, unbelievers and scoffers. God wants to show them He is powerful. He is able to do the impossible. God also wants to increase our faith, and help us to persevere.

Why did they start to panic? They put their eyes on the obstacle. The brevity of the situation hit them. They were outnumbered. They were overpowered, and no match for what they were coming against. The situation was actually worse than they ever imagined. That's exactly what happens to us. Sometimes our situations don't improve. They actually become worse. We see no way out. There doesn't seem to be a feasible resolution. Whether you find yourself in an overwhelming financial situation, an illness, have wayward children, a failing marriage or some other crisis; this is God's word to you:

Exodus 14:13-14... "Don't be afraid. Just stand still and watch the LORD rescue you... The LORD will fight for you while you keep silent."

Fear can paralyze us. It can make us spiral downward very quickly.

Exodus 14:15... "Get moving!"

Go forward!!! Fix your eyes on Jesus!!!

Exodus 14:16 Pick up your staff and raise your hand over the sea. Divide the water so the Israelites can walk through the middle of the sea on dry ground.

We have an equivalent to that staff: prayer. Sister, lift up your prayer without doubting! Moses could've said, "I'm not doing that. That's ridiculous!" But he didn't. He believed God. The power did not lie in the stick, but in our mighty God! Moses was out of options. With raised hands and a bowed heart crying out to God; he saw the impossible happen. God literally parted the sea. He made a way where there seemed to be no way. Moses had no more power than we do. We can "part the Red Sea" too!

John 14:12-13... anyone who believes in me will do the same works I have done, and even greater works, because I am going to the Father. You can ask for anything in my name, and I will do it, so that the Son can bring glory to the Father.

The same power that was available to Moses is available to us!

Perhaps you have been praying for something or someone for a very long time. You may wonder if God is even listening. Has He forgotten me? God does hear. He cares deeply. He has not forgotten you. Quite the contrary! Every one of your prayers is heard! They are never wasted. If you don't get what you're praying for today, pray all the more. Tomorrow if you don't get what you're praying for, pray all the more. And the next day, if you don't get what you're praying for, do the same thing. Don't give up until the Lord answers. He will answer.

Habakkuk 2:3...though it tarries, wait for it because it will surely come...

Dear God, we need you to break through our doubts. Break through our fears. Increase our faith God. Some of us need small things. Some of us need big things, and some of us need a miracle. The size of the task is irrelevant to You God. Nothing is too big for you. We ask you to break through in each one of our situations. Bring a peace to our hearts that passes understanding. Help us to rest while You work. Thank you, in advance, for answering each one of our prayers. It is in Your Name we pray, Amen.

May 23

Is your to-do list growing, and your private time shrinking?

Luke 10:42...one thing is needed...

Perhaps the hustle and bustle of the last week has left you exhausted. And the list is beginning to pile up for the week ahead. You may find yourself too tired to even think about those things. Or you may be ready to jump right in because you just want to get it over with. There are more things to do with less people to do them. We can end up taking on too many tasks, and not doing any of them really well. We had good intentions. We love people. We love Jesus. We want to be helpful. But, in doing so, sometimes we can take on too much. We get in over our heads. We end up losing our focus. Serving and ministering to others is wonderful. It is a necessary ingredient to growth in our Christian walk. But, we have to be very careful. We can be so busy ministering to others that our own spiritual life will be left lacking, dry and deficient. Sometimes we reason that we don't have time to spend with the Lord right now.

We don't have time not too!

If we are to be effective ministers, one thing is needed. We must hear and receive personally from Jesus Himself. If we don't, we'll burn out. Eventually, we will have nothing left to give others. People will irritate us.

Luke 10:40 But Martha was distracted with much serving, and she approached Him and said, "Lord, do you not care that my sister has left me to serve alone? Therefore tell her to help me."

Martha found herself burdened with the thought that she was doing all the work. She even became critical of her own sister. We can do the same thing can't we? We can find ourselves saying, "Why am I doing everything? Why aren't they helping? Why aren't they doing more? Look at what I'm doing?" The heart of ministry is lost.

Her to-do list crowded out the most important thing which was sitting at Jesus' feet.

Jesus was like a guest invited into her home, but left sitting on the couch. He was ignored. It was as though she was cleaning the bathrooms, picking up toys, vacuuming the floor, dusting the furniture, making the bed, and doing the laundry while he just sat there alone.

Jesus doesn't care about those things. They are only the minor details.

He cares about you.

He wants you.

He doesn't want what you can do for Him.

He wants you.

He wants to spend time with you. He wants your full attention.

Luke 10:41 And Jesus answered and said to her, "Martha, Martha, you are worried and troubled about many things."

Martha was anxious about nothing. All the tasks at hand began to weigh her down.

She lost her compassion, love and purpose. We can find ourselves in the same place. We end up putting our eyes on the people. People will disappoint us. Their burdens are heavy. Some of them are staggering. Somehow we wind up thinking we have to carry them. We have to do everything and be everything to everybody.

If we don't slow down, the effects can be devastating. One word spoken in the wrong tone can break someone's heart. We'll have resentment. All our joy will be gone.

People will notice.

Luke 10:39...Mary...sat at Jesus feet and heard His word.

Mary stopped serving to sit at Jesus feet. We need to do the same. It's the only way to hear Him. We try to converse with Him from the "other room." We think we'll just pray while we're driving to work. We'll read a few verses when we get there. Or when we get home from work and put the kids to bed, then we'll spend time with Him. This just won't do.

He has a special word just for you straight from His heart. That won't come from a book, devotional or commentary either. All those are good, but His word is what is needed; a word directly from His heart to yours.

Luke 10:42...one thing is needed...

Jesus, your word is the vital life and breath we so desperately need. In You we live, move and have our being. Help us to take a time out. Revive us Lord. Bring calm to our hearts. Fill us with a peace that surpasses understanding. Restore our joy. Overflow our hearts with love for all of your people; the people you have purposely brought into our lives. Give us strength to serve you well. Right now, let us just trust you to take care of everything while we sit at your feet. In Your Name we pray. Amen.

May 24

Close your eyes for a moment and think about what it would be like to be blind. You can't see anything. On top of that, think about what it would be like to be deaf as well. That was Helen Keller's reality. She was deaf and blind her whole life, yet she declared, "I know life is given to us so that we may grow in love. And I believe that God is in me as the sun is in the color and fragrance of a flower, He is the Light in my darkness, and He is the Voice in my silence." How could she say that?

Oswald Chambers says, "The songbird learns to sing in the dark".

When there is darkness in my ministry, darkness in my marriage or darkness in my workplace, I know God is trying to teach me a new song. God is trying to teach me to hear and obey Him. Songbirds are taught to sing in the dark. One morning I set out to find out if this were true. It is indeed true. A songbird does learn to sing in the dark.

If there were no darkness, no long winter, no night; she could not sing. So it is with us. God is giving each of us a beautiful song to sing. Every long night that we experience is producing a song of faith, hope and love. When we are in the dark, if we will listen, God will give us a precious song, a beautiful message for someone else, when we are back in the light.

Fannie Crosby is a true example of a songbird who learned to sing in the dark.

Fannie Crosby wrote over 8,000 songs; one of my favorites being "Great is thy Faithfulness." Despite becoming blind shortly after birth. Fanny Crosby was born in NY to poor parents, John and Mercy Crosby. At six weeks old, she caught a cold and developed inflammation of the eyes. The family physician was not available, and a quack who came in his place recommended mustard plasters as treatment. The botched procedure blinded her.

Her father died when she was one year old, so she was raised by her mother and grandmother. These women grounded Crosby in the Christian faith, helping her, for example, to memorize long passages from the Bible.

It is also important to note that Fannie Crosby did marry and have a child. Her one and only child died when she was just two months old. Her life was filled with tragedy and yet she praised the Lord.

Crosby was never bitter about her disability. At the age of eight she wrote these verses about her condition:

Oh what a happy soul I am,

Although I cannot see;

I am resolved that in this world

Contented I will be.

How many blessings I enjoy,

That other people don't;

To weep and sigh because I'm blind,

I cannot, and I won't."

She later remarked:

It seemed intended by the blessed providence of God that I should be blind all my life, and I thank him for the dispensation. If perfect earthly sight were offered me tomorrow I would not accept it. I might not have sung hymns to the praise of God if I had been distracted by the beautiful and interesting things about me.

I thought about what she said. If perfect sight were offered, she would not accept. Could I say that? If a healing were offered for my son (Camden has autism), could I say I would not accept? If the Lord came to you tonight and said, "I am going to take back that darkest time of your life, would you give it back?" Wow. That was a tough question.

That would mean going back to the way things were before. Ah. I have been given over to thoughts of what it was like BC. Before Camden. But, I am quickly reminded of Lot's wife. The Lord had mercy on her. The Lord's messenger took her by the hand and brought her out of the city of

Sodom; out of the place of sure destruction. He told her point blank, "Don't look back!" But, she didn't listen. She looked back longingly at what her old life was like and ah what could've been...what should've been.

Genesis 19:26 God turned her into a pillar of salt.

Useless.

She was rendered useless.

I think physically she was moving. She was going through the motions. But, her heart was still in Sodom. Her heart was looking back at what she was denied.

Philippians 3:13 forget those things that are behind and reach forward to those things that are ahead. I press toward the goal for the prize of the upward call of God in Christ Jesus.

I think about Lot's wife. I think about what she had to give up. Her life was about to be turned upside down. She was being asked to give up everything. She was being denied the very thing she wanted. She had to give up life as she knew it. She had to sacrifice everything.

Sometimes the Lord brings us to that very place. Sacrifice. He wants us to sacrifice our desires for His. He wants us to sacrifice our pride. He wants us to sacrifice the idea that we are in control. If we want to be like Him, Paul tells us we must suffer.

Philippians 3:8-10 I count all things loss for the excellence of the knowledge of Christ Jesus my Lord, for whom I have suffered the loss of all things, and count them as rubbish, that I may gain Christ and be found in Him; that I may know Him and the power of His resurrection, and the fellowship of His sufferings, being conformed to His death.

Lord help me to accept my situation with grace. Give me grace to persevere. Fill my heart with a new song. Use this time of my life to change me. Mold me into Your image. Remove the dross from my life. Help me to know You more, being conformed to Your death. Show me Your resurrection power. Come alive in my heart anew.

May 25

There is a scarlet thread that weaves through the Bible. Scarlet is symbolic of the blood of Jesus.

Jesus sacrificed His life for mine. Jesus prayed "Father take this cup from Me, nevertheless, not my will but Yours."

His plan and purpose for my life are infinitely better than my own.

Jeremiah 29:11 For I know the thoughts I think towards you says the Lord, thoughts of peace and not of evil to give you an expected end.

In the above verse the word for hope is the same Hebrew word used in Joshua 2:21

Joshua 2:21...she (speaking of Rahab) bound the scarlet cord in the window.

By doing so she put all her hope in God that He would save her.

The scarlet cord in both of these verses are the Hebrew words "shaniy" and "tiqvah". They speak of the female scarlet worm. This amazed me. No one could make this up. The symbolism is no coincidence and we don't want to miss the message.

"When the female of the scarlet worm species was ready to give birth to her young, she would attach her body to the trunk of a tree, fixing herself so firmly and permanently that she would never leave again. The eggs deposited beneath her body were thus protected until they were hatched and able to enter their own life cycle. As the mother died, the crimson fluid stained her body and the surrounding wood. From the dead bodies of such female scarlet worms, the commercial scarlet dyes of old were extracted. What a picture this gives of Christ, dying on the tree, shedding his precious blood that he might 'bring many sons and daughters into glory' (Hebrews 2:10). Zondervan encyclopedia says in three days those eggs will come to life. Death brings life.

An amazing picture of the scarlet thread of sacrifice woven throughout the Bible and throughout our very lives! The scarlet thread of sacrifice brought resurrection. That same scarlet thread can resurrect anything dead thing in our lives. Is your marriage a wonderful façade of the happy little family, but inside it is nearly dead. Maybe it has been dead for longer than you can remember. Is there a friendship that you thought could never be mended? A wall has been built up so high you think it will never come down? It will take the same sacrifice that Jesus made. What stands in the way? Pride. Pride is a relationship killer. Firmly plant yourself; willingly give up your pride. Jesus is able to resurrect your relationship. He makes all things new. There is no one and nothing beyond His touch.

Micah 1:4... mountains will melt like wax under a fire when brought before Him.

Have your dreams been crushed? Has someone disappointed you? Do you have a special needs child that is very demanding? Do you see no hope in your situation ever changing? Maybe the Lord hasn't given you all of your heart's desire. Has he asked you to just wait on Him?

The circumstances that have caused our deepest sorrow are not a coincidence. There is not a moment in time when God forgot about us. God is in everything. Big and small; He is involved in every detail. We think, "How can this be possible?" His thoughts are not my thoughts. His ways are not my ways. It takes sacrifice to live for Christ. Dying to the way that we think things should be. It is a humbling task.

There will be a resurrection. Death precedes life. Always.

May 26

Jesus hasn't lost sight of us.

Luke 12:6-7 "Are not five sparrows sold for two copper coins? And not one of them is forgotten before God. "But the very hairs of your head are all numbered. Do not fear therefore; you are of more value than many sparrows.

Do not fear. Don't be afraid.

I see you. I hear your heart. I am keenly aware of every detail of your struggle. I haven't taken my eyes off of you. You are always before Me. On my mind and my heart. You're my precious daughter. Could anyone know how many hairs are on the head of another? I often think of this verse with Camden. Could I ever know how many hairs are on that thick head of hair? Impossible for me. But his God knows exactly how many. Our God knows every intimate detail of our particular situations. He cares about the most trivial things in our lives.

Satan wants us to worry. He wants us to doubt our God.

Does God see me? Does He really know me? Insignificant unimportant me?

Romans 5:8 God proved His love towards us that while we were still sinners He died for us.

He died for me. For you.

You matter. You are His daughter. Think how precious each of your children are to you. You are precious to our God.

Your faith is precious to Him.

Job 23:10 But He knows the way that I take; When He has tested me, I shall come forth as gold.

He is with us.

We can feel so alone.

2 Timothy 4:16-17... no one came with me. Everyone abandoned me... But the Lord stood with me and gave me strength so that I might preach the Good News in its entirety for all the Gentiles to hear. And he rescued me from certain death.

The Lord is standing with us. We are not alone. He is teaching us to trust Him. Refining our faith, so that we can share it with a lost and dying world. So we can go and tell what great things He has done for us.

May 27

I had a mole on my face for as long as I could remember. I noticed it started to subtly change color. I knew that could be a sign of skin cancer. I also knew that I had 2 very bad sunburns when I was young which also made me more susceptible. I made the appointment. I didn't tell my husband Ray that I had made the appointment. A little while after I made the call, Ray said, "Did you hear what Camden just said?" I said, "No. What did he say?" He said, "Cancer is not impossible." I was just so floored. I said, "Well I hope that's not a word for me from the Lord! I just made an appointment to see the dermatologist about this mole on my face!"

I went to the doctor. I really just hoped the doctor would tell me it's nothing and send me on my way. But, she didn't. She was very concerned that this could be skin cancer. She did a biopsy right then. I was so scared and the whole time I just kept thinking about what Camden had said that day, "Cancer is not impossible." I had to wait 7-10 days to get the results.

Of course, when she said she was going to do the biopsy I went into panic mode. My mind was racing and I was filled with anxiety. Am I going to die? When the possibility is made so real you really begin to evaluate your life. Am I on track Lord? Am I doing what you called me to do?

And then...Satan brings his condemnation.

Immediately I began to recollect all the things I had done wrong. I was filled with feelings of regret. I was swamped with guilt over the things I wish I had done different.

I was overwhelmed with so many emotions. I couldn't even think straight. I couldn't focus on anything. I was immobilized. The Lord woke me up during the night with a verse.

John 3:14 "And as Moses lifted up the serpent in the wilderness, even so must the Son of Man be lifted up..."

It was speaking of a story in the book of Numbers:

Numbers 21:4 Then they journeyed...and the soul of the people became very discouraged (impatient) on the way.

Numbers 21:5-9 And the people spoke against God and against Moses: "Why have you brought us up out of Egypt to die in the wilderness? For [there is] no food and no water, and our soul loathes this worthless bread." So the LORD sent fiery serpents among the people, and they bit the people; and many of the people of Israel died. Therefore the people came to Moses, and said, "We have sinned, for we have spoken against the LORD and against you; pray to the LORD that He take away the serpents from us." So Moses prayed for the people. Then the LORD said to Moses, "Make a fiery [serpent], and set it on a pole; and it shall be that everyone who is bitten, when he looks at it, shall live." So Moses made a bronze serpent, and put it on a pole; and so it was, if a serpent had bitten anyone, when he looked at the bronze serpent, he lived.

The Lord said, "You're not going to die. Keep your eyes on me."

The next verse is what is so significant:

Numbers 21:10 *Now the children of Israel MOVED ON.*

The people who looked up to the bronze serpent lived. The people who didn't, died. God made it pretty simple. Look up to Me and move on!

What happens if we don't look up to Jesus, but rather we keep our eyes on the problem?

We die spiritually. Death sounds so final and drastic here, but it's true. When we choose to focus on the problem we die a slow death.

I desperately wanted the Lord to tell me everything was going to be ok. But I couldn't hear Him.

"Speak to me! Unveil Yourself to me! Show Yourself to me! I need to hear from You!

We are desperate to hear from the Lord. We want to see Him. We want know all that He has for us.

What will keep us from seeing Him? Sin.

Sometimes as soon as the word sin comes up we as Christian ladies take a sigh of relief, this doesn't apply to me, because I'm not in sin. Remember sin means to "miss the mark". On a bulls eye...you may not be hitting dead center of what God wants for you.

We know that sin veils our eyes. Sin blocks our view of Him. Perhaps it may only block Him partially. I want to know ALL that He has to say, not just some of what He would tell me. I want to see and hear everything! I want to remove every hindrance.

What was hindering me?

My eyes were on the problem. I was completely consumed by it. All my thoughts were on cancer. And then guess where that took me? That took me to feeling guilty. Why do women always feel so guilty??? I was feeling guilty for all that things I wish I had done differently, all things I wish I would've done but didn't. I was feeling guilty for all of my failures.

Jesus said, "Look up to me."

I have a choice to make. Am I going to keep my eyes on the difficulty or am I going to look up to Him?

God did not make a mistake. He brought me to this place for a reason.

Revelation 1:7 *Behold He is coming with clouds and every eye will see Him...*

Throughout the Bible clouds are associated with darkness. Clouds are those dark times that we don't know what is happening. Uncertainty lingers in the air. We may find ourselves in a very uncomfortable place. If you're like me, I don't like being uncomfortable. I don't like when things don't go my way. Or, maybe God called us to do something we don't feel qualified to do or our children aren't where we desire them to be spiritually...

Jesus said, "Look to me and move on."

Take your eyes off of yourself, the problem, the doubt, the guilt, the self-pity-(I lost so much, gave so much up).

I don't think it was a coincidence that the very next day we were doing an outreach at the high school. I had a big white bandage on my face that stuck out like a sore thumb. I didn't want to be embarrassed. I would've preferred to just stay home. That would've been much easier for me and definitely more comfortable. And besides that I could've felt sorry for myself for another day.

But, God said, "MOVE ON!"

James 4:17 To know to do good and not do it is sin.

Ray said, "What time do you have to be there tomorrow for the out-reach?"

I said, "Oh, I don't know if I'm going. I'm still praying about that...look at my face!"

He said, "I think you should go."

The Lord spoke so clearly:

There's a time to pray about something. But, then there's a time to act.

Stop praying.

You've heard from the Lord. Now do it! PUT IT INTO MOTION!

Your mind can't conceive how much more God has for you!

What would've held me back from doing the good that God called me to do? Worry, guilt, self- pity...sin skews our perception of the truth. When I did finally take my eyes off of the problem, my mind was healed. I was revived, refreshed and quickened.

Ephesians 4:16 He makes the whole body fit together perfectly. As each part does its own special work, it helps the other parts grow, so that the whole body is healthy and growing and full of love.

If you keep your eyes on the problem and you don't look up to Jesus, you will not grow. And not only will you not grow you will hinder someone else's growth. Each one of us has been given a special work to do in the body of Christ. If you don't do your part, the other parts suffer.

What do we do if we have missed opportunities? I've missed plenty.

Should we feel guilty? No. That only begins this cycle over again. Condemnation is from the enemy!

Jesus said, "Woman where are your accusers?"

MOVE ON!

Now I want you to see where God took the people after they looked to Him:

They began in Oboth/Ije which means wilderness and ruinous heaps.

They camped towards the sun rising...

It may seem very dark right now, but the sun is rising. The day will break.

Then they camped in Zered which means exuberant growth.

Then they camped in Arnon which means rushing streams.

Then they camped in Beer which means well.

Then they camped in Mattanah which means gift of Jehovah as He is able.

Then they camped in Nahaliel which means torrents of God! Living water rushing through our lives!

Then they camped in Bamoth which means great high place in the valley.

So we can still be in the valley but in a great high place above our circumstances! We can be filled with joy and overflow with life despite the outward appearance of things!

Finally to the top of Pisgah which means cleft. When we take our eyes off of the circumstance and put them on Jesus, he moves us from the wilderness to the top of the mountain and hides us in the cleft of His hand!

Today, what is it that seems impossible? Cancer? Your child? Your job? Your marriage?

Fill in the blank: _____ is NOT impossible!

May 28

1 Kings 3:5 At Gibeon the LORD appeared to Solomon in a dream by night; and God said, "Ask! What shall I give you?"...Solomon replied, "I am like a little child who doesn't know his way around..."

The Lord had given Solomon an incredible responsibility. But he had no idea how to carry out all of his duties. He felt like a little child.

So many times we can be in the same predicament.

We have no idea what we've gotten ourselves into. No clue.

We take things on and suddenly reality hits.

We definitely don't have what it takes. We are in way over our head.

God's very simple reply to Solomon's cry for help, "Ask. Just ask Me. What is it that you need?"

I picture Camden when he was a toddler. His little innocent eyes filled with fear. Tears brimming over; running down his rosy cheeks. When he lifts up both hands as if to say, "Pick me up." Would I ever refuse him? Of course not. Oh I delight to pick him up and squeeze him tight. All of his fears dissipate. I've got you now. He lays his head on my shoulder and relaxes. Everything is safe now.

God will do the same for us. He has everything I need. He is everything I'm not. Thank you Jesus!

God was pleased Solomon asked for wisdom.

James 1:5 If any of you lacks wisdom, let him ask of God, who gives to all liberally and without reproach, and it will be given to him.

If you lack wisdom ASK!

God not only gave Solomon what he asked for, but He gave him so much more.

Ephesians 3:20 Now all glory to God, who is able, through his mighty power at work within us, to accomplish infinitely more than we might ask or think.

May 29

And then there's this fistful of tiny green. Small white flowers peeking out of dirty little hands. The boy brings them to me.

Just because.

It may be just a weed to some. To him, it was his gift.

He did it for me. Just wanted to make me smile. To see me happy.

And it did. I lit up.

You know what I didn't say? I wish you gave me roses. Sure wish you had given me a few more flowers here kid. No, I didn't ask him if this was it. Is this all there is? Is this the best you got? Those things didn't even cross my mind.

Lots of days we beat ourselves down over things we didn't get done.

God is not disappointed in you. No way. He is pleased with you. Beyond pleased.

All your work, whatever you do for Him, He is delighted over. Anything set apart for Him, blesses His heart. It is never wasted. You know why? Because He sees your heart behind it. He sees our little weeds. Soft hands holding out what we have as an offering to Him. For Him. No one else.

That makes His heart smile.

You may feel unimportant. Insignificant. Overlooked. Not by your God. Never.

Sometimes we only see dirty diapers. I'm just a mom. All I do is clean up messes. I'm just a chauffeur. Only thing I do is cook all day long.

There are no insignificant jobs in the Kingdom.

God took the time to record a cook.

1 Chronicles 9:31 Mattithiah... had the trusted office over the things that were baked in the pans.

The man was entrusted with baking pans. This was his calling. His appointment. His divine assignment.

Not prestigious in the eyes of the world, but God recorded it.

He records.

He hasn't missed one thing you've done for Him either.

Hear these words:

He loves you. He sees your heart behind it. He doesn't compare you to others. He doesn't wish you did something else. Something more important. What you're doing is important. He made you for your specific job. Whatever He has called you to do, do it with all of your heart. For Him. An audience of One. The only One to whom we look for approval.

He sees your little weeds. They make His heart smile.

May 30

Malachi 3:10 Bring all the tithes into the storehouse,

That there may be food in My house,

And try Me now in this,"

Says the LORD of hosts,

"If I will not open for you the windows of heaven

And **pour out** for you such blessing

That there will not be room enough to receive it.

These words "pour out" literally mean to completely empty.

You know who is going to be emptied in our giving?

Jesus.

Jesus is going to pour Himself out. Completely empty Himself for us. He'll give us so much blessing we won't have room for it.

God's math.

When we give, we get more.

More than we ever dreamed of.

This is the only place in the Bible God says, "TEST ME!"

It is speaking of the tithe. A tithe was typically a tenth or more. When we give God the best we have straight off the top, He totally blesses it.

Whether we give God our money, time, energy, resources or anything else, God will multiply it.

That is His promise.

You can't lose.

Something else I don't want you to miss.

When you give like this, you're the one who receives such happiness. You think you're blessing someone else, and you are, but you always get more in the end. You end up getting a bigger gift.

Your heart is what will be overflowing with such blessing; joy unspeakable.

Go ahead. Test Him on this today!

May 31

Marriage...don't let it get pushed to the backburner...

Perhaps this week finds you extremely busy. In fact, every week seems to be bursting at the seams with work, activities for the kids and demands of ministry. We can quickly lose the focus of where our priorities should be. I am no different. I was struck by a verse in Nehemiah. It's in a chapter I tend to skim over. It seems redundant and unnecessary to read all those names...however I found a little treasure that really spoke to me. It's my prayer that it speaks to your heart as well.

Nehemiah begins with his call to build. God put a call on his life and he went. He jumped right in. His enthusiasm is admirable.

Nehemiah 3 tells us who came along with him in the work. It points out where each one was working.

The next verse is what jumped out at me:

Nehemiah 3:10 Next to them Jedaiah... made repairs in front of his [own] house.

Jedaiah was working on his own house. Quite often we can get so caught up in our work, ministries, and helping others that we neglect our own "house." We can't work on other homes until our own house is in order; that even includes our church home... Sometimes we're busy doing some really great things. We might make dinner for a family in need, go visit a sick friend, lead a Bible study, etc. While all of those things are wonderful, if we don't have anything left at the end of the day for our own husband and family something has to go.

God has an order of priorities that cannot be circumvented:

Jesus

Husband/children

Others

Maintaining a vibrant relationship with Jesus is our first priority. It is vital. We can't allow anything to take us away from it. God wants all of us. That may mean saying no to a lot of good things (yep, even Facebook). But, it will be worth it. If our relationship with Jesus is lacking and weak, our marriage will be as well.

My husband and children are my next priority. At the end of the day if I come home and my house is a wreck, kids haven't eaten and there's no dinner for hubs I really haven't done what God called me to do. God called me to be a wife and mother. It's a high calling worthy of my all. They don't deserve my leftovers. If I neglect my husband, a distance will begin to grow; that plays right into Satan's hand. His plan is to divide and conquer. We have to be on guard. We need to be proactive. Do you know why? Very simply, the enemy is proactive. Our husbands are constantly bombarded by images, innuendos, and suggestions. Satan continuously assaults. He waits for the opportune time. Let's not provide that opportune time.

Song of Solomon 2:16 My beloved is mine and I am his.

He's the only one I've got. I need to treasure him. Yes, he knows I love him. But, I want to show him. Don't take it for granted that he knows. Love proves itself out in action. Go all out! Lavish him with your love and attention. Write him a love note. Send him a suggestive text. Surprise him when he gets home tonight. It's much easier to build on a strong foundation than try to rebuild something that's falling apart. Even if you find yourself in the latter of the two, God can create something out of nothing. Try to commit to doing something special for him for one whole week. Give it a lot of thought. Go all out. Give it your all. He's worth it! You'll be so glad you did.

Lastly, pray for him. Pray with him. While praying together may feel a bit awkward at first, the vulnerability that's created is what will knit your hearts together.

Ecclesiastes 4:12 A person standing alone can be attacked and defeated, but two can stand back-to-back and conquer. Three are even better, for a triple-braided cord is not easily broken.

June

June 1

My flowers are singing in the warm sunshine.

But they weren't always this way.

They were just dead bulbs.

Lifeless.

It wasn't until I buried them that they came alive.

Last fall I decided to make a change in my garden.

I could've left it alone. It was just fine the way it was.

I wanted change.

I bought some bulbs. It was grueling work to plant them. The ground was so hard to dig up.

But I did it.

Change never comes easy.

It's much the same way in our lives. If we want change, we have to do some difficult things.

Bury some stuff. Let go of it.

If I never buried the bulbs, they would've remained just as they were.

Dead seeds.

Beautiful tulips would've never arisen.

So many times we want to hold onto our plans. Our will. Our time frame. Our sin.

We remain unchanged.

Dead inside.

John 12:24-25 "Listen carefully: Unless a grain of wheat is buried in the ground, dead to the world, it is never any more than a grain of wheat. But if it is buried, it sprouts and reproduces itself many times over. In the same way, anyone who holds on to life just as it is destroys that life. But if you let it go, reckless in your love, you'll have it forever, real and eternal.

Letting go, we blossom. Flourish.

Real life springs up!

Isaiah 55:8 "I don't think the way you think. The way you work isn't the way I work."

God has something radically different. Profoundly better than what we're holding onto. Nothing like we could ever think up.

Much of the time we think the things we've done keep us from Him. And they do. But when those things are buried. Forgiven. Let go of.

We become new.

Old things pass away.

Those broken things we despise, draw us closer to Him. They show us our need for Him. Make us want Him more. Not less.

Sometimes we want change, we just don't know how. Don't know where to begin.

Hear Him whispering to your heart:

Come to Me. You are wasting your time on all of these worthless things.

They make you empty. I want to make you full.

I'll help you go through the change.

Pour yourself into Me.

I'll make you full.

Fill your soul with good things.

Come to Me. Run to Me.

Revelation 21:5...*I make all things new*

You'll blossom into something beautiful.

Unrecognizable.

June 2

It was a beautiful day.

Life was good.

We were relaxing on the beach. Camden was so content. Soft waves gently made their way to his little feet. He was at the edge of the water building a sand castle. It was coming along well.

Out of nowhere this snake pops up.

All building stopped.

We cleared the immediate area. After a period of waiting it seemed safe to go back. So that's what we did. But we used caution. We were suspicious. And sure enough that snake came right back! That was it for me. Abruptly I grabbed the dog. I ordered Camden to get his shoes and we high tailed it out of there. I think Ray would've stayed. Not me. I was terrified. Not willing to risk it. I'm not getting bit by a snake. Nor am I going to allow my child to get bit.

The following week Ray wanted to go back. Camden emphatically replied, "We can never go back there. That snake might be there."

Isn't that just like Satan? Rears his ugly head. He appears out of nowhere. Right in the middle of what God's building. Comes into our church, marriage or home. Ruins everything good. He puts us on the run. We run and run and some of us have never been back. We're still running.

Perhaps that ole snake came along and tempted you. You fell for it. Did something stupid. Now you think God will never have you back. Not after what you did.

Or maybe someone said something or did something to you...they hurt you or let you down and you went in the other direction. And you're still going. As far away as you can get.

And that's exactly what Satan wants. He wants to separate you from God. He wants you as far away as he can get you. Away from all that is good. That is always his goal.

He comes to steal, kill and destroy.

It isn't obvious. Never is. He is subtle. He makes his appearance, wreaks havoc and moves on. Only problem is we haven't moved on.

When he left, he took our peace, joy and contentment with him.

All gone.

In a moment.

It may be years later and we're still miserable.

If you say:

I can never go back there again.

I can never let anyone hurt me again.

I can never get close to anyone again.

Those are all lies from the father of lies. Period.

And as long as you continue to believe them, Satan will continue to have the victory.

John 8:32 You will know the truth, and the truth will set you free."

The capacity to be hurt is always there.

But love is willing to make itself vulnerable.

Revelation 2:4...You left your first love...

Satan used this event to send you running.

No matter what the reason, God is calling you back.

God was doing a great work in you and Satan couldn't stand it. So he reared his ugly head and you've never been the same since.

God hasn't changed His plan, nor His mind.

He still wants to use you.

He gave you gifts and they are going to waste.

Go back.

Get plugged in.

Be all in.

Romans 11:29 The gifts and call of God are irrevocable.

June 3

Judge not...

Recently I had occasion to meet up with an old friend. We were enjoying our time together when she began to open up about some sordid details from her not too distant past. Things she wasn't proud of, and clearly she was sorry for. I wasn't expecting it. I felt uneasy. I did my best to muddle my way through dinner and I headed home. I tried to work on some chores, but my mind was still preoccupied with our conversation. As I recounted her obvious bad decisions, I began to wonder, "How could she have done that? I can't believe she did that. Isn't she supposed to be a Christian?"

Later that evening when I went to bed I couldn't sleep. I was tossing and turning. Finally, I got up. I began to have a conversation with God. "Ok, what gives here? Why am I so unsettled about this? What is going on with me? Why can't I sleep?"

God very quickly and poignantly brought up my past. "Remember when you did that?" I knew exactly what He was talking about. "Remember what you did?" I'll never forget.

"Gee, your sin looks terrible on her, doesn't it?"

Jesus called me right out.

Matthew 7:1-2"Judge not, that you be not judged. For with what judgment you judge, you will be judged; and with the measure you use, it will be measured back to you.

"Do you want Me to judge you with the same standard you're judging her?"

I was silenced.

Everything became crystal clear at that point. My inner turmoil was the result of my hypocritical spirit. I could quickly see the things I didn't like in my friend because they were in me. Either I've done them, or thought about doing them. It is only by the grace of God that I am where I am today. Forgiven.

Isaiah 38:17... For You have cast all my sins behind Your back.

I was so humbled. If God has cast my sins behind His back, who am I to throw her sins in her face, so to speak?

Romans 2:4 Don't you see how wonderfully kind, tolerant, and patient God is with you? Does this mean nothing to you? Can't you see that his kindness is intended to turn you from your sin?

It's the goodness of God that leads to repentance.

God was tolerant with me while I was in my foolishness. In fact, He still is. It amazes me that He just hasn't crushed me yet.

But I love this story:

Luke 7:37 And behold, a woman in the city who was a sinner, when she knew that Jesus sat at the table in the Pharisee's house, brought an alabaster flask of fragrant oil...

Let's pause right here a second. How would you like to be the woman in this verse? It's recorded forever that you are a sinner. That's how she was known. She was a sinner. But, I think that was her past. Here she was humbly trying to do whatever she possibly could for Jesus. She had nothing to give Him..

Luke 7:38-39 Then she knelt behind Him at His feet, weeping. Her tears fell on His feet, and she wiped them off with her hair. Then she kept kissing His feet and putting perfume on them. When the Pharisee who had invited Him saw this, he said to himself, "If this man were a prophet, He would know what kind of woman is touching Him. She's a sinner!"

In this situation I had taken on the role of Simon looking down his nose and pointing his finger.

Luke 7:40, 44 Then Jesus answered his thoughts. "Simon...I have something to say to you. Look at this woman kneeling here. When I entered your home, you didn't offer Me water to wash the dust from my feet, but she has washed them with her tears and wiped them with her hair."

Jesus called him right out. Then and there Jesus stopped him in his tracks. That is exactly what Jesus did to me.

I had to take a good look at this woman.

Jesus said, "That is my daughter. I love her. I died for her. Don't you dare judge her!"

She was pouring out her heart to Jesus. Her gratitude spoke through her actions. How could she repay Him? She could never repay Him. God brought me back to the cross. I needed to be reminded of what I had been delivered from, and how far God had brought me.

I spent the morning just praising God for His forgiveness. His mercy is unfailing. His grace is unfathomable. I could never repay Him.

Luke 7:47 "I tell you, her sins—and they are many—have been forgiven, so she has shown Me much love. But a person who is forgiven little shows only little love."

I have been forgiven so much, and so has my friend. I vowed to love her with the love I've been shown.

June 4

The boy and I were playing a game of hide the star. It's much like hide and seek, only we use a green star. It was my turn to find it. He slyly hid it behind the shed. I rarely go back there. It sits in the very back of the yard. I rounded the corner and there it was. Then I looked up.

Blackberries everywhere. Everywhere blackberries. I was so delighted I didn't know what to do. So I ate them. Couldn't get enough. They were so sweet. How many ways could I use these berries? I would bake a pie. Definitely use them in our morning smoothies. Top our ice cream. The sky was the limit. No end to the possibilities.

I couldn't wait to tell my hubs all about the hidden treasure I discovered.

As soon as he walked in the door, I could barely contain myself.

"Honey, guess what I found in our backyard, behind the shed? Berries! Lots of them!

Very seriously he asked, "You didn't eat those berries did you?"

Not so excited anymore, I gave a hesitant, "Yes. Why?"

"You don't know what they are."

"I know what they are. They are blackberries. We used to eat them all the time when I was a kid."

"They look like blackberries, but may not be what you think. How long ago did you eat them?"

I really began to worry then. I quickly Googled it of course. A chart of every imaginable berry appeared. It seems those weren't blackberries after all. While they looked similar, the ones I ate were actually mulberries. Unripe mulberries can be toxic. Even cause hallucinations or death in some cases.

Spiritually speaking, ungodly counsel can have the same effect on us.

It is imperative that we know the source of all our information.

Personal opinions, talk show hosts, and books that don't use the Bible as their source of truth should be thrown out. Not even considered.

There are many times I want to spout my opinion. Never more than when I hear of a man cheating on a woman. I want to tell that wife to run for the hills. But God just may want her to stay. He may be looking to do a resurrection in that man. My opinion doesn't count. That woman needs to seek the Lord. Let her hear from Him.

If we don't know the Bible we can receive some very bad advice. If we implement it, it can have devastating consequences.

It is vital to get into a church that teaches the Bible verse by verse. One that will give you the whole counsel of God. If not, we'll be lacking in knowledge. Limited on the counsel we can give, uncertain of counsel we receive. Diligent study of the word of God in our personal lives is so important.

To know the Word is to know God.

Jeremiah 15:16 Your words were found, and I ate them, and Your word was to me the joy and rejoicing of my heart...

There is nothing sweeter than Your word Lord. Help me to long for Your word. I want to know the truth. It is Your truth that sets me free. I am Yours. Let me be wise about whom I seek for counsel. Give me wisdom to seek Your truth. Let me not be led by my emotions. My emotions can deceive me. I cannot trust them. I can trust Your word only. Give me discernment. Help me to learn Your word. Hide it in my heart. It will guide me continually.

June 5

Completely 'random' my son Camden exclaimed, "You need to go sit in the corner and think about your life." (I assure you I've never directed him to do that)...

Each day he repeated this statement, I chuckled. But today I began to realize God was actually trying to get my attention. Perhaps my little messenger was delivering a message for me. I asked God, "What is it you are trying to say? When I read Psalm 1, I knew.

Psalm 1:2 But his delight is in the law of the LORD, and in His law he meditates day and night.

Delight means what is most precious, treasured, and longed for.

In other words, God was asking me if He was the most treasured thing in my life. Of course He is important. But that's not exactly what He was asking.

He rephrased it.

Am I your all consuming passion?

Truth of the matter is I had been a little preoccupied. I was putting way too much thought into things that don't count for anything. They have no eternal value.

2 Corinthians 13:5 Examine yourself to see if you are in the faith. Test yourselves.

Taking a hard look at our spiritual life is important.

Matthew 24:12...the love of many will wax cold.

In the last days Jesus says love for Him will wane, but why?

When a person has no desperate need for Jesus, He gets pushed to the back seat.

All too quickly God brought me back 5 years. I was desperate for God then. My world was turned upside down and I needed Him to fix it. So when things evened out, I'd begun to relax. I started to cool off.

God hates lukewarm.

In our fast paced culture of super quick everything, it's as though we want a drive thru Christianity. We don't want to slow down and have a nice meal. Relationships don't work that way; especially with God. Investing quality time is vital.

Psalm 46:10 Be still and know that I am God.

God seems to be pleading, "Slow down. I want to linger over a cup of cappuccino with you."

What is most precious to you?

Sometimes we can spend more time thinking about our children than we do God. We can quickly become consumed with their problems. Ministry consumes time, and competes with God. Often our to-do list is preeminent in our thoughts. While all of these things are important, we can't allow them to engulf us. Before we realize it, a distance can grow between us and God.

God wants to be our all consuming passion. He wants that fire to be stoked for the world to see; not just a little ember.

It was good for me to "sit in a corner and think about my life." I pray it is for you as well.

June 6

I ran into an old friend yesterday. I haven't seen her for many years. She asked, "So what do you do?"

Enthusiastically I replied, "I'm a housewife!"

Blank stare; her face said it all. I glimpsed the picture in her mind. A lazy princess lying on the couch devouring Ben and Jerry's while watching 'Desperate Housewives'.

I wanted to share a snapshot of my reality. Child Psychologist, Gastroenterologist, Speech Therapist, Teacher, Launderer, Dietician, Chef, Maid,

Chauffeur, Play Group Coordinator are just a few of the hats I wear on any given day. Oh, and did I mention I'm the best at scrubbing carpets? I'm not sure which category that would fall under.

"What do you do all day?" she asked.

I found myself fumbling for words. As I smiled politely, I feebly managed to say, "Well, I like to write." Somehow the above list escaped me.

I was shaking my head all the way home. It made me chuckle. Why did this question catch me off guard?

I wondered what she might think if I told her I love being a wife to my husband. Cooking a nice dinner for my family brings me joy. I clean a lot (notice I didn't say my house is clean). Although cleaning messes is not glamorous, I do find great satisfaction in doing it. Wiping away tears and kissing the boo-boos blesses my heart. I love being a mom. I used to work full time. That was difficult. While being a stay at home mom is ten times harder, I feel incredibly blessed to be able to do it. It's a privilege to home school. Being a mom carries with it a staggering responsibility. I don't get a redo. Teaching my children to love God and know His word is of vital importance. Nothing trumps it. If I go out and save the world, and my children go to hell, my life will have been a total failure.

Being a housewife is what God called me to do. I treasure my "position".

I couldn't be happier.

Sister, treasure where God has you.

June 7

Revelation 7:9-14 After these things I looked, and behold, a great multitude which no one could number, of all nations, tribes, peoples, and tongues, standing before the throne and before the Lamb, clothed with white robes, with palm branches in their hands, and crying out with a loud voice, saying, "Salvation belongs to our God who sits on the throne, and to the Lamb!" All the angels stood around the throne and the elders and the four living creatures, and fell on their faces before the throne and worshiped God, saying:

"Amen! Blessing and glory and wisdom,

Thanksgiving and honor and power and might,

Be to our God forever and ever.

Amen."

Then one of the elders answered, saying to me, "Who are these arrayed in white robes, and where did they come from?"

And I said to him, "Sir, you know." So he said to me, "These are the ones who come out of the great tribulation, and washed their robes and made them white in the blood of the Lamb.

One of the elders asked John, "Who are they? Where did they come from?" John answered, simply, "Sir, you know" who they are. These questions really stood out to me. Here was a leader, one who would be very familiar with the people, and yet he did not recognize who they were? John simply states, "Sir, you know." Why did he have to ask who they were? Why were they unrecognizable?

They were radically changed! Every aspect of them was changed for the better.

It is a wonderful aspiration for us this year. I want to be radically different! I want to be unrecognizable even to those who are closest to me. How about you? Are you up for the challenge?

Let's take a look at the first question the elder asked, "Who are they?"

"These are the ones who...washed their robes and made them white in the blood of the Lamb."

This can be difficult to understand. It would help to take a look at how two people sealed a covenant in the Old Testament. A covenant, which is a binding agreement, was sealed when two people exchanged a piece of clothing. Symbolically, this is what we have done when we actively chose to accept Jesus Christ's gift of dying on the cross. He took the penalty for our sins. They are no longer counted against us. We are justified (Just As If I... had never sinned). Hence, we are clothed in Jesus' robe of righteousness. It is pure white. Spotless. When God sees us, He no longer sees our sin. He only sees us covered in our white robe of righteousness.

I love new clothes. There's nothing like a crisp white top. I love wearing white, but... it is so hard to keep it clean! If you're like me, you can mess it up before you even leave the house! If I'm wearing something new, I am on guard against anything that can stain it. I'm very protective of it. I may even cover it with something else to safeguard it. We need to do the same with our new robe of righteousness.

How can we keep our new robe spotless?

There are three things that threaten to stain our robe:

1 John 2:16 For all that is in the world-the lust of the flesh, the lust of the eyes, and the pride of life-is not of the Father but is of the world.

Lust of the flesh:

Lust means to crave, desire and long for. Flesh means our human nature apart from God. Basically, I see something, I want it. I want to look like that. I want to wear that. I want to own that. I want to do that. I want, I want, I want...regardless of how God feels about it. Regardless if it is not God's best for me.

1 Timothy 6:6 Now godliness with contentment is great gain.

God wants us to be content with what we have.

Lust of the eyes:

Guard your eyes! We often appropriate this warning to men, but it is equally important for us. Here's why:

We are bombarded by sexual images. The images we see become locked in our brain. Once we see them, we can't erase them. We learn by repetition. If we want to learn a new application on our computer, we do it over and over. After doing it so many times we remember. If we want to learn a new verse, we say it over and over, and eventually we remember. Well, we have that same capacity when it comes to the bad things. The images we see in the movies, TV, and on the computer do have an effect on us; like it or not. Now what happens is when we see these images enough, they become our standard. We start evaluating ourselves by those low standards. We compare ourselves. We may even think, well this isn't as bad as that. At least I'm not doing that. Comparisons bring compromise.

Clothe yourself in the beauty of Holiness! There's nothing more beautiful than a godly women. You don't need to compromise. You know what God has shown you to be pleasing to Him. Don't doubt what He has told you. Stay true to Him. Don't compare yourself to those around you; not even those closest to you. Compare yourself to His standard.

For singles:

If it is His will, He will bring you that perfect man of God who loves you BECAUSE you have not compromised.

For wives:

Comparisons cause insecurities. Insecurities cause jealousies. Jealousies kill a marriage.

Proverbs 6:34 For jealousy makes a man furious, and he will not spare when he takes revenge.

Pride of Life:

Pride is a desire to be noticed for something...looks, possessions, accomplishments, serving, giving, spiritual life etc.

What is it about ourselves that we want people to recognize us, compliment us and lift us up?

Proverbs 16:18 Pride goes before destruction, and haughtiness before a fall.

1 Peter 5:6...Humble yourself under God's mighty hand, that He may lift you up

Everything we have has been given to us by God. Everything we have can be taken at any moment. Let's use what we have to lift Him up, not ourselves...this includes our finances, knowledge of Him, time, energy, our homes, our children...

Matthew 6:4 He sees everything done in secret and will reward you openly.

Jesus chose a violent death so that we could be clothed in His white robe. We need to choose the same. Choose to die a violent death to those things the Lord has pointed out to us. Protect your white spotless robe! Small changes can make a big impact in our walk with the Lord. With these things out of the way, and no longer separating us from God's best, we will be right where God wants us... "before the Lamb" and on our faces worshipping Him...forever changed...unrecognizable!

June 8

Camden and I were sitting at the table doing his schoolwork. When I looked up I noticed he was distracted. He wasn't listening to a word I was saying. He was lost in his own little world. This isn't unusual and I was tempted to scold him. But this time was a little different so I held off. He was staring at me intently, but not into my eyes. He was looking just below my eyes. A grin appeared on his little face. He sat up on his elbows and drew nearer to my face; as if to get a better look. I sensed he was about to say something real good.

He did not disappoint.

With all sincerity he enthusiastically exclaimed, "I love the cracks in your eyes Momma!"

Once again, he had me roaring with laughter. He was soon laughing right along with me. He has no idea that some might find his statement to be a bit offensive. He calls it like he sees it!

In our culture wrinkles are not a sign of beauty. They are something to be ashamed of. We are to hide them at all cost. I began to think about these "cracks."

I embrace these "cracks!"

Every time I look into one of these cracks, I'm reminded of some trial or struggle we've overcome. We've been through so much. Some you know and some you don't. But, my God knows all of it. And for each one He has given me a precious promise to cling to.

He assured me, "I will never leave you. Yes, I'm staying. I'm here for the long haul."

I don't want to remove, hide or do away with any of them.

That would erase the memory. They are part of my identity. They help define me. I want to cherish the memories. They were difficult, but necessary building blocks of my faith. Without trials we wouldn't need faith.

I wouldn't trade even one of them.

I'd be lying if I said I looked forward to more, but I know there will be. More times to cherish with the One who will fix it all someday.

Revelation 21:4-5 "And God will wipe away every tear from their eyes; there shall be no more death, nor sorrow, nor crying. There shall be no more pain, for the former things have passed away...I make all things new."

June 9

While I was on my morning walk, I was enjoying some quiet time when I was startled out of my zone by a young guy who came bolting past me. Quite obviously he was not out for a casual jog. He was running at full speed; as though he were in a race. I chuckled to myself. If I ran like that I wouldn't even make it one block. Ray would find me lying on the corner in need of resuscitation. That's because God didn't give me the ability to run like that. God didn't make me like that guy. That's his race, not mine. So often we try to run someone else's race. It's exhausting.

I thought about how often I tried to make Camden "run someone else's race". I looked at the charts that had age appropriate milestones. Camden was so far behind. In one test he was at infantile level. Panic set in. I had to catch him up. I was determined he would do all those things. He couldn't keep up with my expectations. They were unrealistic. They were a massive weight for me to carry around. I was exhausted.

One day God spoke to my heart. He didn't make Camden like everyone else. He made him different for a purpose. I was trying to make him something he's not.

Hebrews 12:1...let us lay aside every weight...and run with endurance the race set before us

Lay these expectations aside.

Making comparisons brings discouragement. Don't allow the world to dictate to you what your child should be doing. Focus on his strengths, not his weakness. Praise God for the things your child can do instead of always looking at what he can't do. Laying these weights aside allowed me to run the race God has set for *me*.

It is so freeing to know that my child will be ALL that God has called him to be. That burden does not rest on my shoulders, but God's. He began a good work in him, and He will be faithful to complete it.

June 10

Sometimes we set out to do a task and we hit a brick wall. Suddenly, we're stopped dead in our tracks. The situation looks impossible. We can quickly be overwhelmed. We don't have what we need. We don't have any idea what to do next.

2 Kings 2:6...the Lord has sent me to the Jordan.

Elijah came to the Jordan. He certainly had no means to get to the other side of this massive river. His situation looked impossible. Three things to note:

1. Elijah didn't panic.

2. Elijah didn't second guess.

3. Elijah didn't doubt.

Where did Elijah's confidence come from?

Elijah remembered: "The Lord sent me to the Jordan."

It was the Lord who sent him there. He was exactly where God wanted him.

Jordan means "descender." God descended down to part the water for Elijah. He performed a miracle, and Elijah crossed over on dry ground. He will do the same for you, if need be. Remember, it's the Lord who sent you here. If you're facing an impossible situation, trust God.

Pray.

God will do something amazing at your "Jordan."

June 11

1 Kings 10:13 Now King Solomon gave the queen of Sheba all she desired, whatever she asked, besides what Solomon had given her according to the royal generosity.

What is royal generosity?

It is something from the King Himself; from His treasure trove.

What a picture of us coming before Jesus.

He is King of Kings and Lord of Lords.

Nothing is off limits. He owns everything. All the kingdom is at His disposal, and thus is made available to us. All she had to do was ask. It delighted the King to give her whatever she asked.

It delights God to give us what we ask, when we ask according to His will. Let's not limit God with our paltry request for scraps when He owns the buffet!

He is a big God. Let's come boldly before Him. All His resources are at our disposal.

It honors God to ask big things.

His treasury is endless.

His wisdom is wiser than all of the wise men of the world. He is infinitely wiser than all of the doctors, therapists and experts.

Whatever your desperate need is today, ask.

He delights to give you your heart's desire because He loves you. You are His daughter.

The Queen left the presence of the King with a treasure trove of gifts. Our King desires to load us up with gifts from the treasury of His heart. We only have to ask.

Matthew 7:7 Ask, and it shall be given you; seek, and ye shall find; knock, and it shall be opened unto you.

June 12

I took the dog out early one morning. It was dark with a slight glow from the moon. The air was still and silent. We were meandering around when suddenly a brisk wind whipped up out of nowhere. It began to howl loudly. So loud it stopped me in my tracks. Even the dog became motionless and looked up.

That wind came out of nowhere.

It was unexpected.

God does that sometimes.

He surprises us.

That's what He did to Moses. God told Moses He would give him enough meat to feed 600,000 people for a whole month. Moses was a wise leader, but it really didn't take much smarts to realize there was no way this was going to happen.

It was impossible.

There would never be enough.

And he was right.

But where he went wrong was he questioned God.

I do that sometimes. I look at a particular situation and think, 'No way. How's He's gonna pull this off?' That will never be. Or I consider the amount of time I've been waiting and start second guessing. Even though I already know God said He was going to do it, I still doubt.

Never underestimate God.

Numbers 11:31 Now a wind went out from the LORD...

In the old language this word "wind" was used of the very breath of God. When God sends his wind, He breathes life into seemingly dead situations. Everything changes. He revives. He provides in ways we wouldn't think of.

He can intervene at any time, and you can be sure it will be the right time.

He comes when we least expect it.

If today finds you thinking, "No way..." remember God can do anything!

He just may surprise you.

June 13

1 Kings 17:9 Then the word of the LORD came to him, saying, "Arise, go to Zarephath, which belongs to Sidon, and dwell there. See, I have commanded a widow there to provide for you."

God takes Elijah from the place of "cutting" to Zarephath which means "refinery". God separates, and then refines. God called Elijah to arise. Rise up and get going. But sometimes we can become so comfortable in our place of isolation that it's difficult to move on. Sometimes when we go through a trial we can begin to feel sorry for our pitiful selves. Self-pity can hold us back from doing what God called us to do. We don't want to hinder God from taking us to a new place. God gave Elijah the power to rise and move on. He will give you the power to do the same.

Just as God sent Elijah to the place of cutting, so too He sent him into the "refinery".

Gold is refined in the fire. It has to reach a certain temperature in order for the impurities to rise to the top where the goldsmith can remove them.

What is it that God wants to remove?

Laziness is one thing I find in my own life. God brings about situations to try me. He wants to show me how my slothfulness is hindering me.

Insecurity can really keep us from God's best. All our security comes from Christ.

Fear is something I have been plagued with all of my life.

Fear paralyzes, but courage mobilizes.

Fear has stopped me dead in my tracks countless times.

2 Timothy 1:7 For God has not given us a spirit of fear, but of power, love and a sound mind.

Fear of failure, fear of the unknown, and fear that I won't have what it takes. None of that is from the Lord. If it's not from the Lord, then we know who it's from.

Lord God, take my fears. All of them. Fill me with courage to face whatever comes before me today. Help me to find all my security in You. I have no resources. No ability to do anything on my own. With you I can scale a wall. I can do anything when I'm holding Your hand. Walk with me through the Jordan I face today.

June 14

I see the world through a whole new set of eyes. I have Camden glasses on now. As we were walking down the street Camden was delighted to find a caterpillar inching his way along. After watching him closely for a few moments, he concluded the caterpillar was cold. He quickly ran and got a leaf. Tenderly, he covered him up. Just as fast, the caterpillar found his way out. He scurried away in the other direction. Camden was undaunted. Over and over he reached out to love that little caterpillar. He tried several different approaches. Each one was futile. But, he never gave up. Perhaps he had felt like that caterpillar. Something inside him makes it difficult to allow people to get close to him. He wants to be loved. He wants to be close to people. He just doesn't know how. It's easier to run away. It takes a lot to be his friend. But, it's so worth the effort. There are lots of caterpillars in our lives. Perhaps one will cross your path today. Reach out to them. Don't be deterred by past rebuffs. Love them anyway. Your efforts may be the tool in our Lord's hand used to transform them into a beautiful butterfly.

June 15

Whoooooa he's a big Mac! Is he a big Mac?

As we were walking up to the register at the Dollar Store, a big beefy guy cut in front of Camden. He was burly and wearing all black; quite intimidating. With a giggle in his voice, he exclaimed, "Whoooooa he's a big Mac! Is he a big Mac?"

Camden was not phased in the least by the magnitude of his presence. He actually seemed quite amused for some reason. I began to think upon his attitude of confidence. When we are face to face with the staggering presence of an obstacle, person or difficulty we should have a joyful confidence in our God.

Psalm 37:13 The Lord laughs at him (His enemies), For He sees that his day is coming.

We can have lots of enemies, but sometimes doubt is my biggest enemy. I allow my doubts to take over. They laugh and mock me; causing me to doubt God's promises. The longer I wait for a promise to be fulfilled, the more difficult it is to believe it's going to happen.

Our adversary or difficulty may be intimidating, but it is no match for our God.

God's word never fails. You can trust His promises.

We can trust even when we can't see.

Lord give me the confidence that my situation is not too difficult for you. Nothing is too hard for you. No one is out of Your reach. Father, reach down. Show Yourself strong. Increase my faith.

June 16

Genesis 22:2 "Take your son, your only son—yes, Isaac, whom you love so much—and go to the land of Moriah. Go and sacrifice him as a burnt offering on one of the mountains, which I will show you."

Abraham did not hesitate. He obeyed God immediately. God said, "Go", and he went.

Romans 4:20 He did not waver at the promise of God through unbelief, but was strengthened in faith, giving glory to God.

He took a few guys to help carry his stuff. When he was nearly there, he told them to wait there. He was going to worship and come right back.

Worship at a time like this? He was on the verge of losing his son.

Worship and bowing down to God is what increased his faith. He became stronger and more resolute than ever. If we will spend time worshipping God, we'll be encouraged and come away strengthened as well. Our circumstances may not change, but our outlook will. Supernaturally God will equip us to face that challenge and become stronger in our faith because of it.

When we worship, God assures us He is in control. We are acknowledging His mastery over the entire situation. Abraham lifted his hands as if to say, "This child is Yours Lord. He belongs to You. You are able to raise him from the dead, if need be." He was fully convinced God would do what He said He would do. God never ever goes back on His word. Although every outward circumstance may contradict His promise, we can still believe. God is faithful. He will come through.

Romans 4:17...God, who gives life to the dead and calls those things which do not exist as though they did...

Abraham was thanking God in advance as though he already had been given his son back from the dead. We can do the same. God knows the end from the beginning. He knows every detail of the situation. Essentially, we can celebrate before we actually get our answer to prayer.

1 Corinthians 13:13 But for right now, until that completeness, we have three things to do to lead us... Trust steadily in God, hope unswervingly, love extravagantly.

You can trust God will show up. He will be there for you. Expect Him.

Hope in God. Don't put unrealistic expectations on the doctor, your husband or friends. They will let you down. God never fails.

Love is willing to sacrifice. Pour yourself out. Don't hold back. Give your all. You won't be disappointed.

Revelation 19:6 Alleluia! For the Lord God Omnipotent Reigns...

I want you to take notice of that one seemingly grazed over word: Omnipotent.

Omnipotent means that God is the One who still holds sway over all things. He is still on the throne. We can trust Him.

God, You are still King. You still have the final say. You are the authority over everyone and everything, whether they acknowledge you or not.

Abraham made that acknowledgement when he worshipped. He had the greatest revelation of Jesus Christ ever. God provided for him. God will provide for you. It may not be in a way that you expect. It will almost definitely not be in your time frame. Nevertheless, He will provide.

June 17

"Look Mama, the moon is smiling at me!"

1 John 1:4 And these things we write to you that your joy may be full.

God doesn't just want us to be "happy." I believe God wants us to be overflowing with joy. He wants us to exude joy. I don't know about you but the last thing I've been doing is exuding joy. I'd rather stare down at my disappointments. It's easier to complain and grumble about the hardships of my life. Let's put it this way, if I were to make a list, I think my list of complaints (legitimate complaints) would far exceed my list of "good things."

Perspective is everything.

Camden always has a way of putting things into proper perspective for me. Recently I ventured on a very long road trip. We drove down to Georgia and then we made our way to Florida. One evening we returned from a late dinner. As we were heading in the house Camden stopped. He was staring into the sky. I hadn't noticed but it was a beautiful evening. The sky was crystal clear. The moon was just a sliver; like the letter C.

Camden exclaimed, "Look Mama, the moon is smiling at me!"

I looked back down at him. He was completely bent over. His arms were stretched out so that he could peer under his left arm. He said it again, excitedly, "Look Mama, the moon is smiling at me!"

Who thinks like that?!

I felt my heart smile. I knew God was delivering a message to me.

This child always gives me a new angle. Sometimes we need to bend over backwards to get a new perspective. Little did I know I would need to live this message out when I returned home the following week.

My entire house was flooded when the small line linking our ice maker to the refrigerator busted. It spouted water for hours while we were sleeping. My whole house flooded.

Sometimes life has a way of throwing curves at us. Things don't always go our way. We can be so burdened by the stress of life that we lose our joy. We begin to focus on the negative things in our lives. Or put all of our attention on the things our children aren't accomplishing. All of their appointments, all of the financial burdens, all of the things they can't do, and all of things we can't do. We begin to compare our lives to others, look at what they can do, even worse if we compare our children to others. Despair can set in very quickly.

Philippians 4:1 Therefore, my beloved and longed for brethren, my joy and crown, so stand fast in the Lord, beloved.

V 2 I implore you

V3 I urge you...

V4 Rejoice in the Lord always. Again I will say rejoice!

I believe verses 6 and 11 reveal Paul's secret:

V6 Be anxious for nothing, but in everything by prayer and supplication, with thanksgiving, let your requests be made known to God; and the peace of God, which surpasses all understanding, will guard your hearts and minds through Christ Jesus.

We can quickly forget all the things we have to be thankful for. If Jesus is our Savior, we have eternal life in heaven. That's a big deal.

It's important not to take the small things for granted either. Be thankful for everything. It could be taken away at any moment.

Joy and contentment go hand in hand. A woman's contentment is not found in the "things" that she possesses. But contentment is a state of mind.

V 11 Not that I speak in regard to need, for I have learned in whatever state I am, to be content.

Paul says he had to learn contentment. I believe we do too.

Contentment can be defined as a state of peaceful happiness, to be satisfied, or to desire no more than what one has.

Contentment is a choice.

When we find ourselves needing a new perspective we should go outside and look up.

Is the moon smiling at you?

Be willing to bend over. Be willing to be flexible. Go out of our way to love and be kind and have kind words.

How?

Philippians 4:13 I can do all things through Christ who strengthens me.

For the next week I'd like to suggest that you keep a little journal of the things you are thankful for; things big and things small. Start looking for the little things. Do you love the rain? Write it down and thank God. Did your child have a good day at school? Write it down and thank God. Stop to admire the beauty of an oak tree. Slow down as you pass a lake and admire its serenity. Purposely look for things to thank Him for and it will bring you a new perspective!

June 18

Jeremiah 20:9-10 His word was in my heart like a burning fire...I hear many mocking.

I want my heart to be burning like a fire for the Lord, but it's not. This morning finds me discouraged. I sat down and read a few verses. I love this verse. Typically, it moves me. It stirs up passion, but not today. I'm so down. I get up and do some laundry. I put some dishes away.

What's wrong with me?

I know what it is. I don't have to think upon it for very long.

I'm disheartened by a situation that I've been praying about. Every morning it's at the forefront of my mind. Every evening it's the last thing I think about.

I hear the mocking voice of Satan saying, "God has not answered you. This isn't going to change. Something very bad is going to happen." His voice always seems to penetrate my inner thoughts. I become overwhelmed. I don't even want to pray. I've been praying so long; it seems hopeless. I don't even see the point. But as I looked back to my journal from 3 years ago I become overwhelmed with sheer delight. I'm a little breathless. I realized the prayer request I had written down was a big one. God answered in a big way. It seemed impossible at the time; almost hopeless. My heart seems to be fluttering with glee as I remember. My hope is restored. The enemy's mocking voice is silenced for the moment. I begin to find my strength. Praise is coming forth from my heart. Praise silences him. It keeps him at bay; depletes him of his power over me. I think to myself, "God, You are working. You do hear me! You saw my need then, and You see my need now. You care about me!"

Praise leads to renewed intercession.

Jeremiah 20:11 But the Lord is with me as a mighty awesome warrior.

The Lord is our fierce defender. He is on our side. He will never leave us. He is fighting on our behalf. The Lord is our sword and shield. Darkness cannot penetrate the light. From all outward appearances everything seems pretty grim. But, the enemy won't prevail.

I am certain of that.

Jesus You defeated Satan at the cross. Our battle is already won. You will get the victory. Father lift my head. Take this discouragement lingering in my heart. Fill me with hope. You are my hope. You are the reason I can sing. Give me a new song.

June 19

"To misunderstand the nature and threat of evil is to risk being blind-sided."

Joel Rosenberg

Revelation 2:24...you do not know the depths of Satan

You do not know how far Satan will go to destroy you. His schemes are vast. His tactics are endless. This truth holds even more weight if you are an active servant of Jesus. You and your family become a larger than life target. Why is that? You are a threat to him.

We have to take a close look at this word "depths" in order to fully grasp the meaning of it. Every single word of this Bible is intentional, and this is no exception.

In the original language, the root of this word is 'bathys'. It is used in several places in the Bible, but there is one in particular that grabbed my attention. It's used in a story from the book of Acts to describe a "deep sleep". Maybe you're familiar with it.

Acts 20:7-9...Paul, ready to depart the next day, spoke to them and continued his message until midnight. There were many lamps in the upper room where they were gathered together. And in a window sat a certain young man named Eutychus, who was sinking into a deep sleep. He was overcome by sleep; and as Paul continued speaking, he fell down from the third story and was taken up dead.

This story almost makes me want to chuckle. It sounds so ridiculous. I mean really? How could this happen? It doesn't sound possible. Paul pointed out it wasn't dark in the room. There were a lot of lamps, and it was bright. He also noted that this is a young guy. He's not an elderly man. We could expect this to happen to someone else; but, this young guy? This is such a picture of what is taking place in the church today. Satan is attacking the church. He is attacking us personally. When we get weighed down by the cares of this world, exhaustion overwhelms us. We are overcome, and soon we are lulled off to sleep by Satan. Spiritually speaking, we cannot afford to sleep. Our enemy never rests. He is constantly roaming about. We must stay alert. We say to ourselves, 'How could this happen? This is ridiculous. How did I end up here?' I wish I could say Satan's tactics were unexpected, but they are not.

Most often, his strategies are very familiar to us. We just become complacent, and the enemy begins to lull us into a deep sleep.

Maybe you are familiar with the sleep cycle of the human body. There are 5 stages. The stages are very similar to the "sleep cycle" used by Satan.

Stage 1: A person in Stage 1 of the sleep cycle is still in a state of wakefulness. They can hear voices. They are easily awakened. If a person is awakened in this stage of the sleep cycle, they may say they really weren't asleep. Some report a feeling of falling.

In the same manner, Satan lulls us to sleep with complacency. He begins with subtle lies. We lose our attention for detail. We no longer find it very important to obey God in the "little things". This is the beginning of the fall. We feel something is not right in our spirit, but we ignore it. However, if someone brings it to our attention quickly, we still have the ability to "wake up" and go in the other direction.

Keep in mind that a sleepy person is not effective for anything. Inevitably, they're not giving their all to the ministry God called them to. They're not helping, in fact, they're hindering. They're hindering their children, their friends, spouse and church. They are groggy. They make poor decisions. Others must carry their load.

Stage 2: A person in Stage 2 of the sleep cycle experiences a decline in heart rate, body temperature drops, and their eyes stop moving.

In choosing to ignore the warning to go in the other direction, we see this person's heart for the Lord begin to slow down. Compromising leads to sin every time. The heart is no longer fluttering for the Lord. The love that was once there starts to grow cold. When you take your eyes off the Lord, you cease to see the plot of the enemy. You become very vulnerable.

Stage 3: A person in Stage 3 of the sleep cycle is very difficult to awaken. If awakened, they are disoriented.

Likewise, if you or someone you know has entered this stage you may not recognize yourself. Things are proceeding from your mouth that you thought you would never say. You are doing things you said you would never do. But, you still have a sense of right and wrong. You can be brought to your senses. You can still be awakened.

Stage 4: A person in Stage 4 of the sleep cycle has a very erratic heartbeat. Brainwaves are extremely slow.

Similarly, when you enter this stage you're clearly not thinking. Your heart hardens, and you just don't care about the consequences of your actions anymore.

Stage 5: A person in Stage 5 of the sleep cycle has entered the dream state. Their muscles are paralyzed.

In the same manner when you enter this stage, discernment is completely blunted. Truth is so skewed you believe every lie of Satan. You are incapable of doing what is right because you are so weak spiritually. You are paralyzed. Your ability to think, feel and decide is cut off. You cease feeling shame or remorse. You are callous; apathetic to the pain that you're causing. Although your own will may agree with God, in your flesh, you are powerless to do what you know you ought to do. In this stage, you are completely held captive by the power of Satan.

Typically paralysis is irreversible.

Are you without hope? Absolutely not.

What can you do if you find yourself in one of the stages of Satan's "sleep cycle"? WAKE UP!

John 5:14...stop sinning, or something even worse may happen to you.

Today, Jesus Christ can set you free. Who the Son sets free, shall be free indeed.

What can we do if someone we love is in one of the stages of Satan's "sleep cycle"?

We can use Paul's example with Eutychus:

Paul went to him. Often I have found instead of going to that person we want to alienate ourselves from them. We don't want anything to do with them.

Romans 2:4...not realizing God's kindness leads to repentance.

Paul literally fell on him. Paul didn't keep him at a distance. Paul grabbed hold of him and did not let go; as if to take possession of him. Sometimes that's what we need to do. We need to bring assurance of our unconditional love. Otherwise the person may feel condemned as though everyone is judging them. It's helpful to remember from where it is that Jesus picked us up.

2 Corinthians 2:7 so that, on the contrary, you ought rather to forgive and comfort him, lest perhaps such a one be swallowed up with too much sorrow.

Paul embraced Him with prayer. We know this because that is who Paul was. He was a prayer warrior. He so thoroughly encompassed this kid with prayer that he was awakened from the dead. The same can be true with our loved ones.

Do you have a person in your life that is paralyzed by sin?

Completely envelop their life with prayer.

Revelation 2:24...you do not know the depths of Satan

Dear Jesus, we don't know the depths of Satan, but you do. Wake us up! Protect us this day from every plot of the enemy. Give us a piercing conviction of sin deep within our hearts. If our children take one step off of Your path, be there to gently lead them in the right way. In the areas where the enemy has already begun to destroy, we ask that you rebuild. Restore back to us the ground the enemy has stolen. We ask you God, be our eyes when we can't see. We desperately need You. Help us to know that You are near. In Jesus Name we pray, Amen.

June 20

This week I was taking a nice walk. It was still dark out, and I couldn't see very well. I was strolling along having a good ole time singing and worshipping the Lord. I happened to look down. Mid stride I see a snake and I'm about to tread right on it! I lunged over top of the thing and took off running. Now I'm not sure if the snake was chasing me or not. I didn't wait around to find out. I took off!

When I slowed down enough to think straight, I began to question myself. "Was that really a snake? Was it just a stick? Was I overreacting?" So often something similar happens in our spiritual lives. The Spirit prompts us to be on the lookout for something. But Satan comes along and causes us to question God.

God was warning me. Be on the lookout for Satan and his evil schemes.

God has a plan for your life. Equally so, the enemy has a plan.

There are many things I want you to know about this enemy. You know why? How can you be on guard against an enemy you know nothing about? Knowledge is power. The more you know the better equipped you will be.

First thing I want you to know about your enemy is this: Satan is NOT the opposite of God. That is a great misconception. He is the great counterfeit of God. When someone tries to pass a counterfeit bill they try to make it look as close to the real thing as possible. Satan does the same thing.

Oh can he ever make bad things appear to be good!

2 Corinthians 11:14...Satan transforms himself into an angel of light.

We have to be on guard.

Satan doesn't always try to get us to do really bad things. Sometimes he settles for getting us to compromise. Sometimes he tries to take us away from God's best for us.

Ephesians 6:12 We don't wrestle against flesh and blood but against powers and darkness and evil host of wickedness in heavenly places...

The Bible tells us not to be deceived. How is it that you can be deceived so easily? Perhaps it's because you're still young and you haven't matured in learning God's word.

Ephesians 6:10 Be strong in the Lord and in His mighty power. Put on all of God's armor so that you will be able to stand firm against all strategies of the devil.

This Word will make you wise to the schemes of the enemy.

As I continued along in my walk, I was rounding the bend when there was another snake! I lunged over and ran away from that one too! Now there happened to be even more light on the horizon and upon further inspection I realized that wasn't a snake, but just a large slimy worm. But, did it matter????

If it looks like a snake, run from it!

You can look back in hindsight and question all you want. But I guarantee you if you think of this message and you have to question, "HMMM is this good or bad for me? RUN FROM IT!

Here are three examples of how the enemy will try to deceive you and make something that could potentially be bad for you look good.

He will tell you that you don't need to go to church.

Listen, you have to find a church to get plugged into. It's extremely important and a huge lie the enemy tries to get you to buy into that you don't need to go to church. I just want to warn you it will set a weak foundation for the rest of your life.

Build your foundation on the Rock of Jesus Christ; otherwise you're building on a foundation of sand that will fall.

Secondly, church isn't all about you. Church is also about how you can love and serve others. Church is often a place that people go to seek solace and find help in time of need. You could be the friend someone is looking for and you could encourage one another.

Thirdly, the enemy wants you to believe you don't need this word every day.

This Word is life! This Word is wisdom!

This Word is a refuge. It hides us and protects us. Can I just encourage you to absorb this word like a sponge? Take in as much as you can as often as you can.

There is so much power in this Word. If you don't know it, you can't apply it.

Father, give us wisdom to see the schemes of our enemy. Help us to flee from him. Guard us from his plots. Help us to fall in love with your word. Help us to find a church that teaches Your word. Help us to get plugged in there. We want our family to have a strong foundation in You.

June 21

Daniel 3:15...and who is that God that shall deliver you out of my hands?

Nebuchadnezzar built a large statue and demanded everyone in his kingdom bow down to it. It was the only acceptable response. If you didn't bow down you would be thrown into the fiery furnace. I think this is such a great illustration of how fear works in our lives today. We face scary situations that dictate a response of fear. Everyone around us would agree fear is the only proper choice. We see no way out. The only possible ending to this dilemma is disaster.

Quite often I find myself standing face to face with the unknown. I simply don't know what to expect so I fear the worst. Fear of the unknown has been one of my greatest adversaries. The hands of fear often tighten their grip, and strangle the life right out of me.

Daniel 3:16 Shadrach, Meshach, and Abed-Nego answered and said to the king, "O Nebuchadnezzar, we have no need to answer you in this matter."

When things look threatening, don't respond.

Don't let your mind assume the worst.

Don't replay all the horrible scenarios in your head.

Don't run.

Daniel 3:19 Nebuchadnezzar was so furious with Shadrach, Meshach, and Abednego that his face became distorted with rage. He commanded that the furnace be heated seven times hotter than usual.

When we face our fears with courage, the enemy gets furious. He may heat the fire up.

Expect things to get worse.

God is walking through the fire with you.

Daniel 3:24-25 Then King Nebuchadnezzar was astonished; and he rose in haste and spoke, saying to his counselors, "Did we not cast three men bound into the midst of the fire?" They answered and said to the king, "True, O king." "Look!" he answered, "I see four men loose, walking in the midst of the fire; and they are not hurt, and the form of the fourth is like the Son of God."

Look! They saw the Lord clearer, closer; their spiritual eyes were opened wider than ever in their lives while they were in the fire.

The boys saw Jesus Christ in the fire with them.

He removed their chains in that fire.

What chains are you bound by? What is holding you captive? Are you a prisoner of your own fear? Jesus Christ came to set the captives free. Right here and right now.

The boys saw Him walking in the midst of the fire with them. The sight of God, and the knowledge that they weren't left alone in this, sustained them. They were able to handle the heat. God has not left you alone.

Daniel 3:26...Come out and come here...

When we realize the Lord is with us, He lives inside us, the hands of fear lose their grip. We find ourselves set free! We are freer than we've ever been before!

1 John 4:4 You are of God, little children, and have overcome them, because He who is in you is greater than he who is in the world.

Shadrach, Meshach and Abednego chose courage over fear. God may not choose to rescue us out of the situation. But, He will walk through it with us!

God is greater than our fears!

June 22

Ruth 2:11 And Boaz answered and said to her, "It has been fully reported to me, all that you have done for your mother-in-law since the death of your husband, and how you have left your father and your mother and the land of your birth, and have come to a people whom you did not know before. "The LORD repay your work, and a full reward be given you by the LORD God of Israel, under whose wings you have come for refuge."

Ruth lost her husband. In a moment, life as she knew it was gone. Instead of falling down in despair, she rose up. She chose a path that not many of us would have taken. She stuck by her mother in law. She gave up her life to care for her.

If life has dealt you a blow, you may be facing some difficult demands. When God blesses you with a special needs child or perhaps a wayward teenager, or a trying marriage it is physically and emotionally exhausting. God wants you to know through His word that He is well aware of how challenging these demands are. He knows all that you're doing. Others may not take notice, but nothing gets by Him.

Matthew 6:4... and your Father who sees in secret will Himself reward you openly.

Ruth could've gone back to what was familiar, but God called her to step out of her comfort zone, and she went. It was not convenient, nor pleasant. Ruth knew God was her provider. She had to trust solely in Him. She left her family and her hometown to go to an unknown land. She had no job or any other financial means. She had no friends she could fall back on. There was no family she could turn to. Ruth gave up everything. She did it willingly. She stood beside this woman with a loyalty that is to be admired. Ultimately her devotion was to her God.

I want to trust God like that.

Isaiah 26:3 You will keep him in perfect peace, whose mind is stayed on You, because he trusts in You.

Ruth found her confidence in God. She didn't trust her own ingenuity.

If you've been running in every different direction trying your best to fix everything, slow down. This anxiety and fretting is not necessary. God knows this situation inside and out. Doctors and psychologists don't have all the answers. People will let you down. Our best efforts will fail.

God never fails.

He knows what is needed. He will provide. Flee to Him. He'll hide you under His wings. If you feel like no one in this world understands you, confide in God.

Psalm 91:2 This I declare about the LORD: He alone is my refuge, my place of safety; He is my God, and I trust him.

June 23

Psalm 119:92 Unless Your law had been my delight, I would have perished in my affliction. I will never forget...

I was super excited to go to Colorado. I had never been out west. I couldn't wait. A few days before our departure, Ray got us tickets to ride on a train up Pikes Peak. Pikes Peak is one of the tallest mountains in the world. I was terrified, but I went along with it. Feigning a smile so as not to disappoint him nor the rest of the family.

The day of the train ride, I was wiped out. Fear is exhausting. By the time I reached the top I was physically and emotionally spent. I tried my best not to reveal my inward turmoil. I don't know what gave me away. Perhaps it was my eyes squeezed shut all the way up. Or maybe it was my head tilted down while my lips uttered silent prayers for help. When I not so bravely stepped off the train, my niece skittishly asked, "Aunt Renee are you ok?"

How did she know?

I headed into the gift shop. I bee lined it to the popcorn. The conductor had me sold as he talked about it being the best on the west coast. I like to snack when I'm nervous. I was lightheaded and nearly hyperventilating. The smell of popcorn wafted through the air. I grabbed a bag and headed outside. I knew God wanted to speak to me; fact of the matter is, I wanted to get this over with. This place was crawling with people; tourists were everywhere. I had to find a little spot to be alone. There aren't many places to go at the top of a mountain. The view is everywhere. I know that sounds ridiculous but I didn't want to see over the sides. It made me woozy. I chose a rock on the outskirts of the public parking lot. I got right down to business. "Ok Lord, why did you bring me up here? What is it that you want to say?"

I was irreverently demanding an answer.

None came.

I began to focus on the only thing I could think of at the moment; my box of popcorn. It was the best popcorn I've ever eaten. It was light and airy, not too much salt. The buttery goodness caused me to get lost in my thoughts. Absent-mindedly my popcorn slowly disappeared; my fears went with it. I began to recall a few years back. Popcorn was my evening solace. After I put son to bed, the hubs and I would sit together and share a bag of popcorn. I would somberly reflect on the day's events and comfort myself that I had actually made it through the day. I didn't know how, but I did. How would I make it through tomorrow? I didn't need to worry about tomorrow. Tomorrow had not yet come.

My eyes began to sting with tears. God spoke so clearly, "I got you through that difficult time didn't I?" I sheepishly replied, "Yes, You did."

He whispered, "The current crisis you're facing, I'm going to get you through that too. You don't need to know how."

He is able. He will perfect that which concerns me. He is strong and powerful. I am unable to solve this, fix this or otherwise change this current situation. I am powerless. But that's what makes it so much more of a victory. God will get all the credit. I have no way to make it happen. I can't force the situation; manipulate it, nor resolve it.

I have to go back down to the valley, and wait.

I must trust God. He will do this. He will provide. He can and He will. I don't know how. I don't have to figure it out. I have to trust that He will.

Hebrews 7:24... He is unchangeable...

Unchangeable is one of the best character traits of God. He is the same yesterday, today and forever.

He is the same as He was three years ago. He did not fail me then and He will not fail me now. He will save to the uttermost; completely and all the way, not halfway. Unchangeable, I love that about Him.

June 24

Luke 11:6...I have nothing

This week may find you encountering someone you don't really care for. And if you were to be honest that is an understatement. You really loathe them.

I have nothing. I have no words. I have no heart for them. I have no love.

Luke 6:32 "If you love those who love you, what credit is that to you? Even 'sinners' love those who love them.

It's very easy to love those that love us. However, it is extremely difficult to love the unlovable. When we encounter abrasive people we want to be abrasive right back. They rub us the wrong way and we have no tolerance for that. Jesus says we must love them if we want to be like Him.

How do we do this? Should we just put on an act?

1 Corinthians 13:1 If I could speak all the languages of earth and of angels, but didn't love others, I would only be a noisy gong or a clanging cymbal.

I know I'm dating myself here, but have you ever seen the Gong show? It was a game show back in the 70's. Amateur contestants would perform their "talent" before a panel of judges. If the act was particularly bad, one of the judges would bang the "gong."

If I try to put on some act or feign some sort of pleasantry, it will fall flat. I will be gonged.

However, if I go to God as a begging pauper, He will give me what I need. My feeble words can become a sweet melody to a broken heart (even if that heart is not yet revealed to you). You see, the person who stands before you may actually have a legitimate reason for the way they act or the things they say.

There is always a story behind the story. You just don't know it.

Romans 8:26-27 Likewise the Spirit also helps in our weaknesses. For we do not know what we should pray for as we ought, but the Spirit Himself makes intercession for us with groaning's which cannot be uttered. Now He who searches the hearts knows what the mind of the Spirit is, because He makes intercession for the saints [believers] according to the will of God.

The Holy Spirit is striving right alongside us. He'll help us in three ways:

We're weakened by our own feelings. The Holy Spirit will give us the desire to reach out to this person.

The Spirit will show us our need to understand this person.

He will give us the ability to refrain from saying the wrong thing.

Lord God, I need your Holy Spirit. Saturate me with Your Spirit. I desire to please you. Fill my heart with love for this person. I want to see what you see. Give me your overflowing grace. Let me be that voice that speaks life into a dead situation. Change my heart. Let me be the first to change. Help me to take the lower position. The humble will be exalted.

June 25

Exodus 1 finds God's people afflicted, and put under harsh burdens. A funny thing happened though. The more they were afflicted, the more they grew. It was quite the opposite of what the enemy had in mind. Pharaoh took drastic measures. He demanded every male child that was born be killed.

While maybe not as apparent, the enemy still has the same desire today. He seeks our children.

Why does he seek the babes? How threatening can a child be? Well, Satan knows what they will become. He tries to lure them away from God as early as possible. He knows if they love Jesus, they will be a force to be reckoned with. He knows they will lead us into the arms of Jesus. He wants to divide us from our children.

The Lord wants us to be as close as possible to our children. Slow down. Enjoy them. Spend time with them.

When Moses was born, his mother was desperate to save his life. She set him in a basket by the river's edge. His sister stood watch to see what would happen to him. God sent the most unlikely woman to help. Isn't that just like God? He always works in ways I don't expect.

In the midst of this attack on the children, Pharaoh's daughter is the one who stumbles upon this little bundle of joy.

Exodus 2:6 When she opened it, she saw the child, and behold, the baby wept. She had compassion on him, and said, "This is one of the Hebrews' children."

What did she see?

She saw a child who needed love.

She realized she was looking at a tender baby who needed attention. A reality swept over her that there is a mother out there who "lost" her child. She named him Moses. Moses means "draw out." We have the same opportunity she did. Take a look around you. There are teenagers sinking under the pressures of the world. Depression is rampant. We have a chance to "draw them out." Reach out to them with a kind word of encouragement. Take them out to lunch and just give them a listening ear. Small attempts can make a big impact.

She had a heart of compassion.

Her heart was stirred when she saw him crying. She was sympathetic. She wasn't cold and unfeeling. I think sometimes today we see so much need we become indifferent to it. We walk away; turning a blind eye to it. Pharaoh's daughter grew up under her father's callous dictates. If anyone should've been indifferent, it was her. But, she wasn't.

She had a heart of courage.

She was willing to take a big risk. Her life was at stake. Her reputation could've been marred. Life as she knew it would be forever altered. She didn't care. She considered it worth it.

We must not allow ourselves to procrastinate until the opportunity is lost. Doing nothing is not an option.

She had a heart of action.

She took it upon herself to provide for him. She had resources in abundance. Moses' mother was helpless. She had no means to care for him.

But, God saw her need and He provided in advance. He will do the same for us.

Exodus 2:9 Take this child away and nurse him for me, and I will give you your wages.

When we step into someone's life and try our best to help, it is God who sees. I was thinking back to my earliest recollections of my relationship with God. Warm sentiments flooded over me as I realized it was a Sunday school teacher who first established the idea that God loved me. I didn't have a Dad, and my mom had to work so she sent us to a babysitter. That babysitter put us on a bus to go to a local church on Sunday mornings. She didn't go with us. While I don't remember very much, I do remember feeling loved. It was there that I was taught Jesus loves me. Those teachers have no idea the impact they made on my heart. Those seeds planted so long ago grew, and blossomed. I am grateful to them. I don't know their names, but I know God does.

Matthew 6:4... your Father, who sees everything, will reward you.

Most importantly, it is actually Jesus Himself that we are helping.

Matthew 25:44-45...'Lord, when did we ever see you hungry or thirsty or a stranger or naked or sick or in prison, and not help you?' "And he will answer, 'I tell you the truth, when you refused to help the least of these my brothers and sisters, you were refusing to help me.'

God help me to be sensitive to the needs of others. Give me Your eyes to see. Don't allow me to walk by another hurting child. Remove my callous unfeeling heart. In those areas I've become cold, warm me up with Your love. God prompt me to do something. God give me a willing heart to reach out. Let me not consider the loss of time and energy. Help me to remember you will replenish all of that supernaturally. I want to give You my all. Everything I have is Yours. It doesn't belong to me. I want to make a difference. Use me I pray.

June 26

I was enjoying the warm breeze and taking in a morning stroll when I stumbled upon a little ladybug. She was scurrying along the sidewalk when I passed her. She seemed to beckon my attention. I couldn't stop thinking about her.

Why are ladybugs so captivating? They just make me smile.

She's just frolicking along enjoying life. Nothing seems to be to be bothering her. She isn't complaining that she's alone; in fact she seems to be enjoying herself; even having fun. She is just plain content.

I noted a few things about her.

I look at her shape. She is quite round. I began to wonder if her shape bothers her. I wonder if she wishes she was a butterfly. I don't think so.

She is perfectly content to be pleasingly plump! I could learn a lot from her! Why do we women have so many insecurities? We're never happy with the way we look. We compare ourselves. We try to impress people by being someone we're not. When I look back the more insecure I was the more immodest I began to dress. One day God asked me a question, "Whose attention are you trying grab?" As if to reassure me, He said, "You have Mine. You don't need to wear that." I still need to remind myself of this. We should only strive to please an audience of One. This One is so taken by us. He doesn't care what we look like. Yes, we should try to be in good health but shouldn't agonize over our weight or shape.

1 Samuel 16:7 The LORD doesn't see things the way you see them. People judge by outward appearance, but the LORD looks at the heart."

We are not defined by the way we look!

I can't help but notice her black spots. They really stand out in contrast to her vibrant red color. Is she self-conscience about them? Does she wish they weren't there? My conclusion: absolutely not! Indeed, it's her spots that make her so cute! We always want to get rid of our seeming imperfections. We don't want anyone to know about our weaknesses. God wants to show them off!

2 Corinthians 12:9 Each time he said, "My grace is all you need. My power works best in weakness." So now I am glad to boast about my weaknesses, so that the power of Christ can work through me."

We should learn to embrace our "black spots." Reveal them. It will set us free.

Most of all, I note her playful attitude; I love it! If she's worried about anything you can't tell. I'm pretty certain she knows her Heavenly Father is watching over her. He is her protector and will shield her from danger. Since she's so small she really can't see what lies ahead. But that doesn't seem to bother her either. She knows her Dad's eyes see further than hers. He's her eyes when she can't see.

He made her perfect just as she is. You know what? He made you perfect just the way you are, spots and all. You're beautiful! Just be you. No one can do it better than you!

June 27

Divorce: A separation of two things that were once connected.

I was trying to enjoy a peaceful morning walk, listening to some music. Quite unexpectedly, my phone died. Well, actually it wasn't all the unexpected. There were warning signs. I ignored them. Kept on my way.

It wasn't until I lost it all that I that I decided I had to do something about it.

Every phone has to be charged every day. It is so simple. Why do we neglect it? We forget. We put it off. We get busy.

Suddenly we lose connection with everything.

This is exactly what happens in our lives when we lose our connection to Jesus.

It is not intentional.

Everything is going well. We get busy. It's so easy to forget about the Lord when things are comfortable.

Revelation 3:17 You say, 'I am rich. I have everything I want. I don't need a thing!' And you don't realize that you are wretched and miserable and poor and blind and naked.

When things are good, we forget that we need Him.

Every last thing in our lives goes downhill from there.

Divorce doesn't happen overnight.

It happens when one or both have lost their connection to Christ. When we don't connect to Him every day, we lose our connection to one another. Self sets in. Focus on self instead of focus on Christ results in a major system failure. It can happen before we realize.

How do we reconnect?

It takes work. Good marriages take effort. Marriage is not all rose pedals, and fluttering butterflies.

Love is a choice. Love is not about feelings. We don't always 'feel like' loving. Or being kind. We don't always 'feel' attracted.

We choose to love despite our feelings.

Staying connected is a choice.

What if connection has been lost? It seems hopeless.

With God all things are possible.

John 14:6 I am the way, the truth and the life...

He is the way to Eternal life. He is the way to have life in your marriage. Life again. The way to real life. Real connection. There is no other way. He makes a way when there seems to be no way.

He is truth. Truth is not relative to our feelings. Truth is black and white as it is found in the Bible. When we lose our connection to Christ, we can be easily deceived into believing the lies of the world.

The world tells us if we're not happy, just get a divorce.

Matthew 19:6 Since they are no longer two but one, let no one split apart what God has joined together.

What God has joined becomes a permanent bond. One.

When you attempt to separate, it's never a clean cut.

It's ugly.

Divorce literally rips your hearts apart.

Children lose the most.

Even adult children are broken inside. It's devastating.

There is nothing you can't overcome.

Revelation 12:11 And they have defeated him [Satan] by the blood of the Lamb and by their testimony. And they did not love their lives so much that they were afraid to die.

There is strength and power in that blood. That blood washed. It cleansed. It is precious.

Costly.

It brought life. Eternal Life. It gives life for today. And power. Power to overcome whatever disconnect has come. Power to change you. Power to change your husband. It is not a weak maybe. It is a definite Yes. He can. Jesus Christ overcame death. The grave. There is nothing He can't do. Nothing He can't fix.

He has the power to stop the march to separation.

He has power to resurrect even the worst of situations.

Reestablish your connection to Him. Pray to Him. Cry out to Him.

Pray for your husband. Pray without ceasing.

Watch what your God can do.

 Ezekiel 36:26 And I will give you a new heart, and I will put a new spirit in you. I will take out your stony, stubborn heart and give you a tender, responsive heart.

June 28

What is the secret to a good marriage?

Since I didn't have a dad growing up, I had no idea what it should look like.

Cinderella?

Cinderella never had kids.

Real marriage includes real problems.

When those problems come, and they always do, the world says trade it in for a new model.

I'll tell you what, that something shiny and new with all the bells and whistles couldn't compare to what I have now.

No matter how ugly.

No matter how many wrinkles.

No matter how many stretch marks.

He knows how I got them. How we got them.

The pain we've been through.

The fights. The struggles.

The hospital visits.

When I promised yesterday to give you some practical ideas for having a good marriage, I thought I might share some fun ideas to do with your man. I was going to suggest writing him a love letter, kiss him in public, go for a walk, spend the whole day with him without your phone, or linger over a cup of coffee. All of these are wonderful.

But, for me and my man?

I'll have dark chocolate covered malt balls waiting for him. We used to get them every day at St. Agnes hospital when Camden was in the NICU for two weeks struggling for life. We would come home and collapse on the couch; finding sweet solace in the chocolate together. It was the worst of times.

It wasn't romantic.

It was the fight of a lifetime.

The bonds of war forge comrades for life. I will never forget that time. I never thought I'd say it, but I thank God for it. It made us stronger. It made our relationship with the Lord so much stronger. We needed Him. Together, we cried out to Him. He didn't fail us. He held us together.

We've been through so much. I know you have too.

I don't want new.

I want the old. Tried. Worn. Comfortable. Familiar.

That's lasting love.

Your marriage is worth fighting for. Give it everything you got.

"No one gets left behind. You know that."

-Mark Bowden, Black Hawk Down

June 29

Camden asked to join me for my morning jog. Reluctantly I agreed. After a few blocks I was surprised he was still keeping a good pace. One might think the old lime green Crocs he was sporting would slow him down, but not today.

He proudly exclaimed, "Look Mom I'm running!"

As I looked over to make some cursory comment to acknowledge him, I was captivated by the look on his face. Sheer delight emanating; I was swept back in time. For just an instant time stood still. I was brought back to the year before. My life was so different. There were no smiles on his face, at least not that I can remember. I could only remember the terrible cries; every morning sobbing and more sobbing. Irrational fears plagued him. I had no idea how or if I would ever get through that. But, I did. Suddenly, unexpectedly and in a way I would've never chosen, God changed the situation. I would not trade that experience for anything. What I learned was priceless. When no doctor has an answer and all of the experts stared in silence, that is when I had no other choice but to look to God. When I did, He did not let me down. He will never let you down. Not ever.

Philippians 4:19 My God shall supply all your need according to His glorious riches in Christ Jesus.

As we continued our jog, I could not take my eyes off of him. Nor could I remove the smile from my heart.

Thank You Jesus for what You did. Thank You for what You are doing now. And thank You for what you are going to do.

June 30

We visited Grandma and Grandpa in Florida. Our drive home was exceptionally long and grueling. Fourteen hours straight and we were exhausted. I didn't even unpack the car. I just went straight to bed. A few hours into my sleep I awoke with a startle. For some unknown reason I went to check on Camden. As I opened my bedroom door I heard the sound of rushing water. The sound of rushing water is never good at 2 a.m.

My mind was spinning. What is that?

Did Camden stick something in the sink and turn on the water after I went to bed? Did he overflow the washer? All of these questions raced through my mind while I ran downstairs. As my foot splashed into the kitchen I realized it was none of the above. Two inches of water covered nearly the entire first floor of my house. I darted down another flight to the basement. Water was gushing from the ceiling and pouring through every vent.

It was a disaster of monumental proportions.

My mind was reeling. I couldn't think straight. I felt paralyzed; unable to move. Ray sprang into action. He went to the garage to get our handheld shop vac. I didn't know whether to laugh or cry. That thing was no match for all of this water.

We began to realize the magnitude of the situation.

It was much too big for us.

We needed help.

We couldn't clean this thing up.

We called our insurance company. They sent help out immediately. Within a few hours a whole team arrived on the scene. I felt so much better. There was no way we could've done it on our own.

Isn't it the same way in life? There are people and situations that are just too much for us. We don't know what to do.

This team knew exactly what to do. First, they ripped up the carpet. Part of the floor was removed. The entire ceiling in the basement was torn out. Even the baseboards had to go. My anxiety began to take over again. Would my house ever be the same again?

Sometimes things have to get worse before they get better.

A few hours later the demolition was complete. Giant fans were set up to "create a vortex" in the home. The goal was to remove every trace of moisture. Before leaving for the afternoon, the team leader took me on a tour. He thoroughly explained every detail of what they were doing and why.

One thing he repeated over and over: "This is a slow process."

Indeed it was.

After many months of delays, interruptions and countless mishaps the repair was complete.

My house was never the same.

Many changes were made. Changes I would've never made had this not happened. That is exactly what happens in our trials. They're too big for us. We have to call for help. There is only One who can come when we call. God comes when we need Him. He is never too busy. Nothing is too big for Him to handle. He has a whole host of angels at His beck and call. Depending on the situation He may use them. He works in ways we don't understand. But He does work. He is always there.

He will never fail. Before you know it, everything will be changed for the better and you'll be thanking Him.

Lord, help me to remember change often comes slowly. I want it now. Increase my level of patience. You have a reason for everything. I will trust You, even in this.

July

July 1

My Black-Eyed-Susan's look so downtrodden.

Defeated.

Pitiful.

Poor little souls.

Just a few days ago they were upright.

Singing.

Cheerful and exuberant.

Even giddy.

A nasty storm blew through here yesterday.

It rained and rained.

Pelting them.

Now their heads are hanging low.

They'll have joy again.

I am reminded of 10 brothers and sisters who were imprisoned, beaten and bound. They had been sharing the gospel on the streets of China. Many people were looking on, Christians and non-Christians alike. Many people hearing the word forgot to eat, work, or even return home. The authorities came and dragged the Christians off one by one, binding them with ropes and beating them with electric-shock poles, knocking them unconscious. When they revived, they continued to pray, sing, and preach. Many people noticed the expression on their faces; to their amazement they were smiling. Their spirit and appearance were so lively and gracious that many were led to believe in Jesus by their example.

When I suffer, I want to smile like that.

Maybe a storm has recently blown through your life.

You may be beat down.

Feeling depressed.

Not up to doing anything.

Even hopeless.

2 Timothy 2:9-10 And because I preach this Good News, I am suffering and have been chained like a criminal. But the word of God cannot be chained. So I am willing to endure anything if it will bring salvation and eternal glory in Christ Jesus to those God has chosen.

These little flowers are beginning to perk up.

A fresh wind is blowing through today.

Psalm 30:5...Weeping may endure for a night, but joy comes in the morning.

If God has allowed suffering into your life, He'll bring good from it.

In unexpected ways.

Keep praying, singing and sharing...

Oswald Chambers says, "A songbird learns to sing in the dark."

July 2

As we arrived at church on Sunday Camden asked, "Why is it so blurry?"

I chuckled. I love his perspective. Everything was gray and dreary. Fog was lingering in the air making it difficult to see. Indeed, everything did look "blurry," and I thought how appropriate that question was for several situations I am dealing with in my life right now.

It was a question I pondered for several days.

"Why is it so blurry?"

God allows fog in our lives for a reason. The same rules we use for driving in the fog can be applied to the "foggy" situations in our own lives.

Rule 1: Slow down.

Fog has a way of slowing us down, doesn't it? To proceed when we can't see is dangerous. We don't like to slow down. We have our time frame. When things don't work according to our plan, we get upset.

I have found God never works in my time frame; never. If He seems to be delaying His answer right now, don't be discouraged. In fact, thank Him. It may take a little longer than expected. And that's ok. God may be protecting you from something that you can't see up ahead.

Rule 2: Pray.

Prayer is our lifeline to God.

Sometimes God allows us to be in circumstances where we can't see any way out. It's in those times we have no other choice but to look to Him for help. That is exactly what He wants us to do. Seek Him; not our friends, not our coworkers. We need God Himself.

Rule 3: Read the map.

Our Bible is our map. When we're in unfamiliar territory we don't know what lies ahead, but God does. He'll warn us, and keep us alert. Many hazards may lie ahead. We need His direction. When we can't see which road to take, He'll point the way.

Psalm 119:105 Your word is a lamp to my feet And a light to my path.

You can be sure the God who allowed you to be in this situation will be the God who leads you out. One day you'll look up, the fog will be gone and the sun will be shining again.

July 3

I was relishing an early morning walk on the beach. Camden was right beside me. Thoroughly enjoying his company; we walked in stride together. It was a warm breeze. Not another soul in sight. I just love being with him. He is so delighted with the beach. So many exciting things to get into. New sights to see. Fun things to pick up.

He began to run ahead of me.

He was veering off to the right. I didn't want him over there. Some tractors were milling through the sand picking up trash. Not going at high speed, but they posed a possible threat.

I called to him, but he couldn't hear me. I tried again, still couldn't hear me.

Too much distance had gotten between us.

He finally looked up and realized I was nowhere in sight. When he turned to find me, I tried again.

To no avail.

He was trying to hear me. I could tell. His eyes were looking at me.

But he couldn't discern what I was saying.

He was still too far away.

He just needed to come a little closer. Then he would hear my voice.

It is this way with our God too.

There are times in life we need to know which direction to go. There doesn't seem to be a black and white answer for our situation. What should I do? Which way should I go? Questions need to answered, but answers don't seem to be coming.

If you can't hear His voice, come closer.

John 10:27 "My sheep hear My voice, and they follow Me."

If you're in the right place, you will hear Him.

Be still before Him. Wait patiently. Sometimes He speaks in a gentle whisper.

If you have sought Him diligently and you still feel turmoil that just may be your answer. Don't proceed.

Matthew 11:28,30 "Come to Me, all you who labor and are heavy laden, and I will give you rest...My yoke is easy and My burden is light."

Camden ran back towards me. Soon enough we were talking again. Enjoying our walk together.

July 4

My morning walk was a tough one. There was no breeze. The humidity was stifling, almost suffocating. There was a palpable darkness in my heart. It's hovering over this nation as well.

Today is the Fourth of July. Bold red letters from the local food store circular shout out, "Celebrate Independence Day!"

I'm having a difficult time celebrating independence.

Like never before in this country we are losing our independence.

Dictionary.com defines independent as:

Not influenced or controlled by others in matters of opinion, conduct, etc.; thinking or acting for oneself: an independent thinker.

In this country Christians are losing their freedom. Personally it scares me to death. Everyone in this country is allowed to his or her opinion, but if one Christian stands up and shares it, the backlash is nearly intolerable. It seems to be coming like a tidal wave.

If you are a Christian that means you follow, obey and adhere strictly to the teachings of Jesus Christ. You don't get to pick and choose. It is all or nothing.

The Bible is the sole authority on everything we do.

That puts us in a great position.

My opinion doesn't count.

My feelings don't count.

It doesn't matter what this author thinks. I need not look any further than the Author of life. He made this earth and everything in it. What He says goes.

The Bible is the sole authority on all matters big and small.

God hates all sin: lying, adultery, homosexuality, fornication, stealing, drunkenness etc.

When congress enacts a law that tries to force me to accept something that goes against the Bible, it hurts deep. It robs my freedom. It is an attempt to undermine the authority established by God Himself.

I shudder to think of the utter devastation this is wreaking on the children of this generation. There is a strict accountability to those that stumble God's little children. Anyone who would teach something contrary to the Bible should take heed:

Mark 9:42 "But whoever causes one of these little ones who believe in Me to stumble, it would be better for him if a millstone were hung around his neck, and he were thrown into the sea.

Today my heart is in mourning for these misguided children. I've just heard of another child who is so depressed she wants to take her life. There is a very real enemy wreaking havoc through this new agenda. He is destroying the moral fabric of our society. The powers that be want to extinguish the only light that can bring hope to these hurting souls. These new laws are not freeing, they are enslaving a generation to sin. When a country wants to do what's right in its own eyes, it is the children who pay the price.

Proverbs 14:34 Godliness makes a nation great, but sin is a disgrace...

God we turn our eyes to You. We beg you to save our nation. Hold our children close to your heart. Give us wisdom to raise our children in Your ways, not veering to the left or the right. Fill the emptiness in their hearts with love for You. Help us to share your love with those who are deceived. God please bless our nation. You and You alone make it great.

July 5

I got started a little late this morning. By the time I got outside the sun was already brutal. The air or lack thereof was stifling. It was hard to catch a breath. I could already tell today was going to be a scorcher. I was wondering how long I would last out here.

Just then I stumbled upon a little flower.

What are you doing there?

Flowers aren't supposed to grow in the sidewalk. Weeds may grow, but flowers?

This sidewalk is made of solid concrete. It is not a conducive environment for seed to take root. And in this heat it was quite a surprise.

How did it get there?

Seeds are typically planted by individuals. But they are often scattered by the wind to the most unlikely places. The same thing happens to the "seed" we plant. We often share a word of encouragement and we have one idea in mind of what's going to happen with it, but God often has so much more in mind. The wind of the Holy Spirit takes that seed and carries it along to its desired destination; quite unbeknownst to us. It germinates for a while. Sometimes it's a long while. At just the right time it springs up. It grows into a beautiful plant. Just like that one in the sidewalk.

We often think our words are falling on deaf ears, but they're not.

God's word is alive!

Every one of God's magnificent words is a seed. Not even one will fall to the ground without producing fruit. Can I reiterate? Not even one word will ever return void.

Isaiah 55:11 My word shall not return to Me void, but it shall accomplish that which I purpose...

This word "void" in the old language gives us a picture of a gift. Every time we share a verse with someone we are giving them a gift. It is the greatest gift they could ever receive. They may not be crazy about the gift initially. Perhaps they may not quite understand the gift at first. They may not even acknowledge you (such is the case with special needs children). No matter, we keep on giving. At some point that "gift" will produce fruit.

I don't know who you may be dealing with, but this hard concrete sidewalk is a picture of God's word flourishing in the most unlikely places.

Give the gift that keeps on giving!

July 6

Nehemiah set out to work for the Lord. God called Him to do a job and he was working at it with all of his heart. Things were going well and he was making some real progress. I can picture the scene: I bet he had a smile on his face and a skip in his step to go to work every day. In fact, he probably was whistling while he worked.

Nehemiah 4:7...the gaps were beginning to be closed...

He was making great headway. The end was in sight.

Don't you know someone had to come and rain on his parade. In our story, Nehemiah's enemies have names: Sanballat, Tobiah and Geshem. Each name representing a godly heritage.

Nehemiah 4:8 and all of them conspired together to come and attack...and create confusion.

Whenever we set out to do something for the Lord, the enemy always comes to attack. This is never truer than when we are close to a break-through or completion of the task. He brings all he has.

The enemy always has one goal. He wants to destroy the work of God.

He does this in three ways: He distracts, divides and discourages.

He distracts you from your task.

Doubt distracts us from our task. It only takes one discouraging word to make you doubt. You may begin to question, "Did God really call me to do this? This is hard." Nothing you do for the Lord will ever be easy. Now is not the time to fade out, but persevere!

He divides the workers.

Don't look at what other people are doing! You may feel like you're doing more, and they're doing less. Your animosity will build and soon enough you'll be fighting amongst yourselves. If we fight against each other we certainly cannot fight against the enemy.

He discourages.

The quickest way to become discouraged is to look at the "progress." It may appear to be none. There may be no apparent fruit; no indication you are making any difference at all. Never mind that. Do what God called you to do. Let Him be in charge of the progress. After all, He did not say, "Well done good and successful servant." He said, "Well done good and faithful servant."

Nehemiah happened to be building a wall. What are you "building?" In every building project, from homeschooling to church building to relationship building you will encounter attacks. Don't allow the enemy to destroy the work. Go at it double time. Are things falling apart? Good. It just may be an indicator that you are closer than you think.

July 7

When the rain keeps coming, there is refuge.

Genesis 8:9 But the dove found no resting place for the sole of her foot, and she returned into the ark to him, for the waters were on the face of the whole earth. So he put out his hand and took her, and drew her into the ark to himself.

She had been through so much.

It wouldn't stop raining. It just kept coming.

Is this over yet?

Please God, let this be over.

But it wasn't over. She found no rest.

Until.

She returned to Him.

Her place of security until the storm ended.

He put out His hand.

Gathered her into Himself.

Gently.

Lovingly.

Drew her near. Near to His heart.

And she waited. Another week.

Waiting safely in His arms. Snug and secure. Sheltered.

Many things can make us feel like they will never end.

The wait can seem so long.

Being single. Living in a painful marriage. Illness. Mourning. Having a wayward child.

These things make us weary.

Every day we wonder if today will be the day the water recedes.

In your waiting, rest. Rest in His hands.

Draw near to Him. He is extending His hand. Grab hold.

The water will recede.

The sun will shine again.

Life will come again.

Many times when we lose everything, we gain all.

Proverbs 3:5-6 Trust in the LORD with all your heart; do not depend on your own understanding. Seek His will in all you do, and He will show you which path to take.

July 8

Jesus Christ came with one mission. He came to die. It was a sacrifice. In much the same way He has given each one of us a "mission". It is not easy. It is incredibly difficult. It is a complete life of sacrifice.

2 Corinthians 3:5 Who is sufficient for these things?

Well certainly not me.

This mission is much like a garden.

Gardens are wonderful. Even the thought of fresh vegetables delights me. Gardens take a lot of work to begin. They don't start out fruitful. I decided to have a garden in my back yard one year. All of the ground had to be dug up by hand. It was back breaking work (if Ray was standing by me right now he'd have a smile on his face and one eyebrow raised, looking at me silently thinking, "really Renee tell us how back breaking it was since you didn't lift one shovel full of dirt!" But that's beside the point.) Digging up hard ground filled with big rocks is exhausting. I couldn't do it myself. God gave me a partner to help. I'm so thankful for this "tool" He has given me. He has provided all of the "tools" I need to tend this garden. It will produce fruit; when and how much is not up to me to decide.

It is God who gives the increase.

We are farmers planting seed. The seed is the word of God. The farmer never looks at the seed and says, "how does this dead little piece of nothingness amount to anything?" But rather he tills, he plants and he trusts.

God never fails. God's word never returns void. It will always produce fruit. Sometimes it is fruit that we can see. Other times it is fruit we can't see. But we can trust our Father to bring from this garden what He desires.

1 Corinthians 2:9 Eye has not seen nor ear heard nor has it entered into the heart of man the things God has prepared for those that love Him

We can't look at the outward appearance. We have one mission. Raise our children to know Christ. That begins with planting God's word.

There is a battle going on for our children. Satan is doing battle. It is real. He will do anything to stop you from teaching your child God's word.

Before we can teach it, we have to receive it. We have to get ours first. Much like on an airplane. Put your mask on first.

2 Corinthians 4:17-18 For our present troubles are small and won't last very long. Yet they produce for us a glory that vastly outweighs them and will last forever!

So we don't look at the troubles we can see now; rather, we fix our gaze on things that cannot be seen. For the things we see now will soon be gone, but the things we cannot see will last forever.

We should ask the Lord to take us behind the" veil" to see the eternal value of the things we are going through. We are developing spiritual muscle. We are learning things when we're in the dark.

Lord God, help us to stay focused on this mission you've called us to do. Help us to die to ourselves in every aspect of our lives, so that we can live for You. We want to bring forth fruit for eternal life. Fruit that lasts. Show us the distractions in our lives that Satan is using to build his kingdom. Give us the power of Your Holy Spirit to overcome them.

July 9

2 Kings 6 finds the king on a quest to find Elisha. The king doesn't under-stand how his enemies keep finding out his plans. It was as though there was a trader in the midst. Elisha seems to know where the king is going and what he's doing before he ever does it or tells anyone. One of his men says, "Elisha knows what you're doing in your bedroom."

That is personal and invasive.

But that is our God. He is all knowing and powerful and able to convey secret things to us, in advance. That's what He was doing with Elisha. He was supernaturally revealing these things to Elisha. The king feels if he can get a hold of Elisha then he can go about his business of destruction. This is a reminder to me that our enemy will do anything to silence our message. He'll use our fears. What are you afraid of today? Give this fear to the Lord so He can give you courage in the face of it; otherwise the enemy will use it to deter you.

The king sends a great army with many chariots and horses to surround the city where Elisha is. When Elisha's servant got up and looked out the window his heart sank. He was terrified. The enemy was surrounding the house as far as he could see. There was no way out of this. They were doomed.

Do you feel like that today? Are you backed into a corner with no way out? Are you facing an impossible situation? Do you feel the odds are stacked against you?

Elisha's servant asked, "What will we do now?"

2 Kings 6:16-17 *"Don't be afraid!" Elisha told him. "For there are more on our side than on theirs!" Then Elisha prayed, "O LORD, open his eyes and let him see!" The LORD opened the young man's eyes, and when he looked up, he saw that the hillside around Elisha was filled with horses and chariots of fire.*

Why was Elisha so confident facing this great multitude coming against him?

He could see that God's army is bigger, stronger, and more powerful than anything this army could bring. We can't always see that, can we?

God has people in places we don't know about. God is working even when it doesn't look like it. God will find a way when there seems to be no way.

Today I pray that God will open your eyes to see He is so for you. If He is for you, who can stand against you? You keep praying. He is able.

July 10

Jeremiah 1:5 "Before I formed you in the womb I knew you;

Before you were born I sanctified you;

I ordained you a prophet to the nations."

In its simplest definition, a prophet can be defined as a messenger of God.

Special needs children have a purpose.

They are little prophets.

They speak without having to say a word; little wordless books.

They shout the heart of the gospel.

Charles Spurgeon coined the term wordless book. He spoke of a book that consisted of only three pages; the first was black, the second was red, and the third was pure white.

It had no words.

He told them that he hoped they would all know and understand it, but that there was not a single word in it.

The old minister asked them to gaze upon it...

This book delivered a beautiful message. It showed them their need for a Savior.

As I gaze upon these children, they have a message.

They speak without having to say a word.

These precious wordless books shout out our need for a Savior.

We desperately need to be rescued.

Someone needs to fix all this brokenness.

And Someone will.

The black page represents the unknown.

There are many dark and unknown things about Autism. Bad behaviors, confusing thoughts, and even more puzzling actions all combine in this dreaded disability. Many aspects are just plain baffling. Each individual a unique maze that frustrates even the most prominent physicians.

The red page represents sacrifice.

Individuals with special needs live a life of sacrifice. They are exposed to ridicule. Feelings of inadequacy pervade them. Their parents give up everything. Every aspect of their lives change the moment this child is born.

The white page represents heaven.

It won't always be like this. Someday the struggle will end.

In heaven there will be no more sorrow, no more crying and no more pain.

If you are facing a struggle today may this knowledge bring you comfort. You won't always struggle.

John 16:33 "I have told you all this so that you may have peace in Me. Here on earth you will have many trials and sorrows. But take heart, because I have overcome the world."

July 11

I saw the boy from across the park.

Midair.

I couldn't believe he did it.

Jumped right off the ledge. Between the sliding board and the fire pole. It was real high up.

I had mixed emotions pulsing.

What if he gets hurt?

But he didn't. He made it. And just like that he was climbing up again.

Only this time he was shouting for me, "Momma, come here. Come here. Watch this."

He didn't know I saw.

I ran to him.

All giddy and out of breath, "You can call this my leap of faith."

He leaped again.

No fear.

Pure power. He landed firm.

Has God called you to take a leap of faith?

Sometimes a leap is just taking a baby step. The boy didn't get a running start. He just took a step forward.

Stepping into something new or out of something old can be scary.

You may be hesitating.

If I step out, what if things don't work out?

I would rather be alone in the will of God, than miserable out of the will of God.

What will people think?

It's a real good thing the boy didn't ask me first what he should do. I would've definitely said it was a no go. Don't do it. I like the sure thing. Predictable and comfortable.

Proverbs 29:25 The fear of man brings a snare, but whoever trusts in the LORD shall be safe.

You may fear the future.

Fear and unbelief go hand in hand.

1 John 4:18 There is no fear in love; but perfect love casts out fear.

The boy had no one and nothing to depend on.

He had his faith. He had his God. More so, his God had him.

Your God has you.

If God called you to do it, He will give you everything you need to accomplish it.

Physically, emotionally, and spiritually.

2 Chronicles 16:9 "For the eyes of the LORD run to and fro throughout the whole earth, to show Himself strong on behalf of those whose heart is loyal to Him..."

God wants you to wholly rely on Him for every detail.

You are safe in His hands. Safe to give Him all.

July 12

We were at the beach. One day the waves were rough. Loud. Angry.

Much like I can be as a Mommy.

Another day they were soft. Gentle. Loving. Barely a whisper.

Much like I can be as well.

Sometimes God can seem like this too. He can seem callous and indifferent. He can seem so harsh. When He takes things away from us or He doesn't give us what we want, we don't recognize Him. I'm not even talking about selfish stuff here. I'm referring to good things. Like healing. Returning wayward children. Restoring marriages.

His ways come with His heart. The heart of a Dad who knows what's best for His kiddos.

His ways take us out of our comfort zone.

Job 23:10 But He knows the way that I take; when He has tested me, I shall come forth as gold.

Gold is purified in fire. Heat. Lots of heat.

God allows us to be refined through the heat of trials. He removes the things that are not good for us. The things that don't matter. That have no eternal value.

He can seem angry. He isn't. Quite the contrary. He loves us. So very much. Just as we do for our own children, we take things away that we know aren't the best for them. They can't understand it at the time. When they mature, often many years later, they understand completely. You may even hear a thank you.

We can thank our Daddy for all things. No good thing will He withhold from those who love Him.

God, help me to see that You love me no matter what's going on in my life. Help me to accept these things I don't understand. Help me to accept Your time frame. You are in control of this situation. Not me. Give me wisdom. I need Your discernment. Tell me when to speak. What to speak. Restrain me when I should be quiet. You go talk for me.

July 13

Proverbs 6:6 go to the ant you lazybones; look at her ways and become wise.

The ant is a fascinating little creature. She has many admirable qualities.

She is reliable. She isn't waiting around for someone else to do her work for her. She is not putting off until tomorrow what she knows she should be doing today.

Others can depend on her. Let your yes be a yes. Honor your word. If you commit to it, follow through.

She is determined. She does not allow obstacles to get in the way of her work. If something or someone is blocking her way, she will search for a way around.

She is stable. She doesn't allow circumstances to move her from her work. No matter how difficult the terrain, she keeps going.

She is strong. An ant can lift twice her size. When she must carry a heavy weight she isn't crushed under the pressure. She carries on; undaunted.

Daily spending time before our God will replenish our stamina. We'll be prepared to meet the demands of the day; no matter how heavy they may be.

She is focused. She is not fazed by what the other workers around her are doing.

Keeping our eyes focused on what our King called us to do will keep us from comparing our load to others.

She is diligent. She will keep working until her task is complete.

What has God called you to do?

God chose you because He can depend on you. He knows what He can expect from you. You're the best one for the job.

2 Timothy 2:15 Work hard so you can present yourself to God and receive His approval.

Lord Jesus fill me with strength to keep going today. I want to be diligent and complete what You have for me today. Remove any tendency to be lazy. I am determined to do my best for you. I give you this day and ask you to bless it abundantly.

July 14

Have you recently set out to do something new for the Lord? Maybe you want to try a new ministry, a new work or even just decided to have a new attitude. Perhaps you've found things didn't go as planned. It may seem to be falling apart. Everything is going haywire and you don't know why.

When Israel ventured out to take their "new land" these are the words the Lord spoke to Joshua:

Joshua 1:5 No one will be able to stand against you as long as you live. I will be with you... I will not fail you or abandon you.

Attacks will come.

They are inevitable. It is important to recognize we are waging warfare against an unseen enemy who will not stop his pursuit to destroy the work.

Ephesians 6:12 For we are not fighting against flesh-and-blood enemies, but against evil rulers and authorities of the unseen world, against mighty powers in this dark world, and against evil spirits in the heavenly places.

If things have heated up with family members, coworkers, friends or even strangers, recognize the source; Satan himself is at work.

Don't go to war with your family and friends. Your beef is not with them. Wage warfare in prayer.

Ephesians 6:13 Therefore, put on every piece of God's armor so you will be able to resist the enemy in the time of evil. Then after the battle you will still be standing firm.

The closer you get to completion, the more prevalent the attacks will be.

Nothing can stop the plan of God.

"I will be with you."

God is with you. He will not abandon you. He won't let you go. He is holding onto you. He is not sitting around idle. He is behind you even if you can't see Him.

"I will not fail you."

God won't wander off and desert you.

Joshua 1:7 Be strong and very courageous.

It will take all the strength you have to do the job God called you to do. It won't be easy. So you have to be determined to pursue this no matter the cost. Be constant. Be consistent. Be urgent. Don't put off for tomorrow what you know you need to do today.

If you've had some setbacks don't be discouraged. God can easily recover the ground you lost. If you had a bad experience don't dwell on it. Let the criticism roll off of you. He can make up for lost time.

"...don't turn to the right hand or to the left"

Do what God called you to do. Do not deviate. Get right back to the work. Don't become lax. You're the one He chose to do this.

Stay focused.

God is doing something special with you that He isn't doing with other people.

July 15

Luke 3:2...the word of God came to John the son of Zacharias in the wilderness.

Why was John by himself? As I ponder this question others come to mind. What was he doing out there? Was he out there by choice? If so, did he feel rejected? Was he misunderstood? We know he was a quirky guy. Was he so different he was forced out?

We may never have the answers to some questions. But what we do know is this: God's word came upon him in power. It was so compelling he had to act. God gave John a message in that place. If you find yourself in that solitary place I can assure you God has something to say to you. It will eventually be a message that you share with someone else.

We hate feeling alone. We can even become critical when we find ourselves in that place. We can think things such as: Nobody cares about me. They don't understand what I'm going through. They don't realize what this is like.

God has to get us to that solitary place because it's the only way we'll hear Him. When there's too much going on around us we get preoccupied quickly. Too many people can drown out the voice of God.

Did you ever have so many things go wrong for so many days you just stop telling people? You feel they probably wouldn't believe you even if you did tell them.

God knows; talk to Him about it.

John's personality and gene make up were not by accident. He was eccentric; a misfit by today's standards. But the very qualities that seem to make him a recluse would seem to contradict his being able to speak in a public forum. But God came to him.

It seems John didn't have any friends. But, God was his best friend. If he wasn't out there perhaps he would've been somewhere on Wall Street or making a name for himself in Hollywood.

Why was he out there? God's divine sovereign will.

If you feel like you're in that desolate lonely place, you're in good company.

God is with you in this. Don't despise this place. Consider it a blessing. Thank God for this experience. Expect Him to speak a life changing message to your heart.

July 16

Hebrews 4:16 Let us therefore come boldly to the throne of grace that we may obtain mercy and find grace to help in time of need.

For the past few days Camden has been asking to go to Florida to visit his grandparents. My in-laws live in Florida. We live in Maryland. Florida isn't right up the street. It's a monumental task for us to go visit Mom-Mom and Pop-Pop. That is irrelevant to him. He keeps on asking. The intensity of his plea is building. He doesn't grasp the fact that Florida is a 12-14 hour drive. He doesn't worry about the financial aspects of paying for gas or the price of airfare, should we decide to fly. He is not the least bit concerned about how utterly absurd his request may sound.

At first I chuckled. He wasn't laughing though. He was serious.

Today his polite request has turned to begging.

"Mama, can we go to Florida, today? Please, please, please?"

I try to explain to him that we can't just pick up and leave for Florida. It's impossible. We have commitments and responsibilities that we need to attend to. Besides that, it's really expensive.

I try to gently answer him without giving him false hope that we may go sometime soon.

"Camden, today's not going to work for us to go."

He cannot be persuaded. He cannot be convinced otherwise. He knows and believes with all certainty that we can.

He confidently replies, "How about tomorrow?"

I begin to ponder his audacity. You've got to love it. I need to have this kind of child-like faith when I am asking God for help. There are certain situations and people I am dealing with that are really getting me discouraged. I'm ready to give up. They seem impossible. They seem like they are never going to change. In fact the more I examine them, the more certain I become that they really aren't going to change. In some cases, I've even stopped praying for them. Change would take a miracle.

God still does miracles.

Be persistent. If God doesn't answer today, don't give up. Ask again. Keep on asking until you are certain He has answered.

Be certain. Keep your eyes on Jesus, not on the surrounding difficulties or seeming impossibilities. If your need is financial, remember God owns the cattle on a thousand hills. His resources are endless.

Be fearless. Don't be intimidated by the enemy's tactics. He persuades us to doubt.

Let us boldly come to the throne. It honors God when we ask great things of Him.

What would you ask God for if you believed with all your heart that He could do it? Not only could, but would. He'll do it just because you're His daughter! If we ask anything according to His will, He hears us. He'll answer, just because He loves you. Just because He can and He is just waiting for you to ask so that He can knock your socks off by granting you your request.

Don't set limits on God. Go all out!

James 4:2 You have not because you ask not.

ASK!

...P.S. I left for Florida on that Monday!

July 17

John 16:33 In this world you will have tribulation; but be of good cheer, I have overcome the world.

Even our little children must go through the struggle. It is necessary. They too must learn to depend on Jesus.

I'll tell you, the pain is unbearable at times. Watching children struggle so much nearly broke me. I've wanted to trade places many times.

Am I a victim of circumstance? Absolutely not.

God doesn't always choose to heal. Does He have the power to heal? Oh yes He does! I believe that with all of my heart. If He doesn't heal, He has a better plan. If God healed my son, I would have no ministry in the special needs community. I could not relate to them. I would have no idea what they were truly going through. I would not be able to understand their deep need and the overwhelming pain they experience on a daily basis.

I just read a clip of my journal from 4 years ago:

I cry because I don't want to see him struggle.

Sometimes God sends us where we don't want to go. We cry. We kick and scream the whole way. We want to do His will, until it's something we don't like.

I KNOW NOTHING.

When David came up against the giant, he knew the odds were against him. He knew in his own strength he couldn't beat him. This was bigger than he was. It was a monumental task.

God was on his side. He could not lose.

1 Samuel 17:34-35 But David persisted. "I have been taking care of my father's sheep and goats," he said. "When a lion or a bear comes to steal a lamb from the flock, I go after it with a club and rescue the lamb from its mouth. If the animal turns on me, I catch it by the jaw and club it to death."

They say when someone or something attacks your child something supernatural happens in you. Suddenly you have power you never knew you had. That's what happened to David.

Doing the small things prepared him for the really big.

The same was true for me.

God had already equipped me. I just didn't know it. Just as he prepared David with prior encounters with lions and bears; so God had done the same for me.

What did I have to take on this giant called Autism?

I had God's word! There is so much power in God's word! As I read it each day, God was planting seeds in my heart. He taught me what His Word could do.

God's word has the power to: move a mountain, break a bone, open the eyes of the blind, and make the speechless speak, heal the sick and raise the dead just to name a few things!

WHAT MORE DO I NEED???

My friend, wherever God has you today, it is not an accident. It is not by chance. It is the sovereign will of God. Not a distant God, but a deeply loving Daddy who cares about His child. He is a Dad who distinguishes the cry of each of His children and comes running at the faintest whimper. Whatever challenge you are facing today, He has already prepared you. All you need is found in Him.

July 18

James 1:5-6 If any of you lacks wisdom, let him ask of God, who gives to all liberally and without reproach, and it will be given to him. But let him ask in faith, with no doubting, for he who doubts is like a wave of the sea driven and tossed by the wind.

What are you lacking?

I love the picture this word gives us from the old language. It is one of a runner who has been left behind by her rival in a race.

Do you feel like the enemy just keeps getting ahead of you; stealing the victory? Try as you might you seem to be lagging behind every time. All of your efforts seem to fall short. You seem to be inferior and failing.

Do you feel inferior for the task at hand?

God is able to make up the difference. He can fill in the gap.

He can restore the years the locust have eaten; fully and completely.

God will give you what you need.

Ask.

Sounds too simple, doesn't it? If you're like me you tend to complicate things. I like to go through all the possible scenarios first; most of the time they end in disaster. After that the anxiety takes over. Fretting and fear dominate my thoughts. This can go on for days. Stop the cycle. God says, "Ask."

Ask.

Psalm 84:11 For the LORD God is our sun and our shield. He gives us grace and glory. The LORD will withhold no good thing from those who do what is right.

If you have a decision to make and you fear making the wrong one, ask God to give you wisdom and then trust Him. He is your shield. He will protect you.

Ask.

If you need to talk to someone and you don't know what to say, ask God.

John 12:49...the Father who sent me has commanded me what to say and how to say it.

Ask.

Do you need a friendship or relationship restored?

Ask.

Our generous God gives solely because of His desire to bless. He does not throw our past mistakes in our face. He simply gives us what we need because He loves us. It is not because we deserve it.

Romans 5:8 But God showed his great love for us by sending Christ to die for us while we were still sinners.

Ask in faith, no doubting. Don't waver back and forth.

God is able. He created the world and upholds it. Nothing is too hard for Him.

Ephesians 3:20 Now all glory to God, who is able, through his mighty power at work within us, to accomplish infinitely more than we might ask or think.

Keep it simple.

Ask.

July 19

Be a difference maker. Bring change one heart at a time.

One person can make a difference.

Jeremiah 29:11 I know the plans I have for you...plans of peace and not of evil to give you a future and a hope.

Will you have trials? Oh you bet. But when you are right in the middle of Gods will, you will have a joy that is deep and a joy that is full. Joy is not happiness. Joy is deeper than that. Happiness is typically dependent on our outward circumstances. Joy is not. Joy comes from knowing that no matter what happens in my life I know Jesus is enough. You will have sorrow and pain.

John 16:22 So you have sorrow now, but I will see you again; then you will rejoice, and no one can rob you of that joy. At that time you won't need to ask Me for anything. I tell you the truth, you will ask the Father directly, and he will grant your request because you use My name. Until now you have not asked for anything in My name. Ask and you will receive, and your joy will be complete.

The joy that Jesus gives no one can rob you of that joy.

The things that this world has to offer can bring a smile to your face, but the joy the Lord gives can bring a smile to your heart and no one can take that away.

As we set out to be that one person who makes a change, I found a verse that Paul spoke to Timothy when he was encouraging him to go out and make a difference.

1 Timothy 4:12 Don't let anyone think less of you because you are young. Be an example to all believers in what you say, in the way you live, in your love, your faith, and your purity.

A lot of times you may think, I'm just a new believer, what can I do? Don't let anyone think less of you because you're a newbie.

One person can make a difference.

Be an example. Be a blue print. Be an exact replica of Jesus in everything you say. Memorize His word so you can share it. Love His word. Fight for His word. There is power in His word.

Be an example in what you say. Don't be silenced. Don't be silent. This word can move mountains. Heal the sick. His word is life. I love His word. It gives power to live out what God requires of you. This life is not easy. You will need it.

One person can make a difference.

Be an example by the way you live. Can people look at your life and know that you are a Christian? Don't blend in. Stand out.

One person can make a difference.

Be an example in love. Jesus loved the unlovable. He went a hundred miles out of his way to reach one person. One person is precious to Jesus. If you see someone hurting go to them. Depression is rampant. You have the answer to their depression. Jesus is the answer. Lead them to Jesus. Give them a Bible. Take them to youth group with you. Pray for them. Little things can go a long way.

One person can make a difference.

Be an example in your faith.

When I think of faith, I think of David when he faced the giant. This giant was towering over David. It was bigger than he was. He was more equipped. After all, he had state of the art sword and shield. David had every right to be intimidated. He should've been scared. But, he wasn't. How did he face this giant with such confidence? David wasn't confident in his own abilities. He knew he was no match for this giant. His confidence was in the Lord his God. David knew if the hand of the Lord was upon him, no one and nothing could touch him.

A simple stone is all it took to take down the giant David was facing.

The power did not lie in the stone. His power came from God.

Sometimes the Lord uses the smallest ordinary things and people in unexpected ways to conquer the giants in our lives. David was not an expert rock thrower. He wasn't an expert marksman. He simply took God at His word.

1 Samuel 17:45 David replied to the Philistine, "You come to me with sword, spear, and javelin, but I come to you in the name of the LORD of Heaven's Armies—the God of the armies of Israel, whom you have defied.

It's the Lord who saved me then, and it's the Lord who will save me now.

There is power in the name of our God.

Psalm 18:10 The name of the LORD is a strong tower; the godly run to Him and are safe.

David was staring death in the face. It was imminent. David was no match for Goliath. He was the smallest and the weakest.

2 Corinthians 12:9-10 Each time He said, "My grace is all you need. My power works best in weakness." So now I am glad to boast about my weaknesses, so that the power of Christ can work through me... For when I am weak, then I am strong.

Be an example in purity.

There are giant temptations.

One person can make a difference.

Be an example in what you say, in the way you live, in your love, your faith, and your purity.

Be that one that makes a difference!

July 20

Matthew 14:24 But the boat was now in the middle of the sea, tossed by the waves, for the wind was contrary.

When our plans go awry, we get so confused. Everything is so unfamiliar.

Is this You God?

It's important to remember: Jesus sent them there to the middle of the sea.

If Jesus sent them there then He surely knew where they were.

He knows where you are.

He hasn't lost sight of you.

They were tossed by the waves...

In the old language this word "tossed" has an interesting meaning. It was the same word used to describe a touchstone. A touchstone was a stone used to test the purity of gold by the color of the streak produced on it by rubbing it with the gold. It was much like the pens we use today in stores and banks to see if money is counterfeit.

Trials show us the truth about ourselves.

When things don't go as we expected will we still trust God?

Will we still give Him thanks in the storm?

Jesus came to the disciples.

At just the right time, He came walking on the water.

Jesus rescued them.

Jesus immediately reached out and grabbed Peter. He asked Peter a question: "Why did you doubt Me?"

When my I found myself in the middle of the Atlantic with the storms raging all around, the waves just kept on coming. Relentlessly. When I looked at them, I began to sink. I didn't know if I would make it. But my God grabbed hold of me. He lifted me up and placed me safely in the boat. Near Him. The safest place I could ever be. He'll do the same for you.

July 21

Jeremiah 1:5 "Before I formed you in the womb I knew you; Before you were born I sanctified you; I ordained you a prophet to the nations."

"How can my son be a prophet?" My mind was reeling as I pondered the thought.

A prophet is a messenger of God. How could my son be a messenger of God? At two and a half, he couldn't speak more than 2 words at a time? Nonetheless, God firmly impressed upon my heart that this verse would be Camden's life verse. It would define his entire existence. As every outward circumstance contradicted what God had just whispered to my heart, I began to debate with Him. This baby is behind. He can't talk.

I would soon discover that you don't need words to speak.

The day of Camden's evaluation arrived; it will be etched in my mind forever. When he woke from his nap, I lifted him out of his crib and onto my lap; the warmth of his little body enveloped me. I didn't want to go to this evaluation. I didn't want my world turned upside down. I started reading his little Bible to him. Then I paused, placed my hand on his mouth, and prayed silently: "Lord, please touch his mouth that he may speak in Your name."

Camden turned around on my lap to face me and said, crystal clear: "Nothing is impossible with God."

I was stunned. I knew God was speaking to me through Camden.

Where did these words come from?

God can do anything; at any time.

He may just surprise you.

July 22

Every morning my beautiful little peonies seem to be singing a cheerful song to me. Their innocence warms my heart. They haven't been scorched by the summer heat yet. No disease to speak of. They are happy and content just as they are.

I notice they are bent over; nearly in half. That's odd. I wonder why? Impulsively I start heading in to get some string to hold them up right. If I tie a string around them it will help them grow in the right direction. My intervention is a necessity. On my way back out I get a better perspective. I'm standing farther away. I realize the large tree is hovering over them. It's blocking their view of the sun. They're doing everything in their power to see the sun. But they're so small it proves difficult. The tree is big and holds more influence. They don't give up. They are persistent. They have a natural instinct in them. They crave the sun. They desire the warmth of it. The sun is a necessity in their lives. Any hindrance to that causes their growth to be stunted. Without it they will wither up and die.

I think our children are a lot like these flowers. They crave the Son. Children have an innate desire in them to know God. He placed it in them. We as parents must cultivate that desire. We have to be that string that guides them to grow in the right direction. They can't be left on their own.

The world is hovering over them; always insisting on endless activity. This persistent bustle keeps them from growing closer to God; as they were designed. Am I allowing this inadvertently?

Proverbs 22:6 Direct your children onto the right path, and when they are older, they will not leave it.

I love the meaning of the word "direct" in the old language. It's surprising, but very applicable. It means to be narrow or to make narrow. Narrow has taken on a negative connotation in this culture.

Matthew 7:13 "You can enter God's Kingdom only through the narrow gate. The highway to hell is broad, and its gate is wide for the many that choose that way."

Jesus said the way to life is narrow. Should we apologize for that? I don't think so. He knows what is best and therefore we should heed His word. It is extremely difficult to parent this way today. It means we have to say no to a lot of things many parents say yes to. This won't be popular and it certainly won't win you accolades from your child. Have I made mistakes? Yes, tons of them. If I can help one person not to have any regrets, then this writing will have done its job. We don't live to please the world. Aren't you glad? At the end of the day, I must give account to a greater authority. I will answer for how I raised these children.

I take that very seriously.

God needs me to be Mom more than He needs me to be friend.

There is so much at stake here. Eternity lies in the balance.

July 23

A baby bunny grabbed my heart. Little fella hopped across my path one morning. I love little babies of every kind. They are so captivating. For me, I think it's their innocence. It beckons my heart away from the harshness of the world around. There's vulnerability in them that is a rare find. They are defenseless in every way. They are solely dependent on their momma and papa for protection.

This little fellow was alone.

I can't help myself. The momma in me begins to worry. He might get hurt. Who will protect him if I'm not watching?

He is helpless.

Sometimes we find ourselves in this exact situation; completely helpless. But we are not alone. We are at the mercy of our Heavenly Father. Now this took a while for me to grasp. I don't have a dad. I've never met him. He really never wanted anything to do with me, nor my brother (I have a twin).

God is so very different.

He has proven Himself a faithful Father. He is very interested in every aspect of my life. He knows everything about me. He knows exactly where I'm at. He's never taken His eyes off of me, not even for a moment. How much more so my children?

He is a father to the fatherless.

As I gaze at this sweet bunny, I just want to fight for him. I want to keep him safe. I want to be his lookout. But, I can't possibly be there all the time. As I pondered this thought, Camden meandered outside. I drew his attention to the bunny. I cautioned him to go slow so he wouldn't scare the bunny. Camden only had one thought in his mind: He'll make a great pet! He lunged for the bunny. That bunny took off so fast. Camden bolted after him. But that bunny surprised even me. I couldn't believe how fast he was! Not only that, he was smart. There was a small space under the shed that he fit into perfectly. He darted under there and remained.

There are real dangers in our lives that we can't see coming. God is always one step ahead. Often our children are vulnerable, it's important to remember God is our eyes when we can't see. He is protecting them when we can't be there. He gives wisdom when to run.

Just as He did for my little friend, He will do for you too. God sees and He foresees; therefore He had already provided a shelter of safety to protect him. That's just what a good Dad does.

Psalm 91:1... "God, you're my refuge. I trust in you and I'm safe!" That's right—He rescues you from hidden traps, shields you from deadly hazards. His huge outstretched arms protect you— under them you're perfectly safe; his arms fend off all harm. Fear nothing—..."

July 24

A few years ago we had some painting down at the entrance to our home. There are two columns on the front porch. At the time, one of them had a lovely vine growing up and around it; a Carolina Jessamine. I had planted it a few years back. I trained it to wrap around the column. While it hadn't reached its full potential, it was doing well. After the painters left, I went outside to find the vine had been completely cut off the column.

This is not at all what I wanted. It was not what I expected. I was devastated.

I didn't know what to do. I was tempted to remove the whole thing. Just let it go. Start all over.

Perhaps today finds you in a similar situation.

You may find yourself not knowing what to do and ready to give up.

Psalm 27:13 I would have lost heart, unless I had believed that I would see the goodness of the LORD in the land of the living. Wait on the LORD; be of good courage, and He shall strengthen your heart; wait, I say, on the LORD!

I did wait. I didn't give up on that vine. I made the decision to keep it.

I gave her extra special attention. Doted on her. Loved on her.

I would encourage you to do the same.

Give it time.

Place it in His hands.

Your marriage. Children. Ministry. Finances.

Depend on God and keep at it because in the Lord God you have a sure thing.

Isaiah 26:3 You will keep h[er] in perfect peace, whose mind is stayed on You, because [s]he trusts in You.

Today my vine is glorious. Filled with dainty yellow blossoms. She has grown above and beyond what I ever could've imagined. God can do the same in your life as well.

July 25

There are days our thoughts are monopolized by certain difficult situations. Try as we might, we can't focus on anything else. Darkness seems to be looming. Not just outside, but inside our spirit. There doesn't seem to be a good viable solution to the matter. I found myself in just such a state; mind reeling. I was supposed to be praying. But I couldn't focus on anything else; I was exasperated and joyless.

I looked up and there was God painting the sky with a lovely sunrise. My view was somewhat limited though. There were houses and trees blocking me. I tried to crane my neck to get a better view, but to no avail. Just then this airplane flew straight into that view; completely unobstructed.

I want that view.

God whispered, "I can give you that view."

"If you come to Me, I will take you above the problem. I want you to see things from My perspective."

God wanted to open up my eyes to the unseen.

He wanted me to take my eyes off of the situation just for a moment. Even that was a struggle. While I was supposed to be "praying", I was really going over all the details of a conversation. Recollecting every word that was said; examining and reexamining.

John 16:24 "Until now you have asked nothing... Ask, and you will receive, that your joy may be full.

I have a better understanding of what this verse means now. I wasn't asking the Lord for anything. I was reminding myself how bad the situation was. I wasn't praying at all; just spinning in a vicious cycle. The more I mulled over the problem, the madder I got. It hurt, and that's all I could think about. It was wearing me out.

My view was so limited, and what I could see was exhausting me.

Matthew 11:28 "Come to Me,... I will give you rest."

He seemed to be shouting, "Come now! Stop what you're doing."

When I did the situation didn't change, but my thinking did.

God took me above the obstacles so I could have a better view.

Our feelings can be so deceiving. It's important not to speak or act when we're in the state that I was in. We might say the wrong thing, in the wrong way, or make a bad decision. Hold off until you can hear the Lord speak clearly.

Isaiah 40:31 But those who wait on the LORD shall renew their strength; They shall mount up with wings like eagles, They shall run and not be weary, they shall walk and not faint.

For me, He said, "Wait." I did, and the situation resolved itself within the day.

Coming to Jesus and sharing my heart with Him altered my perspective. He revived me and gave me peace. He will do the same for you.

July 26

This morning was lovely. There was coolness in the air that was quite soothing. I was thoroughly enjoying my walk. Looking at the garden's in full bloom always delights. I noticed how each yard was so well maintained; meticulous and beautiful.

Then there was this one house.

It was obviously vacant. The grass was overgrown. Weeds were overtaking the lawn. Nothing has been kept up. Even the sign was falling apart.

What happened here? I can't help but wonder. How did this piece of property end up in such disrepair? I am certain it was once filled and overflowing with activity.

Did the owner file bankruptcy? Did he invest in the wrong things? Did an illness come upon this home and it slowly fell apart? Maybe the owner made some real bad choices and this is the result.

Our lives can look like this sometime.

Exhaustion catches up and we begin to feel unkempt.

Discouragement overtakes our confidence in Christ.

We have voids that we're too afraid to speak of.

Empty hearts long to be filled; they cry out for someone to help.

There are dreams sitting unfulfilled.

Marriages longing for repair. Where has the love gone?

Weeds of depression are growing instead of joy.

There are questions that beg to be answered:

Who can fill the emptiness?

Who can put this back together again?

Who can bring light into this looming darkness?

Psalm 18:28 For thou wilt light my candle: the LORD my God will enlighten my darkness.

The Lord my God can and will bring light into any dark corner.

What does He know?

Revelation 2:2 "I know..."

Our God knows fully and completely; He sees what no one else sees. He knows the inner depths and longings of your heart for this child, this man or situation. He knows your disappointments, He knows your failings, He knows when you've been hurt. He knows actions that caused you pain. But, He also knows the pain that you've caused. Nothing turned out the way you imagined. Disappointment is an understatement. He knows how hard you've tried. All of your efforts don't go unnoticed by Him. It takes hard work to do what you're doing.

Every moment may be a challenge.

There are some things we just don't tell.

Some things are obvious.

The state of this house is obvious; the overgrown weeds and broken sign speak for themselves. What does the inside look like? That's a little more difficult. I can't see in, but He can...and He can see inside the heart. He knows the desires of our heart.

Psalm 20:4 May He grant you according to your heart's desire, And fulfill...

One of the greatest paradoxes of the Bible:

Emptiness is the prelude to fulfillment.

I cannot hold onto what used to be. If I let go, then my hands can grasp what lies ahead.

Forget those things that are behind.

When we are still holding onto what used to be...our plans, hopes and dreams...anger, fear and depression...God cannot complete that perfect will that He has for us.

God's purpose will make us complete. Accomplish more than our minds could even fathom. He'll make us so full that we overflow! He will satisfy every longing...in His timing and in His way. In turn we will share what we've learned. We will be equipped to help mutually fulfill another's vacancies.

Pretty soon that house and heart will be full again.

July 27

Isaiah 32:2 A [wo]man will be as a hiding place from the wind, and a cover from the tempest, as rivers of water in a dry place, as the shadow of a great rock in a weary land.

I heard a raucous upstairs one afternoon. I paused to listen. Camden was by himself. There were no obvious reasons for all that tumult; I thought I better go check it out. As I crested the top of the stairs I could see into his room. All of his blankets were strewn on the floor. His multitude of stuffed animals were scattered all over the place. Books were everywhere. Even the lamp was knocked over. He is on a path of destruction. Since he has done this countless times before I already know there is something wrong. What that "something" is, I may or may not find out. His behavior does not correlate with the problem at hand. He does irrational things; things that don't make sense. That's just what he does. When something is wrong, he will often try to hurt himself or his stuff. He's even thrown his Sony DS, his most valuable possession, over the fence in the back yard.

I try to remain calm and ask, "Why are you doing that?"

Tears brimming, he angrily replies, "I'm going to destroy all my stuff!"

I ask him the same question several times; each time I am met with the same reply.

If the average person looked in from the outside, all things appear normal. Contagious smile and beautiful curls that frame a gorgeous face, he is the epitome of "normal."

Things are never as they appear.

So it is with each of us. There is always a story behind the story.

We do things that don't make sense. We make bad decisions. We hurt our 'most valuable possessions': spouses, children and friends. We cause pain. Perhaps because we're defending ourselves from past hurts. Maybe there was abuse in the past. Sometimes we see these irrational behaviors in our friends or coworkers. Much of the time they are going through something we don't know about.

We ask ourselves, 'Why did they do that?'

Fears, frustration and anger manifest themselves differently in each one of us.

Many times they just need someone to listen, someone to understand and not judge. I remember when I was in the midst of the biggest storm of my life, no one knew. But God knew. He would prompt someone to send me a card. Out of the blue a simple card became a 'stream in the desert.' A phone call became a 'refuge in the storm', strength to endure one more day.

If you have someone in your life that appears to be doing things that don't make sense, perhaps on a path of destruction, be patient. They may be depressed and you just can't see any obvious reason for it, love them through it. Try to reach out to them, even if it's just in some small way.

Inside each one of us resides the ability to be 'as a hiding place from the wind, and a cover from the tempest, as rivers of water in a dry place, as the shadow of a great rock in a weary land,' to another.

Lord Jesus, give us eyes to see what You see; the story behind the story. Give us ears that are open to listen to the cry of these desperate hearts. Give us a heart willing to do something about it. It is in the magnificent name of Jesus we pray...Amen

July 28

We pulled up to Play Zone. It's one of those places that have the huge inflatable slides and moon bounces. Camden loves it here. We go there all of the time. I turned off the car and got out. I opened his door and waited for him to get out. He wasn't budging. I asked him what was wrong.

He whimpered, "I don't have my socks."

I told him, "It's no big deal. Let's go."

He very hesitantly began to put his lime green Crocs on, but abruptly stopped.

I began to coerce him.

He whimpered again, "I don't have my socks."

Now I'm getting annoyed. This is such a trivial matter. Let's not turn this into a major drama. I'm sure they'll let him get away with it just this one time.

Again, I urged him to get his shoes on and get out of the car.

Now fear is written all over his face, half crying he said, "I don't want to go to jail!"

Go to jail? What? Where does he come up with this stuff? I had to think for a moment, and then I realized Camden comes here all of the time. He is very well versed in the rules. He knows them and wants to abide by them. One of the rules is this: You must wear socks. Now I'm trying to get him to break the rules. Things are very black and white in his world. Rules are meant to be followed. If you don't have socks, you don't bounce; plain and simple.

I began to think about this. There are things God wants me to follow. He doesn't want me to skirt them. They are written in His word. He simply wants me to obey them. But do I follow them fully and completely? Do I obey only when I feel like it? Or do I obey only when I think others are watching?

Proverbs 9:10 Fear of the Lord is the beginning of wisdom.

What is 'fear of the Lord?' It is simply this: We should fear displeasing Him. Does this mean we should cower in fear, in hopes that we don't get beat? No, that is not the heart of a Father. Rather the 'fear of the Lord' is a desire of a child to please his Daddy. A Father has only the best intentions for his child. He knows what is best for him. He can foresee danger. He desires to protect his little one from peril; even when the child can't see any harm.

Compromise in any area will bring inevitable harm to you.

His words echoed in me all day, "I don't want to go to jail."

He really isn't far off. When we sin we compromise our freedom. We become slaves imprisoned to that "thing" we don't want to follow.

Everyone is a slave to something or someone.

Here are just a few I want to be free from: Seeking the approval of people, worry and unforgiveness. Your list may look a little different.

Galatians 1:10 Am I now trying to win the approval of human beings, or of God? Or am I trying to please people? If I am still trying to please people, I am not a servant of Christ.

We must strive to seek the approval of One, and that is God Himself.

Philippians 4:6 Don't worry about anything; instead, pray about every-thing. Tell God what you need, and thank him for all he has done.

Does God really mean 'anything? Anything?' He really does! Countless times He tells us, don't worry. Worry holds us captive. It steals our joy at the very least.

Colossians 3:13 Bear with each other and forgive one another if any of you has a grievance against someone. Forgive as the Lord forgave you.

Forgive. When we don't forgive, we're the ones held prisoner.

Romans 2:1 You, therefore, have no excuse, you who pass judgment on someone else, for at whatever point you judge another, you are condemn-ing yourself, because you who pass judgment do the same things.

Don't judge. The very thing you see in that person is the very thing you're guilty of...that's why it's so easy to spot...we need to look in the mirror before we look beyond.

God is our Dad. He loves us and only has the best for us. If there are any areas where you can say, "I don't have my socks", stop at once. Don't go any further. Even if everyone around you has their socks off, don't do it. God is trying to protect you.

July 29

Luke 10:40-42 But Martha [overly occupied and too busy] was distracted with much serving; and she came up to Him and said, "Lord, is it nothing to You that my sister has left me to serve alone? Tell her then to help me [to lend a hand and do her part along with me]!" But the Lord replied to her by saying, "Martha, Martha, you are anxious and troubled about many things; there is need of only one thing. Mary has chosen the good portion [that which is to her advantage], which shall not be taken away from her."

Martha was overly occupied. Weighed down.

And carrying too much.

When we start looking around, instead of looking up, we know our heart is in the wrong place.

I've been here so many times.

"Lord do you see? Do you see this? Look at everything I'm doing. I need some help here!"

In a gentle whisper, He says, "Do you see Me? Come here. You've lost sight of Me."

Matthew 11:28 Come to Me, all you who labor and are heavy-laden and overburdened, and I will cause you to rest. [I will ease and relieve and refresh your souls.]

Sometimes we may say, "But, I'm too busy Lord. Don't you see what I'm doing for You? I have this, this and this to do. I don't have time for You right now Lord. Maybe later." Later I am even busier. The next day comes and I try to catch up from the day before.

"No time for You this morning Lord."

Before long we become critical. Cranky. Overwhelmed. Nothing to give.

All the small things can add up. Pretty soon we're carrying this massive load.

If you find your spiritual life suffering on a consistent basis, it may be time to let something go. Maybe even a few things. In general, women like to be people pleasers. But sometimes it's at the expense of our own spiritual life. We want to be God pleasers. I can only do a few things and do them well. If I do too many things, I don't do any of them well. Recently I found myself doing too many things. I was doing a ministry that I loved for several years. It was growing and thriving. It was wonderful. But, it required a lot of my time in the morning. I felt like the Lord wanted me to let that particular ministry go. I prayed for quite a while about it. Still, I felt the Lord saying, 'let it go.' I had such conflicting emotions. First and foremost, who would take my place? The only reason I began doing it was because no one else could do it. And several years later there were still only two of us doing it. I didn't want to disappoint my partner. What would she think if I "quit"? Oh me of little faith. Many months later, I still kept going and waiting for my replacement; praying along the way. The Lord said to me one Sunday, "Look, I want you to let that go. It is not your responsibility to find the replacement. That is My job. I created the world. I really don't need your help to find your replacement. You are just disobeying me at this point." And so I conceded. I said, "Ok Lord. I will let that go. I will let my partner know this week." During service that same day, the Lord spoke to me. "Your replacement is sitting right next to you. Talk to her about the ministry." Turns out she had just gotten a new job after 20 years at the same company. This would open up her schedule to do the ministry. The time slot fit perfectly. On top of all that, she felt it was a ministry the Lord had put on her heart for many years.

It is okay to let some things go if they are hindering your personal relationship with the Lord.

God I want to serve you. You know my heart. Give me discernment. Help me to choose wisely. Show me if I have taken on too much. Teach me how to let go, if need be.

July 30

Matthew 13:24-28 "The kingdom of heaven is like a man who sowed good seed in his field; "but while men slept, his enemy came and sowed tares among the wheat and went his way. "So the servants of the owner came and said to him, 'Sir, did you not sow good seed in your field? How then does it have tares? "He said to them, 'An enemy has done this.' The servants said to him, 'Do you want us then to go and gather them up?'

...An enemy has done this.

This word "enemy" is composed of two words in the old language. The first one is 'echthros' which means 'hostile opposition'.

The second one is 'anthropos'. It is very significant. It means a human-either man or woman. You see, quite often we tend to blame Satan for stealing our joy, robbing our children or taking from our marriages. But this verse is stating a man or woman has done this. In other words there are things that we as individuals need to take responsibility for allowing into our homes. There are things that aren't good for our children that we introduce or allow in that should not be. These things produce bad fruit in their hearts and lives. We bring 'tares' into our marriage by allowing flirtatious conversations, websites, gossip, movies and other things that tear down and have no business being there.

We cannot be complacent. We have to be more vigilant than ever.

These things create a hostile environment. These things are not conducive to a rich environment that encourages growth and fruit. But rather they destroy the seed. They corrupt the garden of our hearts, our children's hearts, our marriages and even our churches.

If it doesn't match up with God's word don't do it.

It could be made even simpler than that: When in doubt don't do it.

Galatians 6:7 Do not be deceived, God is not mocked; for whatever a man sows, that he will also reap.

This is a law of God that cannot be circumvented.

A man cannot look at pornography and think his son won't.

A woman cannot find her value in her outward appearance and think her children won't as well.

A man cannot be defined by his position and think his son won't as well.

A woman cannot commit adultery and think her children won't.

A church cannot compromise with the word of God and think its people won't as well.

A nation cannot turn its back on God and think God won't do the same.

In our original verse it tells us these things happened while men slept; we cannot afford to become drowsy.

Lord Jesus help us to have wisdom as parents. Give us sensitive hearts. Prick our hearts when we are compromising. Help us to lift you up as the standard in our home. We want to please you at all cost. Give us discernment and help us make good choices.

July 31

Crossed paths with a little frog one morning. Alive and well. Made me think of Pharaoh. And the plagues. And the frogs all over Egypt. They were everywhere.

Destroying everything.

Have you ever wondered why Pharaoh was so stubborn?

Why didn't he just let the people go?

God tried to be gentle with him. He sent others to talk with him.

Warn him. Exhort him. Beg him.

But he still refused to listen.

Pharaoh wanted things to change. He begged for a reprieve.

One was available.

Let's be clear. He had a choice.

Exodus 8:9-10 You set the time!" Moses replied. "Tell me when you want me to pray for you, your officials, and your people. Then you and your houses will be rid of the frogs..."

So he said, "Tomorrow."

What was he thinking?

This plague was destroying him, his family, his job and everyone around him.

And yet, he wanted one more day with his frogs.

We're not so different than Pharaoh. In fact, we're way more like him than we care to admit.

Each of us have frogs in our lives.

Things that need to go.

Relationships, addictions, pride, unbelief, anger...just to name a few.

God told us to let it go a long time ago. We keep holding on.

We say, "Tomorrow."

Give me one more night with the frogs.

We each have a choice.

John 5:6... "Do you want to be made well?"

The ball is in your court. Things will change the moment you say so.

It is a matter of obedience. We are not at the mercy of some disease that is out of our control. We can't blame our parents nor our circumstances.

In the secular world, sin is often labeled as a disease. Therefore, you are not personally responsible for your actions. No culpability. Just a victim.

That's nonsense.

If you're not sure what you're dealing with, just look in the word of God. That is the only place to find truth.

John 8:32...The truth shall set you free.

You are a slave to sin.

At your choosing, you can be set free.

Jesus Christ came to set the captives free.

Either you are a slave of Jesus Christ, or you are a slave of sin.

Sin is blatant mutiny against God, and either sin or God must die in my life. The New Testament brings us right down to this one issue— if sin rules in me, God's life in me will be killed; if God rules in me, sin in me will be killed.-O. Chambers

If Christ is your Master, give Him full reign of your life.

Straddling the fence with one foot in the world and one foot in the church is painful. There is no rest. No peace. Only constant turmoil.

I know. I did it.

God loves you too much to have you continue on status quo. He is trying to get your attention.

1 Peter 5:6-7 Therefore humble yourselves under the mighty hand of God, that He may exalt you in due time, casting all your care upon Him, for He cares for you.

Today.

Let that go.

Today.

August

August 1

We had an action packed day. Running here and there had taken its toll on all of us. After a long drive, we were nearing home when Camden drowsily asked, "Can we take a ride?" Since we had just driven for 40 minutes, his question was really more of a statement. So I'll rephrase, "Can we drive a little more because I'm almost asleep." I peered into the rearview mirror. His head was turned sideways; eyes were heavy. I assured him he could go lie down in bed when we got home. After all, he had a rough night sleeping the night before. We drove through a few more lights and before you know it we were pulling into our driveway.

He perked up, "Can we go for a walk?"

What?

I thought he was exhausted. The last thing I wanted to do was go for a walk. It was still stifling hot. The humidity was high and my energy low. I tried to persuade him not to go. But he insisted, so off we went. He was on his scooter and I was walking. He made it to the playground about a quarter of a mile away. He stopped and played for a bit. Before you know it he wanted to ride again; but not home. He wanted to go in the other direction. The sun was merciless. I knew there was no way he would be able to make it home, much less any further. He persisted and off we went. At the half mile mark, off came the helmet and down went the scooter. Sweat was soaking his hair. His pudgy hands were hanging down lifeless. His rosy little cheeks glistening in the sun; he could go no further.

He had taken on too much.

Do you ever feel like that? This is way more than I bargained for. Things are not going as I expected. I am exhausted and I don't want to do this anymore. Sometimes it's just out of our control. We didn't ask for this illness or difficulty or wreckage, but here it is. I set out on a nice walk and here I am; melting.

It can all be so overwhelming.

I gladly picked up his scooter and carried it home for him.

Isaiah 38:14... I am oppressed (stressed out); Undertake [this] for me!

God will be glad to pick up this thing that you've taken on. Go ahead and put it down. Sometimes we wonder, 'Are You willing to do this just for me...just because I asked?'

He is. Any Dad that loves his kids as much as God loves us is more than willing to carry it. He knows how hard this is. He sees how heavy this burden is for you.

He understands when we can't take another step.

Mark 6:30-31 And He said to them, "Come away by yourselves to a secluded place and rest a while." (For there were many people coming and going, and they did not even have time to eat.)

Come by yourself. Leave the people behind. Cast your burden and come. He has something to say. You don't want to miss it. His word will help you recover. You'll be refreshed anew.

August 2

Genesis 22:1 Now it came to pass after these things that God tested Abraham, and said to him, "Abraham!" And he said, "Here I am."

God called his name. He got his attention.

Is God 'calling your name'? Quite often He does that through our circumstances.

When He does, you must be willing to respond. God has something to say. He called and Abraham responded. Sometimes that first turning of the head is the most difficult. We're afraid to hear what God has to say. We know we may not like it.

Genesis 22:2 Then He said, "Take now your son, your only son Isaac, whom you love and go to the land of Moriah

Take this thing that is most precious to you. It is that one thing: that plan, that dream, that job, that way of life, or that aspiration. Give it to God, whatever you have your arms wrapped around. He wants you to lay it on the altar of sacrifice. For Abraham it was his son. For you it may be something else. You fill in the blank.

Take now_____.

Are you willing to let it go?

"Go to the land of Moriah..."

Moriah means "chosen by God." The place you find yourself in is no coincidence. God chose this for you. It is not by accident. It is the place that will bring Him the most glory; only if you are willing to obey.

The root word of Moriah means "to see." God is going to use this place to give you a good look inside your heart.

Genesis 22:3 So Abraham rose early in the morning and saddled his donkey, and took two of his young men with him, and Isaac his son; and he split the wood for the burnt offering, and arose and went to the place of which God had told him.

He knew what God was asking and there was some preparation that needed to be done to make it happen. He did what was necessary. First and foremost, he needed to prepare his heart.

Obedience is from the heart.

He didn't like it.

He didn't want to.

He was terrified.

But, he did it anyway.

Sacrifice is never easy.

Genesis 22:5 And Abraham said to his young men, "Stay here with the donkey; the lad and I will go yonder and worship, and we will come back to you."

He arrived at his destination.

What was he thinking?

Was he thinking, 'I cannot believe this is happening to me? God, You know how much I love this child. I had such great plans for him. I hear you. I know what you are asking me to do. It is the most difficult thing I've ever had to do.'

He had to be wrestling inside.

But at some point he chose to obey God. He didn't understand it; who could?

He told his friends, "Stay here."

He had to go this alone. There comes a time when we have to get alone with the Lord and sort this out. We have to leave everyone and everything and take that time with the Lord. At some point, Abraham came to accept God's will.

Obedience is a choice.

Essentially he was saying, 'I know this is where you have me. I offer up my life. I give you my everything. I hold nothing back from you.' Often I have found myself saying, "I want to serve you but only if I get to choose where it is. I want to choose my place of sacrifice."

It's God's choice, not mine.

Sometimes I surrender up to a certain point and not any further. I say, "Your will be done...but only up to this point." God desires a complete surrender. The offering must be whole and complete; not partial and not half way. You can't hold onto part of it.

Do you and God need to take a walk together and sort some things out?

When Abraham did, it helped strengthen him to do what God was asking him to do.

Lord Jesus, I want to submit to your will. Please speak to me. Lead me and guide me. I want to obey you. No matter what the cost. You are worth my all. Take my fear of going it alone. You are with me. I have nothing to be afraid of. I surrender all to You.

August 3

Yesterday we saw how God called Abraham to do something incredibly difficult; something very hard to understand. Abraham took a walk with the Lord. That had to be the longest walk of his life. He sorted things out and then he worshipped. This is the first place in the Bible that this word "worship" is found. It is very significant because worship is equated with sacrifice. The word worship means to bow down.

The very essence of worship is conceding to the fact that I am not in control. Essentially Abraham was saying, 'Not my will but that of my Master. I concede this is NOT what I would've chosen. But, if this is what it takes for God to be glorified then I'll do it.'

He lay what was most precious to him on that altar. In essence, he was saying, "Do as you please. I give you everything. This child is my life. I hold nothing back. "

At some point Abraham had to tell Isaac what God had called him to do.

I cannot help but wonder what Isaac was thinking.

While it's true that Abraham had amazing faith, Isaac had a faith that was at least equal to that of Abraham, if not greater. After all, it was his life that was being taken. Isaac did not run away from what his Father was asking.

There isn't even a mention that he complained.

Isaac did not open his mouth.

Just like Jesus. He was led as a lamb to the slaughter, yet He did not open his mouth.

Isaac submitted to the will of his Father. He willingly offered himself.

Genesis 22:10 And Abraham stretched out his hand and took the knife to slay his son. But the Angel of the LORD called to him from heaven and said, "Abraham, Abraham!" So he said, "Here I am." And He said, "Do not lay your hand on the lad, or do anything to him; for now I know that you fear God, since you have not withheld your son, your only son, from Me." Then Abraham lifted his eyes and looked, and there behind him was a ram caught in a thicket by its horns. So Abraham went and took the ram, and offered it up for a burnt offering instead of his son.

And Abraham called the name of the place, The-LORD-Will-Provide...

God saw what Abraham needed and provided it.

He knows the situation you're in as well. He saw and considered every possible scenario and has chosen the best possible one for you. This place that looks like certain death was one of the most pivotal points in Abraham's life. Sometimes all we can see is the struggle and hardship. The loss. God showed him so much more. God showed him He could be trusted.

God was all he had, but God was all he needed.

For Abraham and Isaac, He provided a substitute. He provided something better and in a way they did not expect. He provided Himself; at precisely the right time. He did the same for me and I know He will do the same for you. So right now, give Him everything. Just give Him everything. What you get in return will be so much more than you expected.

Lord help me to accept the things I cannot understand. I accept Your will. Sometimes I don't understand it, but I trust You. I trust You more than I trust my feelings. Not my will, but Yours be done.

August 4

Psalm 29:4-5 The voice of the LORD is powerful; The voice of the LORD is full of majesty. The voice of the LORD breaks the cedars, yes, the LORD splinters the Cedars of Lebanon.

The Cedars of Lebanon grow in the mountains of Israel, Syria, and Jordan. The trunks of these trees reach 8 feet in diameter and they can grow 130 feet tall. These trees are massive forces to be reckoned with. Often our trials can seem like these trunks; impossible to break through.

As big as that tree trunk is, God's voice is bigger still.

This verse shouts out the awesome power of the voice of God. His voice alone can splinter this tree.

There are obstacles that we are facing that seem impenetrable. They stand as stout as the Cedar. They are a threatening force, but God is able to break them as if they were little toothpicks.

His voice can pierce the hardest heart. It can penetrate even the most boisterous noise of the world. He can bring silence to the taunting voice of fears that attack us without warning. His voice alone can birth new life. It has more influence than all the competing voices of the world. While the enemy hovers as an threatening force and we are overcome with worries, the voice of God interjects to bring a newfound confidence. One Word from the Living God infuses us with strength we never knew we had. Some of us have family that we've been trying to reach for years; unsuccessfully. No matter how far away they are, God can reach them. Distance is nothing for our God. He can reach where we cannot.

No heart, financial hardship, disability, broken relationship is beyond the voice of God.

Jeremiah 32:17 "O Sovereign LORD! You made the heavens and earth by your strong hand and powerful arm. Nothing is too hard for you!"

August 5

2 Kings 4:1-7 A certain woman...cried out to Elisha, saying, "Your servant my husband is dead, and you know that your servant feared the LORD. And the creditor is coming to take my two sons to be his slaves." So Elisha said to her, "What shall I do for you? Tell me, what do you have in the house?" And she said, "Your maidservant has nothing in the house but a jar of oil." Then he said, "Go, borrow vessels from everywhere, from all your neighbors—empty vessels; do not gather just a few. And when you have come in, you shall shut the door behind you and your sons; then pour it into all those vessels, and set aside the full ones." So she went from him and shut the door behind her and her sons, who brought the vessels to her; and she poured it out. Now it came to pass, when the vessels were full, that she said to her son, "Bring me another vessel." And he said to her, "There is not another vessel." So the oil ceased. Then she came and told the man of God. And he said, "Go, sell the oil and pay your debt; and you and your sons live on the rest."

This woman's situation was dire. She was probably hesitant to pour out that little bit of oil that she had. Most likely she wanted to hold onto it tightly. I would have.

Elisha asked, "How can I help? Let's see, what do you have? What do you have in the house? "

She replied, "Nothing...except a jar of olive oil."

This sounded all too familiar to me, in fact it sounded just like me sometimes. While her circumstances were dire, she did have a little oil. It may not have been much but it was something. I tend to over exaggerate my problems. I tell myself, "I don't have enough... I don't have this and I don't have that...I ain't got nothing!"

Listen, this is how our ever present enemy likes to whisper in our ear. 'You don't have enough...look at what they have...why don't you have that? Why don't you get to do that?' In these situations he gets us to compare ourselves to others.

Just like Eve...she could have every tree in the garden except one...but it was that one that did her in. It took her down. Let's not second guess God. If He says NO to something, it's for a reason. It's because He is our Dad and he knows what's best. We always think we know what's best, but we don't. Our Dad has infinitely more wisdom than we do.

Elisha said, "Bring me some empty jars. Take your sons and shut the door behind you. What I'm about to do will not make sense in the natural realm."

God will fill the things that we bring to Him. But He can only fill them IF we are willing to place them in His trust. If not, we will continue to come up empty. We may not have much; but what we do have we need to give Him.

Elijah said, "Don't bring me just a few jars. Bring me a lot!

Ask big things from God... it honors Him!

DON'T UNDERESTIMATE GOD!

BRING MORE THAN WHAT YOU THINK HE CAN DO!

Bring higher expectations!

Ephesians 3:20 Now to Him who is able to do exceedingly abundantly above all that we ask or think, according to the power that works in us, to Him be the glory...

It is important to note:

He used what she had. She didn't need anything else. She had the oil and that was it. It wasn't much, but all she had was all she needed. Sometimes we are always looking at what we don't have, instead of looking at what we do have.

Give God what you have. The widow did and He supernaturally multiplied what she had.

She offered it willingly. She didn't hoard what she had.

SHE POURED IT OUT!

It was in the giving that it was multiplied. If she held onto what she had, it would've stayed the same.

Time, money, gifts, talents, love, forgiveness, grace, energy; all of these things can be more in the hand of God.

God is the great multiplier.

When you give, He will NEVER leave you lacking.

Sometimes we may find ourselves saying, "I'm not wasting my time on that. I'm so busy, I can't possibly do that. I don't even have enough to pay my own bills, how could I possibly help?" And the list goes on.

He takes the little we have and multiplies it. He sees the heart behind it.

Luke 6:38 "Give, and it will be given to you: good measure, pressed down, shaken together, and running over will be put into your bosom. For with the same measure that you use, it will be measured back to you."

You and I just don't have it in us to forgive, to love, to go out of our way. It's just that simple.

If you do it anyways and give what you have, God will use your willing heart. He'll multiply what you have and use it in ways you won't believe.

God help us to trust You with everything. We give you the little bit that we have and ask you to multiply if for Your Kingdom. Increase our faith. All that we have is a gift from You. It does not belong to us. We want to be good stewards of everything You've placed into our trust. Amen.

August 6

The summer was particularly hot. I wondered why all of the flowers in my garden were wilting, but not my limelight hydrangea. She was magnificent; in fact, stunning. She even appeared to be showing off. The summer sun was unrelenting. Many days of scorching heat had taken a toll on all of the other flowers in my garden, but not this one. She was as lovely as ever. I now realize it's because she has the deepest roots. She can go many days without water.

Jeremiah 17:7 "Blessed [is] the [wo]man who trusts in the LORD, And whose hope is the LORD; For [s]he shall be like a tree planted by the waters, Which spreads out its roots by the river, And will not fear when heat comes; But its leaf will be green, And will not be anxious in the year of drought, Nor will cease from yielding fruit.

There may be a year of drought ahead. Struggles. Heartache may come. But if we are growing and thriving now, our roots are spreading far and wide to make a firm foundation. When the time comes we'll be ready for it. We will not cease to yield fruit. Our roots have struck down deep. The deeper the roots, the stronger the tree.

This is so interesting: the Hebrew says she shall "not see" when heat comes. The surrounding circumstances of her life are irrelevant. It doesn't matter what's going on. She doesn't see it.

She sees her God.

Are you in a trial of a lifetime?

The woman who has deep roots in the Lord will not even show the brevity of her situation. She carries on as though nothing has changed.

Her leaf is still green. She is vibrant.

She is still yielding fruit. She continues to grow and be active.

Living water from the throne of God sustains us through the longest periods of drought.

Soak it in as much as you can.

You will need it.

Heat will come. It is not a question of if, but when.

When it comes you will find that you are secure in Jesus. Remaining fixed and firm. Not dropping off, nor fading away. But alive and active. Vibrant and beautiful.

Lord Jesus take my roots deep into your heart. Water them with Your living water. Help me to bear fruit even in long periods of drought. Saturate me. Rain down on me. Keep me from wilting. I want to grow, even now.

August 7

1 Peter 4:8 And above all things have fervent love for one another...

As I was pondering these verses this morning I noticed this word "fervent." In the old language it meant "stretched out." God desires us to have a "stretched out" love. He wants us to love one another even when it is undeserved. That is where the stretching comes.

When I came across a picture of a "Stretch Armstrong" doll I laughed so hard. I had one when I was a kid. You could stretch him in all sorts of precarious positions. He could stretch and wrap his arms around and around his back and legs. His legs could do the same. Here are a few examples of what "stretching" may look like:

People stretch us. But God will stretch us further still. He wants us to love this person.

Just when we think we've reached our limit, He takes us beyond.

I think I know God well enough to say He has brought someone to your mind just now. You probably said, "Nope not them. I can't." That is exactly who God wants you to love.

Matthew 5:46 If you love only those who love you, what reward is there for that?

God is using this person to stretch you beyond yourself.

I love what the outside of the package for Stretch Armstrong reads:

Stretch him long, stretch him thin and watch him go back into shape again.

Grab hold and pull. You can stretch thirteen-inch Stretch Armstrong up to four feet! Squish him, scrunch him, and stretch him out. He always returns to his original shape. Ready for any wild position kids can think up.

No matter which direction he is pulled in, he is pliable.

James 3:17 But the wisdom from above is first of all pure. It is also peace loving, gentle at all times, and willing to yield to others.

Even when stretched long and thin, he never broke. You won't break either. In every circumstance we are called to love. In every instance where people are involved: marriage, children, friendship and even the church God desires us to love extravagantly.

Perhaps you are dealing with an exceptionally difficult person. God will enable you to do what is humanly impossible.

2 Peter 1:3 as His divine power has given to us all things that pertain to life and godliness...

We can't do this on our own. We are depending on His divine power, not our own.

Whether we are dealing with an unreasonable husband, demanding friend, or ungrateful sister our response: love out of a sincere heart.

Love must be intentional, unceasing, and constant in effort.

When we give until it hurts:

James 4:6... He gives more...

The distinguishing mark of a Christian is love.

John 13:35 "By this all will know that you are My disciples, if you have love for one another."

Sometimes we know what we should do, but just don't want to. We feel we've done all we can do.

Malachi 3:8...will a man rob God?

In this particular verse the people were holding back their offering. They had more to give. They knew what God expected but they were unwilling to give it. I think that we can be that way with our love. We can look at a person and size them up by the things they've done or haven't done and say, "I'm not reaching out to them. I won't love them. They don't deserve it. Look at the way they've treated me."

God wants us to give more than we think we are able. He desires us to go all out; love lavishly.

Malachi 3:10 "Bring all...into the storehouse...try me now in this... If I will not open for you the windows of heaven and pour out for you such blessing that there will not be room enough to receive it."

When you bring all that you have and "stretch out" like this, God will pour out His blessing on you.

You may be stretched thin, but you will never be more like Jesus.

Lord, give me Your eyes for this person. Show me what You want me to see. Help me Lord. I am weak. I need Your Spirit. I want to yield to Your will. You loved me when I was unlovable. Help me to do no less. Give me Your heart Jesus. I want to be willing to do what You ask of me. Your honor is at stake.

August 8

A few months ago I felt the need to cut my hydrangea way back. The idea really began the year before. It began to take up too much space in my garden. Instead of complimenting, it began to dominate. When it would rain the blooms would sag down to the ground. It was just out of control. I missed the winter pruning time. I was really hesitant to actually follow through with cutting it back.

Would it still be the same?

When spring came I knew what I had to do. I had to cut its branches way back. I didn't know what to expect. Did I wait too long? Would it bloom at all? Well don't you know this Limelight Hydrangea grew back three times as much as I cut off? It is more magnificent than ever!

Are there some things that need to be cut out of your life?

Maybe you've been putting it off. You know it needs to go, but you've been hesitant. You may be afraid it'll hurt too much. Change is always difficult. But once that weight is lifted, you'll be so free! It will be so worth it! You'll be more vibrant and beautiful than ever!

John 15:1-2 "I am the true vine, and my Father is the gardener. He cuts off every branch of mine that doesn't produce fruit, and he prunes the branches that do bear fruit so they will produce even more."

August 9

The boy shows up with this dandelion.

All shy acting. Reaches out to me, "Here you go Mom."

Just at the right time. It was.

There was the doctor's appointment for him this morn. A routine check-up. And the question that lingered long in my mind, echoing.

"So Mrs. Bollas, would you say he is above average, average, or below average academically?"

I pause. And smile polite.

I want to ask her a question.

"By whose standard?"

My God doesn't compare. He made this guy who He decided He should be.

In His eyes He is perfect. He is WAY above any standard. He brings God's heart joy because He is His son. Not because he can read or can't read. Not because he is better or worse than someone else's kid at Math.

Comparisons bring coveting.

When we compare our children it puts so much pressure on us, and them.

What we're really looking at are deficits.

Should we focus on perceived shortcomings? Not at all.

God doesn't measure. Nor should we.

God celebrates.

He made us each different for a reason. We are unique in every way. For a very specific purpose.

What is that purpose?

To know God, and make Him known.

And God chooses to do that differently in each one of us individually. We shouldn't strive to be someone we're not.

Praise God for who you are. He gave you special gifts. Use them.

If He blessed you with children, thank Him for who they are. If they are "below average" according to the world's standards, God is going to use that in their lives. Be encouraged.

It is in our weakness that we are strong. Strong in Him.

1 Samuel 16:7... For the LORD does not see as man sees; for man looks at the outward appearance, but the LORD looks at the heart."

This boy's heart is big. It makes me smile big.

August 10

John 9:36 Jesus heard that they had cast him out; and when He had found him, He said to him, "Do you believe in the Son of God?"

This man was blind but he received a greater healing than just his sight. This disability opened the eyes of his understanding to see no one else could help him. That's what I found to be in my life. I knew God. I had a wonderful relationship with Him. But if it weren't for this disability I would never have grasped the magnificent power of His word.

God's word has the power to give me strength for another day. It lifts me out of the pit of despair and sets me on firm ground. It takes my shaky faith and shores it up. His word gives me confidence to take the next step. God's word has the power to heal.

God chose to heal the blind man because He knew that would bring Him the most praise.

God did not choose to heal my son. Does He have the power to heal him? I absolutely believe He does. In fact, I prayed for Him to be healed once. But it really was just a matter of going through the motions. I knew deep down that it was not His will to heal him. It was not because of my lack of faith. I wanted to make note of that because a man once told me I didn't have enough faith for my son to be healed. I explained to him that he did not understand scripture. It is not God's will for every child to be healed.

John 9:2...who sinned, this man or his parents, that he was born blind?" Jesus answered, "Neither this man nor his parents sinned, but that the works of God should be revealed in him."

While I did withdraw myself for a time, Jesus found me where I was at.

He asked me a simple question, "Do you trust Me with this disability?"

I answered, "Yes! Yes I do!"

Does your "disability", problem or circumstance have you questioning who God is and what He is doing? You may not understand what He is doing, but you can trust Him. He has your best interest at heart. Maybe your situation is "disabling" you. There are so many things you want to do, but you can't. Your "disability" is going to give you greater "sight." Maybe your financial situation is "disabling" you. Perhaps your situation is making your husband feel "cast out or excluded." Maybe he doesn't quite know how to deal with this yet. Go get him! Don't leave him out there. Satan wants to divide the two of you, but Jesus wants to unite you in this.

God will never fail you.

You can worship and exalt Him even if He never heals. He will change you. He will give you what you need. Today and always.

August 11

John 1:48 Nathanael said to [Jesus], "How do You know me?" Jesus answered and said to him, "Before Philip called you, when you were under the fig tree, I saw you."

Nathanael was going his own way. He was trying to figure things out on his own. Most likely, he had no idea where his life was going. Nor did he have a purpose. He was probably depressed and maybe even ready to just give up.

I have been on that road before. It's a road to nowhere.

Jesus met Nathanael on that road. He showed up at just the right time.

Nathanael wonders how this Man could know everything about him, even though they've never met.

In essence, Jesus replies, "Before you ever thought of Me, I knew you. I saw you."

What did He see?

Jesus saw his past.

Jesus saw his present.

Jesus saw his future.

It is the same for us.

"I saw you when…"

You fill in the blank. He knows it all. Don't leave anything out. He saw you then; and He still loves you.

Jesus knows where you've come from. He sees what you've been through. He knows how hard it's been.

We are never defined by our past.

Jesus will redefine all that you are; if you will allow Him.

2 Corinthians 5:17 Therefore, if anyone is in Christ, he is a new creation; old things have passed away; behold, all things have become new.

He can make all things new in your life.

When?

Today is the day.

Don't say tomorrow. You may not have tomorrow.

What will it cost?

Everything. He wants it all.

He is worthy of all.

You can trust the Man who died for you.

Jesus beckons, "Follow Me."

When you choose to follow Him, it means leaving some things behind; perhaps everything and everyone.

Ecclesiastes 3:1 There's an opportune time to do things, a right time for everything… A right time to hold on and another to let go…

Is what you have so great?

The moment you take one step in His direction, He will run to meet you. He'll take you by the hand and walk the rest of this journey with you. Leave it all behind. He is worth it.

Your life has purpose.

August 12

We were jolted out of our sleep at 2 a.m. one morning by the piercing blare of our smoke detector.

Is this a real fire?

As quick as it sounded it stopped. The adrenaline rush slowed and I was somewhat relieved.

But then it began again.

Ray did a quick sweep of the house; no fire. He unplugged the smoke detector and replaced it with a new one.

A smoke detector goes off for one reason: to warn you of danger. I am relieved that there wasn't a fire. But, I never want to ignore the warning.

Smoke detectors have one purpose; they save lives.

God does the same thing in our lives to protect us from danger. He is gracious enough to send us warnings. He sounds the alarm of your conscience. He sends a friend to advise you of your risky behavior. He tries to block your way.

Romans 2:4 Don't you see how wonderfully kind, tolerant, and patient God is with you? Does this mean nothing to you? Can't you see that his kindness is intended to turn you from your sin?

Don't ignore the warning.

You can silence the voice that's speaking to you, but that won't delay the consequences.

The consequences to sin are devastating.

Proverbs 6:27 Can a man scoop fire into his lap without his clothes being burned?

You will get burned.

Ephesians 4: 17-19 And so I insist—and God backs me up on this—that there be no going along with the crowd, the empty-headed, mindless crowd. They've refused for so long to deal with God that they've lost touch not only with God but with reality itself. They can't think straight anymore. Feeling no pain, they let themselves go in sexual obsession, addicted to every sort of perversion.

Every time you ignore the warning you become more calloused; soon you'll be desensitized. No matter how loud the warning is, you won't hear it.

You are so precious. Your life is so valuable. God wants to protect you and spare you from heartache.

Doing nothing is not an option. The warning requires a response.

Either you will say to God, "Yes, I will obey" or "No, I won't obey."

One response leads to life and freedom. The other leads to death and destruction.

Dear God, please help me to choose life. I want to obey you with all my heart. It is hard. So hard. Help me to do hard. Help me to live for you. I want to let go of everything that displeases you. All of it. I want a clean start. A new beginning. Thank you that you died so that I can have a new beginning.

August 13

Matthew 6:26 Look at the birds. They don't plant or harvest or store food in barns, for your heavenly Father feeds them. And aren't you far more valuable to Him than they are?

Ray and I were on a little escape to Cape May recently. We weren't there long when some unexpected bad news came our way. The impact to our lives could be great. I really wouldn't know the outcome for quite a while.

I was very worried.

I went out on the deck to get a change of scenery. The view changed, but not my thoughts. I was still overwhelmed with my 'what ifs.' What if this happens? What if that happens? None of my scenarios was good.

This was just a bad situation.

Intruding into my pity party came this little birdie. He danced around a bit. Then he flew away; only to return a few moments later.

I was intrigued. He was not the least bit fearful. He actually seemed to be trying to get my attention.

I was sipping my tea and savoring the best toffee cookie I've ever tasted. I thought maybe this little guy might be hungry. I threw him a few pieces. He quickly ate them and stuck around to see if I would give him some more. I happily obliged.

My little friend taught me a lesson.

He didn't know what today would hold.

My few crumbs sustained him for the day. He didn't know that I would be there to do that.

But God did.

God provided in an unexpected way.

Ephesians 3:20 Now to him who is able to do immeasurably more than all we ask or imagine, according to his power that is at work...

I'm pretty sure my little friend would've been happy with a few dry breadcrumbs. But, he got so much more; he got a homemade brown sugar toffee cookie.

Isn't our God awesome?

God sees what you need as well. He is going to provide for you too.

(And I hope a brown sugar toffee cookie comes along with it!)

August 14

My magnolia tree really spoke to me one morning. One large bloom opened wide on the back side of the tree. I could see her through the window of my office. One would never know she was there. From the road, she is hidden. It was only my strategic position that allowed me to see her. She was delightful. Just beckoning me to go get her. When I did the house quickly wafted with her sweet scent.

Our Master had a purpose for her.

Before I ever discovered her, she brought Him joy first. There are many hidden flowers that blossom in the desert. Hidden to the sight of the world. But not hidden from the eyes of the Master. In like manner, there are many insignificant people that please the Masters heart. Quietly working, unseen by the world.

Mordecai was just such a man. His name means little, small, and humble.

A man, seemingly unimportant. Inconsequential. Average.

But it blessed our Master to use him.

In essence, he adopted Esther when her parents died. He played a crucial role in God's plan. He took on an enormous responsibility. One that he could've easily looked at and said, "No way. I am not doing that. I am not cut out for that. Let someone else do it." He could've stepped back. God would've and could've used someone else. He didn't step back. He stepped forward.

He said, "I can do that."

Philippians 4:13 I can do all things through Christ who strengthens me.

Mordecai made a choice. He chose to do this for the King. There are people and situations before us that are a challenge. They may not be our responsibility, but God is asking us to step in.

So often we want a cookie cutter life. A life that's predictable. Relatively the same as everyone else.

God uses different. Embrace your uniqueness.

Romans 12:2...present your bodies a living sacrifice...

Give your life into the hands of the Master.

Mordecai's life was a sacrifice. He gave his life to raise Esther. It was humbling. It was heavy.

In his littleness, God's bigness was magnified.

Taking the lower position put him in a strategic position.

There are no accidents with God. No coincidences in His kingdom.

When we commit our plans to Him, He will direct us on the right path. So many times the things we take on become too much for us to bear. We can feel so overwhelmed.

Proverbs 16:3 Commit your works to the Lord and your thoughts will be established.

This word "commit" in the old language could mean "to roll." In other words, "Roll your works to the Lord and your thoughts will be established."

Typically we roll very heavy things. Heavy things are not meant to be carried by ourselves.

God comes softly, "Let me help you with that."

We forget.

This is your show Lord.

This child, he is Yours. This cancer, it's Hour's. This ministry, it's Hour's.

When we try to carry it on our own, the weight is unbearable.

When we give it over to the Lord, our burden becomes light.

We feel secure again.

Jeremiah 29:11 I know the plans I have for you says the Lord; plans for peace and not evil. To give you a future and a hope.

God's plans are so hard to understand sometimes.

He allows things for a reason.

God is always aiming at something.

He placed Mordecai in a very strategic position. God is not always concerned for our comfort today, but rather His plan for tomorrow.

Mordecai raised Esther to know the Lord.

God uses average people.

It was Esther who saved a whole nation. Don't underestimate your small, seemingly insignificant gestures. God can use them in a big way.

August 15

I was startled out of my sleep last night by a repetitive thudding on the wall. It was coming from Camden's room. I made my way through the darkness and into his room. I tiptoed to his bed. His little voice whimpered, "I'm scared." I reached out to find his hand. When I found it, I felt the warmth of his hands envelop my whole arm. He was drawing me nearer still.

"Stay with me Mama," was his plea.

Just my presence was comforting to him.

But what was he so afraid of that he couldn't get out of bed?

I've felt this way quite a few times in my life. I was afraid to move.

Fear of the unknown can paralyze us.

We don't have to fear what lies ahead. We don't know what the future holds, but God does. He knew the beginning and He knows the end. There is not one detail in between that He doesn't know.

Fear of what people think can immobilize us as well.

In the grand scheme of things it would be nice if everyone approved of everything we did and said, but that isn't realistic. There is only one opinion that counts.

Galatians 1:10 Obviously, I'm not trying to win the approval of people, but of God. If pleasing people were my goal, I would not be Christ's servant.

Fear of failure can stop me in my tracks.

Romans 8:31 If God is for us, who can be against us?

If we never try, we'll never know.

Fear of people finding out my past mistakes can halt my attempts at trying.

Romans 8:28 And we know that all things work together for good to those who love God...

ALL things? Yes God even uses our past failures if we will allow Him.

It's time to take God's hand and walk out of the darkness. You don't have to be afraid. As long as your Dad is walking with you, He'll give you the courage to take the next step. Get up and get moving. He won't leave your side.

August 16

I want to walk with my dog Faithful. It's one of the things I hoped for when I got him. I want to do everything with him. I want to share life with him. Walking will be so good for him. Dogs absolutely love walking.

There's only one problem. He won't get out of the garden.

He wants to eat mulch.

I chide him, "No Faithful." He doesn't seem to hear me.

He continues to eat mulch. Next thing I know he has a big piece of bark that he's chewing on. Mulch is toxic. It's sharp and could cut his throat. I run over and get it out of his mouth before he gets hurt.

I call his name.

Nothing.

I call him again.

Nothing. Again and again I try. He still won't come. I tug on his leash. Nothing. I tug a little harder.

I can't do anything to make him come. He just sits there.

I just want him to walk with me.

He doesn't understand.

I don't want anything from him.

I just want to be with him.

He'd rather sit there and chew on mulch. He doesn't know what he's missing.

We do this in our lives.

God calls us to come walk with Him. We don't come. We'd rather chew on mulch.

Maybe that mulch is something someone said to you. It hurt you and you won't let it go.

Or it may be a relationship that you know is not good for you. Instead of coming when God calls you to walk away, you remain in a toxic situation.

It may just be fear of the unknown. It's easier to stay where you're at.

Walk away. Let it go.

You don't know what you're missing!

God has something so much better for you.

You have nothing to lose (except for pain, heartache, bitterness, anxiety, depression etc.) and everything to gain.

August 17

Ray and I were on a little getaway in New York. We were staying at a hotel close to the center of town. The second morning we were there, very early I might add, the fire alarm began to sound in the building. I looked at him and he looked at me. Are you serious?

Is this for real?

We laid our heads back down. Staring at the ceiling, we decided it might be a good idea to go down to the lobby and see if this is a real emergency. We got presentable. I checked my hair and looked at yesterday's makeup. Should I do something before I scare someone? Too tired to care I decided to wait. But I could use a cup of coffee. I opted for a water instead. Now, which shoes should I wear? After overcoming my indecisiveness, I chose my comfortable walking shoes. We moseyed out the door. At the end of the hall we encountered an older gentlemen who apparently just woke up and heard the alarm. He was disheveled. His glasses were half falling off his face. His hair was sticking straight up. He was harried and coming to that elevator with purpose. I was chuckling in inside. Mockingly, I thought he was overreacting. We rode the same elevator, but not with the same attitude. On the way down he expressed his concern that there was a real fire. When the elevator opened I began to think he may be spot on. The lobby was bustling with firemen. It was a chaotic scene. My attitude changed quickly. We were ushered outside. The bellman told us the firemen were indeed there to check for a fire. This wasn't a false alarm. After some time elapsed we did eventually get to go back up to our room. It was only something minor.

But what if it wasn't?

I began to think about my response to the alarm. I was nonchalant; even a bit indifferent. There are times I have this same attitude with God. He sounds the alarm of my conscience.

Don't say that. Don't go there. Don't do that. But I really don't see what the big deal is so I keep on. I don't consider the consequences. I don't see anything wrong with it.

God sees what lies ahead. He is trying to protect us.

Or He will sound an alarm signaling He wants me to do something. I am slow to carry out his request. I decide to get to it when I get to it. He may ask me to write a letter, make a phone call or any number of things. I wonder what people will think of me?

I thought back to the elderly gentleman.

He had a sense of urgency.

Concern was all over his face.

He was not in slow motion.

He was serious.

He wasn't concerned about his appearance at all.

I need to echo his response. When God sounds the alarm I need to get moving. No matter what the situation is, I need to take it seriously. I also shouldn't be concerned about what other people think.

I should run and not look back.

Hebrews 12:1...let us lay aside every weight, and the sin which so easily ensnares us, and let us run with endurance the race that is set before us...

August 18

Numbers 9:23 At the command of the LORD they remained encamped (KJV rested), and at the command of the LORD they journeyed; they kept the charge of the LORD...

When we experience those long days of waiting, we are to be resting.

The root word of "encamped" means grace.

By His grace, He has you here for a reason.

Stick it out. Right here.

This place may be challenging, difficult, overwhelming.

God does understand.

To be anywhere else would be out of His will.

He led you here.

Whether for a day, week or year.

Rest in His grace.

Rest and praise Him.

So often we miss what God has for us in the here and now. We're so caught up planning our next move. Trying to get to the next place we miss the moment. Those soft rosy cheeks that need a tender kiss won't always be there. In those days of being single, the solitude can seem so long. Enjoy the extra time you have with the Lord. Savor it. It may not always be there. Even when illness strikes, we can't wait for it to be over.

Rest.

God has something to say to you.

At the commandment of the LORD they rested...

Is there a respite in the work?

God is our respite.

He is our Resting Place.

God help me to be content where you have me. Show me how to embrace Your grace. Wrap me up in arms. I need Your mercy. This is a hard place. I know you have me here for a very specific purpose. Use me in this season. Be exalted in my life. You are Lord.

August 19

Sometimes we seem to linger in a place for a long time.

Change isn't coming.

Numbers 9:19 Even when the cloud continued long, many days... Whether it was two days, a month, or a year, the[y]... would remain encamped and not journey...

Even when nothing changes. Endure.

Same scenery.

Same bad situation.

It can be exhausting.

Stay put. Don't give up.

Just like a long winter, the clouds keep coming. Every time you see one, I pray you see it as a visible reminder that God is with you in this.

You are not alone.

He is in the misty gray.

Hovering.

The delays are His plan.

Don't move ahead without Him.

Pray.

Don't faint.

Stand firm.

Stand strong.

God has you here for a reason.

Don't give up on that person, dream or situation.

Your God is coming.

Habakkuk 2:3... Though it tarries, wait for it; because it will surely come...

August 20

Matthew 14:24 But the boat was now in the middle of the sea, tossed by the waves, for the wind was contrary. About three o'clock in the morning Jesus came toward them, walking on the water. When the disciples saw him walking on the water, they were terrified... But Jesus spoke to them at once. "Don't be afraid," he said. "Take courage. I am here!"

Contrary means opposite in nature, direction, or meaning.

Sometimes things don't go as we expected. In fact, they go exactly opposite.

NLT Meanwhile, the disciples were in trouble far away from land, for a strong wind had risen, and they were fighting heavy waves.

It was about 3 o'clock in the morning. It was pitch black out. They were in the middle of a monsoon. It is bad enough being in the middle of a storm on land, but being on the water is twice as bad. There is nowhere to take shelter. A small fishing boat would be tossed about mercilessly.

They were all alone.

No one knew they were even out there.

Would they make it?

Sometimes we can feel like that.

Does anyone know what I'm going through?

This ship is sinking.

It doesn't look good.

There is no help on the horizon.

Jesus came to Peter.

He called Peter to get out of the boat. Walk on the water. He actually walked on the water.

It was only when he took his eyes off of Jesus that he began to sink.

When we begin to look at the waves of our circumstance we become overwhelmed with doubt. That's when we begin to go under.

Keep your eyes fixed on Jesus. He will walk on the waves of this storm with you. Don't be afraid. You God will see you through.

August 21

Why was my child born with Autism?

What have I done to deserve this? Have I sinned? What is it? I need to know so I can make it right. Is this all some big accident? Do you see what I'm going through? What is the purpose of all of this?

Five years ago I was flat on my face crying out to God with these questions. All the while, He was crying out to me, "I made Him like this."

But, why?

I begged to know why.

If only I could know.

After many months of deep anguish I found the answer.

John 9:2-3 His disciples asked Him, saying, "Rabbi, who sinned, this man or his parents, that he was born blind?" Jesus answered, "Neither this man nor his parents sinned, but that the works of God should be revealed in him.

God wanted to display His Power. He saw fit to do that through Autism.

If He could get the most praise by healing Camden, then that's what He would do. If He could get the most praise by not healing him, then that's what He would do.

While I knew in my heart it was not His will to heal Camden, I prayed a little prayer one day asking God to heal him, if indeed it was His will.

I already knew the answer. I was just going through the motions. A formality really. Like checking a box.

It was not God's will for Camden to be healed.

I found out I would need Him more than I ever had in my whole life.

I felt so unequipped to deal with this. I knew nothing about Autism.

But that is how God would get the praise for everything.

Then the LORD asked Moses, "Who makes a person's mouth? Who decides whether people speak or do not speak, hear or do not hear, see or do not see? Is it not I, the LORD?"

God made Camden. He didn't make a mistake. His disability was not an accident. God chose me to have this child. He would equip me to deal with all of his special needs.

I would have to depend on Him every step of the way.

God made Camden different. He didn't want him to be like everyone else.

He made you different as well. He has a very specific purpose in mind.

Isaiah 55:8 My ways are not your ways...

This is not what I would have chosen for his life. But I would not change a thing. Camden is so precious. He is a priceless gift that I would not return for anything.

You are not a mistake.

You are a treasure of the Creator of the universe. He loves you immensely. He wants to use you to bring Him praise.

Celebrate that fact today!

August 22

The Christian life is one of waiting.

What are you waiting for?

I'm reminded of Zacharias and Elizabeth. They were waiting for many years to have a child. Their prayers seemed to go unanswered. They were old; many years past the time when it was feasibly possible. Gabriel, an angel of the Lord appeared to Zacharias. He basically told him 3 things:

Don't be afraid.

Your prayer is heard.

I will give you what you asked for.

Luke 1:20 "But behold, you will be mute and not able to speak until the day these things take place, because you did not believe my words which will be fulfilled in their own time."

The prayer would be fulfilled; just not yet. Therefore God chose to make him unable to speak until that time. Why was that?

Zacharias immediately responded by presenting the impossibility of the situation.

I do it all the time. I look at the outward circumstances and doubt floods in.

Sometimes it's best for us to just be quiet.

Our doubt can cause others to doubt.

Discouragement is contagious.

Gabriel came from heaven and spoke to Zacharias. He told him straight up what was going to take place. He was a messenger of God. Yet Zacharias still questioned. And hey, I'm not down on Zacharias because I know I would've done the same thing. You know what else I would've done? I would've demanded all of the details.

I want to know when.

I want to know how.

And no matter how many details he gave I would've wanted more. That's just me.

Zacharias seemed to say, "Don't you see how old I am?"

He was calculating without God.

Age is not a dynamic that has any bearing on God's plan.

Time is not a factor of any relevance. God is not under our time constraints.

The doctor's prognosis has no merit. God defies doctors every day.

If you are waiting for a prayer to be answered, God is still working on it.

Don't give up.

Your prayer is heard.

God will answer.

It will be at just the right time. Not one day early. Not one day late.

God is always right on time.

Don't look at the impossibility of it happening. The surrounding circumstances are irrelevant to God.

Luke 1:45 "Blessed is she who believed, for there will be a fulfillment of those things which were told her from the Lord."

August 23

"Sometimes your art will only be seen from the sky, from the perspective of heaven." Ann Voskamp

Our art, work, efforts, struggles, hardship, pain and everything in between seem to go unnoticed.

Does anyone see?

Do they care?

That writing you spent days pouring your heart into. It may never get published. No one may read it. It was your love letter to God. It touched Him.

He sees.

The many prayers quietly lifted for that loved one are unseen to the world. They are moving mountains.

He sees.

Those dirty diapers you're changing may never end. He's 10 now. Not one soul knows what that's like for you. You are faithfully raising a soul for Him.

He sees.

Your world may be filled with pain. No one knows the extent.

He sees.

All the hours given selflessly to an elderly parent may go ignored by the family. God sees your labor of love.

The road may seem so long.

God hasn't lost sight of you. He sees you.

One day you will hear Him say those precious words, "Well done, good and faithful servant."

August 24

Recently our friends renewed their vows in celebration of their 25th wedding anniversary. Ray was performing the ceremony and the children were invited to come as well. Camden waltzed in and sat right in the middle, nearly up front. His friends were in the same spot. They each had their handheld electronic games in tow. My Mommy alarm started ringing immediately. I knew he would not be able to sit the entire time his Dad was speaking. There was no way he could be quiet that long. He just isn't mature enough to sit still for an extended period.

I got his attention and called him over. He came.

I whispered, "You have to stay with me. You have to listen to your Daddy."

He reluctantly plopped down next to me.

John 15:4 "Abide in Me, and I in you. As the branch cannot bear fruit of itself, unless it abides in the vine, neither can you, unless you abide in Me.

Abide means to remain, to be present, and to be held.

God wants us to remain in His Presence. Be all there.

That is so difficult.

There is no other place we need to be though. We are drawn away by the littlest things. The news is at our fingertips. Facebook is always buzzing. The Twitter feed is moving.

We have to strive to put everything aside and come into His Presence.

Staying there is what proves difficult.

We do have things to do and places to go. But that doesn't mean we can't remain in His Presence. Our physical position is irrelevant. It's our spiritual state that He's concerned about. He wants our hearts to be open to hearing from Him all day long. There are so many things competing for our attention.

What if we responded to God as quickly as we do to our text messages?

We have to discipline ourselves. It takes practice. I'll put this challenge out to you. Try to spend the entire day focused on Jesus. Ask Him to keep His hand over you and speak to your heart.

Turn off the computer!

Put the phone down!

Come on you can do it!

Your Heavenly Dad has something to say and you truly don't want to miss it!

August 25

As a Pastors wife it's easier for me to write a message than to actually live it out.

Is God who I tell you He is?

I know He's working on your behalf, but what about me? Does He know where I'm at? Can He see what I'm struggling with? Why is He answering your prayer and not mine? Does He hear me? How is He going to fix this?

All of these questions were emanating from my heart one morning.

Then I was reminded of the night before.

Camden woke up screaming. He was crying uncontrollably.

He needed me and I came running.

How much more will my Heavenly Father come running to meet me?

Is God who I tell you He is?

Absolutely.

There is a real God who cares about me, His daughter. He is holding me in His hands. He isn't going to let me go. He is right in the middle of where I'm at. He sees me; even when I can't see Him.

I don't have to be afraid.

These are God's problems to solve, not mine.

I don't have to have all of the answers. I don't need to know how He will fix this. I just need to trust that He hears my cries and is coming to my rescue.

He began this. He will finish it.

I only need to look back at where I've come from. Look at all that He has done for me. He will surely do it again. I don't have to know how. I only need to believe that He will.

God will do the same for you.

Matthew 17:20... if you have faith as a mustard seed, you will say to this mountain, 'Move from here to there,' and it will move; and nothing will be impossible for you.

August 26

Psalm 46:4-5 There is a river whose streams shall make glad the city of God, the holy place of the tabernacle of the Most High. God is in the midst of her, she shall not be moved; God shall help her, just at the break of dawn.

Everything may be falling apart around you. You may not understand what is happening. The future might look uncertain. Every familiar thing may be gone.

You will not fall.

God is your stability.

God is that stream. He is watering us from within. He is our reason to hope. The living God is flowing forth from within allowing us to trust despite what it may look like.

All of our circumstances may change. But our God never changes.

He gives us the ability to worship in the midst of even the most dire conditions.

We worship God for who He is, not for what He gives.

Our soul is secure.

We can stand up and endure.

He is right in the middle of where we are.

Philippians 1:6... being confident of this very thing, that He who has begun a good work in you will complete it...

He began it. He's in the middle of it. And He will finish it.

God will be faithful to the end.

If you need physical energy today, He is the Living God in the midst of you who will strengthen you for the work He has called you to do. If your need is emotional stability, He is in the center of where you are. His strong hands holding you steady. Should you need spiritual support, He is on the inside. Filling you with wisdom. Giving you the words to speak. Keeping you silent when that's necessary.

He is in the midst of us. Everywhere we go. Everything we do.

In the middle of it all.

August 27

My lovely little hydrangea had me so worried. I planted her a few years ago. I had such great plans for her. I was so disappointed in her last summer. She did not blossom at all. Not even one bloom.

She had brown spots all over her. A sure sign of disease. She seemed wilted all the time.

I actually thought I might have to dig her up.

I almost gave up on her.

I'm glad I waited. She ended up blooming. It was almost fall when she did.

There is yet hope.

God always surprises me!

He can do anything!

At any time!

This is just a glimpse.

Time and seasons are in His hands.

Romans 4:17...God...creates new things out of nothing.

He can soften a hard heart.

Heal a marriage.

Return a wayward child.

He can take a life and turn it around.

Just when you wonder if God is even hearing your prayers.

He is always doing something behind the scene. Underneath the surface.

So when you least expect it.

Expect it.

Nothing is too hard for the Lord.

Ephesians 3:20 Now to Him who is able to do exceedingly abundantly above all that we ask or think...

Are you waiting for a breakthrough?

Psalm 27:14 Wait on the Lord; be of good courage and He shall strengthen your heart. Wait I say on the Lord.

Nothing and no one is out of His reach.

Ever.

Some things just take a little longer than others.

August 28

Camden came bursting into my office with an urgency not to be dismissed.

He was a bit panicked, shouting, "Mom come quick. There's a going up and down. A board. A board."

Me: "Do you mean there's a loose board on the deck?"

Camden: "Yes. Does that mean are whole house is gonna fall apart?"

Me: "No. Do you know why? Our house has a strong foundation. Do you know what that is?"

Camden: "Jesus."

Not the answer I was going for, but better nonetheless.

Are some things falling apart in your life?

A few loose boards?

Some stuff you thought secure, but finding out otherwise?

Every worldly thing may be taken: job, house, car, school, friendship, but my future is secure. My house is built on a Rock that nothing can break.

Psalm 18:2

The LORD is my rock and my fortress and my deliverer;

My God, my strength, in whom I will trust...

No storm, tempest, tidal wave, nor fire can destroy.

You know that.

Do your kids know that? Do your kids know that they have a Savior who can keep them safe when trouble comes? Do they know they have a big God who can handle big problems?

Do they see their Mom and Dad pray? Do they see Mom and Dad reading their Bible?

When everything fell apart in my life, I found out I could trust God.

If this earthly tent does go, we have a home eternal in the heavens.

No one and nothing can take that away.

August 29

This is the story of a sweet little peach. She was beautiful in the store. Perfect in every way. At least that's the way she appeared. As I look down at her she is rotting away. I paid a high price for her. She was worth it. After all, I had big plans for her. She was going to top my yogurt and make it extra special.

But there is a problem.

Mold is growing on her. Couldn't notice at first. After a day or two the mold became very obvious though.

It is taking over my sweet little peach.

Sin acts in much the same way in our lives.

At first you may think it's no big deal. You aren't hurting anyone. Perhaps it's just a little thought; merely a little veering off the path.

But then it grows.

Before you know it, it is taking over.

It never stays the same. It always grows.

It has to be dealt with right away.

What should I do with this sweet little peach? I feel so let down.

That's what sin does; it always disappoints.

It always over promises and under delivers.

God has paid a high price for you. He gave His only Son to die a death that you deserved. You were worth it. He took your place so you wouldn't have to pay the penalty.

Should you continue on in your sin?

Romans 6:1-2 What shall we say then? Shall we continue in sin that grace may abound?

Certainly not!

God is love. And because He is love, He is just.

There are consequences to sin.

Galatians 6:7 Do not be deceived: God cannot be mocked. A [wo]man reaps what [s]he sows.

I assure you if you cut that sin off right now, God will run to meet you. The only place you ever see God in a hurry is when He is running to meet a sinner who has come to his senses.

I bet you're wondering if I was able to save my sweet little peach. Believe it or not I was. I only had to cut the bad part off. I'm glad I did it right away. It really was that simple. My sweet little peach was still useable and able to fulfill the purpose for which I bought her. But I had to do it that day. If I had waited any longer I don't know what would've happened.

I'm so glad I didn't wait.

August 30

It was a perfect morning. The air was crisp and cool. Not a drop of rain in sight. A brisk wind was blowing. I was immediately captivated by the moon. It was brighter than usual. Surrounded by clouds, its light whispered a soft melody. It was radiant. I seemed to drift off in thought and not even 5 minutes later it was gone. Where did it go? Black clouds moved in. They swallowed up my beautiful sky.

Our life can go that way sometimes.

Everything is going perfect one minute and the next it's falling apart. It may be the worst thing that you've ever gone through. What good could possibly come from this? We may wonder why this is happening.

I did.

When Camden was first diagnosed everything went black. My life literally had no color. I saw no purpose for any of it. I could not see God in any of it. I found out He was there the whole time. Even when I couldn't see Him, He was there. Now several years later I realize God allows pain in our lives so we can know He is the pain reliever. He allows everything to fall apart so that He can pick up all the broken pieces and put them back together. He makes something beautiful out of it.

He can fix it all.

Even though you may see no purpose for it right now, God is doing something you can't imagine. He will use this "thing" in your life in ways you never thought possible.

Although I couldn't see the moon, it was still there.

God is still there. He hasn't left. He is with you. He'll see you through this.

You can trust Him.

Isaiah 41:10... there's no need to fear for I'm your God.

I'll give you strength. I'll help you.

I'll hold you steady, keep a firm grip on you.

August 31

2 Samuel 16:1 When David was a little past the top of the mountain, there was Ziba the servant of Mephibosheth, who met him with a couple of saddled donkeys, and on them two hundred loaves of bread, one hundred clusters of raisins, one hundred summer fruits, and a skin of wine.

David is exhausted. He is worn out. Tired. Exasperated. He is struggling.

I want to point out the source of his exhaustion; it's his son.

Can you relate?

Oh, don't get me wrong, David loved his son. His son was precious to him; but this child was wearing him out.

When David was a little past the top of the mountain, there was Ziba. He shows up with all kinds of help. He brings bread. Clusters of raisins. A massive amount of fresh fruit.

Our equivalent?

Ziba shows up with Starbucks. He brings homemade chocolate chip cookies. Chocolate almond bark. Ben and Jerry's New York Super Fudge Chunk. In case you've never had that, it's more chocolate!

Maybe today you feel like you are climbing a mountain, and may never reach the top.

Your struggles don't seem to end. It feels like your patience is being tried like never before.

Exhaustion can be an understatement.

Our Lord knows you are tired. He sees you.

Ziba comes at just the right time. In the nick of time.

We should take note where it was that Ziba met him: It was just over the top of the mountain.

If David had turned back, he would not have met up with Ziba. He would not have found the refreshment. He wouldn't have received that special surprise.

Can I encourage you with that today?

Don't quit. Keep pressing on! Keep going. There is a reward!

David wasn't expecting that special surprise.

He is met on the road.

Our God is going to meet us on the road we find ourselves.

Maybe you have some unfinished work to complete. A challenging child to take care of. A distant husband. A lonely evening ahead.

God is going to meet you on this road.

You may feel maxed out.

God is going to meet you on this road.

He is going to surprise you. The love of God is so surprising sometimes. We know God loves the whole world. But when it comes to us, sometimes we can feel a little slighted. Sometimes our struggles make us question. Where are you God? Do you see me?

But then God just shows up in a big way, usually in something small. Some small little token whispers to our heart, "I love you with an everlasting love." You know deep down it could only be God.

God has never taken His eyes off of you. Not even once. He knows you're tired.

David couldn't see over the top of that mountain. He didn't know what awaited him.

He couldn't see the fruit that was lying ahead.

Nor can you. Keep going.

God is going to meet us on this road. Help is on the way.

Lord fill me with your grace to keep going. Meet me today. Breathe life into these dry thirsty bones. Refresh my soul. Overflow my heart with hope. Show Yourself to me in some small way. A token for good. You are so faithful. I know you called me to this work. You will finish what You began.

September

September 1

"Mommy lets go to the church where it's safe."

As we were preparing to leave for our neighborhood outreach a storm came out of nowhere. Rumblings of thunder penetrated our quiet house. I opened the front door to check out the sky; it was dark and ominous. I scurried to the back to look out the window. Just then a lightning bolt lit up the afternoon sky. Our house literally shook from the boom that resounded. Camden saw the panic in my eyes. I ordered him to the basement, but realized I had left my phone upstairs. I ran to get it. He followed closely behind demanding to know what I was doing. I explained I wanted to get my phone in case there was a fire. That set off all sorts of alarm bells in his mind. We made it to the basement. Camden was very upset. I scared him. He no longer felt safe. He timidly asked, "Is our house on fire?" I assured him it wasn't. But that wasn't enough. He asked repeatedly.

After about a half an hour passed he had stated, "Mommy let's go to the church where it's safe."

He knows there is safety within those walls. Church offers him a refuge from the world.

I went upstairs to check the status of the storm. The rain slowed to a drizzle so I decided to head out to the church; mostly because he asked.

We spent some time there. The rain subsided. On the way home those questions were still weighing heavy on his heart.

"Mommy is our house on fire?"

The momma in me wanted to immediately tell him with absolute certainty that our house was not on fire. But the fact remained; I didn't know for sure.

Bad things do happen.

Storms do come.

Lightning does strike.

Things do fall apart.

But we know the One who can put it all back together.

Children need to know they have a Savior that is strong. They need to know He is able to deliver them when nothing and no one else can. They need to know when everything else lets them down; Jesus never fails. When their world falls apart, and inevitably it will, there is a God who has all of the answers.

As he was searching for affirmation, he half asked and half exclaimed, "Mommy our house is strong."

Our house is strong. It has a firm foundation. But it is not indestructible. It is not immune from the storms. It may fall. But this I know:

2 Samuel 22:3 My God is my rock, in whom I find protection. He is my shield, the power that saves me, and my place of safety. He is my refuge, my savior, the one who saves me from violence.

He is the only stable thing in our lives.

By the grace of God our house was still standing when we returned. But if it were not, I assured him that we could trust our God to rebuild.

God, be our rock and our fortress. You and only you are our firm foundation. We look to You to be underneath all that we are. You are the stability that we so desperately need. Deliver us and save us from anything that would come against this knowledge. We love and trust You Jesus.

September 2

My morning is not complete without my coffee. I can't do anything without it. One of the longest parts of the day is waiting for it to brew. So when I first heard about the Keurig I was excited. It held such promise. A fresh hot cup of coffee in less than one minute.

I was so disappointed.

I've had my Keurig for over a year now. I like the idea of it. But, every time I make a cup of coffee I feel let down. It only gives me a half a cup.

It should be full.

John 2:7...Fill...them to the brim.

That is exactly what God desires for us. He wants us to be filled to the brim. That's tough sometimes. Our circumstances are trying.

People let us down. Illnesses come. Friends frustrate us. Hard times fall.

Regardless of our circumstances, we can be brimming over with joy. Our joy doesn't reside in outward circumstances. It resides in the faithfulness of our God.

He will never leave us lacking.

Our God never disappoints. Don't settle for less.

He always delivers.

He will never leave you feeling empty.

He fills with a joy that no one can take away. It is not fleeting.

It is lasting.

It's exactly what you're looking for.

Don't get me wrong; I still like my Keurig. It's just not as good as my tried and true coffee pot.

If I want to be filled I know where to go. .

I go to my God who gives lasting joy. Peace that surpasses understanding. That's when my cup is overflowing. Yours will be too.

Lord overflow my cup today. Fill me with more of You. Remind me of how much You love me. I thank You for Your unfailing love. Spill your grace upon my life. I pray that all Your love would overflow from my heart onto others. You make me full. Nothing else will do. Be near to me today God. I love you so much.

September 3

Isaiah 63:3 "I have trodden... alone... no one was with me."

There comes a time in every woman's life when she must walk alone.

She is alone, but not without her God.

He is with her.

A hiding place in times of trouble.

God often wants to speak to her, but He can't until she is alone.

He wants to flow a message deep into her heart. Many times He has to get her isolated first.

It's only while she is alone that He can speak and she will hear.

No other voice will do.

When my world fell apart, God called me to come away from everything and everyone. But it was Him I was coming to.

He fed me morsels of bread from His word that sustained me each morning. In the evening, His word fed my soul with good things.

I don't understand how God's word strengthens us, but it does. I found I couldn't live without it. It became my life. I needed His word to give me the courage to step out into the darkness. While it was still night, I could take that step into the unknown because I knew He was with me.

He would get me through that dark night and many more that followed.

I learned to trust Him. And you can trust him too.

He will get you through to the end. He won't leave you.

Jesus I ask you to speak to me today. I need to know that You are with me. Assure my heart. Take all my fears. Replace them with Your promises. You are staying. You aren't going anywhere. Help me to step out into the dark night. I know You will guide my steps. Give me a word to stand on and cling to. I ask this in Your matchless name.

September 4

Revelation 3:20 "Look! I stand at the door and knock. If you hear my voice and open the door, I will come in, and we will share a meal together as friends."

Jesus is near. He is at the door.

Can I ask you a question? When you're having company over for dinner and you hear them knocking, are you like me rushing around in a flurry of activity? You're paying attention to every detail. You're not leaving anything undone.

You want everything perfect.

If Jesus Christ showed up at my door this afternoon and looked me in the eye and said, "Renee, I have a job for you to do. Can you do it?"

I would be on it immediately.

My life would come to a screeching halt.

All of my thoughts would be consumed with how to please Him.

I want to do a good job. Doing anything less would be out of the question.

2 Samuel 24:24...[I will not give God] that which costs me nothing.

I want to pour myself into every detail. God has given me a job to do.

He has given you a job to do.

God wants us to devote all of our time, energy and all of our effort into accomplishing this job for Him.

Giving less is not an option.

Why?

1 Corinthians 10:31... whatever you do, do it all for the glory of God.

I'm doing it because I love Him. This is for Him. My work is for Him.

We must tailor every aspect of our lives to accomplish our tasks.

It may be time to reevaluate some things. You may have too many things on your plate.

We can do a lot of things. But we can't do a lot of things well. We have limits.

God has given us specific jobs to do.

Finish what you started. If you're like me, it is easier to do anything besides what the Lord called me to do. I get sidetracked. More than likely it is easier, more pleasant and preferable to do anything but what the Lord called me to do. It can be mundane, boring and exhausting. We cannot forget it's our mission from the King. Therefore it should be exhilarating! We should be honored, thrilled and taking radical action to complete our task!

John 4:34 Jesus said to them, "My food is to do the will of Him who sent Me, and to finish His work.

September 5

Matthew 26:36 Then Jesus came with them to a place called Gethsemane... He said to them, "My soul is overwhelmed with sorrow to the point of death."

Gethsemane was the place that Jesus was brought right before He was crucified.

He was distraught over His circumstances. The burden of what He had to bear was unimaginable.

Gethsemane means olive oil press. Olives must be crushed to get the essential oil out.

The crushing is necessary. It is the same in our lives as well.

Crushing must come.

Pain is essential.

Yet, who would choose it? Certainly not me.

But I can look back at my own life and say I wouldn't trade it.

Five years ago my son was diagnosed with Autism. I was crushed beyond words. It was only two years ago I enrolled him in public kindergarten. After three months, his teacher spoke words to me that I will never forget. She said, "Mrs. Bollas I don't know if Camden is learning anything. I have no idea whether he can learn at all."

While I adored her and know she did the best she could, I removed him from the school. I began to homeschool him and depend on God and His word alone to work in my child.

My son can learn. He is learning and thriving.

I am so thankful for Autism.

It ended up being the greatest gift I've ever received.

I would've never known the awesome power of God's word if He didn't take me through the crushing; the pressing. No therapy, medication, or intervention can match it.

If today finds you in "Gethsemane" it is not by chance.

These circumstances you so desperately want to get out of will be the place you will see your Savior work.

If you will allow Him, God will use it.

The crushing is essential.

No crushing; no oil.

While it may be the most excruciatingly painful thing you have ever gone through, it will be the most transforming thing spiritually that you have ever experienced.

God help me to go through this painful time of my life. Even when I see no purpose in it, You remind Me Your ways are not my ways. I trust You with my life. Increase my faith. Open my spiritual eyes to see more of You. Help me to give You everything. I love You and bless Your Holy name.

September 6

God has a divine purpose for our lives.

Jeremiah 1:5 Before I formed you in the womb I knew you

God sees the commencing and the completion of everything He does.

He predetermined with His all-knowing sovereignty what it would take to bring us to the end.

Jeremiah 1:6 "O Sovereign LORD," I [Jeremiah] said, "I can't speak for You! I'm too young!"

In the old language we can understand Jeremiah's words to be an expression of grief. He feels overwhelmed by what God is asking of him.

He doesn't want to disappoint Him.

How many times have I been there? I feel overwhelmed by what the Lord has asked me to do.

Jeremiah is giving us a sincere expression of his heart here.

He didn't want to let the Lord down.

He knew, even at this young age, he did not have what it would take to accomplish what God was asking of him.

He was scared, and rightfully so.

Jeremiah 1:8 Don't be afraid. I am with you to deliver you.

Jeremiah was factoring without God.

We do it all the time.

The result: fear.

Fear is not from the Lord. It is from the enemy.

Don't look at the utter impossibility of your task. Keep your eyes fixed on the One who can do anything.

Our God is able to do all the things we can't!

Our confidence is in Him.

Whatever God has called you to do, He will equip you for the task.

Lord You have a very specific purpose for my life. Speak through me. Use me for such a time as this. Take away my fears. Empower me to accomplish what You have called me to do.

September 7

I was feeling gloomy one morning. I decided to go for a walk. It was dark. Everything was quiet and still; except my heart. It was overflowing with anxiety. I was pondering a certain difficult situation. It was so frustrating. Nothing seemed to be changing. It was only getting worse. I'd been praying about it, but still nothing. I began to waver and doubt. Soon I was overwhelmed.

I felt so helpless.

I wanted to do something, but my hands were tied.

I stopped at the house for a moment and then headed back out.

As I looked up, I realized the whole landscape of the sky had changed. The sun rose that quickly.

It was beautiful. Bright orange and yellow. Hints of purple. Magnificent. No darkness at all.

Ecclesiastes 3:11 He makes everything beautiful in His time.

God reminded me: this is just a faint whisper of all that He can do.

Job 26:14... these are the mere edges of His ways...

This is just a glimpse.

He makes the sun rise and set.

If He can do that, He can do anything!

Jeremiah 32:17...There is nothing too hard for You.

What do you need for Him to do for you today?

He is able.

September 8

We brought our new pup home.

He was so scared.

As we drove away I realized he was leaving everything behind. Life as he knew it was over. All he ever knew in his short little life was a cold pen filled with filth. He was exposed to the elements. His life so far was pretty harsh. He was always competing with seven to ten other puppies. He never received the attention he longed for.

He was shaking the whole way. He got very sick. His little whimpers broke my heart.

He had no idea what awaited him.

He'd never experienced unconditional love.

He was made to love and be loved.

Back in that old pen he was missing his purpose.

Ray and I just looked at each other with a knowing.

If he only knew.

We can be afraid of the unknown.

We always want things to stay the same. We need to realize what God has for us is so much better than what we are wallowing in at the moment.

Jeremiah 29:11 For I know the plans I have for you," says the LORD. "They are plans for good and not for disaster, to give you a future and a hope."

The word "hope" in the old language gives us a picture of what I would describe as a cross stitch; something like Gramma used to sew. The back of it is just a bunch of threads all jumbled together in a seeming mess. But the front is a beautiful picture sewn by a caring Maker. Our pup could only see the backside. He would prefer to stay there. He couldn't see the beautiful life that was awaiting him.

It is that way for us sometimes too. Change is difficult to face. Sometimes a new life seems too much to bear. Walking away from it all is tough.

God's plan is so much better than our own.

If we embrace God's plan and surrender to it, our tails will be wagging with delight. We'll be bopping around a new territory filled with exciting new adventures. A loving home beckoning us; if only we'll choose to come.

Dear Jesus, help me go through the changes that You are asking of me. Give me peace. You are my security. Help me to trust you more in the areas that are so uncertain. You are solid. Unchanging. My stability. I need you now more than ever. I thank you from the bottom of my heart that You saved me. Your plan is perfect. I will hope in that.

September 9

Daniel 3:17-18 "If we are thrown into the blazing furnace, the God whom we serve is able to save us...But even if he doesn't..."

Shadrach, Meshach and Abednego knew, trusted, and believed with all of their hearts that their God was able to rescue them, but they also knew it may not be His will for them to avoid the fire.

There are times we pray for healing; it doesn't come.

We plead on behalf of a child; change doesn't come.

We beg for a marriage to be saved; he walks away.

God doesn't always rescue us from the fire.

But, He is always with us in the fire.

If we can see Him, our whole perspective changes.

If you find yourself in the midst of a trial, you can be sure God is right there with you.

These guys didn't know the outcome, but they didn't fear.

They were confident in their God.

You can be too.

Others will see Him through your trial and learn that they can trust Him too.

Often we go through suffering so that we can help someone else.

If you know someone is struggling today, pray for them. Consider sending them a note of encouragement. One verse can change the course of their day. Bake them cookies or even offer to watch their child for a few hours. Small gestures speak volumes to a hurting heart.

If it's you in the fire, God wants you to know through His word that He is with you.

He is there.

He is holding your hand through it all.

You will get through this.

He is your protection.

Jesus hold me a little tighter today. As the fire heats up, increase my faith all the more. Help me to endure. I want to be stronger. Fill me with supernatural strength to face this trial. I love your grace. Overflow me with Your power. I need You.

September 10

The people that Moses was called to lead were complaining and questioning. But, he was just doing what God called him to do.

He was doing the best he could.

Exodus 32:26 Moses stood...and said, "Whoever is on the Lord's side-come to me!"

Some came and some didn't.

The ones who didn't were cut off. This is a great example for us.

There are negative, condescending, and critical people surrounding us every day.

Let go of the negative influences in your life. Don't allow them to take one more ounce of your energy. Don't allow them to steal your joy.

Exodus 32:29 Then Moses said, "Consecrate yourselves today to the LORD that He may bestow on you a blessing this day..."

God has called each one of us to serve him in a unique way.

Consecrate has a surprising meaning here in this verse. In this verse it means to "fill your hands."

It is difficult to "fill your hands" with the things of the Lord if you're still holding on to a bunch of bitterness, anger, resentment, complaining, arguing etc.

Jesus wants all of you. He wants all of your time. If you're spending time complaining about the negative people, it's wasted.

He wants all your energy. If you're allowing these negative thoughts to consume you, you are the one being robbed.

He wants to fill you completely up with His Holy Spirit. There's no room for anything else. The heart and soul of Jesus is to bring glory to His Father. And that should be our goal as well.

Lord God, give me wisdom. Help me to have discernment about the influences I allow in my life. Bring me godly people who will impart life to my soul. Show me who needs to stay and who needs to go. I trust you.

September 11

We taught Camden to call 911. We went over the basics of what to do in case of an emergency. We placed some hard wired phones strategically throughout the house. I wrote my cell phone number on a sheet of paper. Underneath I wrote with a black Sharpie in large bold print:

IN CASE OF EMERGENCY CALL 911.

Camden has some irrational fears. He has never used the phone before. He usually runs away from the phone when you try to get him to talk.

That day was no different. We tried to get him some practice by dialing my personal cell phone number. It took about an hour of coercion, but he did finally dial my cell number.

Much practice was still needed.

A few mornings later we received a knock at the door. Camden ran to the door first.

He exclaimed, "He saw me!"

He ran back to me. I went to the door and to my dismay there was a police officer standing there.

He's looking at me; I'm looking at him. After a few tense moments I decided to speak skittishly, "Good morning, may I help you?"

He asked, "You called 911?"

I was initially bewildered and concluded he had the wrong house. But I quickly realized it was Camden. He decided to call 911 to see what would happen. He wasn't sure how the whole thing worked. He wanted to see if this was for real.

He got the surprise of his life when a police officer actually showed up.

We can do this same thing with God.

Sometimes we want to know if He's real. If you question that, call to Him and ask Him. He really will show you. He doesn't take offense to that. He will happily oblige.

Jeremiah 33:3 Call to Me and I will answer.

He hears us when we call.

He comes when we need Him.

If you're wondering, He's on the way; even if you can't see it.

God shows up.

He'll never let you down. Our God will be there when we call; every time.

You can trust Him.

Reliable. Constant. Dependable. Sure. That's our God.

September 12

Genesis 16:13 Thereafter, Hagar referred to the LORD, who had spoken to her, as "the God who sees me," for she said, "I have seen the One who sees me!"

"I Have seen the One who sees me!"

Hagar found herself all alone. These circumstances were not of her choosing. She had no way to provide for herself, let alone her son that was soon to be born. She had no one to take care of her. She was humili-ated. She was brokenhearted. She was betrayed. Life had become unbear-unbearable. All of her plans had been lost; all her dreams were gone. If things weren't bad enough, the Angel of the Lord delivered the news that, 'This son of yours will be a wild one—free and untamed as a wild donkey! He will be against everyone, and everyone will be against him. Yes, he will live at odds with the rest of his brothers.'

I know firsthand what she was feeling.

Everything she had was taken away. Life as she knew it was over. It would never be the same again.

The Lord allowed Hagar to be brought to this very specific place. It was not by chance or bad luck. God knew what He was doing in her life.

Hagar found herself by a spring of water in the desert. When He spoke, it pierced her heart. Suddenly, the eyes of her understanding were opened. At that moment, rivers of living water gushed forth in this desert. She was saturated with hope. She would make it. Her child would be okay. The Lord said, "I see you. I see where you're going. Now, right here, I want you to see I AM enough for you. I am all that you need." The eyes of her mind were opened. It was as though a veil were lifted. Suddenly a light was shed on the whole situation; it became crystal clear. What did she see? "I have seen the God who sees me!" She saw the Provider, the Supplier, the One who is able to overcome. She saw the One who finds a way when there is no way.

Hagar was frantically trying to escape her present circumstances. I've done this countless times. God ever so gently brings me back. He reas-sures me that He hasn't lost sight of me. I may have taken my eyes off of Him, but He never takes His eyes off of me. He is right here.

Surely my own child has caused me to say, "I have seen the God who sees me."

How about you? Do you find yourself withdrawing? Have you found yourself in the barren desert? Sometimes God allows us to go so far down so that all we can do is look up. It's then that those torrents of living water rush over our soul. God sees your need.

Faith is trusting when we can't see the way. It's only human to want to see.

Faith is knowing in the deepest part of your soul that "nothing is impossi-ble with God."

Hebrews 11:1 Now faith is being sure of what we hope for and certain of what we do not see.

"You never realize Jesus is all you need until Jesus is all you have." Corrie Ten Boom

If God takes everything away, you still have Him.

Song of Solomon 2:16 My Beloved is mine, and I am His.

God I pray that You will open my eyes to see that well of living water. Flood my soul with this living water. Saturate the depths of my pain. Soothe my aching heart. Give me hope once again. Help me to go through this change. Fill my heart with faith. Let me know you are near. If You take everything away, I am still Yours.

September 13

I go for a walk with the Lord every morning. The weeks immediately following the diagnosis were no different. I went for my walk every day. I usually like to spend that time praying. But now I could not find words to pray, only sobs. God's heart is moved by a mother's cry. I believe the Holy Spirit cried right alongside me. He interceded on my behalf when I could not find the words. I felt His presence. I heard Him speak. He asked me a piercing question, "Am I who you tell people I am?"

I was brought to a crossroads. Is Jesus Christ who He says He is?

John 4:49-50 The nobleman said to Him "Sir, come down before my child dies!" Jesus said to him, "Go your way; your son lives." So the man believed the word that Jesus spoke to him, and he went his way.

Perhaps the man heard what Jesus had already done; He turned water into wine. This man knew where to turn for help. I knew where to turn for help. In his desperation he knew he could turn to Jesus. But, Jesus perceived this man was looking to see the proof of His action right then and there. Jesus said to him, "Unless you see signs and wonders, you won't believe." No sign was given. Jesus said, "Go," and he went. That had to be very difficult; even agonizing. Doubts and fear certainly must have swept over him. This situation brought him to a crossroads. Is Jesus Christ who He says He is?

Can He do what I need Him to do? Can He fix this?

Sometimes we have to go our way, not physically seeing the answer.

"Nothing is impossible with God."

If you're like me you don't want to move on without some visible answer. I want to know how this is all going to work out. As women we want to see the proof. We want it done right now. We want action. We want to make it happen. We don't want to wait. We don't like waiting. When I don't see immediate results my faith starts to waver. Jesus told him, "Go your way..."

He told me the same thing. Keep going.

Press on.

Don't waver between opinions of who I am.

Don't come to a halt spiritually.

"So the man believed the word that Jesus spoke to him, and he went his way."

This man believed. He thought Jesus' words were true. He was persuaded Jesus was able to do what He said He would do. He placed all of his confidence, conviction and trust in His Word.

Doubts, fear, and unbelief go hand in hand. They bring turmoil. We are tormented by scenarios that never happen. A lack of faith is at the bottom of all fear. Maybe you come before the Lord today and you have no faith.

Ask Him for some!

James 4:2 You have not because you ask not.

Faith delivers us from all of these things. We are not consumed.

What is faith?

Hebrews 11:1 Faith is being sure of what we hope for and certain of what we do not see

Faith gives us the ability to wait although all outward appearances seem grim and unlikely to turn out well.

Faith brings us three things: confidence, hope, and perseverance.

Ask for confidence!

Philippians 1:6 being confident of this very thing, that He who began a good work in you will complete it...

Jesus Christ began a good work in my son the day he was born. I am confident He will complete it.

Psalm 118:8 It is better to trust in the Lord than to put your confidence in man.

1 John 5:14 Now this is the confidence we have in Him, that if we ask anything according to His will, He hears us

Ask for hope.

Psalm 39:7 And now, Lord, what do I wait for? My hope is in you!

Psalm 119:114 You are my hiding place and my shield; I hope in your Word.

Jeremiah 17:7-8 Blessed is the [wo]man who trusts in the Lord, whose hope is the Lord. For [s]he will be like a tree planted by the waters, which spreads out its roots by the river. And will not fear when heat comes; but its leaf will be green, and will not be anxious in the year of drought, nor will it cease from yielding fruit.

Ask for perseverance!

James 1:2-3 Consider it pure joy my [sister] whenever you face trials of many kinds because you know the testing of your faith develops perseverance. Perseverance must finish its work so that you may be mature and complete, not lacking anything.

Today if you find yourself weary from waiting, don't sink back, don't be disheartened and withdraw! Remember the power of the Living Word. It will breathe new life into your very being!

September 14

Jeremiah 17:7-8 "But blessed are those who trust in the LORD and have made the LORD their hope and confidence. For [s]he shall be like a tree planted by the waters, Which spreads out its roots by the river, And will not fear when heat comes; But its leaf will be green, And will not be anxious in the year of drought, Nor will cease from yielding fruit.

How I long to be a woman of power! I desire to be that "tree planted by the rivers of water".

There is a surefire way to be just that:

Psalm 1:2-3 H[er] delight is in the law of the Lord, and in His law [s]he meditates day and night. [S]he shall be like a tree planted by the rivers of water that brings forth its fruit in its season, whose leaf also shall not wither; and whatever [s]he does will prosper.

It is the Word of God that brings the power we so desperately need. If you want to be a powerful woman of God you must daily spend large amounts of time feeding your soul with God's Word. Nothing will bring such effective results in your walk.

Hebrews 4:12 For the word of God is full of living power.

Here are just a few things the Word of God produces in your life:

The Word of God feeds your faith.

Romans 10:17 Faith comes by hearing, hearing by the Word of God.

A baby cannot grow as she should without proper nutrition. A Christian woman cannot grow in her faith without deep, frequent and long times spent in God's Word.

The Word of God brings wisdom.

Psalm 119:24 Your testimonies are my delight and my counselors.

When I need advice the first place I need to run to is God's Word. I need to seek His Word before I speak to anyone else. A Word from the Lord is solid guidance I can rely on.

The Word of God reveals the truth.

John 8:31-32 If you abide in My word,...you shall know the truth, and the truth shall make you free.

The influence of the world and Satan bombards us. Truth is no longer black and white. It becomes gray and dull; not so when you are immersed in God's word. Satan is the father of lies. God's word silences the lies, and frees us from his control.

The Word of God gives strength.

Psalm 119:28 My soul melts with heaviness; strengthen me according to your Word.

When facing challenges that seem insurmountable, God's Word gives me the will to rise up and endure. It fills me with determination to continue on steadfastly.

The Word of God brings peace.

Psalm 85:8 I will hear what God the Lord will speak: He will speak peace to His people.

God's Word will bring quiet and tranquility to our heart, despite outward circumstances. When our hearts are fainting, only a Word from the Lord can completely remove anxiety and fear.

The Word of God brings lasting joy.

Jeremiah 15:16 Your Words were found, I ate them, Your Word was joy and rejoicing in my heart.

Nothing kindles joy in a woman's heart like the Word of God. Nothing this world has to offer can even come close.

The Word of God brings wisdom.

Psalm 119:130... the entrance of Your Word gives light; it gives understanding to the simple.

Sometimes we are at a complete loss as to what we should say to our teenager, our friend who is sick, our sister, and sometimes even our own husbands. God's Word brings discernment. It gives us insight into that person's heart that we would not have otherwise.

The Word of God breaks a hard heart.

Jeremiah 23:29 "Is not My Word like a fire?...and like a hammer that breaks the rock in pieces.

Has someone said something or done something to you and you just can't get over it? Are you still angry? Nothing has the power to break that hardened heart like the Word of God.

The Word of God keeps us from sin.

Psalm 119:11 Your Word I have hid in my heart that I might not sin against You.

Don't leave an open door. One day without the Word and Satan is sure to enter. Even Jesus Himself used Scripture to meet and overcome temptation.

The Word of God brings salvation.

If we want to see a person saved we must give them God's Word. We don't need to think of something clever to say. The Holy Spirit takes God's Word and brings it to life in the heart of the hearer.

Dear God, how we so desperately need your Word. Your Word is Power! We want to be women of Power! We want our lives to count for Your Kingdom. We want to be used mightily. Jesus fill us to overflowing with desire for Your Word. Help us to put away every distraction that would take us away from Your Word. By the Power of Your Holy Spirit help us to use Your Word in the lives of others today!

September 15

John 5:6...He said to him, "Do you want to be made well?"

That seems like a rhetorical question; one not meant to be answered.

The answer would seem very obvious.

Who wouldn't want to be made well?

Jesus asked him because he knew there was a part of him that didn't want to do what it would take to be made well. He had to walk away from his sin. We don't know what that sin was. But Jesus was asking for him to give it up.

Sin can become so familiar to us that we become comfortable in it.

Jesus wants to change that.

Change is difficult. Many times it demands a great personal cost. While everyone wants to be well, not everyone wants it bad enough to pay the price.

Are you willing to do what it takes?

The man did not answer. He blamed others. He said, "I have no one to help me."

Jesus said, "Get up."

That's what He says to us.

Get up.

This has kept you down long enough.

Get up. Do this! You don't need anyone's help. You have Me. I am all that you need.

Don't say, "I can't." In doing so, you are essentially saying, "I won't."

Change your mind! Nothing will change in your life until you change your mind.

Philippians 4:13 I can do all things through Christ who strengthens me.

There is nothing you can't do!

This man had come to feel this is the way it would always be. He seemed to be telling Jesus that he can't catch a break.

He was feeling sorry for himself. And the more he looked at himself, the worse he became.

Sometimes that's the way it is with us. We get used to the way things are. Comfortable in chaos.

We don't like change. Even if it's for the better. Change makes us uncomfortable.

We don't like what's required.

Jesus wanted to do more than a physical healing here.

He had some soul work to do.

But it had to start with the renewing of his mind.

This man had a choice to make.

Repent. Change his mind. Agree with Jesus and go in the other direction. Live. Truly live.

Or stay put.

Paralyzed. Unable to move.

Sometimes it's easier to stay where we're at. It takes determination. It takes moment to moment trust in Christ to overcome sin that has held us captive for so long.

He chose to get up and walk.

Hebrews 12:1...let us lay aside every weight, and the sin which so easily ensnares us, and let us run with endurance the race that is set before us...

Your life can change. Today. Do this. Get up and walk. Be free.

September 16

Genesis 5:24 Enoch walked faithfully with God; then he was no more, because God took him away.

We don't know that much about Enoch. It doesn't say Enoch was a great Pastor. Bible scholar. Theologian. President. Dignitary.

He was a prophet though. He spoke for God.

He delivered messages through this man for one reason: he walked with God.

Enoch spoke for God.

He didn't diminish one word. Didn't try to say it nice. Make it palatable.

If you walk with God, you can do that. You don't need to seek the approval of man.

Although he didn't have a title, Enoch was of great use to God.

Don't ever think you're not of great use to God.

If you walk with God, He can use you greatly.

Where are you?

Single? Look around you. If you walk with God, He will give you words of encouragement for other singles. Words to empower you stay pure, and them too.

Sick? Walk with God, He'll be the lifter of your head. Soon enough, you'll be lifting someone else up.

Stay at home mom? Incidentally, Enoch means "dedicated." And the root word of his name means "train up."

Proverbs 6:22 Train up a child in the way he should go, and when he is old he will not depart from it.

If you walk with God, He will enable you to do the most important job in the whole world: be a godly mom who loves Jesus. And who raises up children to know Him and make Him known. That is of great use to God.

Special needs child? If you walk with God, He will fill you with strength to meet the demands of your day with grace.

Enoch lived, moved and had his being in God.

One day he went for a walk and didn't come back. God enjoyed his company so much he took him.

September 17

In the days leading up to his evaluation, the Lord gave me my son Camden's "life verse". His life verse is:

Jeremiah 1:5-6 Before I formed you in your mother's womb I knew you. Before you were born I sanctified you to be a prophet to the nations.

It was a verse that I knew would be significant. It would define who He was in Christ. It is a promise from God that I will cling to for the rest of my life. This verse is prophetic, although I did not know it at the time. I am only beginning to see and understand how this verse defines everything God made him to be. Before he was even a thought in our minds, God knew Camden Graham Bollas deeply and intimately. He knew what his strengths would be; likewise he knew what his weaknesses would be.

Exodus 4:10 Moses said to the LORD, "O my Lord, I am not eloquent, neither before nor since You have spoken to Your servant; but I am slow of speech and slow of tongue."

Here is the Lord's reply, "Who has made man's mouth? Or who makes him dumb or deaf, or seeing or blind? Is it not I, the Lord?"(Exodus 4:11)

This verse transformed my perspective. Autism is not an accident. God allowed it. God did not make a mistake. Camden was created with a purpose. Only he can fulfill that purpose. God will use his imperfections to bring glory to His name.

Psalm 139:13 You made all the delicate, inner parts of my body and knit me together in my mother's womb. I will praise You, for I am fearfully and wonderfully made; Marvelous are Your works, And that my soul knows very well.

When God looks at Camden He is in awe. Camden takes His breath away.

John 9:2-3... his disciples asked him, "Why was this man born blind? Was it a result of his own sins or those of his parents?"

"It was not because of his sins nor his parents' sins," Jesus answered. "He was born blind so the power of God could be seen in him."

Everyone has not been given the gift of sight. Seeing is a gift. Speaking is a gift. Everyone has not been given the gift of speech. Why? God uses our weaknesses, limitations, and disabilities to magnify His abilities, His strengths and His limitless possibilities.

The greater our weakness, the more we have to depend on Him.

God I thank You for the precious gift of weakness. Thank You for Your faithfulness even when I am faithless. I pray that my life will bring You glory. Every one of Your children bring You joy. They are precious in Your sight. Remind the world that You don't make mistakes. Everything You do has purpose. Every life You create has deep meaning. Thank You for life.

September 18

The Bible is so fascinating. I stand in awe of it. It is so interesting to do a word study on this one simple word: myrrh. Myrrh is our modern day henna. Myrrh has many highly beneficial uses. It is used as a medicine to fight off infections of all kinds. It is an antiseptic, antifungal, and an anti-inflammatory agent. It stimulates white blood cells. White blood cells attack infection.

There are things that constantly attack our lives and infect them with despair.

Illness, pain, and uncertainty just to name a few.

They wreak havoc on our thought lives. Our perspective becomes bleak at best. At worst, hopeless. Our thoughts of despair gather together much like cancer. The blackness grows and grows. It invades every part of our mind. It permeates every ounce of our being. It threatens to consume us.

Myrrh exudes from various trees, such as the Egyptian thorn; within a species found in Arabia. The resin hardens into a bitter gum, of a sweet smell, and valuable. Used in incense (prayers of the saints), myrrh is spontaneously distilled from the tree, and on that account superior.

Throughout the Bible, myrrh is symbolic of prayer. When we go to the mountain, we are brought high above our circumstances. We have a clear view. We do see Jesus. He is there. We feel His Presence. We are filled with the certainty that He is with us. My friends don't have to have the answers. They don't need to say the right words. They simply don't have what I need. My needs are way beyond anyone on this earth. I need the touch of my Jesus; my Master Creator. He made me. He ordained the things in my life before the beginning of time. Yes, He is in control. He is not surprised, nor is He caught off guard. He allowed them. When that knowledge flows through my thoughts, I can have peace. I am no longer a prisoner held captive by my own thoughts. I am set free. The events of my life are happening for His glory.

The need to climb this mountain is daily. It is worth the trek. We could not make it through one day without wrapping our arms around the Savior. We have to do whatever it takes to get there. Our hearts are desperate for hope. Our minds need to be renewed every morning so that we can just get through the day.

God draw me close to You. I am desperate for You. I want to see You. Take me to Your throne of grace. Flood my eyes with hope. Fill my soul with joy. Despite what I can see, I trust You Lord. Lift me up with Your mighty hand. I need You. I can't do anything without You.

September 19

Zephaniah 3:3 Her princes in her are roaring lions, Her judges are evening wolves that leave not a bone till morning.

Satan is a roaring lion with a voracious appetite. He isn't content to wreak a little havoc and be gone. Let's be clear, he wants it all. He wants to destroy your children. He wants to rip your marriage apart. Such a violent attack would appear to be obvious. But, it isn't. He is deceptive. He enters into our thought life. He knows where our weaknesses are. He causes us to question God's goodness. He causes us to take our eyes off God and put them on ourselves. I found this to be especially true when Camden was initially diagnosed. I began to doubt God. I doubted myself. I doubted my husband. My thoughts rambled on. "I can't do this. This isn't fair. I have no future. This is hopeless." I was alone all day. Dealing with life's demands had become no small task. Resentment builds. Frustration mounts. Anger boils over. Who comes strolling through the door fresh as a cucumber? You guessed it, my husband. Satan's timing is impeccable. The "evening wolves" began gnawing away. Biting and devouring until there was nothing left.

I wanted him to know what I've gone through all day long. My doubts and fears were making me miserable. In my house things can go two ways. Either I am seething and he gets the silent treatment or I spout off my list of complaints; badgering and grumbling as though it were his fault. This went on for many weeks.

Proverbs 14:1 A wise woman builds her house; a foolish woman tears hers down with her own hands.

I was tearing our marriage down without even realizing it. He came to me one evening and explained how I was making him feel. After spending time with the Lord, I made a decision. Autism will not steal my marriage. I will fight for it every day. My marriage is worth fighting for. I cannot allow the roaring lion to devour anything more from me. Every thought of doubt morphs into so much more than I ever imagined. Doubt is a toxin that kills. What do we do when these thoughts come? Pray immediately. Prayer purifies. It filters out my contaminated thoughts. It enables me to have a calm, collected spirit when my husband comes home. I can make our home a sanctuary of peace despite what has transpired throughout the day.

Autism can be used one of two ways. In the hand of Satan, Autism will divide and separate. In the hand of God, Autism can unite and strengthen. My marriage is made stronger if I allow God to use it. But, it is a choice. Every day I must choose. I choose love. I choose kind words. I choose to bless my husband. This is not easy. In fact, most days it is a monumental task. How do we do it?

James 4:8 Draw near to God and He will draw near to you. Cleanse your hands, you sinners; and purify your hearts, you double-minded.

Being double-minded means to doubt, and waver back and forth with what you believe and know to be true.

God has used these trials and burdens to build our faith. Our confidence in Him has grown. He has proved faithful every time. Without these trials we would not know that we could trust Him.

Proverbs 3:5 Trust in the Lord with ALL your heart...

Trust fully and completely!

God's grace is all we need. It is more than enough for us.

God please bless my marriage. Fill me with a desire to please this man I am honored to call my husband. Show me how to bring him joy. Use our marriage to bring you glory.

September 20

Autism will present challenges in your marriage unlike any other. A fierce war is being waged. The statistics speak clearly: this war has many casualties.

My marriage will not be one of them! My marriage is worth fighting for!

You are under siege. Your husband and your marriage are under attack.

The battle is on and it there is no place for a weak link.

Proverbs 31:10 Who can find a virtuous and capable wife? She is worth more than precious rubies.

I want to draw your attention to the word "virtuous." This word in the original language paints a picture of a mighty warrior who is strong in valor. A virtuous wife possesses these valiant qualities. Powerful and efficient, she is a force to be reckoned with. This is a snapshot of the wife God created you to be.

The United States Army was created for a very specific purpose. It exists to defend and protect this country. It will defeat any adversary responsible for aggression that endangers the security of this nation.

A wife's duty is much the same. In order to carry out her mission, she must be prepared. She must remain on high alert at all times, lest the enemy enter in by stealth. Knowing the enemies tactics is of the utmost importance. The enemy often tries to enter at night. When darkness falls upon us, we are at a disadvantage. We can't see what lies ahead. Training leading up to the battle is crucial. We can't skip a day. We have to train hard in times of peace in order to remain superior to the enemy.

When a soldier enlists in the army, he submits himself to the authority of his commander-in-chief. His life is not his own. His sole interest lies in the plan and objective of his commander. He cannot deviate from the plan. He must remain submissive to the plan set forth by his commander.

Likewise, God has a plan for our lives. We have to give Him everything. Christ is all or nothing. We can't hold anything back from Him. We can have no self-interest. We have to be prepared to give our life with honor. More often than not I find God's plan is not exactly what I had in mind. My self-interest takes over. It is very destructive. I want to do things my way, but I can't stray from His plan. To do so will be disastrous for my family.

A woman willing to go the distance for her husband is more precious than all the gems this world has to offer.

There's a motto in war: No one gets left behind.

In war, if the enemy infiltrates and captures one of your soldiers, you never abandon him and move on. Quite the contrary, you do whatever it takes to get him back. It's no longer about you, or what you have to endure. You never give up. You fight to the death for his safe return. Quitting is not an option!

The enemy may be holding your husband captive. He may feel defeated in his thought life. Our husbands have suffered great loss too. Although they may express it differently, the pain is ever present. He may be unable to escape. He needs your help. Go and get him!

2 Corinthians 10:3-4 We are human, but we don't wage war with human plans and methods. We use God's mighty weapons, not mere worldly weapons, to knock down the devil's strongholds.

You have an arsenal of weapons at your disposal. However, none are more emphasized by your Master than prayer! All of the armies of heaven are at hand waiting to do battle.

Prayer unleashes the power of heaven!

Jesus, make me a virtuous woman. I long to be a woman of prayer. None of my circumstances are accidental. Help me to bring you glory in what I say, and what I choose not to say. Put a guard on my mouth. Speak to my husband. Speak to my children. Set them free from the strongholds in their lives. Bless the man I am married to. Give me a submissive heart. Help me to honor You by honoring him. Lead him. Guide him. Fill him with Your Holy Spirit. Use us together.

September 21

Luke 11:9 Ask and you shall receive...

Many times we will go anywhere and everywhere seeking help. We will talk to counselors, friends and family. When we still don't find the help were looking for, then we may be desperate enough to ask God. This should not be! Go to Him first! He has all the answers. God is able to do things in your marriage that you never dreamed of. I don't think it is a coincidence that Jesus performed His first miracle at a wedding. Every marriage needs a miracle once in a while!

1 Corinthians 13:7 Love never gives up, never loses faith, is always hopeful, and endures through every circumstance.

Romans 8:35,37 Can anything ever separate us from Christ's love? Does it mean He no longer loves us if we have trouble or calamity, or are perse-cuted, or are hungry or cold or in danger or threatened with death? No, despite all these things, overwhelming victory is ours through Christ, who loved us.

There is a fierce loyalty that is built through love that nothing can divide.

The love of Jesus Christ is able to penetrate the prison bars of iron and walls of steal that have been erected. He is able to disintegrate them.

Surely there will be differences of opinion, squabbles, and friction. We work them out, plain and simple. We don't give up. Jesus Christ never gave up on me!

1 John 4:19 We love Him because He first loved us.

Jesus loved me when I was unlovable. When I was an enemy combatant of the cross, He gave His only Son for me. That is love. Maybe you think your husband doesn't deserve this kind of unconditional love. His actions don't merit grace. When this mindset comes upon me, I am reminded of the sacrifice God was willing to make for me. Since He showed such great love for me, the least I can do is the same. Love proves itself out in action.

The bonds of war forge comrades for life.

September 22

When Camden was first diagnosed I could not gather enough information on autism fast enough. I was like a sponge. I knew nothing about this disability. Knowledge is power. I needed to know what I was up against. I quickly learned even the "experts" don't fully understand it. Autism manifests itself differently in every child. That is why it is called the "autism spectrum". Next I needed to know how to "treat" this disorder. The "experts" can only give you their best guess as to what may work for your child. Something may work for one child, but not another. One of the most frustrating parts of dealing with this diagnosis was finding "therapy". An incredible burden is placed on the shoulders of the parents of autistic children. Even the experts have no concrete solutions.

I was determined to give my child the best there was to offer. Now all I needed to do was to find out what that was.

I diligently searched the Internet for answers. I was exploring all of the newest therapies to treat autism. I spent day after day reading. I went to visit Kennedy Krieger. They are one of the best of the best, and my insurance would pay for Camden to go there. Now I just needed a word of confirmation from the Lord. I needed to hear from him before I could make a decision. He would speak, I was sure of it.

God spoke a verse that would be pivotal in my journey.

Exodus 4:11 Who makes a person's mouth? Who decides whether people speak or do not speak, hear or do not hear, see or do not see? Is it not I the Lord? Now go, I will instruct you in what to say.

God told me to teach Camden! Me? I have no qualifications to teach anyone! I never graduated college. I barely made it through high school! Yes, that's very embarrassing to say, but it's true.

"Jesus Christ is able to teach you how to teach!"

Feelings of inadequacy flooded my mind.

"Oh, Lord, send someone else! You can't mean me!"

I prayed to God for Him to speak to me.

"Send confirmation if this is truly from You."

Jesus Christ gave me the authority. If He gives me the authority, He will give me all that I need to accomplish what He is calling me to do.

Matthew 6:30 Why do you have so little faith?

I had a flurry of questions. What will I teach? How will I teach? I can't even get him to look at me. He doesn't pay attention. Am I going to ruin his life forever? Fears gripped me. Exhaustion overwhelmed me. I felt helpless, which put me in a perfect place. I would need to depend solely on the Lord for everything. I had nothing. I was bankrupt. I did not need to worry about how I was going to teach. I didn't need to worry about what I would teach. God would surely provide. I couldn't let these doubts dominate my thoughts. He already knows my needs before I ask! All I needed to do was say, "Yes Lord, I will obey you. I will teach Camden."

God doesn't give us the big picture. We are on a need to know basis only. He will only give us step 1. He will not give us step 2 until we obey step 1. God called me to teach. I surrendered to His will.

Exodus 4:11... Now go, I will instruct you in what to say.

I don't like to take myself too seriously. I like to remind myself that if God can speak through a donkey, He can speak through me.

The Lord Jesus Christ is my "degree." My validation. My authentication. My confirmation. My authority.

I felt Him leading me to the gospels. Look to Jesus. Go see "how" Jesus taught. Go see "what" Jesus taught. He would be my example.

"Teach him my Word. My Word is all you need. I am all you need."

God told me to teach Camden the Word. He reiterated it over and over.

Isaiah 55:11...so shall My word be that goes forth from My mouth; It shall not return to Me void

One morning I was taking a deeper look at this word "void". In the Hebrew it painted a beautiful picture in my mind, one that would stay with me. Every time we read, hear or speak God's Word, we receive a gift. We never leave empty handed. I was so excited when I read this. I will never look at the Word of God in the same way again. The greatest gift I can give my son is the Word of God.

John 1:1 In the beginning was the Word, and the Word was with God, and the Word was God.

When I give him the Word, I am literally giving him Jesus Christ.

Just the entrance of your Word brings light Lord. Help me to be diligent to do what You have called me to do. God bring your word to life . You can do more than anything I could ask or imagine. Your word is more powerful than anything the world could possibly offer. Thank you for the gift of Your magnificent word.

September 23

There are no coincidences with God. He gave me this child. He is not surprised by his disabilities. But with these disabilities come staggering limitations to my life as well. Nothing is the same. I used to be a social butterfly. I love talking to people. I had a great job at the Post Office. I worked at the front counter. I met so many people. I love people. I looked at every person who walked through the doors as a possible ministry prospect. By that I mean I always hoped I would get a chance to share the gospel with them. There are so many people who are hurting around us. I want to give them hope. I want to take away their pain. I know the only One who can do that is Jesus. I love Jesus. I want to share His love with others. The only problem is I am stuck in the house now. It can be very lonely. The silence can be deafening. There are weeks when I haven't left the house. I needed to make a decision. Either I can wallow in my sorrows or I can rise up and make something happen. God's roadblocks are merely detours. His way is better. His way is smoother.

I want my life to count for Christ. I don't want a day to go by when I didn't make a difference.

I didn't always have this perspective. And there are still days when I say, "I can't do this. I won't do this. This is way too much for me."

When I have this mindset, I think of Caleb in Numbers 13.

The Lord told Moses to send 12 men to scope out the land of Canaan. Go find out what the land is like. Is it good soil or bad? Are there many trees? They were there for 40 days. When they returned they gave their report. "We can't go! There are giants there. We were like little grasshoppers. We will never make it." But not Caleb. He said, "Let's go at once and take the land! We are more than able to overcome it!"

Let's be clear, there are giants. They are mammoth. The giants we face are unlike any I've ever seen. We have no idea how to meet these seemingly insurmountable obstacles. They keep coming one after the other. However, we know the One who can melt those mountains like wax. He has all answers.

Caleb's eyes were not on the giants. His eyes were on Jesus.

When every ounce of logic in you says, "I can't!" God says, "Yes, you can!"

Not only can you, you must!

My sister, I have scoped out the land. You can do this!

Philippians 4:13 I can do all things through Christ who strengthens me!

Let's go! Right now! Get up and get moving! We are moving full steam ahead in the power that was conveyed to us by our God Himself! Caleb knew if God was on his side, there was nothing he couldn't do. The same holds true for us! God plus one equals the majority. I love the math behind that!

Are you feeling under-qualified? You are in good company!

Are you feeling like a grasshopper going against the giant?

Ephesians 3:20 Now to Him who is able to do exceedingly abundantly above all that we ask or imagine...

God is so able to do above and beyond what we expect! God is going to supply every need for you and your child.

Do you trust Him?

God I can trust You! Keep my eyes fixed on You. I love you Lord. None of my problems are bigger than You. Give me discernment. Teach me how to walk in Your ways. I feel exasperated. Calm my anxious heart. I want to be an overcomer today.

September 24

What a delightful morning for a walk. A brisk breeze was blowing as Camden and I set out to get some exercise. The leaves here in Maryland were beginning to change. It was absolutely beautiful.

Fall had arrived.

As we rounded the bend, several children were walking to the bus stop; smiling moms streamed behind. As we got closer, the bus came. We watched the kids get on and the bus drive off.

I felt such joy inside as I watched that bus pull away.

I didn't always feel that way. I hated fall and all that it represented. I hated school buses. That school bus was a reminder of all that my child couldn't do. He couldn't go to a "regular" school. He couldn't do what all the other kids were doing, and I wasn't smiling like all the other moms.

I'm in a new season now.

I'm reminded the very thing I hated so much was the very thing that God used to strengthen me. That thing that I felt messed up my life so miserably was the exact thing God used to build a new and better life with a very different focus.

You may be feeling hopeless right now, but joy will come again.

This is just a season.

God is going to speak a very precious message to you that you will in turn share with someone else.

I felt a little hand in mine. I squeezed it tighter and said, "I'm so glad you don't have to get on that bus."

Camden's face lit up and exclaimed, "I love homeschool."

Whatever you're going through God wants you to know through His word that He is with you.

You will overcome.

September 25

Maybe you're like me this morning and you have a lot on your mind...

Matthew 13:22 "The seed cast in the weeds is the person who hears the kingdom news, but weeds of worry and illusions about getting more and wanting everything under the sun strangle what was heard, and nothing comes of it."

Sometimes we can read the word and it literally goes in one ear and out the other. It makes no impact. No change comes. Before it makes it to the heart, it gets choked out.

Regrets from the past, concerns for the future, school, bills, loved ones and many other weeds of worry strangle out the life of God in us.

Anxiety draws us in different directions. It literally tears us up. It divides us from the peace that God desires for our lives. It steals our joy. Robs us of security.

Don't think about these things so much that they become the primary concern of your life.

Our Father knows the things we have need of...before we ask.

Relax. Withdraw to a quiet place. Hear Him whispering:

Psalm 46:10 Be still and know that I am God...

September 26

Perhaps today finds you in a quandary. Do you need to get a lot done in a little bit of time? Are you facing a challenge that is much too big for you? Or maybe just getting out of bed was a monumental task?

Revelation 3:8 "I know all the things you do, and I have opened a door for you that no one can close. You have a little strength, you obeyed my word and did not deny me."

"I know"...

God sees what no one else sees.

He sees all that we are undertaking. Not only does He see the big picture, He sees the small. He sees what it takes to accomplish what's before us today. He knows all the details. He's acquainted with the peculiarities of our particular need. In fact, He's well aware of all that we've gone through up to this point. He sees what's weighing heavy on our hearts. Our fears are sometimes hidden from the outside world, but not from Him. He is familiar with our weaknesses. He knows when our faith is beginning to falter.

If we offer Him the little bit we have, watch what He can do with it!

He can turn a little strength into a lot.

After all, He did feed five thousand with a few pieces of bread.

He still moves mountains with our little bitty mustard seed of faith.

Give Him what you got and He'll take care of the rest.

September 27

We were returning from a delightful visit with Mom. We take the same highway every time. It leads us over the Francis Scott Key Bridge.

Camden exclaimed, "Look momma the bridge is far away."

Although it looked very far away, it was so close. We were actually right up on it.

It only had the appearance of being distant.

Our lives look like this sometimes.

Things look so far away, we think we'll never get there.

There's a few curves in the road.

It's not a straight shot. It never is.

Our journey is filled with unexpected twists and turns.

Detours. Lots of detours.

Roadblocks.

Yes they are disappointing. Frustrating.

But necessary.

The shortest way is easiest. That's the way I would choose.

The long way is always more difficult.

But, we wouldn't get to see the things we saw had we went our way.

Don't let the curves deceive you.

That thing that looks so far may be just around the bend.

Keep persevering.

When a roadblock comes, smile. God has something better.

His timing is perfect.

In the end you won't be disappointed.

Habakkuk 2:3 Though it tarries wait for it. It will surely come.

September 28

"Maybe your son could be a bagger at Giant!"

Those words made my head spin. Trying to process what he just said did not come easy. My mind was trying to take in that reality; my heart completely rejected it. My son was diagnosed with Autism many months prior to this conversation. But I had just brought myself to be able to share this devastating news with a neighbor.

This was his response.

Suddenly I felt the weight of his words pressing in on me. Suffocating me. Stealing the air from my lungs. The dreams from my heart went seeping out. It was more than I could bear at that moment.

He meant no harm.

I just wasn't ready to accept that as a possible scenario. Yet it loomed in the back of my mind for quite a while. In fact, it's been five years since my neighbor so enthusiastically suggested it. Just writing it has me fighting back tears.

I've learned so much about my God since then.

I no longer consider his diagnosis something to be feared.

I embrace it.

Ask any parent of a child with special needs and they will tell you they fear the future.

We cannot live in fear. Fear is not our Master.

2 Timothy 1:7 For God has not given us a spirit of fear, but of power and of love and of a sound mind.

I trust that the same God who has secured my future has indeed secured my son's future.

It is the most difficult thing to trust what you cannot see.

We have no other choice.

To entrust him to anyone else would wipe me out emotionally.

He is safe in the hands of our God.

God will never fail him. He will never let him go.

This I know.

2 Timothy 1:12...for I know whom I have believed and am persuaded that He is able to keep what I have committed to Him until that Day.

God will never fail you. Wherever He has placed you, He will get you through. He will be enough.

God help me to trust You with the future. All of it. I can't control any of it. Open my hands and heart to give this child, this situation, and my life over to You. You are able to keep it safe.

September 29

Genesis 22:7 Isaac said to Abraham his father, "Father?"

"Yes, my son."

"We have flint and wood, but where's the sheep for the burnt offering?"

Abraham said, "Son, God will see to it that there's a lamb for the burnt offering."

And they kept on walking together.

Essentially God was saying, I know you don't have everything you need.

I know.

And that's enough.

Sometimes we know God will provide, but we want to know how. We want to see the big picture. All the details up front. Then we'll fully trust.

Can you go when you don't have all the pieces?

That's where our faith is put to the test.

Isaac realized his very life was at stake.

He asked for the details.

When he didn't get them, he kept walking.

He went forward trusting in the word of his Father.

He didn't stop.

He didn't retreat.

He trusted.

God will provide.

Himself.

He is enough. Always has been. Always will be.

When the time comes, God will see to it that you have what you need.

God will provide what you need, when you need it.

If you don't have it right now, that's okay. You must not need it.

Keep walking.

You can trust the word of your Father.

Philippians 4:19 And my God shall supply all your need according to His riches in glory by Christ Jesus.

John 12:1-2 Then, six days before the Passover, Jesus came to Bethany, where Lazarus was who had been dead, whom He had raised from the dead. There they made Him a supper; and Martha served, but Lazarus was one of those who sat at the table with Him.

They made him a supper. This seems like such a trivial thing to record in the Bible. But, He did. Jesus is taking note of our efforts. He sees the little things.

It made me wonder.

What would it take to make Jesus a supper? I am sure Martha gave her all. How about you? What does it take to do your 'job' every day?

I wonder if people really know what it takes to be you. To do what you do.

They have no idea. You make it look easy. They don't understand. They'll never understand.

They have no idea the time it takes. The energy. The physical investment alone. The emotional investment. Day in and day out. Sleepless nights. Sick children. Rejection. Loneliness.

People have no idea.

Jesus wants you to hear these words, "I see. I see everything you're doing. I know what it takes. I know what you've given up."

"I am recording it in My book. Just like I recorded Martha's supper. I am recording your small acts of love."

"I haven't missed one yet."

Jesus recorded a supper.

There are no insignificant jobs in His Kingdom. Was this a glorious meal Martha made? I don't think so. But Jesus recorded it. He wrote it down. He made sure we would know He sees the small things. The seemingly insignificant jobs we do. No one else sees them. But He does.

He's recording them.

1 Corinthians 15:58 Therefore, my beloved brethren, be steadfast, immovable, always abounding in the work of the Lord, knowing that your labor (beating, trouble) is not in vain (empty handed or without spiritual wealth) in the Lord.

My Lord, You see all. Nothing gets past You. You know all of my efforts, no matter how futile they seem. Help me to persevere through the rugged terrain. I am tired, Lord lift me up. Guard my heart when people don't understand. This is important work for You. It will not return void. For that, I praise You.

October

October 1

Trees don't grow in the desert.

In fact, nothing grows in the desert.

Dry, harsh conditions make it impossible for anything to thrive.

The desert is desolate. Unyielding heat prevails. One thing I noticed while driving through it is that it seems to go on forever.

Like it'll never end.

Sometimes our circumstances can feel like that. Unending. Impossible. Hard.

But then God shows up and changes everything.

Isaiah 41:17-20...I, God...will not leave them thirsty. I'll open up rivers for them on the barren hills, spout fountains in the valleys...I'll plant the red cedar in that treeless wasteland...I'll place the cypress in the desert, with plenty of oaks and pines. Everyone will see this. No one can miss it— unavoidable, indisputable evidence that I, God, personally did this.

God is always writing a testimony.

An open book for the world to read.

God is so good at creating something out of nothing. It is His specialty. He's been doing it since the beginning of time.

It may not be that He changes your external circumstances.

He changes you.

He makes you a strong cedar that is standing in the midst of the arid desert. And not just standing.

Thriving.

Growing.

Strong.

Beautiful.

The world looks on in wonder.

How did this happen?

It could only be our great God.

If today finds you facing some difficult circumstances, be encouraged! God displays His awesome power through our hard places.

He is still filling in the pages of your book.

October 2

I was pet sitting my friend's dog while she was away on a mission trip. The pup's name is Sophie. This little girl gave me quite a scare. I hope you can keep a secret:

I lost Sophie.

I will spare you all of details, but all of our security measures were breached and she wandered out of the house.

I was frantic.

Ray and I bolted out the door. He was on foot. Camden and I went in the car. We drove down every street. We stopped people to ask if they'd seen her. We looked high and low. I was determined I would not rest until I found her. Nope, I would not sleep until she was safely home. I would do whatever it took to find this dog.

Where could she have gone? Was she hurt? Was she scared? She must be terrified. This neighborhood was all new to her. There was nothing that looked familiar. She had no way of finding her way back to my house. There was no one that she knew either. I had to find her.

Perhaps today finds you on an unfamiliar path. Perhaps you don't even know how you got there. There are no signs to guide you in the right direction. You may feel like you've fallen off the radar. Wandering around lost and exhausted, you may wonder if anyone knows or cares. May I tell you that your heavenly Dad has His eye on you? He has never taken His eyes off of you; not even for a moment. You may have taken your eyes off Him, but He knows exactly where you are. As hard as I was looking for Sophie, how much more so is God pursuing after you! He will go to the ends of the earth for you. He cares that much. You are precious to Him.

If you've wandered off, stop right where you are. Put your hand out and ask Him to take it. He'll lead you in the right direction. You'll find He's been right there with you the whole time.

I found Sophie! I was never so happy! I rounded the corner and there she was; safe and sound in the arms of my neighbor.

Psalm 72:12 For He will deliver the needy when he cries, the poor also, and him who has no helper.

October 3

Early in the morning Camden suggested we go to Panera. He always gets the same thing. A big cookie. But this time he decided he wanted something different. When we walked in, he immediately pointed to the top of the bread rack. The basket held long loaves of French bread.

He wasn't distracted by all the other dazzling desserts.

Never wavered.

Just wanted the bread.

Now I'm thinking to myself, is he really going to sit in my backseat and eat this enormous loaf of bread?

That's exactly what he did.

Loved every bite of it too.

The Bible tells us the word of God is like bread.

While bread feeds us physically, His word feeds us spiritually.

It's soul food.

We can't live without it. Lots of it. Everyday.

We need it.

God's word fills the longings of our hearts.

Everything else will leave us empty.

Drained.

They're alluring at first, but will always leave us lacking.

It's just like our physical diet, the more potato chips, chocolate covered pretzels and Twinkies we have, the less we desire apples, oranges and bananas. In and of themselves, there isn't anything wrong with them. They taste awesome, but they have no nutritional value. More importantly, they give us a distaste for the things that are going to give us healthy benefits.

They leave us lacking.

Facebook, Twitter, television will do the same.

Whether we need wisdom, comfort, joy, peace; nothing can replace God's word for these things.

Isaiah 55:10-11 "The rain and snow come down from the heavens and stay on the ground to water the earth. They cause the grain to grow, producing seed for the farmer and bread for the hungry. It is the same with My word. I send it out, and it always produces fruit. It will accomplish all I want it to, and it will prosper everywhere I send it."

Here's hoping you grab some "bread" and feed your soul!

October 4

Remember that bread I told you about?

It was only a few minutes after eating that bread those morsels turned into a sword.

He whipped it through the air; wielded it with precision. Soon enough he defeated his invisible enemy with one swift blow (I felt it in the back of my car seat!).

In the same way, God's word becomes our sword to fight the enemy.

It's our defensive weapon.

Jesus used it when Satan tempted him to kill Himself.

Matthew 4:5-7 Then the devil took Him up to the highest point of the Temple... and said to Him, "If You are the Son of God, throw Yourself down." Jesus responded, "The Scriptures also say, 'You must not test the LORD your God.'"

Satan comes when we are tired, hungry and worn out.

He wants us to give up.

He'll do anything he can to keep us from God's word.

He just lies. He is the father of lies.

Here's what he wants to keep you from:

God's word gives us discernment to make good choices.

It helps us to overcome the enemy's temptations.

God's word helps us to recognize who the enemy is.

Ephesians 6:12 For we are not fighting against flesh-and-blood enemies, but against evil rulers and authorities of the unseen world, against mighty powers in this dark world...

When there's tension in the home or havoc at work, we want to attack back. God's word will help us recognize the enemy isn't the guy we're married to or the person we work for.

Your real enemy doesn't want you in the word.

If you're struggling with depression, Satan says, "You're too depressed. You can't read."

God says, "You CAN. And you MUST."

Satan says, "You don't have time."

God says, "You don't have time not to."

Don't be tempted to skip your morning devotions.

Be determined.

Don't get distracted.

Grab your sword!

You will need this word to combat the enemy today.

October 5

I had this dream one night.

It was quite short and to the point.

The sun was setting over the city. It was very dark.

And calm.

But it was a false peace.

Out of nowhere this lightning bolt strikes over the city.

I woke up before I could find out who lived, and who died.

Much like this dream, the Bible tells us there will be a time when Jesus comes back to the earth.

Matthew 24:27 "For as the lightning comes from the east and flashes to the west, so also will the coming of the Son of Man be.

"Son of Man" is a title Jesus used for Himself.

If He came back today, would you be ready?

All of the signs are there:

2 Timothy 3:1-5... As the end approaches, people are going to be self-absorbed, money-hungry, self-promoting, stuck-up, profane, contemptuous of parents, crude, coarse, dog-eat-dog, unbending, slanderers, impulsively wild, savage, cynical, treacherous, ruthless, bloated windbags, addicted to lust, and allergic to God. They'll make a show of religion, but behind the scenes they're animals.

It's true, no one knows the day or time.

Therein lies the problem.

The father of lies would have us believe we have time. When in reality we may not.

If today were your last day, would you be ready?

As a Christian I think God was asking me this.

He also asked:

Are you looking for My return or have you gotten distracted?

Are you raising your children to know, love and trust Me, or have other things drawn you away?

Have you finished what I asked you to do?

God is so graceful to give us the opportunity to make some adjustments.

Me? I need adjustments.

How about you?

If you aren't a Christian, God may have some different questions for you:

Do you know how much I love you? Immensely...

Do you know there is a problem? Your sin separates you from Me.

Do you know the penalty for that sin is an eternity in hell?

Do you know if you turn from your sin and live for Me I will remove that separation and your reward will be eternity in heaven?

You are God's precious child whom He adores. He has been trying to get your attention for a while.

Now's your chance for a brand new start. Make those changes.

Don't waste any more time on empty things. He has so much better for you.

Every word of God is true...

Joel 2:32 And it shall come to pass that whoever calls on the name of the LORD shall be saved.

October 6

I had one of those moments.

Panic.

Total panic.

I ran to the grocery store to pick up a few things. I reached for my credit card and it was not there.

Gone.

I think I stopped breathing.

Time was standing still.

Where could it be?

I looked again.

Not there.

I took every last thing out of my purse.

Twice.

Still not there.

My mind was retracing every step I made the day before.

Could I have left it at the 7-11? Was it at my friends?

Maybe I left it in the car.

I paid for my stuff and ran out of the store.

I lifted up every last thing in my car. I took things out. I rearranged.

I looked in stuff. Under stuff. Dug through stuff.

When alas I found it.

I was so happy.

Did you know that's how God searches for us when we're lost?

He doesn't give up on us. Never.

Searches and searches. Relentlessly.

He never stops pursuing us.

No matter where we go.

Luke 15:8 "Or what woman, having ten silver coins, if she loses one coin, does not light a lamp, sweep the house, and search carefully until she finds it?"

You are that valuable to Him. His treasure. His child.

He loves you immensely.

If you have lost your way, or even become a little distant, know this: He is pursuing after you.

Draw near to Him, and He will draw near to you.

Lord, draw me close to You. I want to give You all of the things that are keeping me from You. I need You in my life, every moment. I can't take one step without You. I've tried, and failed. I long to be closer to You. Thank you for your everlasting love. You never give up on me. I praise Your name.

October 7

I was at Ground Zero.

That place is surrounded by a sophisticated security system. The most brilliant minds in America have come together to protect this place.

Fences. Walls. Concrete barriers. Barbed wire.

Cameras.

Guards.

And more guards.

And yet a fifteen year old kid was able to breech it all. One week later another amateur thrill seeker snuck right on in.

Unnoticed.

Psalm 127:1 Unless the LORD builds the house, the builders labor in vain. Unless the LORD watches over the city, the guards stand watch in vain.

We are not safe on our own watch.

All of our efforts to protect against the unseen enemy are a complete waste.

If we don't rely solely on our God, we will fail. We will never be secure.

All of these security measures and barriers came up short.

We try to erect similar barriers in our own lives.

Build walls of protection. Try to ease our anxieties. We lie awake, tossing and turning trying to think of every possible scenario, its dreaded outcome and still we are no safer.

Our children, husbands, jobs, churches and futures are NOT in our hands.

All our worries are for nothing. A complete waste. In fact, they will destroy us.

Fear is not from the Lord.

It's from the thief who comes for one purpose; to steal our joy, our hope, and our very lives.

We can't yield to it.

On our own we are vulnerable.

We wonder, "God do you see me?"

He whispers still, "Do you see Me?"

Fears come when we calculate without God. They hide His face.

When we take Him out of the equation, we are quickly overcome.

Don't factor without Him.

Psalm 46:5 God is in the midst of her, she shall not be moved; God shall help her, just at the break of dawn.

He is right here in the middle of all this. Our refuge and hiding place.

Strengthening. Protecting. Providing.

He is holding it all together, not us.

Psalm 46:2 Therefore we will not fear, even though the earth be removed, and though the mountains be carried into the midst of the sea...

No matter what you may be up against this day, God is with you.

He is for you.

Psalm 91:4 He will cover you with His feathers. He will shelter you with His wings. His faithful promises are your armor and protection.

God please take these fears from me. Fear is not from you. Protect me. Cover me with Your feathers of protection. Make me secure in You. My life is in Your hands. I am safe under Your wings. Your perfect love casts out fear. Envelop me in it. Hover over me today I pray.

October 8

Everyone has a story.

What's yours?

Do you have a God story?

You may ask, "What is a God story?"

Nicodemus did.

He came to Jesus at night, suggesting that he didn't want anyone to know he had questions. He was trying to figure all of this God stuff out.

Questions are good.

It's ok if you don't understand everything all at once. No one does.

Nicodemus knew a lot about God, but he did not know Him personally. They did not have an intimate relationship.

Jesus told Nicodemus if he wanted to go to heaven he would have to be born again.

Nicodemus wondered what it meant to be born again.

Jesus explained that all of us have a physical birth. So too we have a spiritual birth.

A God story.

Unless He writes your story, it's inevitably a bad book you're living in.

It means you're holding the pen.

That's what happened to me. I was writing my own story.

Can I just tell you it was a real bad novel?

I chose all the wrong characters.

The setting became very dark.

It was a painful read.

Until God became the author of my life, I lived in a hell on earth of sorts. And I was destined ultimately for an eternity of more of the same. Hell is eternal separation from God. It is the absence of everything good.

All of us will live for eternity.

The author of our story will determine where that eternity will be spent.

There was a time when my story changed.

Every good book has a hero!

Every girl loves a love story. The world has polluted the meaning of love.

True love gives, gives, and gives.

Lust takes, takes, and takes.

John 3:16 This is how much God loved the world [me and you]: He gave His Son, His one and only Son. And this is why: so that no one need be destroyed; by believing in Him, anyone can have a whole and lasting life.

Jesus came to my rescue.

He rewrote the text of my life.

I made a choice to give him the pen. My heart went along with it. He changed my life. All of my goals were different.

I chose to walk away from my life of sin and live for Him.

Everything changed. Everything.

Is God the author of your story?

If not, give Him the pen.

You will be so glad you did!

God, I've been trying to be in control long enough. Here is the pen. Take it out of my hand. Right now I give You full control. Take over. I surrender this life to you. Fully and completely. Make me whole. Use me for Your glory. Make my life count for You. Every detail. All aspects of it. I give it to You. Make me. Mold me. Shape me. Lord, thank Your for your patience with me. I love You.

October 9

Every wave has a limit.

It can go no further than God allows.

Proverbs 8:29...He assigned to the sea its limit

When we feel like we are floating aimlessly in a sea of uncertainty, God beckons us to come to Him.

Genesis 7:1 Then the LORD said to Noah, "Come into the ark you and all your household, because I have seen...

God sees our need.

He knows exactly how much we can handle.

When we don't know if we can take it one more day, remember there is a limit.

God's hand is upon the waters.

Genesis 7:11...on that day all the fountains of the great deep were broken up, and the windows of heaven were opened.

The flood was from heaven. God allowed it. He had a purpose for it.

The waters may still be rising in our lives.

The deeper the water, the greater the grace we receive.

Noah's whole family was at stake.

I'm sure he was terrified.

Anxious. Defenseless. Helpless.

He had nothing to trust in but His God.

That was enough.

God kept him safe until the storm passed.

He will do the same for us.

He will not fail us when we need Him most.

Psalm 147:3 He heals the brokenhearted and binds up their wounds.

God I need you. Keep me steady. Help me trust You implicitly. You know my insecurities. The waters are rising. Strengthen me from within. Fill me with Your Spirit of truth. I can do this. Keep my head above the waters. Let me know You are near.

October 10

I always think I'm going to mess my kids up.

I just do.

Oh if I could just trust the Lord.

I mean I can, but sometimes I don't.

I feel like maybe I just may think of something He has forgotten.

For instance:

I am not a teacher.

I am not a special needs "expert".

I am not equipped.

I am not a lot of things.

What if I miss something really important? There has to be someone that can do this better than me.

I think that is the point.

There is always someone better. Smarter. More qualified.

And if that was who God wanted He would've called them.

1 Corinthians 1:27 But God has chosen the foolish things of the world to put to shame the wise, and God has chosen the weak things of the world to put to shame the things which are mighty...

I reminded Him who I was.

And He graciously reminded me who He was.

Is.

And always will be.

He is God.

He can do anything.

Through anyone.

God spoke through a donkey.

Why do I take myself so seriously?

Sometimes it is just time to step out of the boat and walk.

Go do what God called you to do. Stop looking around.

Don't let your focus be on the things you don't have.

Look at what you have.

You have Him.

I have Him.

He is enough.

Always has been. Always will be.

Lord You are enough for me today. Silence the lies that the enemy is whispering in my ear. You will give me what I need. You're my sole provider. I lack nothing. No good thing will You withhold from those who love You. I love You. I have everything I need. Help me to be content.

✓ October 11

As I walked under the hovering grey clouds one morning, the tranquility was tangible.

All was calm.

Peace was lingering in the air.

Quiet and still.

It stood in stark contrast to the night before.

Hourly screams and shrieks of pain pierced throughout our home.

Breaking the usual silence, and my heart along with it.

I thought we'd overcome these ear infections, but they were back with a vengeance.

Repeated sobs for help. None coming.

There is nothing worse than a child's cry.

Yet I am acutely aware that my God hears.

The Listener.

What He did in the past He will do again.

Perhaps not as quickly as I would like; but He will.

He knows our limits.

Help is on the way.

As morning dawned I found a short respite.

I was immediately brought back to my own childhood sufferings. I had such bad earaches as well. It's like it was yesterday my mom sat up holding me all night. That is why I am so sensitive to his pain. I know what it feels like. I am certain God is preparing Camden for a day when he too will be able to relate to someone else's pain. He'll have a deep understanding. Full knowledge, because he's been there.

Pain is always a prerequisite for a future ministry.

God will use it for good.

Because He is good.

For that I am grateful.

This too shall pass.

Lamentations 3:22-23 Because of the LORD's great love we are not consumed, for his compassions never fail. They are new every morning; great is your faithfulness.

October 12

Psalm 125:2 Just as the mountains surround Jerusalem, so the LORD surrounds his people, both now and forever.

Jerusalem: A mountain enveloped by mountains; untouchable.

Protected. Secure.

And that is what you are.

When God is surrounding a woman, there is a nothing that can touch her. No force can steal her peace. Disaster may crowd in on every side, but there is a constant calm within. The world cannot give this kind of peace. Nor can it take it away.

Even the title of Psalm 125 is called "A Song of Ascent"; implying it will take us higher.

The Lord takes us above our situation.

He gives us a new perspective.

His Presence protects us from invading thoughts.

Isaiah 26:3 You will keep h[er] in perfect peace, whose mind is stayed on You, because [s]he trusts in You.

Still, peaceful, calm and rested.

He gives us a firm steadfast confidence. No wavering.

Without Gods protection we are not secure.

We would be open and vulnerable.

When we trust God we cannot be shaken. No wavering.

Jerusalem cannot be removed, defeated or obliterated.

Nothing can touch her unless our God says so.

And the same is true for us.

1 Corinthians 15:58 Therefore, my beloved brethren, be steadfast, immovable, always abounding in the work of the Lord, knowing that your labor is not in vain in the Lord.

Jesus, no matter what I face today, let nothing move me. Keep my mind stayed on You. I trust You. Surround my mind with peace. Put your hand of protection upon me. Guard me from the enemy. Help me to persevere through every obstacle today.

October 13

Change.

We want change.

Change is difficult.

We know something has to give.

Something or someone needs to go.

God's will is crystal clear.

Larger than life.

Not a cloud in the sky.

No veil.

Not a shadow of a doubt.

We know what He is asking.

Yet we hesitate.

If we want change, we have to be willing to do what it takes.

Be willing to admit that what we're doing isn't working.

He can make you a brand new person. In fact, he wants to.

Desperately.

2 Corinthians 5:17...anyone who belongs to Christ has become a new person. The old life is gone; a new life has begun!

Is the old life gone?

Sometimes we're afraid of what that might look like.

What will people say?

Who cares!

God wants to save us from the court of public opinion.

Our reputation is so precious to us. But, that's just pride. God hates pride.

God wants you to walk away from it all.

Mark 1:15,18... Jesus went to Galilee preaching the Message of God: "Time's up! God's kingdom is here. Change your life and believe the Message."... They didn't ask questions. They dropped their nets and followed.

They left everything. Dropped it all.

In return they received life.

Full and overflowing life.

Is what your holding onto so worth it?

Philippians 3:13...focus on this one thing: Forgetting the past and looking forward to what lies ahead...

You cannot follow one thing without coming away from something else.

Are you holding onto anything in your life that is displeasing to the Lord?

Let go of it.

And you know what?

He'll give you the power to do it.

Lord, I know this is keeping me from you. Help me to lay anything in my life that You don't approve of, at Your feet. You are worthy of a life set apart for You. Take my attitudes, my fears, my pride, my right to myself, and make me new. Renew me. Refresh me. Revive me.

October 14

Afflicted, bad, challenged, crippled, cut, debilitated, decrepit, deficient, delicate, diminished, disabled, diseased, divided, emaciated, feeble, fractional, fragile, frail, gaunt, haggard, half, ill, incapacitated, incomplete, injured, lame, poorly, reduced, run down, scattered, sickly, troubled, unfit, unhealthy, unsound, unwell, weak, worn-out.

Do any of these words describe you today?

Matthew 8:8...But only speak a word, and my servant will be healed.

Do not underestimate the sheer power of the Word of God.

One word from the Lord our God can heal you of any of these things.

You cannot be whole without the word of God. Everyday. All day.

The minute you step out to do something on your own, apart from Him, it falls apart.

It falls into parts.

Divided.

Severed.

Apart from Him we can do nothing. We are nothing.

There is a very important word that is lost in translation, but incredibly powerful...Speak a word ONLY...the word "only" is missing. It is so powerful...too powerful to leave out.

Only: exclusively, wholly, forsaken of help.

God's word doesn't need help. We can solely depend on it, trust in it, lean on it, embrace it, and cling to it.

When everything else fails, He never will.

Sometimes we're just at a loss. We have no idea of what to do. We don't know which direction to go in.

We have His word

Pray it. Speak it. Sing it. Write it. Search for it. Embrace it.

It was at this spoken word the whole earth was created.

He is the only One who can make something out of nothing. That's what He does best.

He has been doing it since the beginning of time.

This word raises the dead.

Notice this isn't past tense.

It always has.

It always will.

The Power of God's word...matchless.

1 Corinthians 2:4 And my message and my preaching were very plain. Rather than using clever and persuasive speeches, I relied only on the power of the Holy Spirit.

October 15

Ezekiel 37:8 Indeed, as I looked, the sinews and the flesh came upon them, and the skin covered them over; but there was no breath in them.

We walk among people who have an appearance of being alive, but there is no breath in them.

No Spirit. Walking dead. Dead in sin. Hardened. Helpless. Under the influence of the enemy. Filled with deception. In the grip of drugs, alcohol, vanity, pride, fear, lust.

Just there. Useless. Dying a slow death.

No power to overcome.

Ezekiel 37:4 Again He said to me, "Prophesy to these bones, and say to them, 'O dry bones, hear the word of the LORD!'"

God gave Ezekiel eyes to see.

He was overcome.

Not only was he God's mouthpiece, he was God's heart piece.

He spoke out of the overflow of his heart.

The words he spoke became life giving.

He called upon the breath of God.

God's spirit breathed life into those dead bones. And they came alive!

Dear God make me Your mouthpiece. Not only that, make me your heart piece. Move me out of my comfort zone. Give me Your Holy Spirit to impel me to act on what I see. Remove any callous indifference I may be harboring. Fill me with compassion. Use me to intercede on behalf of those who are spiritually dying all around me. Soften the hearts of the people. Empower me to speak your word with boldness. Take me out of my comfort zone. Draw these hearts to you. No one comes to the Father unless they are drawn. Draw them. You save. Not me. And I am solely relying on You. Send Your Holy Spirit, I pray.

October 16

The man and I decided on a little getaway in Western Maryland. An old brick farmhouse on the countryside. Tall cornstalks lining the property danced at the coming harvest. A large barn towards the back overflowed with golden hay. The owner escorted us to our quaint room on the second floor. It had a balcony attached. On it, a comfy couch with a small table and chair, perfect for watching the sunrise. We were delighted. As she prepared to head back downstairs, she thought of one more thing. Pointing to the top corner of the balcony, she advised, "If you see a bird swoop down and fly into that hole, don't be alarmed. She lives up there. She moved a brick. Literally. She pecked away at the mortar first. It took her a few months. But, she did it. She moved a brick. We tried everything to keep her out. We finally gave up." And off she went. Back to the farm.

Next morning I was lying on the balcony. The morning air fresh and crisp. Sipping my hot coffee.

There she was. That industrious starling. A tiny little thing at that.

She moved a brick.

How did she do it?

She persevered. Made her mind up she was getting in there. She didn't let anyone or anything get in her way. The size of the obstacle was irrelevant. That brick was way bigger than she was. It weighed vastly more than she could ever carry. And yet she moved it.

Do you have a brick to move?

Is there something that seems immovable in your life?

Matthew 17:20 Jesus said,... if you have faith as a mustard seed, you will say to this mountain, 'Move from here to there,' and it will move; and nothing will be impossible for you.

She didn't look at the impossibility. Indeed, she took it on. Head on.

Matthew 19:26 But Jesus looked at them and said to them, "With men this is impossible, but with God all things are possible."

All things are possible with God.

She wasn't afraid of the hard.

She didn't move the brick overnight. It took many months of work. Hard work.

This girl pecked away little by little.

I'm sure there were days she just wanted to give up. We can feel like that. When things don't progress as we would like. Our efforts are rebuffed. Rejected. Fall short. Painful nights add up.

She kept at it. She wore it away slow.

Her determination paid off.

Luke 18:1...[wo] men always ought to pray and not lose heart...

Don't give up. You're prayers are heard. Be persistent. It pays.

Be the girl who moves the brick.

October 17

I was enjoying the silence of an early fall morning. The only light in the room was the fireplace. Flickering flames danced on the walls. I heard the pitter patter of little feet shuffling across the floor. Camden was only seven years old at the time. He snuggled up on the couch next to me; we were lying next to each other. It was a rare moment I was relishing. He remained quiet for quite a while.

Then he spoke. "Mama if I get closer to the fire will I be in hell?"

Quite a question.

It left me speechless.

I did some explaining. God does not desire for anyone to go to hell. Hell was meant for Satan and his demons and all who reject his Son Jesus.

It was his choice.

Everyone has a choice.

I asked Camden, "Do you want to live for Jesus? Or do you want to live for Satan?"

There is no in between.

Period.

Jesus said, "Either you are for Me or you are against Me."

That leaves nothing in between.

Either Jesus is everything or he is nothing.

So I asked, "Camden do you want to pray and tell Jesus you want to live for Him?" He sighed, "I think I'll have a piece of pizza." I chuckled inside. So that ended the conversation for the day.

But the next morning was more of the same.

More talk about the fire.

Hell.

And heaven.

And on October 17, 2013 Camden made a choice to live for Jesus. He then got baptized.

Baptism is simply an outward telling of an inward belief. In his heart he asked Jesus to forgive him for his sins; past, present, and future. And he believes Jesus died for his sins to pay the penalty that he deserved. He asked Jesus to forgive him and help him to live for Him. He believes Jesus rose again and is alive today in his life.

I was told a few years ago that Autistic children don't understand spiritual things. "They are too abstract."

But you know what?

God's Word brings wisdom. This child understands the saving power of Jesus Christ better than many adults.

Never underestimate the power of God's Word.

Psalm 119:130 The entrance of Your words gives light; it gives under-standing to the simple.

Dear Jesus, I give You thanks for this child and his testimony. It is a testimony of the power of Your word. It gives life. Eternal life. It is alive and active. A path of life to the simple. Use Your word in my life. Guide me continually. I desire to fall in love with Your word. Fan that flame inside my heart for You.

October 18

A crisp breeze was blowing. The scent of wood burning fireplaces was wafting through the air. It was fall in Maryland, and there is little that can top it. As I was enjoying this delightful morning a leaf fluttered by, jostling me out of my thoughts.

It quickly fell to the ground.

As I looked over to its landing spot I noticed lots of other similar leaves.

What if I allowed all of my burdens, doubts and fears to fall to the ground?

I would have a yard full.

Deuteronomy 15:2... for the LORD's time of release has arrived.

This word release means to let go.

There are things we hold onto that need to go.

We hold onto the past; wishing we could change it.

Let it go.

Philippians 3:13...I have not achieved it, but I focus on this one thing: Forgetting the past and looking forward to what lies ahead...

We hold onto fear as though it were a good friend.

Let it go.

2 Timothy 1:7 For God has not given us a spirit of fear, but of power and of love and of a sound mind.

We mull over past hurts and allow them to consume our thoughts. Sometimes the hardest person to forgive is another brother or sister that has hurt you. Doing so will free you.

Luke 6:37... Forgive, and you will be forgiven.

It will allow you to love and be vulnerable once again.

Let it go.

By letting these things go we can welcome the new things that God has in store for us.

A tree does not grow weaker when it lets its leaves go. In fact, next year it will grow back even stronger, fuller and more beautiful. It will be the same for us.

The letting go is necessary for growth.

Just wait until next year!

1 Corinthians 2:9 "Eye has not seen, nor ear heard, nor have entered into the heart of man the things which God has prepared for those who love Him."

October 19

John 20:1 Now on the first day of the week Mary Magdalene went to the tomb early, while it was still dark, and saw that the stone had been taken away from the tomb.

It was empty. The tomb. He was supposed to be there.

She was distraught.

Ever been there?

You just need Jesus and He is nowhere to be found.

Where are You Lord?

As I taught this lesson to a brood of dirty faced little lambs, one of them caught my attention. He listened intently.

Jesus wasn't there because He was alive.

The boy looks down at the simple black cross printed on the coloring page.

His eyes light up.

He gets it.

And he can barely contain himself. Exuberantly exclaims, "That's why the cross is empty. Jesus isn't dead. He is alive."

With that, my heart overflows.

Simple cross. Simple message.

Too many times I have adult faith. Faith that waivers. Faith that's filled with doubts. And questions. My worldly wisdom gets in the way. Cynicism takes over. I've seen it not turn out. Things fall apart. Trust gets broken. Faith that thinks it has fix everything. I want my time frame. In my way. When it doesn't fall into place, faith falls apart.

All the while Jesus wants us to have the faith of this child.

To see an empty cross and trust.

The child who sits at His feet. And waits. Knowing his Dad is with him. And that's enough. He loves His children. With love inexpressible. With love that comforts. And when we experience loss that hurts every ounce of our being, we can be sure God understands. He gave His Son so we could live eternally.

He knows loss. His loss brought life.

But that life is for today. It is our hope today. Hope that our situation is held in the hands of a strong God who overcame death. And there is nothing we cannot overcome in our lives. No dark night can overtake us. The tomb is empty. Jesus is not dead. He is alive. Alive and active. Laboring on our behalf. Working behind the scenes. Just like He did that day when He rose from the dead. He was working in the darkness.

John 1:5 The light shines in the darkness, and the darkness can never extinguish it.

Never.

The darkness of that tomb could not keep Him. No evil can overtake Him. He still rules. And overrules. He is still sovereign.

He still resurrects.

Dead faith. Dead hope. Dead situations. Dead marriages. Dead prodigals.

Jesus Christ is alive. Go live like it!

October 20

Joshua 14:7-8 "I was forty years old when Moses the servant of the LORD sent me from Kadesh Barnea to spy out the land, and I brought back word to him as it was in my heart. Nevertheless my brethren who went up with me made the heart of the people melt, but I wholly followed the LORD my God.

In the old language this verse would read:

"Nevertheless my brethren who went up with me made the heart of the people melt, but Caleb got behind the Lord and stayed there."

While the rest of the guys were cowering in fear, Caleb stood up with boldness.

Caleb spied out the Promised Land. Yes there were giants there, but God told him everywhere his foot tread would be his inheritance.

It was 45 years later. He still had not received that Promise.

Caleb never forgot. He clung to that Word of the Lord.

The Lord did not disappoint him. His word did not fail.

While he was 85 years old, he was as strong as ever. His faith even more so. He knew he was facing giants in his Promised Land. He saw them firsthand. But he had also seen the Power of His mighty God at work for the last 45 years. He knew God brought him this far. He hadn't failed him yet. He wouldn't fail him now. God gave him this land. Nothing could stop him. The Lord was fighting for him, he could not lose. He would not be defeated.

This knowledge is what filled Caleb with such confidence.

Caleb was reminding Joshua of everything they had overcome.

Had Joshua forgotten?

Do you remember how the Lord helped you overcome?

Life and death are in the power of the tongue.

Our courage can encourage others to stand up and fight. It can quiet the fears of those who are afraid. Our fears can have the opposite effect. They can melt the hearts of others, and cause them to give up.

Caleb knew the God of Angel armies went before him then, and He certainly would go before him now.

Joshua 14:11 "I am as strong now as I was when Moses sent me on that journey, and I can still travel and fight as well as I could then. Now therefore, give me this mountain of which the LORD spoke in that day; for you heard in that day how the Anakim were there, and that the cities were great and fortified. It may be that the LORD will be with me, and I shall be able to drive them out as the LORD said."

Caleb said, "Give me this mountain! I got this!"

Caleb was reminding Joshua of a few things. Remember when we saw those giants? They were there. They were big, but our God was bigger. God told us He would do it. We believed Him. We trusted Him then, and He never let us down.

Can I remind you of a few things?

That giant obstacle you're facing is nothing for God. You get behind Him and stay there. God will take care of you. He will never let you down. He will not abandon you. He will not disappoint you.

You can trust your God.

Get behind the Lord and stay there.

You will overcome.

October 21

Isaiah 55:11 So will the words that come out of my mouth not come back empty-handed. They'll do the work I sent them to do, they'll complete the assignment I gave them.

You have an assignment from God. A mission.

You are a word from heaven.

All of your circumstances may change. Your mission stays the same.

James 1:2 Dear brothers and sisters, when troubles come your way, consider it an opportunity for great joy.

Enter Autism.

My mission stayed the same.

Only my mission field changed.

God was sending me to a whole new group of beautiful hearts longing to hear a word of hope from the God of all Hope.

Use whatever challenge you're up against as an opportunity. This isn't some unfortunate accident.

This is your hour of influence.

Go make a difference!

Acts 20:24 But none of these things move me...

But my life is worth nothing to me unless I use it for finishing the work assigned me by the Lord Jesus—the work of telling others the Good News about the wonderful grace of God.

When we surrender our plans for His, life springs up!

Persevere! We cannot swerve from our purpose. Be deliberate. Loyal to our faith. Not even the greatest trials and suffering can persuade us to leave this calling.

Remain steadfast through the suffering.

Endure. Remain under the pressure.

Psalm 30:5... Weeping may endure for a night, but joy comes in the morning.

October 22

Just like Isaiah, Nehemiah overheard a need and he responded. He made himself available. As soon as he did he encountered opposition. Let's find out how he responded...

Nehemiah heard the people of Judah were hurting. He didn't turn away. It would've been easier to block out what he heard and saw. Sometimes we can be so desensitized to the needs of people that we become unfeeling. We put on our blinders and think it's not our problem. It's not my kid. I have enough problems of my own. My needs supersede theirs. Seeing is a choice. Nehemiah chose to open his eyes to the need. Or we may be sensitive to the need but it seems so overwhelming we think, "What's the use?" Change begins in one heart. One spark can kindle a forest fire! Nehemiah didn't dismiss what he heard. His immediate response was to fast and pray. It was in this time of prayer that God gave him a heart of love and compassion for the people. Without love, the work will fail. His heart was brimming over with love. This overflow demanded that he do something. All ministries begin when God places a burden on our heart and we respond.

Nehemiah 2:5 Please...send me...

We see that Nehemiah had a job with the king. I'm sure he was involved in ministry right where he was. Often God will call us out of one ministry and into another. Perhaps it's just for a season, and sometimes permanently. Don't be afraid to step out. You may think there won't be anyone to take your place. But God has a replacement in mind. They may be waiting for you to step out so they can step in. No one will know there's a need if you're still filling it!

Nehemiah begged God to give him success. He needed to find favor with his boss, the king.

Proverbs 21:1 The king's heart is in the hand of the LORD, like the rivers of water; He turns it wherever He wishes.

Not only did he find favor, the king provided his every need. Our King will do the same for us.

Lord Jesus we need you. We want our lives to count for you. We want to make a difference in Your kingdom. Let love be our motivation. Increase our faith. Let us know that You are able to do exceedingly abundantly above anything that we could ask or imagine. Fill us with the confidence that You will supply our every need financially, emotionally and spiritually. Fill us to overflowing with your Holy Spirit. Give us boldness to defy the enemy. Let us rise up and build!

October 23

Today is much like a day I walked through a few years ago. It was cloudy and gray. There was no color in it. I had just experienced one of the darkest days of my life and yet my heart just wanted to sing out to God in thankfulness. You see I had just spent the weekend in the emergency room with Camden. I watched him endure the most agonizing pain no mother ever wants to see her child experience. It was a grueling lesson for me. When we finally left there I was numb. I couldn't do anything but thank God that I was NOT in the hospital. That weekend changed me forever. I became grateful for the littlest things. I began to thank God for sunshine. Roses seemed to sing to me. The color of flowers took on a new brilliancy. I became amazed at all of the things I had been ungrateful for. I never want to go back to such a state of heart.

Psalm 118:1 Give thanks to the LORD, for he is good! His faithful love endures forever.

Give thanks. This word "thanks" in the Aramaic can mean to confess or show yourself guilty. Am I guilty of giving thanks in ALL situations?

Is there enough evidence to convict me?

Take a look at the word "good". The root word in the old language means "better." God has something better than we can imagine that He is going to bring from our current circumstances.

Typically we set limits on when we will be thankful. We set conditions, and if they are met then we'll be thankful.

We will reciprocate only if we "feel" we have something to be thankful for first. Reciprocate means to repay an action or gesture of another. That means someone must go first. We are inclined to wait for the other person to do it first. God wants us to give thanks before the good comes. That means we are looking at His character and we examine what He's done in the past and we trust that He will do the same in this situation.

God is the same yesterday, today and forever.

He did not let me fall.

I will thank Him when not one thing looks like it's going to come through. I will thank Him on this tough day.

God I thank you right now for what You are going to do in my situation. Nothing looks good right now. But I know that you work all things for good for those who love you and are called according to your purpose. As bad as things are, I recognize they could be worse. I praise You that they are not. I love you because You are faithful even when I am faithless. I will bless Your name on this day.

October 24

Philippians 3:10 That I may know Him and the power of His resurrection...

The more you know Him, the more you will know His power.

Trust is built over time.

Because of my background, when I came into our marriage, I was fragile and insecure. I had known Ray for about 3 years before we married. I knew I could trust him. I knew I loved him. But, there were so many things he didn't know about me (I tried to warn him!). Only after spending hour upon hour together did we really start to know each other. Day after day, walking through new experiences reveals our true hearts to each other. Month after month of building a firm foundation. We would spend hours and hours talking. We would plan outings to different places; delighting in each other's company. Each year we spend together we grow closer. Our love deepens.

It works the same way with our God.

The more time we spend in His word, the more we become acquainted with Who He really is. We can hear a lot about Him. Listening to other people's experiences with Him may give us knowledge; but that's head knowledge. Not heart knowledge. He wants our hearts. Our souls. All of us.

The more we know Him, the more we want to give Him.

We learn He can be trusted.

The more we trust Him, the more freedom we have. We are unimpeded by our own thoughts. The things we see become irrelevant. We learn to trust Him with what we cannot see. He detaches us from our fears. How freeing that was for me. Releases us from the dreadful unknown of the future.

Daniel 2:22...He knows what is in the darkness, and light dwells with Him.

Although I walk in darkness and cannot see what the future holds for me, I am not afraid. He put it there.

Micah 7:8 When I sit in darkness, the LORD will be a light to me.

Nothing will slip by Him. He won't give me something that's not good for me. He will never give me more than I can handle. Never. Because He loves me. We will handle it together. He has proven Himself time after time. He is a trusted friend.

I know the real Him; not the superficial. I know what is underneath.

I am ready.

I wait in anxious anticipation for Him to work in my life.

The more I know Him, the more I know the power of His resurrection.

He rose from the dead. There is nothing He can't do!

October 25

2 Kings 22:1-2 Josiah...reigned for thirty-one years...His mother's name was Jedidah...he did what was right in the sight of the LORD...he did not turn aside to the right hand or to the left.

How did Josiah manage to walk in the ways of the Lord? His father was an evil wretch of a man. He definitely wasn't there for him. He didn't even have a Bible growing up.

Everything was stacked against him.

One thing is clear.

He had a mother who knew her God.

Behind every man is his mother.

She lived in the midst of a country that was swamped with perversion.

Everywhere she looked was polluted.

She stood up.

She stood out.

Very little is written about her. In fact, nothing. Only her name is recorded for us. We can deduce a lot from just that.

Her name was Jedidah which means "beloved." Loved by God.

She could stand out. Come out and be separated from all of the perversity of her generation because she knew who she was. The world didn't define her. Her God was the sum total of who she was. She didn't give in to the ways of the world. She lived out her faith. Constant. Day in and day out. It wouldn't have been easy. But she knew God could take care of her.

He saw her needs.

Struggles.

Longings.

He filled them all.

She was at home being a godly mother.

She didn't compromise her son.

It paid off.

Josiah changed a whole generation.

She raised up a son who took a stand for the Lord. He was bold. Just as his mother, Josiah found his identity in his God. He sat on his mother's knee. He learned from her. Watched her. She lived it out. She was authentic and he knew it. Soaked and saturated with the love of God, he had a sensitive heart. The temptation to just give in and be like the rest of the men would always be looming. Overwhelming at times.

He did not give in.

Not only that, he set out to remove the infestation of filth in his country. He stirred the hearts of the people to come alongside him and do the same.

He made a dramatic impact on the lives of many people.

Josiah took a stand.

His mother laid that foundation.

What did it cost her?

There is no mention of the things she gave up for her son. But they are evident. No mention of the time she invested in him. It speaks for itself. No mention of the hours she spent praying for him. It's obvious.

She left a legacy.

It is recorded forever in the words of His Book.

Sometimes it seems we are fighting a losing battle. We can't change the whole world. But we can make a difference in our homes. We are raising children for the King. It's an awesome responsibility. It's so tempting to just go with the flow.

We can't give in.

We have to be women who give our hearts to our God.

Our everything.

Our all.

It will take our all.

There is a battle for our children. They need us to fight for them.

They will never be stronger than what we are.

God knows the struggle we face to make this happen.

He hears the cries of our hearts. Sees all of our tears.

It's worth it. He's worth it.

Lord teach me how to pray. I want to lay aside all of the ridiculous distractions that keep me from prayer. I want to be that prayer warrior for my children. Show me the fleetingness of my life. Give my children a supernatural love for You, and Your word. Meet them on the road today. Overwhelm them with Your goodness. Gently remind them Who You are. Should they turn to the left or the right, let them hear You whispering, "This is the way. Walk in it."

October 26

1 Kings 10:1-2 Now when the queen of Sheba heard of the fame of Solomon concerning the name of the LORD, she came to test him with hard questions. She came... with a very great retinue, with camels that bore spices, very much gold, and precious stones; and when she came to Solomon, she spoke with him about all that was in her heart.

The Queen of Sheba came to Solomon with 3 things.

She brought precious things, hard questions and a trusting heart.

We can bring these same things to our God.

We can trust Him with what is most precious to us. There are some real hard things we're facing. When the therapists don't know and the world doesn't have any answers, we can go to the One who has them all.

Genesis 18:14 "Is anything too hard for the LORD?"

We can speak to Him about all that's on our hearts. There are certain things we just can't trust to anyone else.

Psalm 20:4 May He grant you your heart's desire, and fulfill all your purpose.

The King gave the Queen much more than she came with.

He did not disappoint.

The same will be true for us.

When we come to God with our hard stuff, we'll leave with the peace that passes understanding.

We'll go away full. Overflowing.

Filled with much more than we came with.

Ephesians 3:20 God can do anything, you know—far more than you could ever imagine or guess or request in your wildest dreams! He does it not by pushing us around but by working within us, his Spirit deeply and gently within us.

October 27

We can often become so preoccupied with the here and now, that we forget the promise God gave us.

The enemy mocks us. He taunts us, saying, "You'll never do this. This is never going to happen."

The waiting seems so long.

We tend to want to take matters into our own hands.

This is what happened to Sarah. She got tired of waiting.

She thought she would "help" God out. Her help made a big mess; especially in her marriage.

Sarah waited a really long time. Waiting is so difficult. We would much rather do something, anything other than wait.

Waiting really comes down to trusting.

Do I trust God enough to wait for His timing?

His way?

Genesis 21:1 The LORD kept His word and did for Sarah exactly what he had promised.

Always. God ALWAYS keeps His word.

There are no exceptions to this. None. He never goes back on His word.

You can always trust it. It never changes.

Our feelings change with the tide.

Don't trust your feelings. Don't put your trust in people. When the enemy taunts you, stand on God's word.

His word is the only thing that we can trust.

Proverbs 3:5-6 Trust in the Lord with all your heart. Don't lean on your own understanding.

We believe and then we waver. When things look good we smile and trust. When things don't look so good, we frown and try to force it.

Just as sure as an unopened bud will blossom into something beautiful, so too will your waiting.

If I try to force open a bud, I would destroy it.

God gave Sarah exactly what He promised.

He will do the same for you as well.

He is faithful.

Psalm 84:11 For the LORD God is a sun and shield; the LORD will give grace and glory; no good thing will He withhold from those who walk uprightly...Blessed is the [wo]man who trusts in You!

October 28

2 Chronicles 19:11...Be bold and diligent. And God be with you as you do your best...

Dare: to be bold, to do something terribly difficult, to show courage in an undertaking, to bring oneself to do something...

Being bold requires us to step out of our comfort zone. That's not always easy.

Acts 5:12-13 And through the hands of the apostles many signs and wonders were done among the people...Yet none of the rest dared join them...

This verse suggests many others had the opportunity to be a part of something so amazing it would blow their socks off; and yet they missed it.

They weren't daring enough. They sat on the sidelines instead of getting in the game.

The apostles were average people just like us.

Simple. Ordinary. Unassuming.

No exceptional skills.

God chose to do many wonderful things through their lives. He still uses simple people just like us to accomplish His work.

Our own insecurities, being aware of our own ineptness, examining our inabilities; all of these things keep us from experiencing the amazing things of God.

Being a Christian is so exciting!

You get to partner with God Himself.

God did not need them. He doesn't need us. He gives us opportunities to be used because it's such an awesome blessing.

Don't miss doing something great for God.

Step out of your comfort zone!

Dare to take that leap of faith!

They dared not go. They missed out on all that God did. They could've had a part in it, but they totally missed it. They sat on the sidelines.

Here is what else I love: God still does miracles.

Many believers were still added to the Lord. God just supernaturally used the few men and women he had. He multiplies what we give Him.

Dare to use the strength and capacity that God gave you. Whatever that looks like for you.

Don't waste your gifts! Don't miss that opportunity!

October 29

There is a soft glow to the foyer. Flickering shadows dance on the walls. The scent of apple cinnamon wafting through the air draws me away from the moment.

Takes the exhaustion away and lifts me up.

The fan is blowing softly; sending a fresh wind through the whole house. Along with it a sweet fragrance.

Fire kindles fire.

I lit that candle, and it's gonna stay lit until I say so.

It's mine.

Our joy is much like this candle.

Nothing can blow it out unless we allow it.

No matter what's good. No matter what's bad.

It cannot steal my joy.

It will not.

Joy is a choice.

Nothing can take possession of my joy.

My candle will stay lit. Burning bright.

No darkness. No scheme of hell. No criticism will douse it.

When you encounter darkness, remember where you came from.

Assume the person you encounter is right where you were.

Hold out your candle. Give grace. Overlook. Do a lot of overlooking today.

John 1:5 The light shines in the darkness, and the darkness can never extinguish it.

I will light my world today.

How about you?

Keep your candle burning.

Go light your world!

October 30

2 Chronicles 14:11 Then Asa cried out to the LORD his God, "O LORD, no one but You can help the powerless against the mighty! Help us, O LORD our God, for we trust in You alone. It is in Your name that we have come against this vast horde. O LORD, You are our God; do not let mere men prevail against You!"

Asa was up against a lot.

Sometimes we are up against more than we can handle.

I like the Message version. It says, "God is not impressed by numbers." He isn't intimidated by them...so why should we be?

Asa cried out to "his" God. I like that. He isn't some far away distant God. He is MY God. My Jesus. I am His and He is mine.

Asa didn't fall down in despair when he saw the great multitude coming against him. He looked up.

He cried out to his God. Almighty God. The God that created the earth and the heavens and everything in them...that is our God. But He isn't distant. He is near. Near to help. Sensitive to our need. He hears when we call. Just like when our child is in a room with other children we can pick out their cry and we jump up to listen and see if they're ok. God can distinguish our voice. He knows when we need Him to act.

Asa recognized there was none to help. No one but the Lord. Asa said, "We rest on You. We trust in You alone. It is in Your name that we have come."

When we are feeling overwhelmed we're not alone.

God is with us. God is for us.

Dear God please help me to grasp that You hear my voice. You are listening. Help me to trust You alone. You are my God. I am your daughter. I will rest in that today.

October 31

2 Chronicles 15:8... Asa...restored the altar of the Lord

This one word meant so much to me this week...

Restored: make new...to polish a sword...renew...renew oneself

How do you feel when you get a new outfit or when you clean your house all nice and spic and span?

Feels like a new house. It's refreshing. Puts a spark back in your step.

Remember what your Christian life used to look like? Remember when your faith was strong? Remember when your prayer life was everything to you?

Asa restored the altar. One of the altars spoken of in the Old Testament was the Altar of incense. In the Bible, incense is often a metaphor to prayer.

God wants us to restore that time of deep prayer to our lives.

The newness wears off. It does.

Revive it! Revive that vibrancy you had in your prayer life.

Add some new songs during your prayer time. Go to a different place and take a walk with the Lord. Get a new devotional. Do something different.

Another altar spoken of was the Altar of burnt offering.

What was the Altar of burnt offering? It was the whole bull, lamb, or sacrifice. It was the whole thing; not just pieces that were offered.

The Lord wants to take us back to that time when He was everything.

Maybe you've never quite been there. God wants to take you there. He always does that through our circumstances.

It is through the darkest storms that we find He is our refuge.

He wants us to remember when He was everything to us. And when we gave him everything. There was a time when we just wanted to be with Him. That was the only thing that brought comfort.

God wants our everything. He wants all of our hearts.

Is there any part of your heart you are holding back? Is there an area you don't fully trust Him? Are you relying on yourself? Are you putting too much pressure on yourself?

Asa relied wholly on the Lord at the beginning of his walk. But at the end of his life, it was very sad. He didn't seek the Lord. He relied on himself. His own ingenuity. I find myself doing that sometimes.

The Lord wants to remind us of the things He and He alone has brought us through.

We did nothing. He did it all. And He will do it all this time. We can rely solely and wholly on Him.

Lord, renew my desire for You. Fan me into flames for You God. Revive these dead bones. Breathe new life back into me. I want to be sold out for you. Show me my areas of complacency. I see where I am trying to force things to happen. I just want to give you those areas. My confidence is in You.

November

November 1

Psalm 118:22 The stone which the builders rejected has become the chief cornerstone.

Cornerstone: a stone that forms the base of a corner of a building, joining two walls.

We are "walls" Christ is joining together. One here and one here. On our own we are weak and shaky. Not firm. Not standing solid. But joined together with Christ as the cornerstone, we become strong together. We grow fuller and more mature through our weaknesses. The weaker we are the more we need to depend on Christ.

2 Corinthians 12:10 When I am weak then I am strong.

Wherever God has you right now you can be sure it is no coincidence. If you are going through a trial, God wants to use it for good; to strengthen someone else. If you have gone through a trial and all of us have, he wants to use that thing to bring hope to someone else.

God loves weak things. He adores weak people. Weakness is not something to be ashamed of, or afraid of.

2 Corinthians 12:6... Therefore most gladly I will rather boast in my infirmities, that the power of Christ may rest upon me.

I am convinced the church exists for the weak, rejected, lonely and the hurting. We are a refuge. A shelter. Open arms to embrace them; because we've been there.

As a church body, let's seek them out. Let's open our eyes this week and be on the lookout.

Isaiah 35:3 Strengthen the weak hands, And make firm the feeble knees. Say to those who are fearful-hearted, "Be strong, do not fear! Behold, your God will come with vengeance, With the recompense of God; He will come and save you."

Let's seek out the grieving. Weak. Worn down. Wounded. Sick. Lift them up. Strengthen them. Share our story with them. Bring them comfort. And hope.

November 2

I watch still.

My eyes are locked. I sit mesmerized.

How could anything good come from that black ugliness?

I stay focused; not wanting to miss anything.

Knowing it's out of my control, I breathe.

I blink and there she is before me.

Captivatingly beautiful.

She spreads her wings.

The struggle is over.

I just witnessed the birth of a butterfly.

She emerged from her cloak of darkness. Completely changed.

Many times our Lord clothes our lives with deep darkness. Seasons of intense struggle. It can seem cruel. Too much to bear. Being alone feels overwhelming.

Darkness in necessary.

Every woman must be clothed in darkness for a season. It is there she is given wings to soar to new heights spiritually.

Isaiah 61:3... to give unto them beauty for ashes...

There is an initial spiritual birth.

John 3:3 A man must be born again.

After that, there is a continual transformation of your life.

Birth, but then rebirth.

New life inside the heart. Change. Permanent change. Radical and different.

Our spiritual life is a continual metamorphosis.

God writes, but He rewrites. He makes, but He remakes.

New ways of thinking, feeling, and acting.

This takes place only in the dark difficult days of adversity. The process cannot be avoided, even in our children. We don't want to see suffering. It's painful. But had I stepped in to "help" the butterfly emerge, a crucial part of her wing development would've been missed. She would've fallen out malformed; never able to reach her full potential. Butterflies must go through immense pressure. Their wings must flap and flap to develop strength. It's the pressure that spreads a critical fluid that is so necessary to fly. My misguided attempts to "help" would've stunted her growth.

Darkness is necessary.

Hidden in darkness, but never alone. He is in the darkness.

Psalm 139:7 Where can I go from Your Spirit?

Cancer, autism, abandonment, loneliness and difficult seasons change us for the better.

We enter empty, and come out full.

Go in broken, and come out whole.

Enter in clinging to our will, but come out surrendered.

Hands wide open.

A surrendered will brings peace.

A peace this world cannot give. Peace that surpasses understanding.

Philippians 4:13 I can do all things through Christ who strengthens me.

I can do this. I will get through this. I can be strong in the face of any-thing. Though war may rise against me, I will not fear.

I will rise.

In the midst of an uncertain future I can trust the One who holds it. He is certain.

I am able because God is able.

We don't know the outcome of our trials. But it will be good.

Ecclesiastes 3:11 He makes everything beautiful in His time.

He is good. Everything He does is good.

Isaiah 40:31 But they that wait upon the LORD shall renew their strength; they shall mount up with wings as eagles; they shall run, and not be weary; and they shall walk, and not faint.

November 3

Acts 4:31 And when they had prayed, the place where they were...was shaken; and they were all filled with the Holy Spirit, and they spoke the Word of God with boldness.

I think it is so awe-inspiring to see the Power of prayer in this verse. It is breathtaking. This word "shaken" in the original language gives us a picture of an earthquake of great magnitude. The force of it literally moves everything from its secure place. When an earthquake hits, the epicenter is where the greatest impact is felt. The effects ripple out from there. When we pray the condition we are in spiritually is shaken to the core. We are shaken up; never to be the same again. We are filled with the Holy Spirit. As a result we speak the Word of God boldly. Just like an earthquake, the effects ripple out. Individually, we are shaken, moved and filled. Consequently, we speak boldly to those the Lord brings in our path. We pray for them. By the power of our prayer, they too can be shaken and filled. Boldness overcomes them and they "can't help but speak the things which [they] have seen and heard."

The ripple effect!

An old woman with a halo of silvered hair-hot tears flowing down her furrowed cheeks-her worn hands busy over a washboard in a room of poverty-praying-for her son John-John who ran away from home in his teens to become a sailor-John, of whom it was now reported that he had become a very wicked man-praying, praying always, that her son might be of service to God. The mother believed in two things, the power of prayer and the reformation of her son. So while she scrubbed she continued to pray. God answered the prayer by working a miracle in the heart of John Newton. The black stains of sin were washed white in the blood of the Lamb. "Though your sins be as scarlet, they shall be white as snow." The washtub prayers were heard as are all prayers when asked in His name. John Newton, the drunken sailor, became John Newton, the sailor-preacher. Among the thousands of men and women he brought to Christ was Thomas Scott, cultured, selfish, and self-satisfied. Because of the washtub prayers another miracle was worked and Thomas Scott used both his pen and voice to lead thousands of unbelieving hearts to Christ-among them, a dyspeptic, melancholic young man, William Cowper by name. He, too, was washed by the cleansing blood and in a moment of inspiration wrote:

There is a fountain filled with blood

Drawn from Immanuel's veins,

And sinners, plunged beneath that flood,

Lose all their guilty stains.

And this song has brought countless thousands to the Man who died on Calvary. Among the thousands was William Wilberforce, who became a great Christian statesman, and unfastened the shackles from the feet of thousands of British slaves. Among those whom he led to the Lord was Leigh Richmond, a clergyman of the Established Church in one of the Channel Islands he wrote a book, The Dairyman's Daughter, which was translated into forty languages and with the intensity of leaping flame burned the love of Christ into the hearts of thousands. All this resulted because a mother took God at His Word and prayed that her son's heart might become as white as the soapsuds in the washtub.

~ Mrs. Charles Cowman

One praying woman can change a family.

One praying woman can change a city.

One praying woman can change a nation.

It begins at the epicenter; your own heart. One heart at a time; starting with you!

November 4

As I opened the door for Mary her eyes spoke before she did. They told a story. It's the same story of the colorless life she resides in. I recognize it so well because I've been there. Ashen gray circles envelop her sunken eyes. The dark circles reflect an even darker soul. Her eyes are filled with pain. They tell me of the hope that's been stolen. Dreams shattered. Sleepless nights. And laughter lost.

When you see her she has a beautiful smile, but just below that façade is a heart that is breaking and crying out for someone to see her pain. She pretends everything is ok even when it's not. That's what mothers do. Her world falls apart daily. Every day she has no idea of what to expect. You wouldn't know it though. Rarely will she let anyone break through that concrete barrier she's built up around her. It's too risky. She may fall apart.

I've heard of other mothers recently too. Moms just like you and I. Our dreams start the same. Elated to have a new baby. But that quickly turns into a nightmare.

I've seen blood dripping down an arm; a bite from her son trying to communicate his anger. Head butts into her face; over and over again. Ranting and kicking so hard into her shin until one might think it would break. Overwhelmed by the enormity of the demands placed upon them, some snap.

There are no words to convey what my heart feels. I feel so much guilt. Why do I get such an easy life?

My heart cried out to God, "Why are you showing me these things. I am helpless to do anything about it. I want to do something God. I have nothing to give. Nothing. In and of myself I am bankrupt."

But Jesus.

I have Jesus. He is the answer. The only solution.

Psalm 123:2...as the eyes of servants look to the hand of their masters...so our eyes look to the LORD our God, until He has mercy on us.

I have seen firsthand what the Lord can do.

I found solace in Him. He brought me hope. Everyday. While my world was falling apart, I still had Him as an anchor for my soul. While I had gone so far down, he brought me up again.

Psalm 126:2 We were filled with laughter, and we sang for joy. And... said, "What amazing things the LORD has done for them."

If He did that for me, He can do it for you.

Psalm 126:5 Those who sow in tears shall reap in joy.

God fill the holes of our hearts with the tiny seeds of hope that you have planted. Use our tears as seeds. Bring these seeds to life! We desire to bear much fruit for you. Without You we can do nothing. But with You we can do anything.

November 5

God filled the holes in my heart. He took a trail of tears and made something beautiful bloom in my life.

Each tear a seed.

Those seeds fell into the ground and died.

John 12:14...unless a grain of wheat falls into the earth and dies, it remains alone; but if it dies, it bears much fruit.

God brought life out of death.

I had to bring death to my plans, my hopes, and my desires. When I did, I found a new life.

Philippians 3:7 I once thought these things were valuable, but now I consider them worthless because of what Christ has done.

What has God done?

He raised me from the dead!

After that, He called me to go out and tell what "great things He has done" to anyone who would listen.

He wants to do the same for you! He wants to use you to bring hope into another hurting soul. There are hurting hearts all around us. We have the answer! Jesus Christ is the answer.

God allows brokenness to happen. He does not make mistakes. He wants to use your testimony.

You may say, "Who me? What could I possibly do with this brokenness? And loss? And emptiness?

God uses brokenness to open us up to feel pain. He makes us relatable.

You are uniquely you. God will use you in ways you never dreamed possible.

Romans 8:28 We know all things work together for the good for those who love God and are called according to His purpose.

God can make something out of nothing. He takes that emptiness and fills it. He will bring you back to life and joy again. You will yet praise Him!

Maybe you feel stuck where you're at. It feels like a prison sometimes. There seems to be nowhere to go. I felt like that before.

Jesus Christ came with the key to that prison. He has come to give you the key to your freedom.

You are free! Freer than you've ever been in your whole life.

Christ came to set the captives free.

He wants to use you right here. Right now. In this place you find yourself in.

Don't be looking around and saying, "Who me?"

Yes you!

God is calling you to rise up!

Luke 9:1 Then he called his twelve disciples together, and gave them power and authority over all devils, and to cure diseases. And he sent them to preach the kingdom of God, and to heal the sick.

God has given you the authority.

He has given you the power.

He will give you the strength physically, emotionally, and spiritually.

You can do this!

Do you need Him? Oh yeah!

He'll give you what you need. Strength every day. You will have to call upon His name every day. Day in and day out. It is good to be dependent upon Him.

Jude 1:24 Now to Him who is able to keep you from falling...

You will stand because He is able to make you stand.

You can stand and speak. This is your testimony. There is hope in God.

You may feel like Jeremiah. Young. Too inexperienced. You may think, what could I possibly say or do?

God touched Jeremiah's mouth. He gave him all the words to speak.

You may ask, "What words do I have?"

You have the words of God! Words of eternal life.

John 1:4 In Him is life

There is life in the Son.

He gave me a new life. A Zoe Life. A God life. He is doing the same in you.

God use my testimony. Use me to plant seeds of hope in hurting hearts. You waste nothing. Don't let my pain go to waste. Embolden me to share my story with others. Let Your Name be lifted up. Today. Use me today.

November 6

John 1:4 In Him is life...

Zoe is the Greek word for "life" here in this verse. It means a full life. An abundant life. Vibrant. Complete. Active life.

That life is only found in the Son.

He gave me a new life. This Zoe Life!

God's word is alive! It brought me back from the dead. No more sorrow. No more pain. No more looking back! God called me to rise up! And He is calling you to rise up!

The word of God empowers women.

It is time!

Philippians 3:13 No, dear... sisters, I have not achieved it, but I focus on this one thing: Forgetting the past and looking forward to what lies ahead...

Looking forward to what lies ahead often requires us to turn our backs on the past and walk in step with the Lord.

Psalm 128:1 A Song of Ascents. Blessed is everyone who fears the LORD, who walks in His ways. When you eat the labor of your hands, you shall be happy, and it shall be well with you.

This verse holds the keys to our happiness!

Keys to happiness: fear the Lord and walk in His ways.

When we walk toward one thing, we must depart from another.

When God called me to rise up, I needed to make a decision. I had to decide to be content with where I was. That was not easy. The Lord and I wrestled for a long time. Much like Jacob. He wrestled with God. Initially he tried to get away from the Lord. By the end of their wrestling match, Jacob was clinging to God and begging for a blessing.

It was in that place of wrestling and struggling with God that Jacob came away with a new name.

God changed Jacob's name to Israel that day.

God wants to give you a new name too!

Isaiah 62:4 Never again will you be called "The Forsaken City" or "The Desolate Land." Your new name will be "The City of God's Delight" and "The Bride of God," for the LORD delights in you and will claim you as his bride.

You are desolate, but you will sing again.

God will give you a new heart. A courageous heart to face every day.

He will also give you a new purpose. New goals and aspirations.

Right where you find yourself. Right here in this place.

November 7

My circumstances had me hedged in. I couldn't go anywhere. I couldn't do anything. I wanted to "move". God wanted me to stay.

I wanted a change to my situation. God wanted to change me.

Pain gave me my voice.

It gave me a new ministry.

There is a woman in the Bible that found exactly the same thing in her loss.

Luke 2:36 Now there was one, Anna, a prophetess, the daughter of Phanuel, of the tribe of Asher. She was of a great age, and had lived with a husband seven years from her virginity; and this woman was a widow of about eighty-four years, who did not depart from the temple, but served God with fastings and prayers night and day.

Here is what we know about Anna. We know she was a widow. I am sure the loss caused her great pain.

How did she overcome?

She stayed in church. Literally she camped out there. I can't think of a better place to be!

We know very little about Anna. But what we know is powerful.

Anna found a prayer ministry in her suffering. It says she served God with fastings and prayers.

She withdrew from the outside world. A time of withdrawal is necessary in every woman's life.

We must take time to hear from the Lord. He will speak to us in our time of mourning. Give us the comfort we so desperately long for. Equally important, he will give us a precious message in the dark.

Anna didn't run away. She didn't take herself off the shelf of life. Nor did she fall away.

She gave herself away. To her God.

In doing so she gained the more.

She gained a new life.

Matthew 10:39 "He who finds his life will lose it, and he who loses his life for My sake will find it.

She found a new purpose.

Ezekiel 22:30 "So I sought for a man among them who would make a wall, and stand in the gap before Me..."

Anna became an intercessor. It is a hidden ministry that is invaluable to the kingdom of our God.

She found new Joy.

Psalm 126:5 Those who sow in tears shall reap in joy.

She became a servant of the living God.

A slave.

Everyone is a slave to someone or something.

I was a slave to depression.

I saw nothing good in my circumstances. I was a prisoner. I couldn't get out. I became stuck in an endless cycle of thinking about myself. Self-pity is an ugly sin that masks itself as sorrow. It makes us look at ourselves. Examine ourselves. Evaluate ourselves. Eventually loathe ourselves. We think about ourselves all the time.

That is depressing.

We long for what used to be.

There is a time for acceptance.

1 Timothy 6:6 Now godliness with contentment is great gain.

Contentment is our source of great gain.

It is a step higher to get you something else; more of your God. Your treasure.

Let us choose contentment. And like Anna, let's find our new purpose.

November 8

1 Kings 17:2-8 Then the word of the LORD came to him, saying, "Get away from here and turn eastward, and hide by the Brook Cherith, which flows into the Jordan. And it will be that you shall drink from the brook, and I have commanded the ravens to feed you there." So he went and did according to the word of the LORD, for he went and stayed by the Brook Cherith, which flows into the Jordan. The ravens brought him bread and meat in the morning, and bread and meat in the evening; and he drank from the brook. And it happened after a while that the brook dried up, because there had been no rain in the land.

It's interesting to note the first place the Lord tells Elijah to go is the Brook Cherith which in the old language means "place of separation, cutting or destruction".

Without exception, the Lord brings us to a place of separation for a purpose. God wants to separate us from everyone and everything that is influencing us. God is cutting away everything we depend on so that we can see He is all we need. Elijah didn't end up here by accident. God sent him to this specific place to hide him. It was a place of protection. If that were me, I would've thought God was trying to punish me for something. Maybe he was upset with me? I always think like that. But hide me? No, that wouldn't have been my first thought. We often mistake adversity for discipline. God actually sent him there to protect him. That's what God will do for us. He wants to show us we're trusting in the wrong thing. We have to trust solely in the Lord and His provision. We can't trust in ourselves, our ingenuity or our resources. We have nothing without the Lord. It was God who sent him there and it would be God who would feed him there. He saw in advance what Elijah would need. He sent the ravens to feed him. He used an unconventional way to meet his need. God never works the way we think He will! The separation was the pathway for Elijah to see God descending down in his need (Jordan actually means "descending"). When Elijah arrived at the Brook Cherith he stayed there. He abided. He didn't run away. When God sends you into this place of great need, embrace it. Don't run from it. God is going to meet you there. He's going to provide for you.

Philippians 4:19 And my God shall supply all your need according to His riches in glory by Christ Jesus.

Allow God to do what He wants to do. God wants to remove our independence. When we try to do things on our own we fail. At the Brook Cherith, this place of "cutting", Elijah saw God meet his need supernaturally. God will do the same for us if we permit Him. Give Him time to work. God is not in a hurry.

November 9

2 Chronicles 4:19-22 Thus Solomon had all the furnishings made for the house of God: the altar of gold and the tables on which was the showbread; the lampstands with their lamps of pure gold, to burn in the prescribed manner in front of the inner sanctuary with the flowers and the lamps and the wick-trimmers of gold, of purest gold; the trimmers, the bowls, the ladles, and the censers of pure gold. As for the entry of the sanctuary, its inner doors to the Most Holy Place, and the doors of the main hall of the temple, were gold.

Why are the flowers there?

In the midst of all the utensils used for the sacrifice, there is beauty.

Right in the middle of all the ugly. There is beauty.

God wants us to see there is beauty in all of this suffering. Beauty at the altar of sacrifice.

Flowers are a picture of new life. Zoe Life. Abundant and full. Vibrant and active. The life God intended.

Even in the sacrifice of a broken heart. Even in the pain of it all.

We blossom in the breaking.

Not at first. It's a slow process sometimes.

When we come to Him with our hearts broken open, He can make something real beautiful out of it.

Makes us whole.

We can praise Him. Thank Him. Zoe Life is only found in Him.

John 1:4 In Him is life.

It was only through His death that we could live.

Death brought life.

Philippians 1:29 For you have been given not only the privilege of trusting in Christ but also the privilege of suffering for him.

Paul was given a thorn in the flesh to remind him to be humble. The Bible doesn't tell us what that was.

But we know and can deduce several things.

It made him weak.

It caused him to be humble.

It's caused him to desperately need the power of God upon him.

2 Corinthians 12:9 And He said to me, "My grace is sufficient for you, for My strength is made perfect in weakness. Therefore most gladly I will rather boast in my infirmities, that the power of Christ may rest upon me."

The word "weakness" means a want of strength in the body. It can mean a sickness or an infirmity.

A disability. It can mean the inability to get out of bed, to continue on or to accomplish a task. It can also be applied to our soul needs. We need understanding. There are things we don't understand and we desire to. It could mean we have no ability to bear this trial. We need strength to get through.

But the definition that really spoke to me was this: an inability to produce results.

It seems I am unable to complete the task at hand. I am just spinning my wheels. I'm not getting anywhere. Producing very little result. Whether that be in homeschooling, reaching a husband that is distant or obtaining that breakthrough in your special needs child. Our God is able to do what we have been unable to do this far.

The word "perfect" in the Greek means to complete. To finish. To bring to an end.

God is going to see us through.

To. The. End.

God does not save half the way.

He saves all the way.

He will take us the whole way.

Philippians 1:6 I am sure of this, that He who started a good work in you will carry it on to completion until the day of Christ Jesus.

He will carry out His plan to completion. All of it.

For the marriage that is struggling, He began it. He will give you what you need to sustain it.

For the single woman desiring more, our Lord is in you. He will fulfill all your need.

He is enough.

Need makes us weak.

We don't like weakness.

We avoid weakness and need at all cost.

God loves weakness. He loves weak women. He loves humble and contrite hearts. Weakness makes us humble.

It's humility that gives us the ability to sacrifice. May our Lord bring "flowers" at your altar of sacrifice.

God, we are desperate for you. Please come. We need help. We are helpless. Who else do we have, but You? You are enough for our needs today. Come fill our hearts with strength to believe we can and will overcome whatever we are facing today. Equip us. Intervene for us. We can do nothing on our own. Come upon us with power. Show me the beauty in the midst of my sacrifice.

November 10

Face time with God is so crucial. In our fast paced lives we give less and less time to what is most important. God can't be relegated to a few texts. We need quality time alone with Him.

Having a special needs child is a staggering responsibility. It is a high calling of God. In and of itself it is a ministry that takes all you have physically, mentally, emotionally and spiritually.

Each of us are called to unique circumstances. While they aren't all overwhelmingly taxing, they are challenging in their own respect.

Moses felt this weight.

God called him to go to the Promised Land. And did I forget to mention he was to take a few hundred thousand people with him?

Go to a strange land.

Having no idea what it's like. Not knowing what to expect. Not knowing what he would encounter along the way.

He was overwhelmed before he even took one step.

I feel like this all the time.

Moses gives us a good example. He gets alone with the Lord.

Exodus 37:7, 9 Moses took his tent and pitched it outside the camp, far from the camp...when Moses entered the tabernacle the pillar of cloud descended...and the Lord spoke to Moses.

Each of us must get alone with the Lord.

We need to withdraw from the world, people, and distractions. That is often easier said than done. Moses had to get there physically. Getting to prayer is challenging. You will be met with serious warfare.

We have to overcome. Not be overcome by the incessant demand of busyness.

Prayer must be deliberate. Intentional. It is imperative. Non-negotiable.

God disciplines His children. Kids thrive on routine; so do we. It is essential for a vibrant Christian life.

Fitting God into our busy schedule isn't the way to go. It's a sure loss every time. Fitting, molding and shaping our schedule around Him is the best way. Solid, with undeniable results.

Matthew 6:33 "But seek first the kingdom of God and His righteousness, and all these things shall be added to you.

We have to say 'no' to a lot of good things in order to say 'yes' to God.

Make an appointment and keep it.

Show up. On time. Ready mind.

November 11

Exodus 33:6-7 For the LORD had said to Moses, "Say to the children of Israel, 'You are a stiff-necked people. I could come up into your midst in one moment and consume you. Now therefore, take off your ornaments, that I may know what to do to you.'?" So the children of Israel stripped themselves of their ornaments by Mount Horeb... everyone who sought the LORD went out to the tabernacle of meeting which was outside the camp.

The Lord hates pretense.

Israel had all of these outward adornments. God was not concerned with these at all. He is always looking at the inward; the heart. More or less he was telling them to get real. Be honest before Me. I can't do anything for you until you get truthful with Me, and truthful with yourself. Soon after, we find Moses pouring his heart out to the Lord. He gets transparent. And why not? He knows our hearts. He is acquainted with all of our fears.

We can try to put on a good front for people. But we don't have to do that with the Lord. We can't.

Moses cried out to the Lord, essentially saying, "Lord, I know you told me to do this. But, You haven't told me who is going to help me."

All of Moses inadequacies came flooding forth. Fears abounded.

Moses knew what he was capable of. He was not up to this huge task. He was doubting his abilities. I'm sure he felt alone. But He wasn't alone.

His God was with Him.

Exodus 33:14 And He said, "My Presence will go with you, and I will give you rest."

God told Moses He would be going with him.

They would do this together. And that was enough.

I want to assure you God doesn't make mistakes. He knows exactly what He is doing.

Our perceived "inadequacies" do three things:

First, they make us humble.

1 Corinthians 1:26-27 Remember, dear brothers and sisters, that few of you were wise in the world's eyes or powerful or wealthy when God called you. Instead, God chose things the world considers foolish in order to shame those who think they are wise. And he chose things that are powerless to shame those who are powerful.

Secondly, our inadequacies make us rely solely and wholly on God.

2 Corinthians 12:9 My grace is sufficient for you...

Thirdly, our inadequacies show the world the power of God.

2 Corinthians 12:9...My power is made perfect in weakness.

God loves weakness. When we are weak. He is strong.

Hear Him whisper this into your heart:

I am enough for you. Period. Whatever your need. I am enough.

God knows each of us by name. He knows what we are capable of.

He began this work and He will complete it.

Moses realizes something vital.

"These are your people."

This is Your ministry. Not mine. This child is Yours Lord. He belongs to you. He is Your responsibility. Not mine. I don't have to carry this enormous weight. If I try, I will be crushed.

We get to do this together.

Moses goes from panic to peace instantly. He realized he wasn't alone. Peace that passes understanding flooded his heart.

Our merciful God sees. He hears the cries of your heart. He spoke to Moses and He wants to speak to you as well. He is on this journey with you. He will see you through to the end. Just be honest with Him; tell Him your fears. Tell Him your doubts. Tell Him your sins. He already knows and is waiting to hear from you.

Lord Jesus I pray You will come down and speak face-to-face with me. Touch my heart with a special Word from Your heart. Hover over me with Your grace. Let me know how very special You think I am. Fill my heart to overflowing with the knowledge that You love me. You chose me. Lord I can't do this without You. Walk me through it.

November 12

This boy. He challenged me to my core. His picture is embedded in my mind. He is kneeling at the flag pole in front of his school. All alone. Many schools participate in this yearly event. It's called Prayer At The Pole. Christian youth gather at the flag pole and pray before school.

He was the only one that showed up.

While his generation is turning their back on God, he turns his face towards God.

Oblivious to the consequences.

2 Timothy 4:16... no one stood with me, but all forsook me

People fall into two categories these days:

People pleaser or God pleaser. You can't be both. It's impossible.

This boy was left all alone.

What would his friends think?

Galatians 1:10 For am I now seeking the approval of man, or of God? Or am I trying to please man? If I were still trying to please man, I would not be a servant of Christ.

I don't know that he thought about pleasing his friends.

He cared more about pleasing God.

I long to be that free. That bold. That courageous.

He risked all.

His reputation was at stake.

When you give it all, you gain the more.

What does this boy know? Real men love Jesus.

Ezekiel 22:30 "So I sought for a man among them who would make a wall, and stand in the gap before Me on behalf of the land, that I should not destroy it; but I found no one."

God is looking for a man to stand in the gap.

This kid is a difference maker. A game changer. A life maker.

His life has purpose.

And so much value.

He made a statement without saying one word.

All he has is Jesus. All he needs is Jesus. Everything he needs is found at the feet of Jesus.

He's doing the only thing he can do. Pray.

He knows prayer changes things.

We are raising up the most depressed generation of children.

They have no peace because they have no Jesus.

They are so lost. And he knows it. And he is doing the only thing he can do. Pray.

If you want a changed marriage, do something about it. Pray.

If you want a changed church, do something about. Pray.

If you want a changed nation, do something about it. Pray.

If you want a changed child, do something about it. Pray.

Bring them to the feet of Jesus. That's when life happens. That's where change takes place.

Dear Lord, I pray for a heart like this boy. Give me a heart that is sold out for you. Don't let me sell out to the crowd. I want to please your heart. I want to make a difference in another's life. Use me Lord. Give me a heart to do something about the sadness I see all around me.

November 13

My poor pup. I tread on him inadvertently. I stepped on his paw. I didn't meant to.

I really hurt him.

I didn't even realize it. I never heard a whimper out of him.

I turned around to see he was burying his little face. Rubbing his eyes, he was trying not to cry. Holding it all in.

I read Golden Retrievers are good at masking pain. They just want to please. They want to make everyone happy. They just want friends.

Desperately want to be near. They don't let you know if they've been hurt.

People are like that too.

We can step on them with the things we say.

We have to choose our words so carefully.

They last a lifetime.

Be quick to listen. Slow to speak. Slow to get angry.

We never know what's going on behind the scenes.

There is always a story behind the story.

Always.

Proverbs 15:4 Kind words heal and help; cutting words wound and maim.

Jesus please help me not offend. I want to see people the way you see them. Give me graceful words. Help me not to react. Put a guard on my mouth. Use my words to soothe. I want to be kind. Help me to just slow down and take the time to speak a gentle word to a hurting heart today.

November 14

Sometimes we set out on our journey. We know there will be difficulties. We expect them. The winds start kicking up and we cling a little tighter to our God. And we keep sailing. Along comes the rain. Torrential downpours and gusts and hail and suddenly we don't know if our ship is going to make it. This very thing happened to Paul in Acts 27. God told Paul to stay in the boat. Period. You will get to where you're going. I will make sure of it. I called you there. And no matter what comes your way you'll make it through. You will finish. I will make sure of it. Everything, including the ship you were trusting in, may fall apart. But you will get there. Eventually the ship did fall apart. They made it though. Clinging to the boards of the ship got Paul and everyone he was with safely to shore. If they jumped ship they wouldn't have made it. They chose to trust God's word instead of looking at their circumstances. You can trust God like that too. You can never trust your feelings; they change with the wind. You're going to get where you're going. Even though everything you were counting on crumbles. The very thing that you thought was holding it all together may break apart. Stay in the boat. Trust God. He's your safe place...

Acts 27:25...I believe God that it will be just as it was told me.

November 15

It was a nice peaceful morning. Everything was still. There was a crisp chill in the air. Its fall but you wouldn't know it.

No wind.

Quite comfortable.

Nothing was really moving. All was quiet. I was lost in thought.

I approached a bend in the road.

Awakened out of my false sense of security; headlights beamed directly in front of me. I was startled. It was a large truck. Loud.

It got my attention.

It began to veer off the road. It was heading straight for me. I froze in my tracks. Is this guy really going to hit me? I didn't know which way to go. I was frozen. It was obvious he was texting. Not paying a bit of attention. He looked up at the last second; barely negotiating the bend in the road.

As this guy was looking down, distracted and foolish, his entire life could've been wrecked by one imprudent decision.

This same scenario can happen in our lives if we're not careful. If our eyes aren't focused and looking up, Satan can wreak havoc.

Be watchful.

Wake up.

1 Peter 5:8 Be sober, be vigilant; because your adversary the devil walks about like a roaring lion, seeking whom he may devour.

This was a warning.

When there are contentions between you and your husband do not withdraw yourself from him.

Draw near to him.

Put everything aside when he gets home.

Make him the center of your attention. Let him know he's important.

Respect him.

Love on him.

Even if you have no inclination to do it.

The same goes for your children.

Be vigilant.

Know what your children are doing. Know who they're with at all times.

Beware.

Don't give your children open access to the Internet.

There are predators at every click.

Galatians 5:9 A little leaven leavens the whole lump.

God has a special plan for His children. We have to do everything we can to keep them pure.

Matthew 5:8...the pure in heart...shall see God.

Why does Satan always go after the children?

Because he knows what they will become.

He wants to destroy them.

That is his mission.

John 10:10 The thief's purpose is to steal and kill and destroy...

If you have to say no to something, consider providing an alternative. You can't watch this, but how about this? You can't go there, but how about here? You can't hang out there, but how about here?

We must do everything in our power to protect them.

We need to pray for our families.

Pray for our husbands.

If we don't who will?

We need to be his biggest fan.

We need to pray for our children.

If we don't who will?

They need our covering.

James 5:16...The effective, fervent prayer of a righteous [wo]man avails much.

Stay on guard!

November 16

I had a dream one night. It was so vivid. My front yard was filled with water; much like the Arctic. There were a few polar bears scattered about. Some were above the surface and some below. One polar bear in particular stood out. He was large with a commanding presence. He had two little cubs following closely behind him. They were swimming in a circle; playing and romping about. Noticeably, he was looking down. His head was below the surface. All the while very large storm clouds were rolling in. Things were getting dark and ominous, but this bear was oblivious.

This is such a picture of what is happening in our world today. Things are getting darker by the minute.

The Bible tells us there will be a day when the Lord returns for His people. Everything around us points to the fact that the time is imminent for this to happen. While the Bible clearly states that no one knows the exact time, it does point to things that will happen. There are telltale signs.

2 Timothy 3:1-5 You should know this... in the last days there will be very difficult times. For people will love only themselves and their money. They will be boastful and proud, scoffing at God, disobedient to their parents, and ungrateful. They will consider nothing sacred. They will be unloving and unforgiving; they will slander others and have no self-control. They will be cruel and hate what is good. They will betray their friends, be reckless, be puffed up with pride, and love pleasure rather than God. They will act religious, but they will reject the power that could make them godly.

If this verse doesn't describe our society, nothing does.

Discern the signs and the times.

Matthew 24:37-44 "When the Son of Man returns, it will be like it was in Noah's day. In those days before the flood, the people were enjoying banquets and parties and weddings right up to the time Noah entered his boat. People didn't realize what was going to happen until the flood came and swept them all away. That is the way it will be when the Son of Man comes. Two men will be working together in the field; one will be taken, the other left. Two women will be grinding flour at the mill; one will be taken, the other left. So you, too, must keep watch! For you don't know what day your Lord is coming. Understand this: If a homeowner knew exactly when a burglar was coming, he would keep watch and not permit his house to be broken into. You also must be ready all the time, for the Son of Man will come when least expected."

If that polar bear had been looking up, he would've seen what was coming. He could've protected his cubs.

Look up.

Your cubs will follow you anywhere. You can't afford to miss this. Knowledge is power. You owe it to yourself and to your children to know and watch for the signs.

The only place to get your answers is found in the Bible.

Don't put it off. The time is short. Don't ignore it and hope it goes away. The storm clouds are rolling in.

God is trying to get our attention.

November 17

Two workers dangled precariously over New York City; hanging by just a cable.

One cable snapped.

Unexpectedly.

Would the other?

Life and death were hanging in the balance.

When they left for work, did they know their life may be required?

Everyday life hangs in the balance for each of us.

Joel 3:14 Multitudes, multitudes stand in the valley of decision! For the day of the Lord is near in the valley of decision.

We know the fate of these two workers.

They were saved.

But do you know your fate?

If you died today, where would you go?

Everyone will live forever.

God's word is true.

Heaven and hell are real.

Hell is a real place.

A lake of fire burns forever.

And ever.

With no escape.

God wishes none to go there.

He gives us free choice though.

We have to choose heaven.

While we still have a chance, we have to repent of our sins. That is where the difficulty lies. Repentance means to actually turn from it and go in the other direction. Don't be deceived, you cannot live in a habitual lifestyle of sin and go to heaven. That is a lie and completely contrary to the word of God.

Your Rescuer, Jesus, stands with Hand stretched out inviting you to come into safety. He has already paid the penalty for your sin.

John 3:16 "For God so loved the world that He gave His only begotten Son, that whoever believes in Him should not perish but have everlasting life."

Turn from your sin while there is still time.

You are not promised tomorrow.

Live for Him.

Do whatever it takes.

He is worth it.

God loves you immensely. He wants you to know that.

November 18

My eyes hurt.

Heart hurts.

Sigh.

What's a girl to do?

This girl?

She's blossoming.

It's fall. You don't bloom in fall.

Do you?

People disappoint us.

Disabilities overwhelm us.

Things don't go the way we want.

We can revile.

Get angry. Spout off. Fret.

Or we can smile. Smile big.

God, You are still God.

Even when people are ungodly.

And ugly.

We are misunderstood.

When words hurt, I have a choice.

Joy is a choice.

I have a rose bush in my front garden called a Joseph's Coat Rose. It is spectacular. Each new bud starts off pale yellow. When it opens up it is dark yellow with hot pink edges. As time progresses and the heat comes, it changes to a deep glorious salmon color. In the book of Genesis we find a story about Joseph. He was given a coat of many colors. Symbolic of his many trials. He was able to thrive through a life of continual adversity. He was thrown in a pit by his own brothers. Found himself a literal slave. Thrown in prison and forgotten about by everyone.

Except His God.

God never left him.

God was with him.

And for him.

Joseph chose to be content.

We can do the same.

Ephesians 5:20...giving thanks always for ALL things to God the Father...

We can praise Him for the good things. And the bad.

Ann Voskamp says, "giving thanks is only this: making the canyon of pain into a megaphone to proclaim the ultimate goodness of God... But this is not easy: that which I refuse to thank Christ for, I refuse to believe Christ can redeem."

God is able to make goodness come out of this person, situation, disability, and even death.

Even if we can't see how.

I will praise Him for that.

If I don't, I become a prisoner of my circumstance. Held in chains.

Joseph was in a literal prison. But he was free. He chose to die to his plan, his way, and himself. He chose to accept where God placed him. He knew nothing in his life was an accident. Everything had a purpose.

Genesis 50:20 You intended to harm me, but God intended it all for good. He brought me to this position so I could save the lives of many people.

No matter where you find yourself today, know this: God is for you. He is with you. You have nothing to fear. Just like the rose, God is making something beautiful from the heat of your trials. Give Him thanks.

November 19

As I headed out to get my coffee this morning I was stopped in my tracks. The door was locked. Tightly. I tried several times to open it. The gentleman at the front desk kindly informed me I couldn't go anywhere. The police had stopped all the traffic. Something about a bomb scare. All I could really think about was my coffee. He on the other hand was concerned about my safety. I sure appreciated that. But I really wanted to shout, "Just open the door, I am willing to risk it!"

Okay but I didn't. I went up the stairs to where he was. I am supposing he saw the desperation on my face. He offered me a cup of his coffee. I politely declined. He made several calls to see if I could leave. To no avail. He would not let me out. However he told me I could go out back and sit on the large veranda overlooking the ocean.

Not a bad alternative.

As I sat there in utter darkness I listened to the rustling waves. Looking into the unknown. There was a chill in the air. I began to ponder the situation.

I'm forced to stay in when I want to go out.

I don't understand.

I can't go where I want to go.

I can't do what I want to do.

I don't understand.

I have to sit out back.

There's no one around. No one stirring yet.

Out of the corner of my eye I see one small light moving across the water. A boat moving at a pretty good speed.

I see it so easily because it's so dark.

I ponder some more.

I look up.

That light that was moving across the water abruptly turned and went in the other direction.

It did a 360 and went the other way.

That happens in our lives sometimes.

We are so sure we are headed one way and without warning everything changes.

It's so hard to understand.

Oftentimes difficult to accept.

That boat never turned back.

It's dark and I can't see why. I don't know the surrounding circumstances. I don't have the big picture. I am trusting the captain had his reasons. He knows the seas best. Perhaps the waves ahead were too big. In his desire to protect the boat, he turned around. He knows where he's going.

I don't.

I thought I did. It looked so obvious.

Micah 7:8...when I sit in darkness the Lord will be a light to me.

As I sit in darkness I'll continue to wait and trust. My God knows what's best.

His eyes see further than mine. His eyes see further than yours. If today finds you perplexed, trust the Lord. Lean not on your own understanding. He knows what is best for you. You can trust Him.

 November 20

Nehemiah 6:12 I perceived...

Nehemiah spent a lot of time with the Lord. This gave him great spiritual discernment. He could see things others would miss. He saw the enemy's plan to stop the work of God. The enemy tried to intimidate him. But he was confident in the call of God.

When we encounter opposition:

Call to God. Don't call your friends first. Don't add fuel to the fire. Where there is no wood the fire goes out.

Get to work with greater determination.

Remember, if Satan is attacking we know it's a good work from the Lord.

Don't defend. Don't respond. Don't fight back.

Pray.

Nehemiah lived a life of prayer.

Pray! It's your faith builder.

Pray! It's your resource maker.

Pray! It's your boldness to defy the enemy.

Prayer keeps the vision fresh.

Prayer stirs up the gifts we've been blessed with.

Prayer moves in the heart of others so that we find favor in places we typically wouldn't.

Prayer fills us with passion.

If you're not passionate, you need to stop and pray.

Ultimately our service is to the Lord.

People will wear you out. If you're expecting someone to give you kudos and praise and thanksgiving, you may be waiting a very long time.

O. Chambers: You will know how much of a servant you are when people treat you like a doormat.

All of your praise comes from God.

Matthew 6:6...your Father who sees in secret will reward you openly.

Be urgent. Be constant. Be persistent.

God wants all of you.

God needs all of you to pull this off.

November 21

Life can change in an instant.

I rushed out to my car to run some errands. Rush, rush, rush.

Pushed the button to open the garage door. It never moves fast enough.

Threw the car in reverse. Hit the gas.

GASP!

Out of the corner of my eye I saw yellow fur flash in the mirror. It was Faithful our pup.

I slammed the brake. Shaking and breathless, I jumped out to make sure he was safe.

How did he get out here?

It didn't matter.

I was elated when I saw him! Actually overcome with all kinds of emotion.

Relief.

Joy spilling over.

Grateful, just so grateful.

But what is this?

He recoiled back.

Hesitating.

He thought I was going to scold him. With head down and eyes not able to look at

me, he inched his way forward. Uncertainty in his steps. I had no intention of yelling at

him. He already knew he wasn't supposed to be out there.

My arms were stretched out wide.

I didn't care how long he had gone astray. It didn't matter. What had he done while he

was out there? It didn't matter. Why did he run out there? It didn't matter.

How far did he go?

All trivial and irrelevant.

All I cared about was that he was home. He was safe.

He was clearly shaken up. Very nervous. Cowering down. He didn't know if I would receive him. He was so afraid. I reassured him. I couldn't give him enough love and attention. I just kept hugging him and hugging him some more. I was so happy he wasn't hurt. He wasn't killed. He was alive. That's all that mattered. I could've lost him.

Forever.

But I didn't. He was on the loose but he didn't keep running. He came home.

Maybe you've been on the run. You may think God could never receive you.

The only place in the whole Bible we see the Father (a picture of God) running, is to greet his prodigal son who is coming home. When he reaches him, he doesn't beat him. Badger him. Nor remind him of all his failings. He embraces him. Just loves him. Lavishly. We are never defined by our past mistakes. Our identity does not rest in the things that we did or didn't do in the past. Our identity rests in Whose we are. We are God's children. We are His sons and daughters. Sons and daughters need not do anything to earn their parents' love; we love them because they belong to us. They are ours.

Luke 19:10 The Son...has come to seek and save that which is lost.

He will pursue after and never ever give up looking for that one who is lost. Destroyed. Crushed. He came to seek them out. That was His purpose. People who are healthy do not need a physician. But people who are sick. People who are sick know their need for healing. They feel it every day. Their guilt can be overcoming. People never let them forget. They never let themselves forget either. God works differently. So vastly different. He quickly forgets. When a man repents and turns in the other direction, God says he remembers those things no more.

Psalm 103:12 As far as the east is from the west, so far has He removed our transgressions from us.

Our greatest failures can be springboards to greatness.

Luke 7:47 "I tell you, her sins—and they are many—have been forgiven, so she has shown me much love. But a person who is forgiven little shows only little love."

Our failings humble us. Instead of running from God, if we will run to Him, His Holy Spirit will empower us to move on from them.

Paul was a murderer, yet he became a man God used greatly.

David committed adultery, but still God forgave him and went on to say, "He is a man after My own heart."

The moment you turn in His direction He will run to meet you...

November 22

Mark 14:3-5 And being in Bethany at the house of Simon the leper, as He sat at the table, a woman came having an alabaster flask of very costly oil of spikenard. Then she broke the flask and poured it on His head. But there were some who were indignant among themselves, and said, "Why was this fragrant oil wasted? For it might have been sold for more than three hundred denarii and given to the poor." And they criticized her sharply.

Mark 14:8 "She has done what she could." She could've done other things. Some thought this to be a waste of time and money. No one else saw any reason for what she did. But, she did it for her Lord. That was reason enough.

It was an act of devotion.

An alabaster box was thought to be the best way to preserve their finest ointments.

She had very little to give. She was just like us. Maybe everything she had was contained in this simple little stone jar. Everything we are is wrapped up in our children. Or our husband. Or our ministry. Or some other work.

She broke the seal. Opening up her heart.

She gave Jesus her everything.

He is worthy of our all.

Our finest and best.

There's an interesting Greek word that is used along with the word "spikenard." Pistikos is a word used to describe our English word for faith.

This women's act of devotion came from the depths of her heart of faith. She trusted in her Lord.

She wanted to give back to Him what He had given her.

She did what she could. That is all we can do.

Her small act of faith was recorded. God commended her for her act of devotion. God used it to reach the world.

He will do the same for us. Lives all around us will be touched by our small gifts. We don't have to necessarily do "big" things for God. The "big" things come from doing the little insignificant jobs.

It's not wasted.

We do it for Jesus. It is a work that brings Him joy. He delights to see our acts of devotion. He commends us for it.

It may look like a waste to others. Paltry. And trivial.

But not to our Lord.

She did what she could. And that's all that counts!

God help me to be faithful in the little things. You see what no one else sees. I just want to please you today. Humble me before You.

November 23

Camden drew me a picture one morning. It was a simple hand with a round circle in it. But that circle had two more circles in it; much like an eye. I was sure he would tell me it was Jesus' nail scarred hand.

Me: What is this Camden?

Camden: It's a eye.

I began to think about that eye.

Jesus wants us to see ourselves through the eyes of those nail scarred hands.

That's where ALL of our identity is found.

He wants us to view who we are through those nail scarred hands.

It shows us His great love for us. He took the nails so we could live.

Fully live.

That's what makes a heart full. That's what takes away depression. Seeing ourselves through His nail scarred hands.

We can be free. Free to be me. Free to be you.

The message His hands deliver is one that silences the lies we've been believing for so long.

Those hands would speak loud, "I died for you. You. I died so you could live." Not this empty existence we've been masquerading around in.

A repeated cycle of depression. Sadness. And hopelessness.

Waiting for something to change.

Hoping maybe something will change if you lose weight.

Hear this, you are not a number on the scale.

Or when the right guy comes along maybe you'll feel complete.

Hear this, you are complete in Jesus Christ. Completely loved. All of you. Inside and out. Just the way you are. Not when anything changes. But right now. Today. And forever.

Hear His words: I died for you.

No one has ever loved you like that. They never will.

Our identity rests and is held in the hands of our Father.

We are his sons and daughters.

Sons and daughters need not do anything to earn the Fathers love.

When we are able to see ourselves through those nail scarred hands our lives will never be the same again.

Only these hands can get close enough to touch our pain.

Through death comes life. Hear Him, "If you will place that insecurity into these hands I can replace it. I'll hold you close to My heart. I will protect you. These hands are strong enough to defend you."

You are precious.

Cherished.

Loved.

So loved.

The extent that we understand the love of God is the extent of our fullness.

Ephesians 3:19 May you experience the love of Christ, though it is too great to understand fully. Then you will be made complete with all the fullness of life and power that comes from God.

Love is not measured is dress size. We can't earn it. Nor can we lose it.

We are never defined by our past mistakes. Our identity never rests in the things we did or didn't do.

Nor is it found in what we look like. What people say about us is irrelevant.

We are only defined by those hands. Hands that died are outstretched. Ready to embrace. Run into them today. Let them hold you close.

November 24

Yesterday was balmy and warm. Today is ice and snow. How quickly the weather can change. The snow is beautiful; calm and serene. It's delightful to look at. I'm praising God, but still my heart is heavy. My dear friend is not celebrating today. She is going to have her son "evaluated" at Kennedy Krieger on Monday. For her, I doubt she can see the snow. I doubt she can see anything. For me it was the most dreaded day of my life. I couldn't see anything for months. When I reflect back on that time, the best way to describe it is to say everything was in dark grays, black and white. There was no color. Everything was just a blur.

Recently Camden and I were learning about Paul in Acts 9. Paul was just walking down the road and suddenly his entire life was turned upside down. He was blinded. He couldn't see anything.

Camden softly asked, "Was he crying?"

I don't know if Paul was crying. I would imagine that he was. When my life was suddenly interrupted with Autism, I was crying. I was "blinded" for a very long time. I couldn't see a thing. I didn't understand why this was happening to me. I was just overwhelmed with despair. Much of it came from not knowing what the future would hold. I couldn't "see" what would lie ahead for me or my son. I'm on the other side of that now. I have perfect vision. I can see.

I want to share with you a moment in time that I will never forget. It was the day of Camden's dreaded evaluation. He was two and a half; he could barely speak two to three words at a time. I knew my life was about to change forever. I didn't want to go. Everything inside of me knew what they were going to tell me. I was sitting in my rocker in Camden's room. He was snuggled tightly in my lap. We were reading from his little Bible. I gently placed my hand on his mouth, praying silently, "Lord, would you just touch his mouth that he can speak in Your Name?"

He turned and looked me in the eye; spoke crystal clear, "Nothing is impossible with God."

I have clung to those words ever since. God can do anything! I have seen it first-hand. No matter what the diagnosis, God is in control of your destiny. He will take care of you in ways that you can't imagine. He will show you great and mighty things that you didn't think were possible. And perhaps they weren't possible until God came into the equation. When we take Him out of the equation, things can be scary. Don't factor without Him. He is actively involved in every detail.

I never thought I would say I am thankful for Autism; but I am. It is the greatest gift I've ever received. Don't get me wrong, it is tough. But, I have a greater vision of God now. I've seen God do amazing things! Without it, my life would just be ordinary, but now it's extraordinary! I don't know what situations you are facing, but I do know you will come out of it with a better "vision" of God and His awesome power.

November 25

My granny. How I loved her. She was so soft and gentle. Everything she did was done in love.

So gracious. And kind.

She never ever let me down.

I could always depend on her.

She had a way of fixing things. She did everything by hand. Her loving hands made everything better.

No shortcuts.

When she cooked there was no microwave. She stirred everything with love.

Even when she sewed, she sewed by hand.

Sewing takes time.

She once mended a pair of my jeans when I was a little girl. They were worn and ripped open at the knee. I was in a hurry to wear those jeans.

Granny was never in a hurry.

All was done in her timing.

Sewing takes time.

When the time was right, she began to sew my jeans. I watched her hands as she began. Her knuckles were swollen with arthritis.

This was painful for her. But she continued on because she loved me. She took the needle and thread, and began to stitch. Careful. And precise. Going back-and-forth several times to make sure it wouldn't come apart again. This would be a permanent fix. When she was finished I was quick to put on those jeans. So happy to display her handiwork. On the inside I could feel the seam. It stuck out like a scar. Every step reminded me of her gentleness and love. She did this for me.

God is doing the same for us.

2 Chronicles 7:14...I will heal...

He is taking the threads of our lives, these painful things we've had to endure, and stitches them together tightly.

These threads are not accidental. They are purposeful. Every one intended to draw us closer to the heart of God.

It's the red thread that is most valuable. The thread of sacrifice. The things we've had to give up.

His death brought life.

These scarlet threads He has allowed in our lives will bring us new life. An abundant life. A Zoe Life. A God life.

Jeremiah 29:11 For I know the thoughts that I think toward you, says the LORD, thoughts of peace and not of evil, to give you a future and a hope.

November 26

1 Chronicles 4:9-10 Now Jabez was more honorable than his brothers, and his mother called his name Jabez, saying, "Because I bore him in pain." And Jabez called on the God of Israel saying, "Oh, that You would bless me indeed, and enlarge my territory, that Your hand would be with me, and that You would keep me from evil, that I may not cause pain!" So God granted him what he requested.

Jabez means sorrow. Grief. Pain.

What would cause a mother to name her child Jabez? What had she gone through?

We will never know.

What we do know is this: the painful circumstances caused her child to stand out amongst his brothers.

Jabez was more honorable. Honorable in the Arabic meant "weighty, heavy, deep".

We know this child's pain caused him to go deeper into the heart of his God.

Pain has a way of doing that. Always takes us deeper.

Pain becomes an anchor. It takes us to the deepest depths. Without that anchor we would stay surface Christians. God always desires to takes us further. Closer. Nearer to His heart.

2 Corinthians 4:17 For our light affliction, which is but for a moment, is working for us a far more exceeding and eternal weight of glory, while we do not look at the things which are seen, but at the things which are not seen. For the things which are seen are temporary, but the things which are not seen are eternal.

Sorrow has a way of giving us a whole new perspective. We are no longer concerned about petty shallow things. Things that don't matter. Our focus becomes eternal.

Beautiful things are birthed in darkness.

This child birthed amidst such sorrow came to be a powerful prayer warrior for the Kingdom of God. His name suggests he had to endure adversity more than his brothers.

Adversity makes us stronger. Jabez learned to thrive. He called upon the name of the Lord.

1 Chronicles 4:10 And Jabez called on the God of Israel saying, "Oh, that You would bless me indeed, and enlarge my territory, that Your hand would be with me, and that You would keep me from evil, that I may not cause pain!"

We can glean so much from him. This is the prayer that emanated from his heart:

Bless me.

Lord, bless me only so that I may bless others. Prosper my endeavors.

Enlarge my territory. Expand my borders. Enlarge my borders of trust, faith and confidence in You. Multiply my ministry. Use this suffering to bring something good.

Lord take me further than I think I can go. Help me to take risks on people. Give me more courage. Take me higher spiritually. Expand my sphere of influence. I want to help others that are in a similar circumstance.

Use me. God don't let this pain go to waste. Let me bring You glory through it.

God granted his request.

November 27

Sometimes God asks us to do something that seems impossible. Our finite minds want an outward sign.

I was called to teach my son God's word. He told me not to take him to a qualified Speech Therapist, but teach him to speak by using His word. Seemed impossible. He wasn't even three years old yet. Just diagnosed with Autism, he could barely say anything.

I was immediately challenged by secular therapists. They said Autistic children don't understand such abstract things as God.

Those therapists don't understand the power of God.

1 Corinthians 2:14 But people who aren't spiritual can't receive these truths from God's Spirit. It all sounds foolish to them and they can't understand it, for only those who are spiritual can understand what the Spirit means.

God just needed me to trust Him and obey.

We walk by faith, not by sight.

Mary was called to birth the Son of God. How could this be? It seemed impossible.

Luke 1:35 And the angel answered and said to her, "The Holy Spirit will come upon you, and the power of the Highest will overshadow you; there-fore, also, that Holy One who is to be born will be called the Son of God. "

One thing was clear. The birth had nothing to do with her. This thing would happen by the power of God. His power would overshadow. This word "overshadow" in the Old Testament gave us a picture of a hovering cloud of dew. It symbolized the immediate presence and power of God.

Dew comes quietly. Without announcement. Unexpectedly. It appears in the dark of night. Dew saturates.

This is exactly the way the Spirit of God operates in our lives. He comes without fanfare. And usually when we least expect it. When everything is dark in our understanding, He appears. He overtakes the situation.

Nothing is too hard for Him.

God is birthing something in each of our lives. This process takes time to develop. What do we do in the meantime? Wait in faith. Obey in the small things. Don't strive to make it happen. It will only come about supernaturally.

November 28

As God is birthing something new in your life, Satan is waiting to devour it.

Revelation 12:4 And the dragon stood before the woman who was ready to give birth, to devour her Child as soon as it was born.

Baby churches. Baby ministries. Baby believers.

Why does Satan always attack the babies?

He knows what they will become.

He desires to silence them. He needs to snuff them out before they grow.

His tactics are subtle. Lies come in whispers. Day in and day out, he murmurs things such as:

My life is worthless.

God could never use me.

God could never make something good out of this tragedy.

But God does. He can. He will.

He is building a testimony.

There is no testimony without the test.

Job 23:10... When He has tested me, I shall come forth as gold.

Never give up. Lift up your hands to heaven. He will fill you with strength to make it through.

Moment by moment.

If you find yourself in the wilderness, take note:

Revelation 12:6 Then the woman fled into the wilderness, where she has a place prepared by God, that they should feed her there one thousand two hundred and sixty days.

God never lost sight of this woman. He knew where she would find herself. God had already made provision for her.

Psalm 46:1...God is our refuge and strength, a very present help in trouble.

Her days in the wilderness were numbered. They were exact. We will find our days to be the same. God knows exactly where we are. Be strong. Take heart.

Revelation 12:11 "And they overcame him by the blood of the Lamb and by the word of their testimony, and they did not love their lives to the death."

Use your testimony. Don't be ashamed of it. God wants to speak to another soul through you. Do not allow Satan to silence you. Is it messy? God will use it to clean up someone else's life. Is it sad? God will use it to restore joy to another hurting heart who may be wondering if they will ever feel joy again. Is it ugly? God will use it to bring beauty out of ashes into a similar situation.

Speak in boldness. Share in power. Rise up.

Jesus, embolden me with the power of your blood. Help me to overcome Satan by using my testimony. Silence his lies in my life. Give me words to speak to that person in my life who is struggling. Fill me with your Holy Spirit. I want you to bring something good out of this painful time in my life. I know that you can. You will. Help me to trust you.

As my life spun out of control, turmoil abounded. The thoughts of my heart like mud and muck churning in the waves of doubt. Rain kept on coming. It seemed it would not end.

Would I make it through another day?

Many mornings I awoke with that question on my heart.

Revelation 4:1... the voice I first heard...said, "Come up here..."

He called me to come every morning.

An invitation to the throne.

Pain always comes with an invite.

Come up here.

Revelation 4:6 Before the throne there was a sea of glass, like crystal...

No matter what havoc is in my life, I can always find solace at the throne of God.

Time and again, He is the lifter of my head.

His words bring everything to a halt.

My problems don't cease, but my anxieties do.

Philippians 4:6 Be anxious for nothing, but in everything by prayer and supplication, with thanksgiving, let your requests be made known to God; and the peace of God, which surpasses all understanding, will guard your hearts and minds through Christ Jesus.

He brings me right thinking. My feelings are not reality. They can never be trusted.

God's word is reality. And truth.

It can always be trusted.

Psalm 37:7 Be still in the presence of the LORD, and wait patiently for him to act.

Our inaction can be more powerful than our action.

Exodus 14:1... Camp on the shore of the sea

The Lord instructed Israel to camp out. Stay right where you are. Don't go any further. The enemy will think he has you trapped. It did seem that way. Even to Israel. Pharoah brought his A game. It was no match for the Lord.

Exodus 14:13-14... And Moses said to the people, "Do not be afraid. Stand still, and see the salvation of the LORD, which He will accomplish for you today. For the Egyptians whom you see today, you shall see again no more forever. "The LORD will fight for you, and you shall hold your peace."

Father God, sometimes we forget that you are fighting for us. Keep this in the forefront of our minds today. Fill me with courage to face today. Arm me with your strength. Take my fears away. They are not from you. They are from the enemy who seeks to destroy my determination. Help me to rise above. Take me before your throne of grace. Still these anxieties. Calm my anxious heart I pray.

November 30

Hannah didn't get what she asked for.

She prayed. She begged. She pleaded.

Still, her prayer wasn't answered.

What do we do when we don't get what we ask for?

1 Samuel 1:12... she kept on praying...

Hannah's prayers multiplied. They increased. Her desperation was apparent.

When our prayers go unanswered it can feel like we're running out of time.

Days go by. Weeks. And years. Blowing by like fall leaves in the wind.

As Hannah's desire grew, her perseverance began to wane.

1 Samuel 1:6 And her rival also provoked her severely, to make her miserable, because the LORD had closed her womb.

When someone else has what you want, seeds of bitterness can grow quickly.

In our minds, they can be perceived as the enemy. A rival.

Every word they say can become like fingernails screeching down a chalkboard. Just their very presence irritates you. An unpleasant reminder of your unanswered prayer.

A provocation reminding you of what they have and you don't.

It was the Lord who gave children to Peninah. But it was also the Lord who closed Hannah's womb.

Both were from the Lord.

This is so crucial to remember. We have to surrender to the Lord's will. His timing. His way. We don't have to strive to make things happen. He gives. In His way. And His time.

Get real before the Lord. If you don't, you'll get real angry. Be transparent before Him. Give Him access to your heart. Let Him console you.

1 Samuel 1:8... You have me—

You have Jesus. He is enough in the waiting.

Don't look at what you don't have. Bless God for what you do have.

There is always a scene behind the seen.

Penninah had children. But there is no mention of their usefulness for the Lord. Hannah raised up a prophet. God is always doing something spiritual. Prayer matters. If you are still waiting, intensify them.

Don't quit praying.

Psalm 20:1 May the Lord answer you in the day of trouble.

Oh Lord, help me to keep my eyes on You. I don't want to covet what You're doing in another person's life. I want to be content where You have me. Your plan for me and my child is unique. It is good. Best for me. Keep my heart fixed aright. I love You. Help me to be patient as You unfold Your plan; in Your time. I trust You.

December

December 1

Sometimes our worst fears are confirmed; the doctor delivers a diagnosis we weren't expecting. Maybe a bank statement comes in the mail; we don't have enough to cover the bills. Or a debilitating illness strikes out of nowhere. It is stunning. We are floored; dismayed to say the least. Immediately, our mind spins. Doubts swirl round and round. We play out every possible scenario, none of them good.

In the story of David and Goliath, Israel was facing some grim odds. No one could defeat this giant. They knew it and so did Goliath. He was mocking and scoffing at their attempts to beat him. When he spoke they trembled.

1 Samuel 17:10... Goliath said, "I defy the armies of Israel this day"...

He was daring them to try to beat him. When Saul heard these words he was terrified. He knew what they meant.

Goliath strutted in front of Israel for forty days and nights. Taunting and mocking, his threats were very real. They had every reason to fear. Goliath was much bigger than they were. They weren't equipped to defeat him. They didn't have enough men. Death was looming and they knew it.

David jumped in as if to say, "What are you afraid of?"

Was David blind?

He was well aware of his stature. He looked in the mirror every day. He was the youngest and the smallest. He was the least skilled out of all of his brothers.

In essence, David said, "So what if he is bigger and stronger! If God is for me who can be against!"

David tried to get some kind of encouraging word from those around him, but none came. Each one confirmed David's inability. All of them reiterated the staggering odds. This did not deter David. In fact, I think it spurred him on.

The greater the odds, the greater the victory.

David wasn't looking at how small he was; he was looking at how big God was. He didn't see the obstacle, he saw the obstacle mover. He defeated that giant with a sling and one small stone; very unlikely weapons.

1 Samuel 17:45, 47 David said, "You come to me with a sword, with a spear, and with a javelin. But I come to you in the name of the LORD of hosts...the battle is the Lord's."

The Lord doesn't work in conventional ways. His ways are higher than ours. I ask you today, what is it you are facing? It is nothing compared to the greatness of our God. He is stronger. He is wiser than the doctors. He is the Great Physician. He does not always heal, but he does carry you through. He will never let go. The money does not always come, but He will make another way.

Proverbs 3:5-6 Trust in the Lord with all your heart; do not depend on your own understanding...

You can trust Him with your life; David did.

Lord you are bigger than this thing I am trying to overcome. Silence the voices that instill fear. Strengthen my heart with courage to face this giant. The battle is Yours. Fight for me. I sing Your powerful name, Jesus, over this. I will not trust in myself, nor my abilities. I will trust in You.

December 2

With the holidays approaching, instead of joy, we may feel dread. We know we're going to see a friend that we've had a disagreement with or a family member who always has a way of ruining our beautiful day. How can this year be different?

Colossians 3:15 And let the peace of God rule in your hearts...

As we usher in another holiday season, fond memories come to mind. They take us back to a simpler time. As we reminisce we are filled with delight; Grandma's buttery mashed potatoes overflowing with gravy, pumpkin pie smothered in whipped cream and sitting by a warm crackling fire. But, suddenly the flames are doused. You are brought back to reality. A not-so-fond memory rushes to the forefront of your mind. It seems to take over. Abruptly, you can recollect every detail of a conversation that hurt you. Word for word you remember how you were insulted. Painful words were said that you haven't forgotten. You may act like you've forgotten, but you truly haven't. Or perhaps a family member or friend did something to you or your child, and try as you might, you've never put it behind you. Just the thought of it makes you angry. Tranquility is gone. Pumpkin pie is out. Fury takes the preeminence as you hit the replay button over and over in your mind.

Seeing them is inevitable. You can't avoid it.

Now what?

Taking a deeper look at our verse will help us:

Colossians 3:15 And let the peace of God rule in your hearts...

The word for "rule" in the old language gives us a picture of an umpire. In Major League baseball, an umpire has a great deal of responsibility. An umpire's decision can change the outcome of a game. It is imperative that he make the right call. His decision is final. It cannot be reversed.

We will be in a similar situation when we encounter friends and relatives with whom we have animosity. In a sense we get to be the umpire. We get to decide the outcome. Since we are Christians, and we represent Christ, we bear a great responsibility. Our response to this person could literally change the outcome of their lives. It's imperative that we "make the right call." We must allow God's peace to rule. There's a lot at stake. Our decisions are final. Nothing we say or do can be taken back. We get to decide. Will the "peace of God" rule in our heart?

How will you react when you see this person?

4 things to remember before making your decision:

1. Remember how much you've been forgiven.

Colossians 2:13 You were dead because of your sins... Then God made you alive with Christ, for he forgave all our sins.

God didn't hold onto any of our sins to throw in our face at a later date. Rather, he cast them away; as far as the east is from the west. Shouldn't we be willing to do the same?

2. Remember to be thankful for the time you have with them.

We don't know what tomorrow holds. We aren't guaranteed another day. We may not have another Christmas to spend together. Don't waste precious time holding grudges, and repaying wrongs. Don't let your pride get in the way.

3. Remember to seek to please the Lord, not man.

Colossians 3:23-24 And whatever you do, do it heartily, as to the Lord and not to men, knowing that from the Lord you will receive the reward of the inheritance; for you serve the Lord Christ.

You are not forgiving them because they deserve it. They may not deserve it at all. But, you're forgiving out of reverence for the Lord. He will reward you for it. It will bring Him honor, and it will allow peace to "rule" in your heart. Love them lavishly; "do it heartily". Go all out. That's what Jesus does for us.

4. Remember you are not warring with flesh and blood.

Ephesians 6:12 For we are not fighting against flesh-and-blood enemies, but against evil rulers and authorities of the unseen world, against mighty powers in this dark world, and against evil spirits in the heavenly places.

Truly, your battle is not with a family member; although that's what it may appear. Your battle is with the enemy of their soul. There's a lot riding on this decision. If we respond harshly, we may push this person further away from Christ. That's exactly what Satan wants. He wants to separate and divide. Don't play into his hand. Christ wants to unite and bring peace.

What will "rule" in your heart?

Make your decision now. Don't wait until you see the person.

Get alone with the Lord. Allow Him to remove that anger completely, and give you His heart for this person.

Luke 6:45...Out of the abundance of the heart the mouth speaks.

If you have anger in your heart it will be obvious. It'll come out in the things you say and do.

Matthew 5:9 Blessed are the peacemakers...

A peacemaker is willing to do what it takes, no matter what the cost.

It's your call. What will you decide?

December 3

Did you ever have one of those days where you wake up and first thing out of bed your day becomes unmanageable? Or perhaps half the way through, you get some unexpected news. Bad news. On any other day, it wouldn't be all that bad. It's just something trivial. But, it's the straw that broke the camel's back. You just don't need one more thing. And one more thing happened? Do you feel like running away from it all?

That's exactly what happened to Elijah. He had just come from a major victory. Defeating 450 prophets of Baal was no small task. He was bold. Valiant. Stood against them in fearless courage and they were defeated. Moments later he prayed down rain from heaven.

Next thing you know Elijah is running for his life from a little women. Scurrying away with his tail between his legs. We find him under a Juniper tree, praying that he might die.

How did he get there?

I have found myself there on more than one occasion.

It's never something major that happens. In the grand scheme of things, it's usually some small trivial thing. Nothing we haven't overcome before. But it's the straw that broke the camel's back.

It's one more thing.

It's the silly little things that can take out a strong man. Leave him hiding.

Maybe you're hiding out. Rest assured, our Lord knows where you're at. He is coming to meet you. Just like He did Elijah. He touched him gently.

1 Kings 19:5 "Arise and eat."

Some pretty simple words. You just need to get up. Get yourself something to eat. He did just that. He laid back down and got some rest. The Lord came to him again. He spoke the same words, essentially saying, "Rise up and eat. I know this is a lot for you. I understand you're feeling overwhelmed. I see where you're at. We'll get through this together."

God just pours out His grace.

He provided food and cold water for him. God gave him enough for the journey that was lying before him. He went another 40 days. And soon enough he found himself hiding in a cave. Feeling sorry for himself. God comes to meet him in the cave. He always knows where we are.

Psalm 139:7-10 Where can I go from Your Spirit? or where can I flee from Your presence? If I ascend into heaven, You are there; If I take the wings of the morning, and dwell in the uttermost parts of the sea, if I make my bed in hell, behold, You are there. Even there Your hand shall lead me, and Your right hand shall hold me.

We can't escape the Lord. He so graciously finds us. He asked Elijah gently, "What are you doing here, Elijah?"

1 Kings 19:10 "I've been working my heart out for the God-of-the-Angel-Armies," said Elijah. "The people of Israel have abandoned your covenant, destroyed the places of worship, and murdered your prophets. I'm the only one left, and now they're trying to kill me."

I've felt like Elijah. I've asked, "Don't you see what I'm doing for you Lord? Look what has happened! It's all useless. No one wants to follow you. They don't want to listen to you. There aren't any Christians left in all of the United States of America. I've only tried to be a witness for you. Now I am being attacked."

1 Kings 19:11 Then He said, "Go out, and stand on the mountain before the LORD." And behold, the LORD passed by, and a great and strong wind tore into the mountains and broke the rocks in pieces before the LORD, but the LORD was not in the wind; and after the wind an earthquake, but the LORD was not in the earthquake; and after the earthquake a fire, but the LORD was not in the fire; and after the fire a still small voice.

Our Lord came in a whisper. He spoke soft.

Go anoint Hazael, Jehu, and Elisha. I am sending them to you. They will walk with you. They're gonna help you. God will help us as well.

You never walk alone. He has never left you.

If today finds you in some unexpected struggle here is what you can do:

Psalm 77:11 But then I recall all you have done, O LORD; I remember your wonderful deeds of long ago. I will also meditate on all Your work, and talk of Your deeds.

Use this time of difficulty to give a testimony! Sometimes the testimony is just to ourselves. Remember what the Lord has done in the past. Write it down. Meditate on it. Hope will rise.

Do you have a physical need?

Isaiah 40:29 He gives strength to the weary and increases the power of the weak.

Is your need for God to provide?

Philippians 4:19 And my God shall supply all your need according to His riches in glory by Christ Jesus.

God will provide. He always has, and He always will.

God is doing something. Always doing something we can't see. The Psalmist says I will remember what you've done in the past. I will talk about it. Talking about it brings glory to God. It takes others to the heart of God. His goodness is brought to the forefront, and suddenly you aren't so overwhelmed anymore. You're praising Him.

December 4

Camden: "Mom could I go for a walk with you? I want to talk to the Lord."

Me: "You sure can..."

Camden: "God is big and strong and mighty. We don't have to be afraid of the rain. It makes the flowers grow."

I couldn't think of a better Christmas message.

God is big. He was a big enough Man to come as a little vulnerable baby into this dark world. He can relate to our struggles. He struggled and overcame our biggest enemy. He took on sin. He Himself was sinless. Yet He was willing to suffer for me? Me?

I could learn a lot from His humility.

He came to die.

I care so much about my rights. He cared nothing about His rights. He could've spoken up, but He didn't. He was beaten and hung on a cross for me and for you.

That is strong.

But the greatest part of the Christmas story is that He didn't stay dead. He defeated death. He rose again. And that means, if He rose we will rise again too. For those who have accepted His gift, turned from their sins and made a commitment to live for Him, we will live forever in heaven with Him.

That is mighty!

And whatever you may be going through I want you to know that nothing is too big for God. He is still resurrecting circumstances and people. He is still actively working in your life.

You don't have to be afraid of the rain.

God is using it to make you grow.

Wow God You are so awesome! Sometimes I just don't have the words.

December 5

There are times the Lord calls us to do things that look utterly impossible. Monumental tasks that seem hopeless to complete. He brings us into situations that we see no way out. There are obstacles to overcome. Long stretches of highway with little distraction. No respite. And frankly we're not up to the task. Absolutely not qualified. Undermanned. Underfunded. Definitely don't have the resources to bring this task to completion.

Moses knew all about this.

God called him to take six hundred thousand people through a desert. Do you know what it would take just to feed all those people? Not to mention give them water? Toiletries. Basic necessities. There were no internet signals in that desert. No Amazon Prime to deliver.

The only way to pull this off would be the power of God.

Exodus 33:7 Moses took his tent and pitched it outside the camp, far from the camp, and called it the tabernacle of meeting.

Alone time with God is a must.

It's impossible to serve the Lord without extended quiet times with Him. Moses was wise to go far from the camp. Each of us must also withdraw from everyone and everything; every day. We cannot allow the needs of the ministry to supersede our need to be alone with the Lord. If we don't get refilled each and every day, we will have nothing to offer. We will get burned out quickly.

We cannot do God's work without God's power.

Ephesians 5:18...be filled with the Spirit...

We need a constant replenishment from His heart.

We often think to ourselves, 'I can't afford to take that time with Him today.' But the fact of the matter is, we cannot afford not to. I've tried. And failed miserably.

John 6:63 "It is the Spirit who gives life; the flesh profits nothing. The words that I speak to you are spirit, and they are life.

Human effort amounts to human results; nothing supernatural.

When God speaks a word, life happens. Real life. Spirit infused outcomes.

We need the power of the Holy Spirit when we are working for the Lord. A Spirit filled ministry is vital. You only get a Spirit filled ministry from a Spirit filled heart. We are leaky vessels; we must be refilled daily.

Lord take us past the needs of the people to see our greatest need; alone time with You. We can do nothing without You. Show us the areas where we are relying on ourselves. Our hope is in You. You alone Lord can do miracles. Help us to find the balance. We trust You to take care of the needs while we are with You. Help us to recognize the enemy who relentlessly pursues our time with you. Don't let us cave in to his pressure. Fill us with Your Holy Spirit to accomplish great things today in Your Name and for Your glory.

✓ December 6

Silent night, holy night

All is calm, all is bright

Round yon Virgin Mother and Child

Holy Infant so tender and mild

Sleep in heavenly peace

Sleep in heavenly peace

Picture this:

A young woman has her cell phone in her left ear. In her right ear her iPod is playing Christmas music. Her laptop is in front of her. She is checking her email. The timer is going off in the kitchen. Her cookies need to come out of the oven.

Does this scene look vaguely familiar?

Now let's rewind the clock.

Suppose this young woman was Mary? When the angel of the Lord spoke to her, do you think she would've heard Him?

The Christian woman's life is overflowing with activity. We somehow think we are not accomplishing anything unless we are always busy running back and forth. We think more is better. We will actually accomplish more if we attempt less and spend more time in silence waiting upon God.

I believe Mary had many silent nights.

Luke 2:19 Mary quietly treasured these things in her heart. She thought about them often.

When the Lord spoke to Mary and told her she would bring forth a son, she was troubled. Her circumstances were dire. She faced humiliation. There was a possibility she would be a single mother for the rest of her life. Her life was turned upside down. But she remained poised. She was not moved. Her faith remained unshakable. How was she able to overcome her fear?

She had ears to hear the Lord.

Luke 1:30...Don't be afraid, Mary, for you have found favor with God.

Perhaps Mary would have missed what God had to say to her if she was talking on her cell phone, listening to her iPod and checking her email. She wouldn't have had time to hear from God.

This Christmas season lets dare to turn it all off. Dare to be alone.

Nothing is more profitable than setting time to be silent before God.

John 14:27 I am leaving you with a gift—peace of mind and heart. And the peace I give isn't like the peace the world gives. So don't be troubled or afraid.

When we really hear God speak, we will not be afraid. When we really see Jesus face to face, we will not be troubled. We will leave His presence with a gift; peace of mind and heart. There is not a gift more valuable than Heavenly Peace.

I pray with all my heart that you will have a silent night with the Savior. One silent night may change the course of your life forever.

December 7

There is such a cold chill in the air. My cheeks hurt. My hands are numb.

Fall is coming to a close. The last of the leaves are disappearing. Nothing left.

Emptiness is palpable.

Our hearts can feel like this sometimes.

Seasons come upon our soul. It seems like the whole landscape can change without us realizing it.

How did this happen?

Nothing looks like it used to. All is unfamiliar.

Illness enters our lives. Hardships come. People are taken. All these things leave us distraught. That sense of loss is painful. Makes us vulnerable. Longing to be protected. Crying out for comfort.

When everything is taken from us, we can see what remains.

Loss reveals what's underneath.

Deuteronomy 33:27 Underneath are the everlasting arms.

Lord You are there when everything in my life is taken. When loss is so profound, I feel you enveloping me in Your strong arms. You are able to keep me from falling. I am safe. Keep my mind stayed on You. I trust You. Everything in my life may change, You stay the same. Give me strength for today. Lift me up with Your strong hands.

December 8

Let's take a look at the Garden of Eden. Eden means pleasant and delightful. That is where God placed Adam and Eve.

Imagine what it was like to walk with God every day in the garden. It was perfection. Perfect weather. Perfect circumstances. No worry of being late. For me I wondered what it would be like to have no stress. No doubts, no insecurities, no worry about what I look like, no worry that I would say the wrong thing, no worry that I would be embarrassed, no stress that I may not be smart enough or not understand, no worry that I would be sick; just relaxing with my Lord every day.

We know the story well...

The enemy deceived Eve. She was expelled from the garden.

2 Corinthians 11:3 But I fear that somehow your pure and undivided devotion to Christ will be corrupted, just as Eve was deceived by the cunning ways of the serpent.

Satan caused Eve to question God.

"Did God really say...?"

Satan's lies bring lack of trust.

I think that is the most devastating thing. Eve walked with God. God spoke to her. She heard His voice. They talked together. And then separation. She had to have a heartache at what she was missing.

Trust was broken. Insecurity began for women that day.

Insecurity can manifest itself in many ways.

It influences every aspect of our lives.

It sets limits on our ministries. It determines who we date.

Insecurity affects our marriage.

It affects our friendships.

It causes us to do things we don't want to do.

The cycle of insecurity repeats itself in our children.

It influences our decisions.

Insecurity causes depression.

It affects our quality of life and is destructive in every way.

God wants to remove our insecurities and lack of trust.

Eve had that perfect trust and then it was gone. Her innocence was stolen.

The serpent deceived her. She began to question God.

I began to think about when that innocence was stolen from me. When was it that the enemy started working in my life? His lies began early in my life. They do for all women. Someone hurts us. Abandons us. Leaves us. We blame ourselves.

We begin to put up walls. We hide behind them. Maybe they've been up for years. As the walls grow higher, so do our insecurities.

John 20:19 Then, the same day at evening, being the first day of the week, when the doors were shut where the disciples were assembled, for fear of the Jews, Jesus came and stood in the midst, and said to them, "Peace be with you."

The disciples were behind these closed doors. They were surrounded by walls.

The walls didn't stop Jesus.

He came right in.

He wants to come behind our walls. To come in and take those insecurities. Trade them in for peace. Hear these words: God loves you just because you're you. He loves everything about you. Not because of any accomplishment. Not because of your looks. But because you're His daughter. We need not fear being ourselves. Give these fears to your God. Let Him make you a new creation. He wants to renew our minds. We must find our security in Him.

Lord saturate my soul with Your love. I believe You love me. Help me to leave the past behind. I trust You. Help me to get close to people. I want to love like you do. Show me how to do that. I want to hear you speak. Take down these walls I have allowed to be built. Come in. Speak to me. I need to hear Your voice. My security is in You. Renew my mind. Transform these thoughts into something beautiful. Heal me I pray.

December 9

Exodus 33:1 The LORD said to Moses, "Get going..."

Some days you may feel like me. My "get up and go, has already gotten up and gone."

I don't have anything left to face the day. I am overwhelmed, and the day hasn't even begun. Certain more challenges lie ahead, I feel like pulling the covers back over my head.

Exodus 33:12-13 Moses said to the Lord, "See, You say to me, 'Bring up this people, but You have not let me know whom You will send with me'... And [Lord, do] consider that this nation is Your people."

Moses must've been overwhelmed too.

He seemed to be asking, "Who is going to help me with all of this? I know You called me to do this, but I simply don't have what it takes. How am I gonna get through this? Lord, show me what to do. These are your people."

I can relate.

There are so many days I feel like I am in way over my head.

It appears Moses is reminding the Lord, but I think he is actually reminding himself.

We should remind ourselves:

These are your people. This is Your marriage. This is Your child. It's Your church. Ministry. Illness.

This is Your gig Lord.

Exodus 33:14 And the Lord said, "My Presence shall go with you, and I will give you rest."

God told Moses He was going with him. That's what He is telling us.

I am going through this with you. We'll face this together. You and me.

And I will give you rest.

Isn't that what we really want?

Rest. Peace. And to know all is well.

All doesn't have to be well on the outside, but on the inside. That's where it counts.

We want peace.

Every outward circumstance may be crumbling, but Jesus is still with us. Should He call us to face an enormous challenge, we need to know one thing:

He is with us.

He called us to do this.

We have two choices.

Be overwhelmed by it all or be overwhelmed by Jesus. I choose the latter.

Ephesians 3: 20 Now to Him who is able to do exceedingly abundantly above all that we ask or think, according to the power that works in us, to Him be glory in the church by Christ Jesus to all generations, forever and ever. Amen.

Lord overwhelm me with Your Presence. I can't do this without You. Help me to keep going. Keep moving me forward despite all of my outward circumstances. Give me rest. Help me to sleep soundly tonight. My life is in Your hands. Jesus, you are good when nothing else is good. We will do this together.

December 10

Recently we had a birthday party to celebrate the true meaning of Christmas: the birth of Jesus. Happy hearted children flowed out of every room of the church. There were some great crafts and games for them to play. One game in particular stood out. It is a classic from my childhood: Pin the Tail on the Donkey. I had so much fun watching them play. Some of them were apprehensive about the blindfold. They reluctantly put it on. After spinning them around, we sent them on their way. They completely missed the mark. They weren't even close.

This reminded me of what my life was like before Jesus came into it and saved me. I was wandering around aimlessly in the dark. I had no purpose. Life was meaningless. I was blinded to all the good that God had for me.

2 Corinthians 4:4 Satan, who is the god of this world, has blinded the minds of those who don't believe. They are unable to see.

Maybe you feel like I did back then. Satan was holding me captive. I had it all, but I had nothing. There was always a smile masking the emptiness. There had to be more to this life. There was, but my life was not in the hands of the One who could change it.

Jeremiah 29:12-14 "When you call on Me, when you come and pray to Me, I'll listen. When you come looking for Me, you'll find Me. Yes, when you get serious about finding Me and want it more than anything else, I'll make sure you won't be disappointed...I'll turn things around for you."

I had to get serious about finding Him. So that's exactly what I did.

That's what you need to do as well.

God wants to remove that blindfold. He wants to give your life direction. Place your life in His hands. Every detail. He will fill it to overflowing.

God does have a purpose for your life. It is precious to Him. Commit your life to Him and He'll direct your path.

Lord, I am serious about knowing Your will. Reveal it to Me. I want to do Your will God. Not mine. Not what I think or feel. But what You desire. Remove the blindfold that is keeping me from seeing Your plan for My life. I give you my pride. I want to be humble. I give you my plans. Give me Your plans. Lord I can't do this life without You.

December 11

John 1:38-39 But Jesus turned, and as He saw them following Him, He said to them, what are you looking for? [And what is it you wish?] And they answered Him, Rabbi—which translated is Teacher—where are You staying? He said to them, Come and see. So they went and saw where He was staying, and they remained with Him that day.

Jesus invited them to come.

What an invite. He invites us to come to Him today. It's an open invitation. Will you drop everything and go. Are you available? Don't miss it.

So simple. Jesus just wants to be near us. I can't think of anything else I'd rather do today than hang out with Him. Keep it simple.

Jesus asked them a question.

What are you looking for?

Take the time to mull this one over. What is it that you're searching for? What do you crave? What is your heart's desire? What are you aiming for? What do you need?

Nothing can top what He can give you.

If you are willing to leave everything behind and come follow hard after Jesus you will finally find what you're looking for.

Come.

A simple invitation, but difficult to achieve sometimes. Coming often means we have to leave some things and people behind.

It often means saying, "No" to some good things. Good, but not God's best.

Jesus answered with a simple reply. Come. It wasn't complicated. It was a simple message for a simple day.

They came right away. We need to do the same. Don't put it off. Don't tell yourself you'll do it later, you won't. Do it now.

They came expectant.

They got what they came for.

Jesus will never disappoint you. At the end of the day, if His invitation is swept aside and covered over with my to-do list, it will be my loss.

God you bless me every time I come to You. Help me to fight the temptations of my phone, the television, or just plain apathy. Fill me with desire. In the areas I have cooled for You, set me on fire. Speak to me. I need you. I need your strength and guidance. I love You Lord, please speak to me now.

December 12

Isaiah 1:18-19 "Come now, and let us reason together," Says the LORD, "Though your sins are like scarlet, They shall be as white as snow; Though they are red like crimson, They shall be as wool. If you are willing and obedient..."

What a delightful surprise awaited me; snow! Something about it beckoned me to take a closer look. Its majesty was captivating. I've seen snow hundreds of times, and yet I was still drawn to it. It's purity matchless. Yesterday everything was brown and dead; lifeless. Today a blanket of beauty covered it over. There was stillness; quiet emanating. What a beautiful picture of the human heart when at peace with God. But when it's not at peace, it's always crying out to be made right.

Sin wreaks havoc. It wrecks your life. Before you know it you end up in a place of blackness trying to figure out how you got there. Satan wants to pin you there. You have a difficult choice to make. Accept and yield, or deny and refuse.

Come now.

This is a summons from the Lord that demands a response. He provides us with an irresistible offer to make things right. The heart longs for a covering only He can provide. It's only by the blood of Jesus that our sins may be washed away and we be made white.

Let us reason together. God seems to be saying, "Let's talk about this. Let's come out of darkness into the bright clear sunshine." Repentance brings you out of the dark cave you're hiding in. You can't hide from God. You have to come into agreement with Him. This is sin. There is only one response; complete obedience.

Though your sins are like scarlet, they shall be as white as snow.

Yielding to Gods way brings that covering we long for. It is a peaceful blanket to cover you over. Refusing will bring an unsettling feeling that something isn't right. There is never peace, only a sense of being exposed. When God puts His finger on something in your life He will not remove it until you obey Him. It is no longer something to be prayed about. We can't pray about repenting. We have to repent. God's word demands a decision.

John 8:36... If the Son sets you free, you shall be free indeed.

There is an unparalleled serenity in the soul after concession is made.

This promise holds two conditions: You must be willing and obedient.

Your desire to please the Lord must be stronger than your desire to please yourself.

This is not easy.

God increase our faith.

This word "obedient" is the Hebrew word for "hearing." How interesting...

As I was writing this a barking dog interrupted my silence. It wouldn't stop. The incessant bark began to rattle my nerves. I was trying to keep going, but this dog was causing my thoughts to spin. It was a deep loud bark. This intrusion caused me to lose my concentration. My focus was diverted. I could no longer hear what the Lord was saying. This loud bark was pursuing me. I couldn't seem to escape it. I believe that is precisely what the enemy does. He comes to silence the voice of God. We know the truth, but the enemy comes as a barking dog. Soon the voice of truth is drowned out by the loud insistent bark. He is relentless in his pursuit. He will use anything and anyone to silence the voice of God; even a barking dog. He'll persuade you to wait one more day. Today, if you hear His voice, don't harden your heart. Silence all the "barking dogs" in your life. Then you can hear God clearly beckoning you, "Come now." Come into agreement with God.

A matchless tranquility awaits all who will come.

December 13

Christmas is approaching! How exciting! I can't wait to bake my chocolate chip cookies. I always stick with the basic recipe that's on the Nestle Tollhouse bag. It has never failed me.

Year after year it is tried and true.

I need to make sure I have all of my ingredients on hand.

After all, how would a chocolate chip cookie taste without the chocolate chips? Or what if I left the butter out?

I suppose it would be very disappointing.

It would not be what you expected. It would be lacking. Something would be missing.

It's the same way with the Christian life.

God's recipe for success:

Acts 2:42 And they continued steadfastly in the apostles' doctrine [for us the Bible] and fellowship, in the breaking of bread, and in prayers.

Read the recipe. Stay in God's word. If you don't know His word, you won't know how to do life right. Things will keep falling apart.

Do life with other Christians. It's difficult to do the right thing by yourself. Find yourself a church and go. Get involved as much as possible.

They "broke bread" to remember the Lord died on the cross for them. We should not take this lightly, but always come back to that place of realizing Jesus died because of our sin personally.

Prayer keeps you in touch with your Heavenly Dad. It is a must. Where would a child be without guidance from his Dad? His assurance is vital. We need His discernment every day to make wise decisions.

All of these ingredients come together to make a Christian complete; lacking nothing. A perfect recipe for success.

Colossians 1:17...in Him all things consist...

Without Him everything falls apart. If He is not the foundation of your relationship, marriage, children, home etc. it will fall. We can't do anything without Him.

Stick with the basics and you'll be thriving no matter where life finds you.

December 14

There are tasks. And then there are impossible tasks. Unreachable people. Impassable situations. Things that appear to have no solution. All the surrounding circumstances even seem to confirm what we feel in our heart. There is just no way.

I was thinking about one such situation in my own life. It was an early morning; not yet dawn. Nothing moving yet. The air was still. Hardly a breath. As I rounded the bend, there in front of me was a hovering cloud. It was at street level. What struck me odd was the fact that it wasn't there 15 minutes ago. I had just walked this block. It came out of nowhere. I continued to walk through it. When I got some distance away, I noticed my hair was soaked. My jacket was thoroughly saturated as well. I didn't feel it getting wet. The mist wasn't discernible. How did this happen?

I thought of Mary, the mother of Jesus. The angel came to her, a teenage girl, and told her she would birth the Son of God. Having no husband, and still a virgin this was impossible. She asked a legitimate question.

Luke 1:34... "How shall this be...?"

It's the same sort of question I was asking. Maybe you're asking your own questions.

How is this going to happen? Who is going to reach this child? How will I get through this?

Luke 1:35 The angel replied, "The Holy Spirit will come upon you, and the power of the Most High will overshadow you. So the baby to be born will be holy, and he will be called the Son of God."

This word overshadow in the old language spoke of a cloud representing the immediate Presence and Power of the Holy Spirit coming upon Mary. It is the Holy Spirit that will come upon us, giving us the Power to accomplish whatever it is we need. Much like the dew I walked through, He will come upon our situation with unmatched power; saturating it. Usually when we least expect it.

Zechariah 4:6 Not by might, nor by power, but by My Spirit.

Lord, there is none but You. Saturate my soul with hope. You are my only hope. I need you. Please hover over me. All things are possible with You. I will trust you. Take away all of my doubts and fears. Overshadow me with your Presence. Bring this to pass I pray.

December 15

1 Samuel 17:3-4 The Philistines stood on a mountain on one side, and Israel stood on a mountain on the other side, with a valley between them. Then Goliath, a Philistine champion from Gath, came out of the Philistine ranks to face the forces of Israel. He was over nine feet tall!

Israel had already been defeated so many times they'd lost all hope of the situation ever changing. They cowered before Goliath. All he had to do was look at them a certain way and they ran in the other direction. They tried everything. Nothing worked. Goliath came out using the same words.

Same scenario. Different day.

We can be in much the same position.

Same challenges. Different day.

Same giant.

Maybe your giant is exhaustion. A wayward child. A child with a disability. Perhaps you're one paycheck away from bankruptcy. Every month. And then you may be facing all of the above along with it. These giants come out to taunt us every day. And every day there is no change on the horizon. Nothing to steal us away. We even despair of life.

No rest.

No chance of the situation changing.

Doubts come as shooting arrows assaulting the soul.

How am I going to pay for this? What should I do?

Depression threatens to sink us below the surface.

But God.

The Living God.

Psalm 84:2 My soul yearns, yes, even pines and is homesick for the courts of the Lord; my heart and my flesh cry out and sing for joy to the living God.

Not a dead God.

Not a defeated God.

An alive God who is fighting on our behalf!

He steps in.

We have no power against these giants.

But our God who rose from the dead has power over them.

He is able to sustain us and protect us from sinking.

We cannot allow the enemy to taunt us anymore.

Your situation is not hopeless.

The greater the impossibility, the greater the victory for our God.

He is strength when we have none.

Grace in the moment.

Goliath means exile.

Exile is defined as being away or restricted from coming to a certain place, usually as a result of a punishment.

These giants restrict us from coming into a place of peace. Thus being left in a place of torment.

Jesus came to set us free. He can give us peace in the midst of turmoil.

Doubts and fears hold us hostage.

2 Timothy 1:9 God has not given us a spirit of fear but power love and sound mind.

Lord help me not to allow the enemy to taunt me any longer. I will overcome this. By the power of the Living God. You are alive and acting on my behalf. I trust you with my whole heart Jesus. Let your peace that surpasses understanding guard my heart and mind. Permeate my soul with your peace Lord.

December 16

Judges 1:1-2 Now after the death of Joshua it came to pass that the children of Israel asked the LORD, saying, "Who shall be first to go up for us against the Canaanites to fight against them?" And the LORD said, "Judah shall go up. Indeed I have delivered the land into his hand."

Israel was facing the challenge of a lifetime. They were terrified. They asked a question, "Who will go first?" I'm sure they didn't want to know the answer. I never want to be first.

The Lord said, "Judah will go first."

Judah means praise.

When we are facing challenges, trials and battles of a lifetime we get so overwhelmed we don't know what to do. We sure don't want to go through this. We can cower in a corner for days. That is exactly where the enemy would have us; cowering before him. Fear perpetuates a cycle of anxiety that overtakes our lives. It robs us of our joy.

On the other hand, praise causes us to ascend high above our troubles. The higher we climb the smaller our problems become. Praise will withdraw us from what we can see and release us before the throne where we will meet with God Himself. Encountering the Lord will change our perspective. The problem may not change, but we will.

Praise enables us to see behind the struggle. Whatever task, challenge or mountain you must climb today, send up the praise.

Indeed, God said they would overcome. The Lord was emphatic about this. There are certain things we are unsure of. We don't have a definite answer for. And other times the Lord gives us a Promise. When He does this we have to cling to it; no matter what things look like on the outside. Irrespective of the current circumstances and no matter what the doctors say; God's word trumps all. Financial advisors and well-meaning family don't have the final say; God does. He knew the fierce battle that was lying ahead of Israel. God said, "I got this. You praise me." He knows the challenges we face. He's got them!

Praise is training for the battle. Sometimes it is just plain hard to praise Him. Do it anyways! It is a choice. God is good. You may not see one good thing that can come of this, but praise Him anyways! Offer up your life. Concede. If this is what it takes to bring God glory, then bring it on!

Job 1:21... "The LORD gave, and the LORD has taken away; blessed be the name of the LORD."

God I want to praise you before I do another thing. You are going before me to pave the way. I am thankful You choose to be in this with me. I am not alone. Take away these fears that daily taunt me. Bring a calm to my heart that only You can give. The battle is Yours. Fight for me. With me. In me. I believe in You. I trust Your way.

December 17

It was one of those days where you relish the serenity. Not a soul in sight; and quieter than usual.

Yeah, that didn't last long.

I rounded the bend. I was met with loud squawking. Obnoxious. Rude.

What is that? Where is that coming from? It didn't take me long to figure it out.

I looked up. I saw a big ole black bird. That black bird was screaming at an owl. Screeching and shrieking.

The owl didn't flinch.

When the annoying squawks didn't work, the dive bombing began. Over and over again. Flying as close to his face as possible. Shouting insults. Obviously provoking him.

The owl didn't flinch.

I thought for sure that owl was going to take that black bird out. He certainly could have. He was definitely bigger. And from the looks of things, he had every right.

Sometimes we find ourselves in the same position as this owl.

Under attack. Insulted. Offended.

How should we respond?

We can learn a lot from this wise ole owl.

Take a deep breath. Keep silent. If you respond immediately most likely it will be in the wrong tone. You'll say things you don't mean.

We can never take our words back. Words hurt.

I like to ask myself, "Is there any truth to what this person is saying; even a sliver?" If I am honest, I would say there usually is some portion of truth. I need to figure out how to make that right.

Matthew 18:15...if your brother sins against you, go and tell him his fault between you and him alone.

In private. Not on Facebook, Twitter, or in a group setting.

Allow a little time before responding. Emotions need to settle.

Pray.

Ephesians 4:15...speak the truth in love...

There are times when you have to speak. Not always though.

Sometimes there is more power in silence.

Take the hit.

James 3:17 But the wisdom from above is first of all pure. It is also peace loving, gentle at all times, and willing to yield to others. It is full of mercy and good deeds.

Wisdom chooses peace.

Blessed are the peacemakers.

They recognize what's at stake.

Quite often we can win a battle, but lose the war. Am I striving to get this person heavenward or just trying to be right?

Mercy is showing kindness towards someone who does not deserve it. They deserve your wrath, but you give grace instead.

Remembering all the mercy we've received makes it a little easier.

"Father forgive them, they do not know what they are doing."

Jesus spoke these words while hanging on the cross, amidst the insults, offenses, and mocking. If you've been offended, take a step back. Satan loves to divide. Especially during this holiday season. Don't be lured into petty provocations. You don't have to be in a hurry to respond. Pray. Ask God what you should do. As Christians, we need to do a lot of overlooking. You can never go wrong by taking the humble position. The lower place. God will always honor that.

Loving the unlovable is difficult. But worth it.

1 Corinthians 14:8 Love never fails.

December 18

"Dear Jesus, it hurts so much. It's not fair. God, what have I done to deserve this? Why me God?"

Self-pity is a snake that must be avoided or it will slowly kill you. The Lord gave me this dream to illustrate His point...

It was vivid. I was walking in front of my house and right there in front of me was the shed skin of a huge snake. It was at least 8 foot long. Immediately I thought to myself 'this means there is a huge snake lurking around here and it is close.' I should have run away. I know I should've. I have no idea why I didn't. I continued down the pathway to the front door. I heard a rustling in the bush. Again, I should've run, but I didn't. This time I felt completely powerless to do so. I was almost numb. The snake slithered out of the bush and rapidly, with precision, sunk his fangs into my hand. I was flailing my hand wildly in the air trying desperately to shake it off.

There is an enemy of our souls. He is a snake whose tactics have not changed since the garden. Slither in, observe, and attack. Nothing new. Then why do we fall for his trickery? The answer is quite simple. He is devious. He is a master of disguise. Just like a snake sheds its skin, Satan transforms himself into an angel of light.

He can make bad things appear good. But, God gives us warnings. I saw the snakeskin. It was right in front of me. The warning was there, but I didn't listen. In my mind I knew I shouldn't keep walking down that path. I have done this quite often in my walk with the Lord. There are big red flags, but I don't heed. I rationalize that I have every right to feel this way.

I compare myself to others. I think I'm doing pretty well, in comparison. But you see, my standard is different than theirs. For me, God has already spoken, "I don't want you to have this attitude." Now I have a choice. I must tell the Lord one of two things. "Yes, I will obey You" or "No, I won't obey You." When I say, "No, I won't obey You," this little snake grows a tad bit bigger and my heart grows a tad bit harder. Did you know a snake sheds his skin by rubbing up against something hard? Every "no I won't" causes me to grow harder and more callous. It doesn't seem like that does it? This thing He doesn't want for me seems so trivial. It seems like no big deal. That is where the deception has begun my sister. A snake sheds its skin because it has grown bigger. One seemingly innocent "no I won't obey" turns into another. It always grows into much more than when it began.

A snake sheds his old skin when the new skin is formed underneath. In the same way, Satan's influence has grown in our heart. He already has his game plan for the next take down. His plan is already in place. Likewise, we need to have a plan in advance for next time. We have to stay one step ahead. When a snake grows a new skin it has the same colors and all the same patterns. Satan has not changed colors since the beginning. He will continue to go back to what works. If his scheme worked once it will work again. Never say, "I have every right" or "I would never do that." The moment I say that is the very moment I let my guard down, and inevitably become vulnerable. Once the snake has bitten, he has one goal. He wants to devour you. He wants to disqualify you from ministry. He wants to blow your witness to your friends. He wants to destroy your marriage. He wants to annihilate your children. He will not be shaken off easily. Why? Once he has control of one area, he wants more. He wants all of you. Sin must be taken seriously.

Satan will fight to the death. Someone must die here. The choice is yours.

James 4:7 Submit yourselves therefore to God. Resist the devil, and he will flee from you.

December 19

2 Kings 6:6 "The ax head floated up."

Ax heads don't float.

They sink.

For an ax head to float, it would defy gravity. All laws of science would be defied.

The ax head did float.

Things impossible with man are possible with God.

There may be some challenges lying before you, don't give up.

If you have a person in your life who seems hopelessly lost under the murky water of the world, don't give up.

Or perhaps there is a need. You have no way to provide for it; don't give up.

2 Corinthians 9:8 And God will generously provide all you need. Then you will always have everything you need and plenty left over to share with others.

God is able to make all grace abound to you. He can send help from afar. Places you would never expect. So too is He able to soften a hard heart. Give desire where there is none. He can defy doctor's prognosis. They don't limit His healing ability.

The ax head did float. Contrary to all expectation.

Don't give up. Persevere in prayer to our Heavenly Helper.

Lord you have been doing impossible things since the beginning of time. Speak a word into this situation. Breathe Your breath upon me. Revive my hope. Fill me with Your Spirit to believe that all things are possible to him who believes. I believe in You. Help my unbelief.

December 20

We walked out of the store and there it was.

This car. It was filled with so much junk, I wondered if it was abandoned. Could someone have driven that thing?

Even my son was taken aback.

Is this really someone's reality?

The driver's side door opened. Very slowly.

Even slower, a middle aged gentleman struggled to get out. He shuffled into the store. Where would he put any more stuff?

As I examined each thing individually, old newspaper, picture frames, even trash, I wondered why he didn't just throw it away.

Get rid of it.

I began to think about all that clutter.

Our lives can begin to look like this sometimes. Before we realize it, we're carrying around a bunch of junk that doesn't belong.

Here are some things that need to go:

Old hurts. Yeah we say we let it go, but we're really holding onto it for future ammo. We'll use it someday.

1 Corinthians 13:5 [Love] keeps no record of wrongs.

Past regrets.

Philippians 3:13... I focus on this one thing: Forgetting the past and looking forward to what lies ahead.

Fears. Worry. And more fears. And even more worry.

"Worrying is carrying tomorrow's load with today's strength-carrying two days at once. It is moving into tomorrow ahead of time. Worrying doesn't empty tomorrow of its sorrow, it empties today of its strength."

-Corrie ten Boom

Maybe this week has brought many heavy things. Unexpected things. Commit them to the Lord. They are His to carry. Not yours.

December 21

Deuteronomy 15:2 This is how it must be done. Everyone must cancel the loans they have made to their fellow Israelites. They must not demand payment from their neighbors or relatives, for the LORD's time of release has arrived.

If the Lord sets you free, you shall be free indeed.

At the word of the Lord the release is made. He has the authority.

This is the year of Jubilee.

There are some things in our lives holding us captive. They possess us. Instead of us possessing them, they possess us. Often we think we're "controlling" them, but they have taken control of a part or all of our lives. We can no longer serve our Master well. The Lord wants to release us of those things.

Sometimes it is our pride. I care about what people think of me. There is something I won't do because I'm afraid of what others may say about me. Or for others, their possessions possess them. I can't do this because I love my stuff. I could never do that, I don't have the skill for that. Still others are held captive by drugs and alcohol.

My right to myself, my time, and my energy can keep me bound to a mediocre life. For others unforgiveness consumes them. They are unable to fully live. For me, laziness is always looming. It holds me back from doing all that God has asked me to do. Fear is another big thing that we need to let go of. Our fears hinder us from so much. We fear failure. We fear the future. We fear getting close to people.

At the bottom of all fear is a lack of trust.

And lastly we have the dreaded diagnosis. This "diagnosis" impedes our child's spiritual growth. I found it so freeing to "shred" that diagnosis. While it was freeing to finally get it, it began to possess me. It captivated my thoughts. When new things came, whether it was new opportunities to socialize or new things to learn or even new concepts from the Bible, I thought to myself, "he'll never understand that."

A diagnosis will never define your child. First and foremost, your child is a child of the Living God. He will be ALL that God has planned and purposed. Nothing can stop that.

If I continue to hold on to this thing, whatever this thing is, it holds me captive. I am its prisoner.

When you give that thing up, it's because you trust the Lord. It's not even because you may want to, but rather out of obedience. This is what my Master is asking from me and I will do it. You see, when you let that go you'll realize that God has something so much better for you.

There will visible results in your spiritual walk.

Deuteronomy 15:4... for the LORD will greatly bless you in the land which the LORD your God is giving you to possess as an inheritance—

He will take you into a new territory. Places you've never been spiritually. You never thought they were possible. He'll show you things you've never seen. This is your inheritance. This is what you get in return.

Deuteronomy 15:5 You will receive this blessing if you are careful to obey all the commands of the LORD your God that I am giving you today.

Shama shama is the rendering in Hebrew for these words "if you are careful to obey." It puts the emphasis on not just hearing, but doing.

Be careful. Watch. Be on the lookout. Treasure this in your memory. Protect yourself at all cost.

Let it go.

The time of the Lord's release has arrived.

Deuteronomy 15:6 The LORD your God will bless you as he has promised. You will lend money to many nations but will never need to borrow. You will rule many nations, but they will not rule over you.

As soon as you let it go, you are free. The great paradox is that you become a slave again, but to Christ. It is willingly and gratefully that we become servants of the Master.

Deuteronomy 15:15-17 Remember that you were once slaves in the land of Egypt and the LORD your God redeemed you! That is why I am giving you this command. "And if it happens that he says to you, 'I will not go away from you,' because he loves you and your house, since he prospers with you, "then you shall take an awl and thrust it through his ear to the door, and he shall be your servant forever. Also to your female servant you shall do likewise.

Release brings radical action.

Thrusting an awl through your ear is radical. It is painful.

This is an outward sign of an inward commitment of the heart.

God wants to use you in a radical way. To do so, you must release these things.

The time of release has come.

December 22

I had a dream I was in a boathouse. Rectangular. Three walls on one side and the backside completely open. It had a sturdy floor that I was sitting on. Solid foundation. I was facing the open side. Ray was facing me to the right. A friend was standing to my left. We were enjoying the solitude of a quiet day on the Chesapeake Bay. Clear sky. Calm seas. Just small lapping waves; relaxing enough to lull us to sleep. Out of nowhere, a large black cloud started forming in the distance. The more we talked, the larger it got. They couldn't see it; their backs were to it. Oblivious. As I brought it to their attention the cloud seemed to erupt like a volcano spilling dark grey ash over the entire sky. The boathouse that was stationary just a few moments ago quickly lifted up. All at once I was being tossed about every which way. I was so scared. Ray and my friend were suddenly gone. I found myself alone on these open seas with no place of protection. No one to help. Nothing to hold onto. Nothing to keep me from sliding right out into this raging sea. Floating debris became a real threat. But not pieces of wood or tin cans; large pieces of buildings. Since there was no door or outer wall, my safety was in real jeopardy. If it entered the boathouse I would have nowhere to go. It would crush me. I looked around desperately trying to find something to anchor me. Something to hold onto. There was nothing.

Did I think I could save myself?

I noticed in my dream I didn't cry out to the Lord at first.

I tried to figure it out myself.

I did everything in my power to keep from falling.

Looked all around me before looking up.

It was only after all my futile attempts that I realized I had no power to make it through this on my own.

I was at the mercy of the Lord.

Joel 2:32 Everyone who calls on the name of the Lord shall be saved

Much like this storm, many things come into our lives quite unexpectedly. Maybe you already see that dark ashen cloud looming on the horizon of your own life.

Now is the time to call out to Jesus for help. You don't need to figure this out by yourself.

James 1:5-6 If you need wisdom, ask our generous God, and he will give it to you… But when you ask Him, be sure that your faith is in God alone. Do not waver, for a person with divided loyalty is as unsettled as a wave of the sea that is blown and tossed by the wind.

You may already be right in the middle of that storm. Feeling all alone. Everyone else may desert you, but God never will. Call upon Him. First.

He has never failed. He wouldn't now either.

And He won't fail you.

I may not know what tomorrow holds, but I do know Who holds it.

He has strong hands.

Psalm 18:2 The LORD is my rock, my fortress, and my savior; my God is my rock, in whom I find protection. He is my shield, the power that saves me, and my place of safety. A refuge in the storm.

How did my dream end?

The storm remained a raging sea. But in the midst, the waves of my heart were stilled. A calm peace settled in. A knowing.

My God is in this with me. I am secure. And so are you.

Hebrews 6:19 We have this hope as an anchor for the soul, firm and secure.

December 23

Luke 1:28-30 Rejoice, highly favored one, the Lord is with you; blessed are you among women...Do not be afraid, Mary, for you have found favor with God. And behold you will conceive in your womb and bring forth a Son and shall call His name Jesus...He will be great and will be called the Son of the Highest...Then Mary said to the angel, "How can this be?"

I don't know how blessed Mary felt. I'm pretty certain I would have felt anything but blessed.

Scared, terrified, uncertain, and anxious are just a few of things I would've felt.

As parents of a special needs child, we face these feelings every day.

The angel said, "Rejoice."

In the Greek, we can get a better understanding of the word rejoice. In its context, it means to celebrate, to be glad, to be well and thrive.

Are you thriving or just barely surviving? God wants us to thrive. He wants us to be doing better than expected. To have a song in our heart despite the adversity. In spite of the pain, through the trial that we face today, God wants us to celebrate.

The angel told her she was highly favored, and I believe the same is true for us. God chose to give us this child. Out of all the mothers in the world He chose me. Wow. He saw the big picture. He saw the magnitude of his needs and said, "I choose you." I choose you because you are the best person for this enormous task. And the reason that would be so overwhelming is because we don't have what it takes. We need Jesus.

2 Corinthians 12:9 My grace is sufficient for you; for My power is made perfect in weakness." Therefore most gladly I will rather boast in my infirmities that the power of Christ may rest upon me...for when I am weak then I am strong.

We can't do anything without Him. I have nothing for this child. I have no idea what I am doing. But, by the power of Christ I trust He will give me what I need. I have no other choice but to depend on Him for everything. But, it's a good place to be. God's grace is more than enough for me. Jesus is enough to fill every need I have. I need His wisdom. He will allow us to see things and learn things that even the doctors don't know. This will give us discernment to make decisions.

We are not alone. We don't have to fear anyone or anything. God will never leave us. He is with us. He is fighting on our behalf.

If you are facing a financial struggle right now God wants you to know through His word that He and He alone will provide for you.

Philippians 4:19 My God shall supply all of your needs according to His glorious riches in Christ Jesus.

Or maybe today finds you exhausted. As you read this, God's word is filling you with strength to endure.

Isaiah 40:28-29 Have you never heard? Have you never understood? The LORD is the everlasting God, the Creator of all the earth. He never grows weak or weary. No one can measure the depths of his understanding. He gives power to the weak and strength to the powerless.

We cannot exhaust God. His supply is endless. Ask Him. Come to Him. He will breathe new life into you. He'll give you the physical energy you need to put one foot in front of the other.

Isaiah 40:31 But those who trust in the LORD will find new strength. They will soar high on wings like eagles. They will run and not grow weary. They will walk and not faint.

When we fix our eyes on Jesus He lifts us up. All of our hope is in Him. All our expectations are in what He can do.

Luke 1:31 you will conceive...

Your mind cannot fathom what God is going to do in this situation.

God is going to birth things through this situation, this trial, this child that you wouldn't believe.

Luke 1:34 How can this be, since...?

Mary said, "Since I don't know a man"...quite obviously this would make conception impossible.

So you fill in the blank.

What is that impossible thing in your life that's dogging you right now? Satan may even be mocking you. He may be taunting you and saying you'll never overcome it; whispering the lie that you will never get past this. Or this person will never change. These circumstances are too much and you can't do it anymore.

Luke 1:35 The angel answered and said to her, "The Holy Spirit will come upon you and the power of the Highest will overshadow you therefore, also, that Holy One who is to be born will be called the Son of God."

God is birthing something new in your heart and your life through this. He is building a testimony for Himself. So He can get all the glory. He makes it so impossible that you and those around you will say, and agree, "Yes this could only come about from God Himself."

God will "birth" a stronger faith. He will build a stronger relationship with His Son Jesus. These kinds of things are only birthed through trials and difficult circumstances; challenges that are beyond us.

Thank you for Jesus. God You are birthing new things in my spirit. Help me to be patient as you bring this about in my life. Although your birthing process is painful, I will trust you. Every good and perfect gift is worth waiting for. I praise You for what You are going to do in this situation.

December 24

A Christmas Story

Once upon a time there was a little boy named Camden. He had curly brown hair, big blue eyes, and the longest black lashes you've ever seen. With sweet rosy cheeks that needed to be squeezed and tiny pink lips; one might think he was an angel. The week before Christmas Camden was scheduled for dental surgery. Everything went without a hitch.

Until he woke up.

Screaming in terror, he could not be quieted. Throwing fists, kicking and biting. Tears and more tears. All the way to the parking lot he screamed and flailed. The doctors and nurses had such compassion. They truly felt for him and his parents. Their hearts crying out for someone to fix this. To make it better. On their way home it was like a switch went off. Crying ceased. Peace and contentment returned. This little guy was as happy as could be.

But that's not the end of the story.

Here is the rest of the story. The true Christmas Story.

God sent His Son Jesus to come into the world as a little baby. He came to die on a cross for the sins of the world. Pain and suffering were never God's intention. Pain entered when sin entered; all the way back in the garden. Jesus came to die. To pay the penalty for that sin and every other sin. All who repent of their sin will live forever with Jesus in heaven. In heaven there is no more sorrow, no more crying and no more pain. That is why we celebrate Christmas. That little baby came to fix it all. That is the hope of Christmas for all who believe. That is the hope Camden's parents have.

Whatever trial or adversity you may be struggling with, there truly is Someone who can fix it all. There is hope. His name is Jesus.

For all who believe in Him, heaven awaits.

Revelation 21:4 "And God will wipe away every tear from their eyes; there shall be no more death, nor sorrow, nor crying. There shall be no more pain, for the former things have passed away."

December 25

Camden: "Mama, I prayed for your nose."

Me: swooning... "Camden, that is so sweet of you. Thank you."

Yeah, I'm betting you've never had a Christmas morning quite like this one.

It started out rather blissful. I sipped coffee by the fire. Drinking in the sight of my tree. White lights twinkling. Treasuring the memories of each ornament. I'm quite sentimental.

Camden decided to put some Legos together in the other room. I heard a raucous. Our pup was causing quite a stir. He was getting into all the Legos. Camden was not happy. I decided to put the dog outside. He decided to bust loose and run in the other direction. He about barreled me over.

Knocked me right into the hutch. Before I knew it, I heard teacups clashing and things falling over. Next thing I know, this large metal star (at least one foot in diameter) came falling from the top of the hutch and busted me right in the nose. It about knocked me out.

I saw stars. Literally. Camden saw the blood and began hollering, "We have to take you to the hospital." Over and over again. He was so scared. Obviously it was very painful for me, but I tried to keep it together as not to scare Camden any more than I already had. All that and it was only 5 a.m.

I found myself lying flat on my back crying out to God for help.

Not exactly the peaceful morning I would've chosen.

Much of life happens like this. Not at all what we would've chosen.

No way.

I thought of another star that led to an unlikely place.

Matthew 2:9...the star which they had seen in the East went before them, till it came and stood over where the young Child was.

That star led them to the Savior.

Sometimes that "star" leads us through some very dark nights. Oftentimes painful.

It may lead you through divorce. Financial ruin. Drug addiction. Abandonment. Loss. Disability.

Who would choose this?

But what if all that brokenness opened us up to the heart of our God?

The deepest depths of Who He is. He is love. He loves us with a love that is so wide, and high, and long, and deep. It is difficult for us to grasp this kind of love. God loves brokenness. It leads us to His Son.

His Son is His heart. He gave His only Son to die for us. That's how we know He loves us.

You may lose it all. It's exactly in that place you gain all. All of Him.

As unpredictable as life can be, God is always predictable.

Psalm 23:4 Even though I walk through the valley of the shadow of death, I will fear no evil, for You are with me...

He is constant. Steady. And strong when we are weak. It's precisely when we have no strength, we take His.

Isaiah 40:29-31 29 He gives power to the faint and weary, and to him who has no might He increases strength [causing it to multiply and making it to abound]. Even youths shall faint and be weary, and young men shall feebly stumble and fall exhausted; But those who wait for the Lord [who expect, look for, and hope in Him] shall change and renew their strength and power; they shall lift their wings and mount up [close to God] as eagles [mount up to the sun]; they shall run and not be weary, they shall walk and not faint or become tired.

In the midst of the pain, blood and the bag of ice on my nose, I burst out laughing.

I mean I could not contain myself.

Why can't my life be normal????

If God brings some unexpected things your way, embrace them. Don't be afraid.

Laugh with your God. He is with you, even in this.

You will get through it. Together. You and your God.

John 8:29 The One who sent me is with me; He has not left me alone...

He is Faithful.

December 26

Proverbs 14:1 The wise woman builds her house, but the foolish pulls it down with her hands.

We want to always be building our house. Our homes need a strong foundation. A foundation is being laid daily. Our words are building our children and husbands with confidence. It is so easy to always be critical. It is so easy to point out what they are doing wrong. It's not so easy to find the good. But we want to seek that out. We want to "catch them" being good. Praise them for it. Even if it's the smallest thing. Small things add up to big things. A lot of times kids will do anything to get attention; even if that means negative attention.

When they're sitting the way you want, praise them.

If they share something, praise them.

If they come right away, praise them.

Eye contact, holding the pencil, whatever is good for your child; tell them. Tell them often that you think they are doing a great job. Tell them often how much you love them. Show them often. It is easy to overlook these little things. Because Camden is not affectionate I can let days go by without hugging him. You just get caught up in life and then you realize you're not doing the really important things.

Lord help me to remember to be on the lookout for opportunities to praise my children. Show me ways to build their confidence in You. Teach me Your ways Lord. Use my words to build up my husband. Help him to feel needed. Bless my marriage. Let it be a reflection of my relationship with You. Give me kind words to build up my children. Put a guard on my mouth against negative words that tear down and have no value. Touch my mouth with Your love. Let me flow words of life giving power.

December 27

I had a dream one night. It was very dark. Pitch black of night. Nine o'clock to be exact. I was around the bend from my home and a car pulled up slow. Headlights dim. I had an ominous feeling. I thought someone got out, but wasn't sure. I couldn't see if someone was approaching. I felt the presence of evil. I grabbed my phone and pretended to call for my brother to come get me. I couldn't see a thing. Only about a foot in front of me and that was it. Next thing I saw was a large knife coming at me. Everything went into slow motion. I reached for the knife with my left hand. I bent the blade in half. It literally melted like butter. I didn't have a scratch on me.

Immediately I woke up with this verse:

Isaiah 54:17 No weapon formed against you shall prosper.

I bent the knife in half. With my left hand. My weak hand. That is impossible. But that is the power that we have against the enemy.

1 Corinthians 1:25 The weakness of God is stronger than man.

He cannot kill us. He cannot silence our testimony. His power is limited. He can most certainly disrupt, but he cannot stop the work of God.

No darkness can extinguish the light of Jesus Christ.

No accusation can imprison us. The prison door is open. No failure can keep us locked in. Or chained up. Jesus Christ holds the key. You are released. Walk in freedom.

The Lord is our defense.

Romans 8:31 What then shall we say to these things? If God is for us, who can be against us?

Go in the power of your God. You are untouchable in His will.

December 28

Camden grabbed a golden piece of cornbread and exclaimed, "I'm pretending this is my Christian bread!"

I quizzed him, "So where do you get that Christian bread?"

He spoke wisdom, "You have to go to heaven up to JESUS to get it."

I don't know about you, but I need some of that Christian bread today. Some soul food.

How about you?

Do you have someone to speak to today? Go to the Lord first. Get your message from Him. Get His words. Mine? They fall flat every time.

One word from the Lord is better than 10,000 of my own.

Commentaries are great. Godly counsel from Christian friends is so helpful. We can even get some great encouragement on Facebook.

Nothing trumps the word of God.

It is matchless.

Do you have a busy schedule today? Go to God and his word first, and He will put your day in order.

Matthew 6:33 Seek first the kingdom of God and His righteousness and all these things shall be added unto you.

Do you have a full plate today, and short on time? Something needs to go but don't let it be teaching your children the word of God. It is the most important thing in their lives. Bread from heaven is the only thing that satisfies and truly makes full; a heart full. All the things of the world will leave them empty and lacking.

Deuteronomy 6:6-8 Write these commandments that I've given you today on your hearts. Get them inside of you and then get them inside your children. Talk about them wherever you are, sitting at home or walking in the street; talk about them from the time you get up in the morning to when you fall into bed at night.

Do you have a difficult decision to make?

Jeremiah 33:3 Call to Me and I will answer. I will show you great and mighty things which you do not know.

Are you feeling down and not ready for another grueling week ahead?

Isaiah 40:27-31 Why would you ever complain...saying, "God has lost track of me. He doesn't care what happens to me"? Don't you know anything? Haven't you been listening? God doesn't come and go. God lasts. He's Creator of all you can see or imagine. He doesn't get tired out, doesn't pause to catch his breath. And he knows everything, inside and out. He energizes those who get tired, gives fresh strength to dropouts. For even young people tire and drop out, young folk in their prime stumble and fall. But those who wait upon God get fresh strength. They spread their wings and soar like eagles. They run and don't get tired, they walk and don't lag behind.

Now go get you some of this Christian bread!

December 29

2 Chronicles 20:17 You will not need to fight in this battle. Position yourselves, stand still and see the salvation of the Lord who is with you...!

Sometimes we look up to find a storm brewing on the horizon. Dark clouds begin to swirl overhead; all looks ominous. Danger is looming. We hope this just blows over, but something deep inside tells us it may be a direct hit.

There are times in our lives when evil is looming. We are getting some whispers of what is stirring. The enemy seems to be gaining ground, and we begin to panic. We don't know what to do next. Our mind is reeling. Try as we might, we are incapable of stopping it. When we find ourselves in a situation such as this, what should we do? There is a great example for us in Second Chronicles. Jehoshaphat gets word that he is about to be attacked. He was deathly afraid. He asked everyone to fast and pray.

He immediately sought God's help. We should do the same.

2 Chronicles 20:12 O our God, won't you stop them? We are powerless against this mighty army that is about to attack us. We do not know what to do, but we are looking to you for help."

We cannot place ourselves in a better position than standing before the Lord, helpless. The Lord allows us to be brought so far down, so that we have no other choice but to look up to Him.

2 Chronicles 20:14... the Spirit of the LORD came upon one of the men standing there... This is what the LORD says: Do not be afraid! Don't be discouraged by this mighty army, for the battle is not yours, but God's.

Oh how comforting it is to remember this. The battle belongs to the Lord.

2 Chronicles 20:16-17 Tomorrow go down against them...You will not need to fight in this battle. Position yourselves, stand still and see the salvation of the Lord who is with you...!

Stand still. Stop doing. Stop moving. Hold your ground. You don't have to do a thing.

2 Chronicles 20:20 Early the next morning the army...went out...and on the way Jehoshaphat stopped and said, "Listen to me,...believe in the Lord your God, and you will be able to stand firm.

Stand firm. Don't waver.

2 Chronicles 20:21-22...the king appointed singers...This is what they sang:

"Give thanks to the Lord, His faithful love endures forever!"

At the very moment they began to sing and give praise, the Lord caused the enemies to begin fighting against each other, and they were defeated.

Sing! Sing, my sister, sing!

Singing brought about the victory!

How could they sing in the face of this adversity?

They were so sure they were going to win this battle they were singing, in advance, to celebrate the victory. So it should be the same with us.

Something supernatural begins to happen the moment we begin to sing.

Whatever battle you are facing today, I pray you will sing with all your heart to the Lord. No matter how grim things may appear, God will win this! The battle belongs to the Lord. God is on your side, therefore, you can't lose!

Romans 8:31 What, then, shall we say in response to this? If God is for us, who can be against us?

December 30

The dreaded clean-up has begun. Christmas is over. And another year gone by. As I was taking down all of the tinsel and glitter I couldn't help but notice how empty the fireplace looked. I kept staring. I began reflecting back on the past year, there were lots of ups and downs; but it was a good year. Even so, there were some things I wanted to see happen and they just didn't come to pass. I am feeling a bit like my fireplace right now.

Something is missing.

Perhaps you feel the same way as you take a look back at the last year. Maybe there were some things you were hoping for: a new job, spouse or baby, an illness healed or a relationship restored and it just didn't happen.

God reminded me He doesn't think like I do.

Isaiah 55:8 "For My thoughts are not your thoughts, nor are your ways My ways," says the LORD.

I see something missing.

God sees a blank canvas ready for the Master to create something amazing. He'll take the blackness of the disappointment and make it the backdrop of something beautiful. Just like my fireplace, your life will soon be displaying something lovely in that empty space.

Psalm 27:13-14 I would have lost heart, unless I had believed that I would see the goodness of the LORD in the land of the living. Wait on the LORD; be of good courage, and He shall strengthen your heart; wait, I say, on the LORD!

Philippians 1:6... being confident of this very thing, that He who has begun a good work in you will complete it.

Wait on the Lord. He is finished yet. He began a good work. He will finish it.

Sit with His word.

His word will NEVER leave you empty. It is the only thing that can fill, satisfy and make you whole. It will always complete that which is lacking in you. So if today finds you feeling a little empty, go get your fill from the one and only God who knows the longings of your soul. He sees your unfulfilled dreams. He knows all of the desires of your heart.

Psalm 107:9 For He satisfies the longing soul, and fills the hungry soul with goodness.

December 31

Today found me reflecting on this past year. I've had a year filled with many joys, and also many sorrows. There were many happy times, and many sad times. There were times of great confidence, and times of great fear. I am thankful to say that my year was NOT defined by fear. Let me explain.

Recently I flew to Florida for a birthday party. Some people love flying. I am not one of them. In fact, I loathe it. Mostly because I am afraid the plane is going to crash. A typical flight for me causes great anxiety. I usually have a death grip on Ray's hand. I ask him to explain every loud noise (certain the engine is falling out). My mind cannot rest until we land. However, this flight was different. I was rather calm. I actually asked myself, "Why are you so calm?" Then I remembered my verse from that morning. I only had about 5 minutes to spend with the Lord before we left. We had to be out the door by 5 a.m. Here is the verse the Lord gave me:

Philippians 4:6-7 Be anxious for nothing, but in everything by prayer and supplication, with thanksgiving, let your requests be made known to God, and the peace of God, which surpasses all understanding, will guard your hearts and minds through Christ Jesus.

I realized the Lord had completely taken every fear away from me. Yes, my fears did try to creep back. But, I just kept repeating that verse and the unrest disappeared. I have given some thought to my fears. Most often I spend a lot of time fearing things that will never happen. I discovered that for me, fear is learned behavior. I fear everything. I think this is something I picked up from my mother who picked it up from my grandmother. Fear is not from the Lord. Fear is from the enemy. It will rob you blind if you let it. This year was filled with very serious threats to my health, and that of my family. But, what stands out to me most is that I can say, as Paul did, "you know how much suffering I have endured...but the Lord delivered me from all of it." Did he remove the problems? No. Not all of them.

But He walked through each and every one of them with me. And I am certain He has done the same for you. As this year closes out, let's thank our God for seeing us through every trial. Praise Him for helping you to rise above every adversity. He is good!